a collection of
ramblings about movies
from the first two years of

Place
logo
here

placelogohere.com

A FUTURE LANDFILL FODDER BOOK

an imaginary imprint of Place Logo Here Ltd

ISBN-13: 979-8-218-65138-1

Cover design by the author

Library of Congress Control Number: 2018675309

Printed in the United States of America

How crap was grouped together in this book

Without rhyme or reason   **351**

A curiously unhelpful index 571

The ramblin' preamble

I don't know who you are, and it is equally unlikely you know who I am. That makes it all the more curious you have decided to purchase a book by an ostensibly anonymous author, the contents of which are already available to read for free on the internet. At least you must be in favor of recycling, as this volume is composed of content already published on placelogohere.com, my blog that is largely dedicated to movies, though I have strayed onto other topics on occasion.

As somebody who has never aspired to make a feature film, it may seem odd I write about movies. The reason is simply that I find cinema the easiest thing to write about. In high school, I was an aspiring writer and employed in the greatest job I can imagine a teenager having: film critic for a small community press newspaper. My work on the blog today sometimes feels like I am coming full circle, writing again about that medium so late in life.

The essays I have compiled into this collection are what I believe to best represent the first two years (2023-2024) of the blog, with the focus largely on older or more obscure films. I noticed older horror and science fiction constitute the bulk of the content. There are also sections on comedies, dramas and musicals. A few documentaries provide even more variety. But my absolute favorite genre is noir, and that is curiously underrepresented. Maybe a future volume will rectify that.

While I may occasionally write about contemporary movies on the site, there isn't much one can say about a film like the latest *Alien* sequel which hasn't been covered already. The same is often true about the works of classic Hollywood which are still popular today. I was amazed by *Singing in the Rain* once I finally got around to seeing it, but there isn't any reason for me to add to the mountains of accolades already heaped upon it.

Exceptions have been made for more recent works I feel have yet to find a significant audience (i.e. *Borderlands*, though not the 2024 film you're thinking of), ones which I feel have been maligned unfairly (such as 2016's *Ghostbusters*) or even some where my critique might be excessively harsh, but at least written in a novel way (please see *Enys Men, The Master* or *The Outwaters*). Classic cinema is largely avoided, with one exception being my essay on *The Sound of Music*, as I believe I have a different perspective on it than anybody I have met. The essay on *A Night at the Opera* is presented with the intention of converting the uninitiated to the joys of the Marx Brothers. My pieces on *Shazam* and its sequel are to share one incident of pleasant surprise and another of severe disappointment.

No matter who you are, you will disagree with something in these essays. You might disagree with everything I have written. That's OK. Different points of view are what makes us human and interesting, and trying to understand the perspectives of others builds empathy and understanding.

But while I may not recommend to others most of what I have seen, I try to find at least one positive thing to say about each. I am not always successful in that goal, unless I start ending some essays with "a nice aspect of the production is it eventually came to a merciful conclusion." Failing that, I like to think some of those observations are funny. That said, humor, even more than beauty, is in some part of the beholder (I assume the elbow, or "funny bone", though nobody has ever laughed after hitting one of theirs against something).

While some reviews say this or that picture is recommended or not, I have largely tried to avoid any kind of ratings system. Even the pictures I eviscerate might have a particular appeal for some readers, and the factors driving that interest might be among the reasons cited by me for why I despised a movie. There is an audience out there for every work, so I believe pass/fail, A-to-F, stars, whatever methods could deprive potential viewers of discovering a film they would enjoy.

Also, despite these essays all having originally appeared on the blog, there have been some corrections and reworking of them in this collection. Hopefully, all previous spelling and grammatical errors have been resolved, so njoy this new asortment of tiepos and other crimes against writing.

As for my anonymity, it is all too easy to determine my identity, but I am nobody of any renown; hence, learning my name and other superficial characteristics is unlikely to change your opinion on the thoughts expressed here. Collectively, these musings *are* me, especially given the personal anecdotes I tend to weave into my work. If there is one thing I can say in my favor, I refuse to allow ads on my site, as I believe having those would add insult to injury for those who subject themselves to my ramblings there.

And so, here we are, the person who pays for something they could get for free and the writer who only loses money from their site, as they refuse to allow advertising to accompany it. We probably deserve each other.

976-EVIL (1988)

Some of the movies I watch I only learned about from books, which is partly why I read so many movie books. That, and I have no life.

I was turned on to Romero's *Dawn of the Dead* in the early 90's because of a piece I read in Chet Flippo's book *Everybody Was Kung-Fu Dancing*. The *Rolling Stone* writer described what it was like on set during the filming of *Dawn*, and I was intrigued by the idea of survivalists clearing a shopping mall of zombies. The result was I fell in love with a movie I otherwise wouldn't have rented at that time.

Similarly, I only learned about *976-EVIL* from a piece in *Satanic Panic: Pop-Cultural Paranoia in the 1980s*, edited by Kier-La Janisse. I doubt I would have seen this movie if I had not been intrigued by the write-up about it there. Unfortunately, this movie is nowhere near as good as *Dawn*, but my increasingly relaxed standards have enabled me to enjoy it.

The lead is played by Stephen Geoffreys, who is best remembered as Evil Ed in *Fright Night*. This role isn't radically different from what he played there: a nerd with a twitchy, barely-suppressed energy that feels like it is always on the verge of being unleashed. He gets bullied at school, infantilized by his mother at home, and longs for an unattainable dream girl.

That's pretty much boilerplate for a movie like this. And, inevitably, there will be some sort of supernatural device that gives the poor sap special abilities, only to eventually corrupt him for its own diabolical purposes. This time around, it is a phone service called "Horrorscope". I have no idea why anybody in the movie would feel inclined to call this service (especially curious to me is the absence of an area code), let alone why nobody hangs up when it prompts you to enter 666 to continue. I wondered what people still using dial phones would do. Could failure to upgrade to a touchtone phone save your soul?

I won't say much more about this movie. I don't want to accidentally spoil anything, though *976-EVIL* largely follows a certain template. Besides, if you're watching this kind of movie, you're not really looking for surprises. You're looking for kills, some snappy one-liners and maybe some nudity as a bonus. Fans of movies like the Freddy Krueger series will especially enjoy the visual aesthetic that is "80's hair metal music video" (I doubt it is a coincidence that Freddy himself, Robert Englund, directs).

976-EVIL is a movie strictly for genre fans and it succeeds on those terms, but it won't win over anybody not already predisposed to like it.

Original version posted on 1/9/2023

Alone in the Dark (1982)

My favorite line in the *Mystery Science Theatre 3000* theme advises viewers to not be too concerned about the scientific aspects of the setup, and to just chill, instead. That is sage advice I tried to keep in mind while watching 1982's *Alone in the Dark*, but I simply couldn't turn off my brain for a film I can't believe I liked just the same.

For example, the plot centers on four escaped violent lunatics from an asylum that is really just an old mansion. The ward they are in is on the top floor, which is only accessible through a door locked via electronic keypad. Now, in the event of a power failure, would you expect that door to stay in the locked position or automatically unlock? I solidly believe the former, but it's the latter which happens.

Now, imagine you are the sole guard in that ward, and you have nothing with which to protect yourself. Given the guard (Brent Jennings) seemed like an intelligent person up until this point, wouldn't you assume he would know the door would be automatically unlocked in such an event? At least, wouldn't you *try* to flee if you were in the same shoes as him? And yet he doesn't, and the same fate befalls him as did most Black characters in movies of this type and vintage.

And the insanity unleased by that power outage spreads to the town proper, where *suburbanites* set fires and loot stores. I suspected that development was meant to be a joke. There is evidence of such awareness in these scenes, as one guy steals a mannequin and another walks away with what appear to be oversized props for a public access TV children's show.

Our escapees are Jack Palance, Martin Landau, Erland van Lidth and a mystery man known only as The Bleeder. We never see the face of that last inmate while he is in the institution, so you know that can only be the setup for a twist later in the movie. I don't want to spoil anything, but any viewer will likely be aware of the concept of Ebert's Economy of Characters, even if they don't know the theory by name. Basically, every character in a movie must have a reason for their existence, which often makes it easy to determine who the killer is in things like this. I immediately guessed who the mystery man was, yet was still disappointed to discover I was right. That it is this particular character is the result of events that are so improbable as to likely be impossible. They are, at the very least, nonsensical.

Palance has convinced the others their new doctor (Dwight Schultz) has killed their previous one, so they find the doc's house and terrorize him and his family. In addition to Shultz, there is his wife (Deborah Hedwall) and a daughter who is amusingly cynical for her young age (Elizabeth Ward). The doctor's 20-something sister (Lee Taylor-Allan) just happens to be visiting. She conveniently has a fear of the dark.

She also is a punk, if more in appearance than in commitment to the lifestyle. When the blackout happens, it is in the middle of a concert she dragged Shultz and Ward to. The band is the Sic Fucks, and I had never heard of them before seeing this film. I'm not tempted to hear more of their music, as it was basically screamy pub rock instead of punk. Still, I was amused the female backup singers were wielding oversize prop weapons like some sort of proto-GWAR.

I was also surprised to see an early appearance by Lin Shaye. I'm sure most people remember her primarily from the *Insidious* series, though she has had a long career that started long before that. It was strange seeing her in this picture, as she was so young at the time. I assume her connection on this film was her older brother, Robert Shaye, as he was one of the writers. He eventually went on to be an executive producer on the *Lord of the Rings* trilogy, so it was interesting to see where he started out.

What I found most frustrating about *Alone in the Dark* is there is a potentially better work here, but it seems somebody was determined to handicap it. The film opens on a dream sequence that is genuinely creepy, and nothing after it lives up to that promise.

Original version posted on 1/16/2024

The Ambulance (1990)

Prior to watching Larry Cohen's 1990 picture *The Ambulance*, I had seen most of his films, though none as late in his career as this one. I was worried that, by this time, the director would have lost his taste for the bizarre quirks which distinguish his work. I needn't have worried, as this film is an absolute blast.

It starts with a mulletted Eric Roberts trying to make small talk with Janine Turner on a busy New York street. You can tell she enjoys the attention but isn't receptive. Suddenly, she collapses on the sidewalk and an ambulance picks her up, though suspiciously faster than help should arrive. Also, this vehicle is of an outdated variety, more like the car in *Ghostbusters* than any real ambulance would have been at the time.

It is that kind of quirk which is a litmus test for whether this movie is right for you. On one hand, the movie requires the vehicle to be something distinctive; otherwise, it wouldn't stand out as something for our protagonist to watch out for. On the other hand, wouldn't such a vehicle be *too* distinctive? It would be something the authorities would notice right away. Maybe even your average New Yorker might take note, though it is my understanding they tend to turn a blind eye to most things.

The only information Roberts gets from Turner before she is whisked away is her first name and that she is a diabetic. When he asks the attendants where they are taking her, they tell him the destination is St. Francis Hospital. It is no surprise when Roberts doesn't find her there, nor at any other hospital.

Instead, she has been taken to a secret facility where she is strapped down in a hospital bed. An effectively creepy guy wearing surgical gloves explains how Turner is going to be subjected to experimental surgery that will either cure her diabetes or kill her.

She has an interesting exchange with him: "You're going to kill me, aren't you?" "Yes, I will eventually. But you'll be in perfect health when you die." He also likes to stroke her face with his glove-clad hands, saying, "I just like to touch human skin through a surgical glove, that's all." Why do I have the nagging suspicion this guy would be an incel nowadays?

Roberts gradually enlists the help of a detective played by James Earl Jones and a cop played by Megan Gallagher. Jones initially suspects Roberts of being delusional or a homicidal maniac. The actor is obviously having a great time and chews the scenery with gusto. In an odd touch at adding character, he also chews a great deal of gum. In a scene where he is in hot pursuit of the ambulance, I believe we see four sequential shots of him putting yet another piece of gum in his mouth.

Gallagher, on the other hand, will become the love interest. Still, it is a far from thankless role, as she has a great personality, is intelligent and is more than capable of defending herself.

Stan Lee appears in an odd cameo as Roberts's boss at Marvel Comics. I wonder if we are seeing the real Marvel studio at the time, as this is obviously a location shoot—I'm just not sure that's the location. I expect their operation now entails more than just the dozen or so artist tables we see here.

Red Buttons makes a welcome appearance in a fairly significant role as a fellow patient when Roberts is picked up by a real ambulance. Playing a retired New York Post reporter, he provides a considerable amount of comic relief.

I thoroughly enjoyed this movie, coming within in a hair's width of saying I loved it. I can't say I would recommend it to everybody, as the amount of enjoyment one will likely get from it is heavily dependent upon how far one is willing to suspend disbelief and accept some deliberately hammy performances.

Original version posted on 5/25/2023

The Asphyx (1972)

One of my favorite recurring characters in Terry Pratchett's *Discworld* series of books is Death. It talks in all capital letters. There is also a Death of Rats, an appropriately sized rodent skeleton in a hooded robe and bearing a tiny scythe. Both versions of Death talk in ALL CAPITAL LETTERS, though all the smaller one can say is "SQUEAK."

In 1972's *The Asphyx*, a wacky Victorian-era scientist played by Robert Stephens has discovered each person has their own angel of death, which is assigned to only that individual. He has also found a way to live forever by imprisoning that spirit, or "Asphyx", at the moment of a person's would-be demise. As long as it is captured, that person cannot die.

His first guinea pig for an experiment to test this theory is an actual guinea pig, thus creating the world's first immortal rodent. Curiously, the animal's Asphyx looks exactly like those we will see later when the same process is attempted for human subjects. Shouldn't the grim reaper for guinea pigs look different than that which is for humans? At least, it sure doesn't look like the *Discworld* Death of Rats.

Regardless of the species the Asphyx is supposed to whisk away into the afterlife, it looks quite laughable. It actually is intriguing when viewed in quick glimpses, if only because the viewer is trying to figure out what the hell they're seeing. Then the picture shows us it way too often, and for too long each time, guaranteeing hearty laughter at the sight of a puppet that moves as jerkily as Kermit the Frog and which is about as threatening.

Making matters worse, every character in this pronounces the spirit's name as "ass-fix". This results in such unintentionally hilarious dialogue as "You're just here because you want to capture the condemned man's ass-fix." I'm guessing these are the kind of people who pronounce, and with a straight face, the name of our seventh planet as "yer anus".

At a public execution, Stephens realizes a spirit lingers nearby when a person's (or guinea pig's) life is in imminent danger. He uses a special beam of light to capture that spectral form. By moving the light, the Asphyx will move with it, until it can be captured in a box. Are you also already thinking about *Ghostbusters*?

I'm not sure why trapping this thing ensures a person will live forever. Consider the guinea pig, which had been poisoned so as to summon its Asphyx. Isn't the rodent *still* poisoned? Given this, shouldn't it live in perpetual pain for eternity? And why does the Asphyx stay in the light, anyway? Is it just an astral showbiz whore who can't help but hog the spotlight?

Stephens next does an experiment on himself where he skirts the edge of death, courtesy of an electric chair of his own design. Once his Asphyx is trapped, he is determined to have his daughter and his adopted son do the same. What is mind-boggling is *he comes up with a different method of near-death for each of them.* Since the electric chair worked for him, I have no idea why he would deviate from that arrangement. So, imagine his daughter's reaction to the guillotine he has constructed in order to trap her Asphyx. Then again, I'm not sure anything could shock a person further when one's father has already built their own electric chair.

This looks and feels similar to the gothic films output of Hammer Films. Unfortunately, it compounds a batshit premise with bizarre gaps in narrative. Remember that "special light" I mentioned that is used to capture an Asphyx? That is a "light booster" we first see being used in the public execution scene, but with no explanation as to why it is there or what it does. We don't learn its purpose until some time has passed. Until then, I was completely, and pointlessly, bewildered by what that apparatus was.

Even weirder are the bookending sequences set in present-day London. Before the opening credits, we see police investigating a head-on collision between two automobiles. They pull a body from between the vehicles and, without us seeing the face, one of the officers announces in a stunned voice the victim is somehow still alive.

So, you know from the beginning one of these characters will achieve immortality, and it is simply a matter of guessing which one will. I won't reveal who that is, though we will see at the end that person has somehow aged drastically. This is accomplished through makeup that is literally, laughably bad. Also, I don't understand why anything that could prevent a person from dying would still let them age. Once again, I ask you to consider how poison still in a body could not kill a person. The kicker is they also still have the guinea pig, and it looks exactly the same as before. I laughed so hard at this that my Asphyx was probably hovering nearby, just in case I asphyxiated. Wait...the name of that thing now *almost* makes sense to me!

The Asphyx is a stupefyingly daft movie, but I have to give it points for being unique. I'll acknowledge there is a kernel of an interesting premise here, but the ineptitude of the film's construction only exacerbates its goofiness. Shockingly, the technical aspects of it are quite solid, with the exception of the creature itself. I think the guinea pig deserves better than a sad Muppet that appears to be the grim reaper for humans. I hope that, when it met its maker, it was welcomed by The Death of Rats. SQUEAK.

Original version posted on 1/29/2024

Black Moon (1934)

It isn't surprising Fay Wray is second-billed in 1934's *Black Moon*, as *King Kong* had made her a star just a year earlier. Curiously, she plays a tertiary character in this at best. Instead, third-billed Dorothy Burgess is the true star here.

Burgess plays a high society woman who had been raised on an island plantation by some of the indigenous Black population following the death of her mother. Since then, she has lived in the States with her wealthy industrialist husband (Jack Holt), with whom she has a young daughter (Cora Sue Collins).

Now Burgess has returned to the island with her daughter to stay in the gated fortress of her uncle (Arnold Korff). She is increasingly spending time with "her people", raising concerns from Korff and his White house staff. The uncle is also concerned about the potential for a revolt. Having stayed behind in the city, Holt is increasingly worried about his wife and daughter. He had sent Wray, as his extremely devoted secretary, to travel with Burgess, and she is soon cabling him to say he must come quickly.

There's good reason for everybody's worries. The island's homegrown religion requires human sacrifice, and Burgess has arrived just in time for that. I doubt the term is acceptable anymore, but everybody is wondering if she has "gone native". It does seem odd she leaves the complex every night and doesn't return until dawn.

It is no surprise this film's portrayal of the local populace would be deemed unacceptable even a couple of decades after this was released. What did catch me off guard is Burgess's defense of those people. She has some good arguments in support of them; however, the perspective of the film will eventually fall on the side of her being delusional when she made such statements. I will concede that a token effort to present the belief system of an indigenous culture is better than no effort at all. It's also interesting to see how strong-willed Burgess is, though women with agency would be another element of movies to fall victim to the Production Code.

Speaking of which, you know this is pre-code when Wray tells Holt there's a certain married man she's in love with. She insists she won't live in sin, though only because he hasn't asked her to. Holt is so dim that he doesn't understand it is he who is the object of her affection. Another scene has a bit I doubt would have survived the code, wherein the radio operator is found dead, and we see the dangling feet of the hanged corpse.

I found it strange nobody just tries to use the radio until Holt finally steps in to do so, as he has a radio operator's license. It seemed daft to me that nobody, regardless of how much or little they know about the equipment, doesn't just start pressing buttons, turning random dials and screaming for their lives.

Black Moon is definitely a relic from its time, but it has a peculiar vibe I liked, one similar to the highly atmospheric *I Walked with a Zombie*. Unfortunately, how the film regards non-Causasians is problematic. What I found interesting is, if one was to take the same movie and change the setting to rural England and the characters to White villagers, you would have a proper folk horror film.

Original version posted on 11/9/2024

Blue Sunshine (1977)

In general, I find low-budget pictures from before the digital age more interesting than contemporary low-budget films, as well as major studio fare from any era. These films tend to take more risks (albeit, not necessarily *good* ones). Also, because film stock and film cameras require significant funds, the minds behind such pictures were usually deeply invested (often literally) in the crazy they were throwing up on the screen.

1977's *Blue Sunshine* is such a film. Although competently made, it doesn't seem to follow its own bizarre logic very well and its star delivers one of the worst performances I can recall seeing in a movie with a moderate budget. On the other hand, I wasn't bored for a single minute.

The plot concerns people who consumed a variant of LSD a decade prior that has now made all their hair fall out. They also get turned into homicidal maniacs. That acid was distributed back in the day by a reformed hippie now running for Congress. Seems like there is any easy joke waiting to be made about Congress and homicidal maniacs, maybe even bald ones.

Zalman King takes the lead here in what is the typical Hitchcock role of a man falsely accused of murder who goes on the run in an attempt to clear his name. Odd how he is pursued by only one police detective throughout the runtime, though he will eventually be wanted for four murders by the end. The police in this place and time must have been seriously understaffed.

King is deliriously, howlingly bad. I'm sure economy mandated only one take be used for most of the shots, but I kinda hope there were multiple takes of some of his line readings and that footage of even worse takes still exists somewhere. He over- or under-acts throughout the runtime. Often, he shifts tone abruptly and radically within the same shot and without any apparent character motivation. He may not be as bad as Tommy Wiseau, but I couldn't help but think I was seeing a predecessor here. A proto-Wiseau, if you will.

The other actors fare better, but it is difficult to imagine an actor of any regard knowing how to properly work such batshit material. One character who almost inexplicably develops into the main antagonist is the congressional candidate's bodyguard, whom I can only describe as "Discount Joe Don Baker". You know, in case premium, authentic Joe Don Baker is too high-brow for you. Also, Brion James has little more than a cameo at the beginning, but he goes gloriously crazy in a way similar to what Nicholas Cage is famous for now.

I'm not sure what the deal is with the psychopaths losing all their hair suddenly, but the effect is not well-done. Somebody will grab a person's hair, which is an obvious wig, which slides off to reveal that person is bald, though that is an obvious bald cap. It's weird how many people in this grab another's hair—something I have never done, nor had done to me, in real life. And, if the tell-tale sign that somebody is about to become a homicidal maniac is their hair falling out, then it seems I should have been on some kind of watch list for a long time now.

I went into the movie thinking it would be horror with tinges of sci-fi, but it is closer to a conspiracy thriller. It even flirts with the possibility of becoming a political thriller, what with a potentially nefarious figure running for office, but it casually abandons that thread before it really develops into anything.

The movie is a strange combination of moments that are effective and others that are hilariously daft. There are a couple of solid, intentional laughs. But there are many unintentional laughs, such as a maniac who somehow manages to consecutively stuff three fully-functioning, conscious women into a fire in a typical home fireplace. Yes, three fully competent adults capable of kicking, flailing or at least RUNNING THE FUCK AWAY WHEN THEY SEE THE FIRST WOMAN DIE.

There are some other aspects of the movie that appeal to me personally, and which I understand may not be of interest to anybody else. Chief among these is the shopping mall where the climactic scene takes place. I'm not sure what location was used, but this is a quintessential 70's indoor mall, complete with lots of wood. The icing on the cake is there's a full disco in the mall and, yes, there will eventually be a maniac—MAYYY-KNEEE-ACK—on the flor-or. And he's attacking like he's never done before.

Possibly the weirdest aspect of this picture is the ending. My best guess is they were filming sequentially and ran out of money. That's the best explanation I have for the strangely arbitrary and abrupt ending which uses text overlays in an attempt to provide closure. It felt like that *Simpsons* bit where "Poochie died on the way back to his home planet".

There wasn't enough of interest for me in *Blue Sunshine* to warrant another viewing, though I did find much to enjoy here. It is solidly of a particular age and it ,does some things a movie with more money behind it wouldn't try.

Puppets, for example. I almost forgot the movie has a puppet show performed in the mall as the opening act for a political rally (insert "puppet government" joke here). The puppets aren't in the movie for long, I suspect for fear they would start out-acting Zalman King. But don't feel too bad about Zalman—he went on to become the producer of highly lucrative, softcore dreck like *Wild Orchid* and *Two Moon Junction*.

Original version posted on 3/25/2023

Borderlands (2013)

Fair warning to those who are particularly averse to spoilers, as I am about to reveal the closing line of 2013's found footage horror *Borderlands* (are there any non-horror found footage films?). Then again, the IMDB page puts that line at the start of its quotes section, so just casually scrolling through the main page for the film will reveal this line (also, alas, which character says it). So, here goes. This is the time to bail if you don't want to know this devastating concluding line before watching this picture. And that line is *"You said it wasn't real!"*

Even just typing that line makes the hairs on my arm stand up. But then, the uninitiated would not know the full content of that exclamation. They won't yet have heard it yelled with such despair, anguish and, perhaps worst of all, the feeling of betrayal. I only hope I can convince more people to give this movie a chance.

Gordon Kennedy stars as a priest who investigates reported miracles for the church. He is cynical and skeptical enough that I was surprised he was a priest. When the film opens, he is in Brazil, uncovering yet another faked miracle. He will later unburden himself to Robin Hill, where we will learn his debunking had tragic consequences on that occasion.

Now he is on a mission to investigate what happened at an ancient church deep in rural England. We will see video footage of that occurrence. During a routine baptism, the baby starts crying. Then the crucifix on the table starts moving and the bells start ringing. What appears to be a minor earthquake gains significance upon consequent rewatchings. And this is a film that definitely stands up to repeat viewings.

Joining Kennedy is Hill's tech expert. One thing I find fascinating about this actor is his primary occupation is editing. Of particular note are the pictures he edited for Ben Wheatley, such as *Kill List*, which is one of my favorite films. Honestly, I wouldn't have suspected he was anything other than a full-time actor, because he seems to have such a natural talent.

The rapport between Kennedy and Hill is amazing, and is more than half of the experience. Most of the dialogue between them either advances the plot or is character development, though many of my favorite moments are from their idle banter. I really like these characters—enough that I would gladly watch a movie that is just them hanging out together. There will eventually be a third member of this group, though this bureaucratic church official played by Aidan McArdle is little more than a killjoy.

Together, these three will investigate the strange happenings at the local parish. This church is of so little importance to the residents that, when Kenneth and Hill ask an old man for directions to there, he simply looks at them in a deeply bewildered way. As they drive off, Hill yells this parting shot: "Have fun with Edward Woodward!" This is a film that assumes (likely correctly) its audience will have seen *The Wicker Man*. Given that, it knows viewers will have certain expectations and will rise to meet some of those, while subverting others.

Things start pretty slowly, though a significant atmosphere of dread gradually builds. The leads stay together in a house where they mount cameras in the ceiling corners. At night, these capture footage of mysterious figures looking in the windows. Eventually, somebody sets a live sheep on fire in the yard. An old journal of a long-deceased priest contains the disturbing line, "I fear I now serve a new master."

The horror...the horror... [the section about horror films]

The picture also succeeds where many found footage movies fail, and that is explaining why anybody would be filming everything we are seeing. The many cameras employed by Hill are to capture any and all evidence they might need in case things go off the rails like how they did in Brazil. There are cameras installed around the house they're staying in. There's also GoPro (or similar) cams they wear a great deal of the time. At one point, I like how the filmmakers anticipate what could be a flaw in the integrity of the found footage conceit, having Hill casually mention he has installed signal repeaters in a certain key location.

Borderlands (retitled as *Final Prayer* in the US) is one of the best found footage films I have seen. I highly recommend watching it on the new Second Sight blu-ray. Although this is a UK release, it is region free. Among the extras are a great interview with the leads, who turn out to have as good of a rapport in real life as their characters do in the film. I suspect this is the only movie ever made where the actors got along as well as these two.

Original version posted on 5/13/2024

The Boy Who Cried Werewolf (1973)

Day-for-night often fails to be fully effective, but some of the most egregious examples I have seen are courtesy of 1973's *The Boy Who Cried Werewolf*. Since lycanthropes are active at…let's see here…the light of the full moon, the vast majority of the film takes place at night, except it is obviously day when these scenes were shot. There are also isolated bits genuinely shot at night, which makes the bad day-for-night stuff look even worse in comparison. To think Universal Pictures released this, when they were doing better day-for-night work in their television fare of the time. One line that made me laugh out loud is: "Hey, little boy. What are you doing out here in the black of night?" This is said in a moment filmed at what appears to be high noon.

That incompetence is a shame, because it distracts from what is a surprisingly unique picture. This PG-rated flick is much stranger than I would have expected. It is also more gruesome than something I would have anticipated from a title suggesting this is akin to Disney's live-action output from the era.

We can tell we're not watching a Disney film almost immediately, when a werewolf falls off a cliff and takes a street sign through the chest. This is after trying to attack a kid played by Scott Sealey. Kerwin Matthews, playing the boy's father, gets bitten in a struggle with the creature, becoming a werewolf himself. A psychiatrist played by George Gaynes later tells Matthews a bit about the history of "werewolfism". None of this high falootin' talk of "lycanthropy" from this highly educated man.

Despite this appearing to be a kid's movie, Matthews really carries the movie as the father who is a danger to his son. Not that he appears to be a fundamentally bad person, but I couldn't help but wonder if becoming a werewolf was a metaphor for something dark lurking in his psyche.

One large strike I found against his character is what an asshole he is to his estranged wife, played by Elaine Devry. Apparently, her need for a career was unacceptable to him. From the perspective of the modern viewer, it may be hard to believe this is not portrayed as him being unreasonable. That is reinforced when she capitulates by the end of the picture, declaring all she really needs is a man. My question to her would be: why does *this* asshole fit the bill?

Sealey, as their son, is ostensibly the star of this, which is a strike against the film, as he is deeply annoying. Not sure exactly why he grated on my nerves, but his character is whiny throughout the picture. Then again, the film is called *The Boy Who Cried Werewolf,* so I guess that's what the main character has to do. All the time. In as shrill a manner as possible.

I found it especially confusing Sealey is so desperate to see a hippie encampment up close. The residents turn out to be literally Jesus freaks, as led by a Bob Homel. This guy looks and acts as if Lebowski had travelled back in time and founded a cult. I'm wondering what's going through the minds of his followers and if any of them are hopeful that Manson guy is still taking new recruits.

Anything has to be better than taking orders from a guy who is very confused about his religion and its rituals. He appears to think a pentagram is people dancing in a circle. He believes doing so will force out from Matthews the evil he perceives in the man.

By the end of the movie, the police force, those hippies and an angry mob are all hunting for Matthews. The people in the mob have torches and Frankenstein rakes, as any proper mob should have. The hippies want to pray the evil out of the monster, which is a new one on me. And the police appear to be largely useless, as the chief examines a cellar door clearly smashed from the inside, yet concludes it is the work of a mountain lion. That would assume the beast somehow wandered in and the door firmly shut behind it.

The strangest aspect is how conspicuous Matthews is when he has turned, as only his head and hands change. You would think at least his wife would realize who the monster is but, after he attacks her and their son, she tells the police it was some sort of animal. She's seen animals that wear green corduroy jackets? And pants?!

Speaking of which, fans of bad clothing staples from the 1970's will find much to enjoy here. My personal favorite is a young woman wearing a suede fringe top that looks like she is cosplaying as Pocahontas.

That's probably as good a reason as any for Matthews to kill her and her boyfriend. He rocks their trailer back and forth until it rolls off a cliff. While rocking the trailer, he somehow also shatters a window by smacking it with *both* hands, which makes me wonder how the trailer is moving. I'll just assume he is dry humping it, per that famous bumper sticker, "If this trailer's rocking, it's probably being dry humped by a werewolf".

All of this leaves me wondering who the intended audience was for *The Boy Who Cried Werewolf*. In addition to the deaths I have described so far, Matthews also strangles a TV repairman to death. That seems to me a hair too violent for a kid's movie. At the same time, it is too tame for most adults. Parts of it, such as the hippies, are so ridiculous that there seem to be moments where the filmmakers realize how preposterous this whole enterprise is. This is a strange animal (well, half-animal, I guess), and that may be the only reason to seek it out.

Original version posted on 1/23/2024

Bug (1975)

1996's *Joe's Apartment* had CGI cockroaches that sang and danced in extensively choreographed numbers. And yet I was more surprised when the things spell out the last name of Bradford Dillman's character in the 1975 horror film *Bug*. I hate to inform the filmmakers, but it had the exact opposite effect of what they intended. I wasn't scared in the least. Instead, I was doubled over from laughing so hard.

This occurs in the second, and weirder, half of the picture. Let's start with the first half, which at least has some action in it.

It begins in a church during an earthquake. The floor undulates like ocean waves, which was impressive, even if it left me wondering if such a phenomenon could ever happen in a real quake. That said, I was more impressed with this sequence than anything in the effects-laden *The Quake*.

After this scene, the characters disperse like...well, roaches. A father and son are going home in their pickup truck when it suddenly stops. The father chastises the son for flooding the engine, which confused me, as I don't think that could result in the white smoke pouring out of the tailpipe. There is enough of it to form its own cloud system. Even more surprising is the truck then explodes.

A previously unseen species of roach released by the earthquake caused that explosion, as well as several more to come. These things look like those fossils of trilobites and have appendages on their undersides they can strike together like flints. They deliver an electric shock when picked up, meaning evolution resulted in something with its own built-in joy buzzer. Add in its own whoopie cushion and these things could be the life of the party.

One of the things I struggled with when watching the movie is, even taking into account the fire-making ability, I still couldn't fathom how these things were making vehicles explode. For that matter, I was a little fuzzy as to why they are attracted to vehicle engines to begin with. Maybe they just like the warmth. It is revealed the things live on ashes, but I just checked under the hood of my car and, while not pristine, the engine didn't have much ash on it.

Even more confusing to me is the discovery roughly halfway through the runtime that these things will perish naturally. In addition to being slow-moving and unable to reproduce, they can't adjust to the low pressure of the surface atmosphere, so they eventually explode. If I never again see a roach's insides exploding outwards in slow-motion, it will be too soon.

But why would the air pressure have been greater underground? One scientist speculates the roaches lived for eons in a cave deep below the surface, a microcosm of just them and their food sources. But I don't think the air pressure would be incredibly high in such a situation. I mean, it isn't like they are in the ocean at that depth. I could be wrong (and I know I am overthinking this), but something about this doesn't scan.

The movie then downshifts for its second half, when it focuses almost exclusively on Dillman and his attempt to ensure the survival of the invaders. The death of his wife seems to be the motivation, though he seemed to have an interest in a preservation effort even before that happens. I would have thought he would have had even more motivation to wipe these things out once they have killed his wife, but what do I know.

Cross-breeding with common household cockroaches results in the hyper-intelligent bugs that eventually spell out his last name as well as "WE LIVE". This was too much for me. I only wish the roaches from *Bug* could be further crossbred with the singing roaches from *Joe's Apartment*, and then we might have insect dance routines in increasingly complex geometric progressions, perhaps as fractals growing into patterns of infinite complexity, pushing bad taste into hitherto unexplored territory.

Original version posted on 1/6/2024

Butcher, Baker, Nightmare Maker (1981)

Susan Tyrrell must have led an interesting life. Being Oscar nominated for Best Actress for 1972's *Fat City* didn't dissuade her from going on to do *Andy Warhol's Bad* or playing Queen Doris in Richard Elfman's deeply weird *Forbidden Zone*.

In 1981, she starred with Jimmy McNichol in the off-beat horror film *Butcher, Baker, Nightmare Maker*. She's his aunt, and she takes him in after his parents die in a horrible collision with a truck that's hauling logs. In an impressively gruesome sequence, we see (in slow-motion, no less) one of those logs go through the windshield, *through the driver's head*, and out the back window.

That happened because the driver discovered too late that the brakes weren't working. I wasn't surprised by later dialogue where a character raises the possibility those brake lines had been cut. And there's only one person we can suspect having done that.

Cut to 14 years later, and McNichol is the star of his school's basketball team. It is made obvious from the first time we see Tyrrell with him that she has strong incestuous urges. This probably doesn't bode well for Julia Duffy, as McNichol's girlfriend. Tyrrell even refuses to let her come to the house for his birthday dinner the next night, as mom will be his "date".

It's no surprise how poorly she will react to the full-ride athletic scholarship he's been offered to an out-of-state college. She will stop at nothing to keep him by her side. In a scene with odd beats and pacing, she seduces a TV repairman making a house call, changes her mind when he gets randy, then stabs him to death. In what seems like impossible timing, McNichol arrives home just when the murder happens, and he ends up holding the bloody knife.

The horror...the horror... [the section about horror films]

As if Tyrrell's behavior wasn't schizophrenic enough, she's upstaged by Bo Svenson when he shows up as the lead detective. For somebody who played detectives in so many movies and TV shows, it's like he forgot how to act like one for this. His behavior is distracting and, as he's playing a detective, far from professional.

You see, he's convinced McNichol is gay and so, according to Svenson's spurious logic, the boy must have killed the repairman. Those offended by the word "fag" will be appalled by the number of times the detective says it. He also holds such interesting beliefs as McNichol must be gay because he was raised by a woman without a man in the house. Svenson will twist any new information to support his theories and reject anything that challenges it, even when fellow detective Britt Leach can tell Tyrrell is the murderer. It might not even be the first time she has killed.

Tyrrell's performance is the most unique aspect of this film, and that's for reasons both good and bad. It is impossible to take your eyes off her in any frame she's in. At first, she has odd twitches that hint at a cracking psyche. In the third act, she flies straight off the rails in a hysterical, deeply batshit manner that a better director would have reigned in.

Go figure, that third act is when the picture succumbs to the conventions of the slasher genre, which is a shame, as it had been an unsettled and unsettling mess before then. The film defies expectations of what one would expect from a murder investigation film, as a viewer would identify with the detective by default. But Svenson is so immediately repellent, I had trouble figuring out where our sympathies are supposed to lie. We were more than halfway through the film when it started to dawn on me this homophobic psychopath is the other villain, and we are supposed to instead champion such figures as a closeted basketball coach.

Earlier, I mentioned the odd pacing of the murder scene, and that is something which plagues the movie throughout its runtime. Just as it is hard to define exactly what makes great editing, it is often just as confusing to pinpoint what constitutes bad editing. All I know is I found myself aware of the seams, which is never a good thing.

In addition to the odd performances from Tyrrell and Svenson, there are some other interesting aspects of *Butcher, Baker, Nightmare Maker*. I was pleasantly surprised to see Bill Paxton, younger than I have seen him before but already fully-formed as an actor. He effortlessly steals the few scenes he's in.

I also always find it interesting when movies wear their influences on their sleeve, such as Tyrrell's shrine to the Virgin Mary, which immediately brought to mind *Carrie*. And if one shrine seems a fair indicator of an unbalanced mind, what does one make of the revelation Tyrrell has *two* shrines?

Original version posted on 12/1/2024

The Cat Creeps (1946)

I can't believe anybody in this age could still be superstitious about black cats. As somebody who has lived with four of them so far in the course of my life, I have experienced first-hand how loving and beautiful they can be. Also, regarding my convoluted writing in that previous sentence: you can't *own* a cat, you can only live with one.

As Kim Newman points out in a bonus feature interview on the Vinegar Syndrome blu-ray, 1946's *The Cat Creeps* is part of a long tradition of black cats being an element of horror films. One thing that distinguishes this movie is it is the only time I have seen a cat allegedly possessed by the spirit of its murdered owner.

According to the daughter of the deceased woman, the cat will identify the killer. This leads to such bizarre moments as a woman freaking out as another holds the cat limply before her: "Just stop pointing that cat at me!" That is some overwhelming ailurophobia.

The movie begins with a newspaper reporter (Frederick Brady) receiving an assignment to investigate a candidate for senate. This assignment comes directly from the editor, whose brother (Arthur Loft) just happens to be the opposing candidate in the election.

The accusation against the other candidate (Jonathan Hale) is that he is responsible for a murder that happened 15 years prior. Brady immediately goes to Hale to let him know the accusations, as he hopes to have him as his father-in-law one day.

Lois Collier plays Hale's daughter. I don't recall ever having seen her in anything before, but she's OK here. Admittedly, it isn't a role that would strain any actor.

The bulk of the movie will have the fairly large cast congregate in a dark old house. Honestly, I was never entirely sure what was happening or even who some of the people were. That's pretty strange, given this is not even a full hour long.

Among the characters are Noah Berry, Jr., as Brady's photographer and comic sparring partner. There's also Brady's potential future spouse and her father. There's a private detective. There's an old woman who seems to serve no purpose except to die early on. Also, there's her daughter, who is only here to convince the others the cat is possessed by the spirit of her deceased mother. There are a couple of other characters I couldn't think of a good reason why they would be there: a male detective and that woman who is terrified of cats.

When our main group of characters arrives at the house, they see a light come on in an upstairs window. Despite this, they proceed to break into the house. I have no idea why they did this. Seems like the leading candidates for an election only two days away should be concerned about the potential negative publicity that could result from an arrest for breaking and entering.

In addition to the murder mystery and the political intrigue, there's supposed to be two hundred thousand dollars hidden in the place. I'm surprised the writers didn't also throw in the Maltese Falcon, the Ark of the Covenant and the Hound of the Baskervilles.

Aside from being an unusual mess, this is a highly entertaining picture. The dialogue consistently has a zing to it, even if the characters didn't strike me as likely clever enough to be saying such things. Some examples: "Terry, you're only saying that because it's true" and "He sleeps with one eye open. He can't even trust himself".

There's also a moment I liked where Brady tries to trick the killer by saying somebody should go get a doctor. He expects only one of three men to seize the opportunity, except all three volunteer. "I thought one of you would tip your hand. You can't *all* be guilty."

The Cat Creeps is obviously a cheap programmer created solely to occupy the second slot on a double bill. Still, it is enjoyable, if you're able turn off your brain and just roll with it. Besides, there is a beautiful black cat that is really the star here. There's a reason one character quips, "Everybody seems more interested in the cat than the murderer."

Original version posted on 9/27/2023

Catacombs (1965)

Gary Merrill had once been married to Bette Davis, after they fell in love on the set of *All About Eve*. He had been separated from her for five years when he starred in 1965's *Catacombs* (later retitled to *The Woman Who Wouldn't Die*), a movie where he conspires to kill his financially successful but domineering wife. One wonders if he thought of his ex-wife while making this.

One thing that was refreshing about this film is that wife, played by Georgina Cookson, obtained her money through her business acumen, when most films of that era would have had her simply inheriting a fortune. Nor does the script make her into some shrill shrew. Instead of simply henpecking Merrill, she treats him as more of a boy-toy, and it is obvious she enjoys being serviced by him.

She doesn't seem to have any romantic interest in the younger man who is her secretary, played by Neil McCallum. Still, she controls him, holding over his head the checks she keeps in her safe, ones where he tried to forge her signature. McCallum chafes under her thumb, and this former prison inmate dreams of offing her.

While she may not have a wandering eye, Merrill does, and his settles upon her niece (Jane Merrow) who has just returned from an art education in Paris. It is obvious Merrow also feels constrained by her aunt, though she only appears to be mildly frustrated. And it isn't like we see Cookson treating her monstrously. There are just little things like her observation of a study of a nude woman Merrow has painted: "Haven't the French ever heard of landscapes?" Well, we don't see the lowest portions of the work, so there could be bush there.

The horror...the horror... [the section about horror films]

I was surprised Merrill's lust for Merrow is reciprocated, given the age difference and, well, he's not an attractive man. Merrow even says at one point, "I think the word to describe you is virile", which I guess is supported by the appallingly dense carpet of chest hair we see when he's lounging with his shirt open. I will concede he may have a certain animal magnetism, but only because he is rather simian in appearance, especially when he is in profile as she sculpts a bust of him.

Anywho, there's at least three people who might want Cookson dead, though her behavior seemed fairly reasonable to me. She's unpleasant enough that I wouldn't want to be around her, but I very much doubt I would suddenly drown her in a sink, as her husband does.

And here is where the wheels on the movie start wobbling some, even if they don't completely fall off. You see, he takes her body to the shed, where he digs a hole in the earth floor. I'm not sure if it is bad acting, but Cookson is breathing, and heavily. I think simply reframing the shots would have made that less obvious. What is more curious is Merrill decides to use a locker as her casket, instead of simply burying the body. There's no real reason for him to do that. Somebody might later notice the locker is missing. It will displace more dirt than just a body. It just doesn't make any sense.

Really, the only reason this is in the film is to make it seem more possible she is not dead once mysterious things start happening. Further evidence for the possibility he did not kill her was a very odd element of the plot introduced earlier, where she regularly hypnotizes herself in a mirror as a way of dealing with pains she experiences. In a moment that straddles the line between creepy and funny, we see her staring bug-eyed into a mirror that reflects a strong light into those eyes. I could not help but recall *Prince of Darkness*, and was waiting for her to stick her fingers into the mirror while going "Faaaatherrrrrr…"

Merrill had the poor timing to spontaneously off her a week before she was going to Italy for a spa trip alone. McCallum had already arranged with Merrill to have Cookson die on that trip. But the secretary happens to know a woman who can transform herself into a stunning impersonation of Cookson— and that's because she is played by the same actress. Admittedly, Cookson's lower-class alter ego convincingly speaks in a different accent when not "on the job". Unfortunately for her, she does not anticipate McCallum hitting her over the head with a rock and putting her in a car he douses with gasoline and pushes off a cliff. The resulting explosion is impressive.

The rest of the film is full of mysterious happenings where it appears either Merrill failed to kill his wife, or she has somehow returned from the grave. There's also the likelihood somebody is causing shenanigans to torment the others. That said, with a cast of seven, there are only so many possibilities.

So, I was surprised I was unable to outguess *Catacombs*. In retrospect, there may have been one or two cheats that make it difficult for viewers to come to the same solution. Still, I accepted this, as well as some quirks that stretch credulity, and not just the ones I mentioned earlier. Crisp black-and-white photography, solid performances and an above-average script made this a more fulfilling experience than what I assumed it would be, and that was yet another remake/rip-off of *Diabolique*.

Original version posted on 9/12/2024

Clearcut (1991)

A small propeller plane flies over a vast wasteland of felled trees in the Canadian forest. In a scene which reminded me of the opening of *The Wicker Man,* it touches down on a lake in what is obviously a very isolated area. A man steps out of the plane, wades to the shoreline and the plane departs again. The man continues into the forest, despite wearing highly incongruous clothing for this endeavor: dress shoes, pressed slacks and button-down shirt. He's also carrying a briefcase.

This unusual and intriguing setup begins 1991's *Clearcut.* This is the only Canadian feature in the folk horror blu-ray box set *All the Haunts Be Ours* from Severin. Not sure why, but I never wondered whether there were any folk horror films from above the 49th parallel. Similarly, and embarrassingly, I also never think of there being Native Canadians, which at least the entire population of Nunavut may want to have a conversation with me about.

Our guy encounters a little girl in the forest who asks him for a light. She proceeds to light a cigarette for herself and he asks her if she knows who he is. "The man who talks for us," she replies.

The two exit the forest and see a huge fight between Native Canadians and police. Right behind the police are bulldozers. A news crew is capturing the whole affair.

Turns out our protagonist is a lawyer for the tribe, returning from Toronto with bad news: he failed in court to block further clearcutting efforts to establish a new road. We'll also meet the instigator of the project, and winner of that lawsuit: the pompous head of the local lumber mill.

Ron Lea plays our lawyer protagonist, and he starts seeing a mysterious figure who is played by Graham Greene. Lea participates in a sweat lodge ceremony, though I wasn't entirely certain why he is invited or why he accepts. As the tribe's chief (played by Floyd Red Crow Westerman) warns him, he should not be scared of what he finds within himself. The lawyer's vision in the ceremony is the laughing visage of Greene.

I was surprised when Greene talks directly to Lea the next day. I thought he had been an imaginary figure up until this point. Greene taunts Lea, asking what exactly the lawyer can do for the tribe now that the case is lost. Like *Strangers on a Train*, Lea jokingly proposes they skin the owner of the mill alive. And like that movie and book, a dubious character takes this recommendation to heart.

Greene's character is fascinating: a mischievous, malicious and possibly supernatural being. He is as funny and witty as often as he is terrifying, and occasionally in the same moments. The folk horror element that comes into play here is when Westerman mentions a trickster spirit known to him. I think it's interesting how so many mythologies around the world have such a figure.

Greene ends up kidnapping the mill owner. It's hard to say whether Lea is also kidnapped or if he is an accomplice. The remainder of the film explores complex and constantly shifting dynamics between the three men, though Greene always has the upper hand. In a way, this is like some weird, homicidal buddy/road picture.

I would describe *Clearcut* as more drama than horror, though it gets quite gruesome towards the end, and it doesn't pull any punches with the gore. Overall, I would say I enjoyed it, though I would be hard-pressed to give concrete reasons why. At the very least, it was interesting to see folk horror from a place and culture I would not normally expect one from.

Original version posted on 6/10/2023

Danza Macabra (1964)

Funny how all the ghosts in 1964's *Danza Macabra* keep telling the protagonist Georges Rivière they are spirits, yet he doesn't believe them. I have to concede I also would not believe them. And yet, I kept waiting for our hero to realize he's surrounded by gh-gh-gh-gh-gh-*ghosts!!!* and then for one of them to respond with "Well, duh."

Rivière has accepted a wager from Umberto Raho to spend the night in his haunted castle. The ante was originally 100 pounds until Rivière, a newspaper man, claims no honest journalist would ever have that much money on him. Instead, he agrees to do it for 10 pounds. I liked that.

Turns out Raho recruits some poor sap every year on that day, November 1st, to try to survive a night in the house. So far, none of the challengers have lived to see November 2nd. I would be apprehensive if I was presented this wager, as I seem to recall that date is an important holiday in some cultures, being the day of the…something. Don't worry, it will come to me.

The castle is sufficiently foreboding just from the gate, with spikes positioned in a manner implying they are to keep people *in* instead of out, as they would make excellent footholds for one trying to break in. Once through the gate, Rivière has to cross a cemetery, and he is so startled by everything that I'm surprised he had enough courage to get into the house. Along the way, he jumps at the sight of a kitten. He also somehow gets thoroughly entangled in tree branches so sparse that I suspect the own way I could get stuck to them is if they were actually sewn to my clothes.

Finally inside the castle, he encounters a great many ghosts, all of which are doomed to recreate roughly the same scenarios on this night year after year. Most notable among these is Barbara Steele, the queen of gothic horror movies, what with her weirdly angular facial features and disproportionately large eyes. Soon, her ghost is reexperiencing her death, then her husband is murdered again, then her lover who killed him is dying all over again, etc., resulting in four re-dead bodies in a bedroom. It's like a bizarre version of the old "The House That Jack Built" nursery rhyme. It also turns out those who tried to win the wager in the past are now ghosts there as well and are endlessly reenacting the night they arrived . I thought that was an interesting touch.

One of the more interesting spirits who isn't Steele is Arturo Dominici, a professor who took up the challenge in a prior year due to his interest in the metaphysical. That he, needless to say, failed and became a ghost himself is a peculiar spin on an academic "going native".

This is a movie that doesn't pull its punches, and I was surprised by the coldness of its ending. There's also a single bit I wish had been excluded, and that is the head being cut off from a live snake. Alas, a real animal was definitely harmed in the making of this movie.

Aside from that, I found a great deal to enjoy in this film, which is more widely known by its U.S. title, *Castle of Blood*. Once one sets aside the jarring sensation resulting from watching a bunch of people in 19th century England talk in Italian, this is a much better than average gothic horror picture. This, despite it being based on a short story by, as the opening credits put it, "*Edgard* Allan Poe". Perhaps it was, because it isn't based on anything written by Edgar Allan Poe.

Original version posted on 8/31/2024

Death Line (1972)

False advertising is a bitch. I bought this import blu-ray because it said Christopher Lee is in it. And he is, for like three minutes.

Lee is in 1972's *Death Line* because he wanted to act alongside Donald Pleasance. The result is they are almost in one scene together. I say "almost" because the camera alternates between either a straight-on shot of Lee or a straight-on shot of Pleasance. At first, I thought they were filmed at different times and places, but the final shot reveals they are there together. So why take the bizarre approach of having them appear to talk directly to the audience?

The concept of the movie itself is intriguing: people have been disappearing periodically from a London tube station. There was an incident decades ago near this stop in which a tunnel under construction collapsed. Some of the workers were left to die there.

From the evidence we will be presented, we can surmise some of those workers survived and then spawned successive generations by abducting and impregnating women from the platform. They also have been killing men and eating their corpses.

That the men could ever escape from what was thought to be their tomb seems me a fatal flaw in the premise. If the earliest survivors of the accident could get out to find victims, why didn't they just get away entirely?

Of course, then we wouldn't have a movie. This gory non-sensical mess full of copiously drooling, puss-oozing, rapey cannibals. Well, *cannibal,* singular, as we are down to the last descendent of his tribe. He looks like the homeless guy from the cover of Jethro Tull's *Aqualung* brought to life.

This is a seriously gross picture. There are some shots which linger so long on things like rotting limbs and decomposing carcasses on meat hooks that it is like a pornography of gore. To my absolute shock, this *wasn't* one of the films singled out my British censors in the 80s as one of the "Video Nasties". And, yet, it isn't scary in the least, unless you count a poster on the wall advertising "The Black & White Minstrel Shows presents The Magic of the Minstrels."

As for the cast, Donald Pleasance is the most notable presence, though he seems to think he is in a comedy. Other than his performance, there are no indications this movie was meant to be tongue-in-cheek (Well, there was that train showing the next destination was "COCKFOSTERS", which made my wife and I breathless from laughing—and which goes to show how immature and easily amused we are). I wish I could see the movie he thinks he's in instead of the one he is actually in. He delivers many bizarre little quips that had to be ad-libbed. At times, it's almost as weird of a performance as Christopher Walken's cameo in *Gigli.*

Our alleged hero in this is played by David Ladd. He and his girlfriend (Sharon Gurney) find a victim of the tunnel cannibal, mistaking him for a drunk. When they report this to the police, Ladd ends up in a confrontation with Pleasance.

I'm not sure if it is just Ladd's performance (which is definitely sub-par) or his rude and abrasive character, but I kept hoping the police would start whaling on him. I was baffled as to why this actor was cast at all and initially wondered if it was because he looks like Jeff Bridges at first glance. Then I noticed one of the movie's "presenters" is Alan Ladd, who just happens to be his father.

Sharon Gurney fares better, both due to greater acting ability and a better role. I write that, even though that role largely boils down to "girl inevitably getting abducted by rapey tunnel troll". Maybe it's just her Ziggy Stardust haircut, but she looks odd—it's as if David Bowie, Charlotte Gainsbourg and Kristen Stewart had a child together. She also has a weird piecemeal coat that looks like one coat ate several others and then coughed up a hairball.

I strongly disliked *Death Line*. Some of Donald Pleasance's shtick is amusing, but not enough for me to recommend it to others. It is similar to 1984's *C.H.U.D.* which, despite being lower budget and made over a decade later, is the superior film. Actually, I love that later film so, not only would I recommend seeing it instead of the earlier one, I would recommend watching that one, period.

Original version posted on 5/12/2023

The Devil's Lover (1972)

As we learned from a legendary Monty Python sketch, nobody expects the Spanish Inquisition. I especially wouldn't expect it in Italy, but yet there's the mysterious red-hooded and black-cloaked figure in 1972's *The Devil's Lover*. At least, it sure looks like an Inquisitor. Instead, it is only the devil (Edmund Purdom) dressed as one—so, somebody slightly less evil than a torturer for the medieval-era Church.

This figure goes around the countryside in medieval Italy, appearing and disappearing seemingly at random. The only deliberate harm he seems to do is pursue Rosalba Neri, distracting her from her love for her fiancée (Ferdinando Poggi). The wedding of those two goes ahead, though Purdom has Neri murder her husband with an elaborate ceremonial dagger on the honeymoon night before they can consummate their relationship. Then she goes skipping to the old, desecrated church while weirdly inappropriately jaunty music plays on the soundtrack. I like to imagine that, if this happy ditty had words, they'd probably be something like "la la la la la/it's my wedding night/but I'm off to have Satan/plug all my holes."

The general vibe of this film is like an old fairy tale I've not heard before, and of the kind the Brothers Grimm collected back in their original versions. There's a poisoned amulet. Neri's wedding dress is cursed when a figure catches a glimpse of it while peeping through a window. But there are elements which were far more gruesome than the Disneyfied versions of those tales everybody is familiar with today.

For example, two friends of Neri are lured into a cave where they are raped and murdered. There's also some girl-girl action, which is portrayed as something evil. There's also a vampire there, which means we have a couple of women raped and murdered by a group which includes a vampire lesbian. I wonder if this is how some far-right conservatives imagine a typical gathering of liberals to be like.

One aspect of the film I thought would be amazing is the cinematography. Instead, many scenes are filmed in what might be the least scenic parts of rural Italy. At times, I was once again reminded of Monty Python, whose *Holy Grail* was intentionally filmed in a way that made England of that period look as shitty as possible.

Still, there is the obligatory beautiful old castle, which such movies have led me to believe are still the predominate form of architecture in that country. The medieval storyline is pointlessly bookended by some business in the present day, where Neri and two female friends arrive at the castle. She's trying to find the truth as to whether the castle was purchased by the owner from Satan. I never knew Old Scratch was a Realtor. Apparently, there's no end to his evil.

I was amused the trio of young(-ish) women arrives at the castle just expecting to be put up for the night, which they are. Their strong sense of entitlement makes me think they would do well in today's world. I can imagine them as successful social media influencers.

Neri doesn't find the answer she's looking for, but she still seems satisfied when she wakes up the next morning from what she thought was a dream, but which is everything we have seen that apparently really happened centuries earlier. That she is so happy seems odd given what we know she just dreamed. Her two friends also seem quite chipper, though we saw their alter egos in the past, one raped and tortured and the other getting branded with a hot iron, and her tongue torn out, by Neri. If Neri had a dream that was her experiencing what had happened in the past, and presumably the other two did as well, I doubt everybody would be so chummy going forward. Even if they didn't share the same vision, they still spent the night in a dank, old castle, which doesn't seem great.

As for the performances, this is entirely a showcase for Neri. I suspect she's not a great actress, but she commands the screen in every frame she's in. Then again, none of her costars have much presence, so it is easy for her be so noticeable, if only in contrast.

I was surprised this blu-ray comes with a soundtrack CD, as I can't imagine that having much replay value. There's one moment that is memorable for entirely the wrong reasons, as it sounds like somebody is playing a pipe organ using their elbows.

A great deal happens in *The Devil's Lover*, except it feels like they were just making it up as they went along, with little consideration for sense or logic. When that approach works best, you get something like *Suspiria*. But more often than not, you get a feature like this, a mess of elements that try to be mysterious, but instead failed to intrigue me. The best of these kinds of film give me something to chew on for some time after. A week from now, I doubt I will recall ever having seen this.

Original version posted on 10/22/2024

Doctor Death: Seeker of Souls (1973)

I am a big fan of the two *Dr. Phibes* movies. Some people seem to find them mean-spirited, but I think they're too goofy to take seriously. Part of what sells it is how much fun Vincent Price is having. John Considine isn't Price, but he channels some of that diabolical glee as the villain in 1973's *Doctor Death: Seeker of Souls.*

Considine's character is hundreds of years old. Back in medieval times, he was an aristocrat and alchemist (alchemocrat?) who discovered the secret to eternal life: transferring his soul to that of a recently deceased man. He navigates through a long series of bodies until he winds up in 1970's L.A., providing this service for others.

The first demonstration we see of his work is startling in its showmanship, as he saws a woman in half—for real. "I don't know what gets into me, but I feel the urge to do everything theatrically." The purpose of this ritual was to move the soul of that woman into a corpse on the stage.

Barry Coe is in the audience witnessing this Grand Guignol transfer of a soul. His wife has recently died, and he is unable to get over the loss. Looks like somebody is about to see the doctor.

Let's go ahead and get something out of the way. You are not going to be able to enjoy this movie if you get hung up on the technical details of what happens to a body after death. In one scene after another, the soul of one person is transferred into a dead body and, regardless of how fresh that corpse may be, it obviously ended up in a state that was unable to support life. I found I had to quickly set aside doubts that putting a soul into a recently poisoned body would be a good idea.

That said, if you can suspend your disbelief, this movie is a hoot. More than half of the fun is watching Considine go audaciously over the top. He is gloriously hammy and relishes it, such as when he tells Coe his life story: "To explain it properly, and I do enjoy telling the story, we start 1000 years ago." Later, he lays a big, wet smacker on a corpse and declares, "This child kisses better dead than Tana did while she was alive."

The production values are OK, but nothing extraordinary. Everything about it looks and feels like a made-for-TV movie. Admittedly, such a film wouldn't have the gore this does, but there isn't much that would have to be trimmed from it today to get a PG-13 rating.

I also want to briefly mention the score, which becomes more cartoonish as it goes along. By the end, it sounds like music from *Scooby Doo*, cult TV classic *The Avengers* and the original *Batman* series are all playing at the same time.

As for the cast, Coe and the supporting actors are all competent, but not much more than that. Of particular note is Moe Howard of the Three Stooges in a cameo that was his final screen appearance.

Doctor Death is less horror than it is comedy, even if it is an especially dark one. And Considine isn't Price, but he is a fair substitute for a film like this. I went in with no expectations and ended up having a good time.

Original version posted on 4/6/2024

Dolls (1986)

Let's face it: dolls are creepy. I think this feeling is aptly summarized in one of the most beloved episodes of *The X-Files*, "Clyde Bruckman's Final Repose", where a psychic played by Peter Boyle gets weirded out by a murdered woman's collection of dolls. "Why did this woman collect dolls? What was it about her life? Was it one specific moment where she suddenly said, *I know... dolls*. Or was it a whole series of things?"

There are shelves upon shelves of the things in the dark, old mansion at the center of 1986's *Dolls*. This is a weird movie. Actually, it feels like two different cuts of the same movie were spliced together almost at random.

One of those movies would be a slightly dark kid's adventure, ala *The Goonies*. Carrie Lorraine plays a little girl who has two deeply awful parents, played by Ian Patrick Williams and Carolyn Purdy-Gordon. The movie is well-served by Lorraine's naturalist acting, and her lines seem to be tailored for such a performer: "What do you want from me? I'm seven years old." As for Purdy-Gordon, she was the wife of the director at the time, and that is Stuart Gordon, of *Re-Animator* fame.

That credit alone should clue viewers into the other path this film will take, and that is a fairly gory and violent one. I have seen films of this vintage which are far more explicit in that regard, but this is still a very solid R. So then: *not* a kid's adventure film.

The family will seek shelter in the creepy-ass mansion after their car breaks down in a storm created by the most fickle rain machine I have seen. Turn the camera one way and there's a deluge. Cut to the opposite angle and there's nary a drop in sight.

The owners of the mansion are eccentric old doll creators played by Guy Rolfe and Hilary Mason. I do not recall having seen Rolfe in anything before, but his performance brings dignity to the film. But I do remember Mason as the blind psychic in *Don't Look Now*, and it was great to see her in something again.

Other shelter-seekers over the course of the night include Stephen Lee as a benign man-child. This overweight man looks more than a bit like Sean Astin gone to seed. He arrives with two hitchhikers he picked up, and these are played by Bunty Bailey and Cassie Stuart. Neither is very believable as a punk rocker, even if this is the 1980s low-budget film idea of a "punk".

Bailey was briefly a thing in the film world after being the girl in a-Ha's "Take on Me" video. Here, she has a deeply risible British accent I assume is meant to be Cockney. Maybe that is her real accent, but the fact it wavers in strength from line to line indicates otherwise.

The kid's thread through the movie, as I have come to think of it, largely has Lorraine and Lee investigating by candlelight weird phenomena around the house. Their encounters with the evil, living dolls are largely benign. Admittedly, these things do try to kill Lee at one point, but Lorraine intervenes, and they all play nice from that point on.

The other guests in the house do not have Lorraine to intervene for them, so they are killed off in various ways. Once again, the gore and violence could have been worse, but it is strong enough here to be excessively jarring in comparison to the other material. One moment that crossed a line for me is when one character rolls over somebody they think is only sleeping, only for them to discover that corpse to have an eye plucked out of the socket and dangling around on the thread of its optic nerve.

The characters are pretty slow on the uptake, making them easy for the dolls to capture and kill. One character says, when they finally catch on to the situation, "Oh my God. They're right...it's the little people." Alas, this is not an adaptation of John Christopher's novel *The Little People*, which is about Nazi leprechauns (no, really--I own a copy).

One area where the film excels is the special effects. I'm sure they would have used CGI if it had been9 cheap and readily available when this was made. Thank God it wasn't, as a combination of marionettes, stop-motion and mechanical-controlled figures were employed. I love practical effects, and the stop-motion is especially effective. One effect I never quite figured out is how the unarticulated dolls' heads change expressions in some scenes. Those isolated moments *deeply* unnerved me.

The movie was produced by Charles Band, who would go on to a kind of fame with the cult hit series *Puppet Master*. Given the physical effects work here, one can see a straight line from this film to a succession of movies centered around tiny toy killing machines.

Dolls isn't the first film I have seen which scans as a kids' movie but which has enough hard-R content in it to disqualify it as such. That element didn't completely turn me off, but it kept me from completely losing myself in it. Even with that, there is still enough here to warrant a viewing by the curious, and the whole endeavor has a certain goofy charm.

Original version posted on 2/21/2024

Dracula (1974)

I would say Jack Palance is among the last of the actors I would consider to play Dracula, if only because he never would have been anywhere on the list of candidates, period. To my considerable surprise, Palance is exceptional in a 1974 telefilm adaptation of *Dracula*. He has the stature for the role and, let's face it, he has always had an intimidating stoicism. Those qualities serve him well here.

I can imagine the snorts and eyerolls of anybody who might be reading this when I wrote this was made for television. Those who immediately dismiss an entire form of media are missing out on some real diamonds, even if you do have to go through the rough to unearth them. In this case, we have a telefilm directed by Dan Curtis and written by horror legend Richard Matheson, the team behind the also excellent *The Night Stalker* and *The Night Strangler*.

It was screened in theatres outside the US, including the UK, which was pretty common at the time. And, honestly, given the solid photography and widescreen shot compositions, I would not have assumed this was primarily made for the small screen. Location shooting in very old locales in Yugoslavia and Croatia definitely makes the most of a budget that had to have been far less than that of a big studio feature film.

Adaptations of the novel have varied wildly in how closely they hew to the source material. This one is fairly faithful, though it is inevitably partly influenced by the Lugosi version and the Hammer series. Other sources might have also been incorporated, but I am unconcerned about that. I'm not a purist, and I don't care which versions of, or elements thereof, the whole vampire mythology it sticks to.

In this take on the tale, we follow poor, doomed Jonathan Harker (Murray Brown) on his way to the count's estate. As always, I like it when we see this part of the story, though it never stops striking me as strange that we have a monster movie begin with somebody going to complete something so mundane as a real estate transaction.

I like the scene where Palance looks at the photos Brown has brought with him of his fiancée and friends. When he sees Lucy (Fiona Lewis), he snarls and contorts his face in a way that reveals a nature which is truly beastly. Even better is when Brown points out her boyfriend, and Palance's expression is as if he suddenly smelled something repulsive.

Once Brown is trapped in the mansion, he discovers a passage into a secret and rundown part of it. I like how there are cobwebs all over everything, yet there are candles lit. So, this area hasn't fallen into disuse, but who is still using it, and for what purpose?

Brown gets his answers in a moment that actually made me jump. He's looking at a very old painting of Palance, only to turn around and discover creepy women standing stock-still at different places around the room. Like some diabolical game of "red light / green light", the brides of Dracula have entered without a sound and then stopped as soon as they were observed.

There's another great moment shortly after, when Palance arrives in England. All we are shown of how he traveled to England is the wrecked ship *Demeter* crashed on the shore, and a man lashed to the wheel, his arm locked outwards holding the crucifix that failed to save their life. This isn't a jump scare, unlike the scene with the brides, but the impact of this brief scene lasts long after the credits roll.

One element which is unique to this version, as far I can tell, is it becomes a police procedural for an extended period of time, as Simon Ward and Nigel Davenport inquire about boxes of earth reported on the docket of the *Demeter* and follow the path they took to their destination. I might have seen other versions with scenes like this, and simply forgot, but this one is noteworthy in how much time is devoted to the thread.

Even at the time it was made, everybody knew the basic story points of the Dan Curtis *Dracula*, as well as roughly how it will turn out. No wheels are reinvented but, for fans of this particular niche of horror, it is quite satisfying simply to see it executed so well. That Jack Palance makes such a surprisingly good Drac is icing on the cake.

Original version posted on 8/7/2024

Enys Men (2022)

2022 "horror" movie Enys Men stars Mary Woodvine, in what is nearly a solo performance as a scientist losing a grasp on reality in her study of an isolated group of strange flowers, on a very deserted island (if you don't count all the ghosts and/or figments of her imagination). For this essay, the critic will be subjected to observation whilst watching the picture.

02 minutes, 52 seconds: Scientist takes temperature of soil around flowers. Ascends rough stone steps in hillside. At apex, grabs a stone, holds at arms-length over a square hole in the ground and lets it fall into the abyss. Enters house. Fires up generator. Waits for apparent daily communication on the shortwave. Records plant temperature in journal as 14.3 degrees Celsius with observation "No change".

06 minutes, 31 seconds: Critic's temperature measured at 96.5 degrees Fahrenheit. Note taken reading, "No change." Slight interest in film, due to it looking as if it was filmed in the time it takes place (1973). Also surprised to see it is in the Academy ratio—the same dimensions as older televisions.

09 minutes, 50 seconds: Scientist takes temperature of soil around flowers. Ascends rough stone steps in hillside. At apex, grabs a stone, holds at arms-length over a square hole in the ground and

lets it fall into the abyss. Passes prominent vertical stone that has lichen growing on it. Fires up generator. Enters house. Waits for daily communication on the shortwave. Records plant temperature in journal as 14.4 degrees Celsius with observation "No change". A girl who obviously is not really there watches her do this.

12 minutes, 17 seconds: Critic's temperature measured at 96.7 degrees Fahrenheit. Note taken reading, "No change." Boredom setting in. Single chip of one of Lay's more bizarre limited-edition flavors sampled. Critic realizes that, despite their classic advertising slogan, there ARE times when a person can eat just one.

17 minutes, 45 seconds: Scientist takes temperature of soil around flowers. Puts ear to ground, hears some sort of mechanical sounds. Ascends rough stone steps in hillside. At apex, grabs a stone, holds at arms-length over a square hole in the ground and lets it fall into the abyss. Passes prominent vertical stone that has lichen growing on it. Obvious ghost girl enters house. Scientist fires up generator. Enters house. Waits for daily communication on the shortwave. Records plant temperature in journal as 14.5 degrees Celsius with observation "No change". Briefly converses with imaginary girl. Night: pulls up dressing gown, revealing scar across midsection.

21 minutes, 32 seconds: Critic's temperature measured at 96.4 degrees Fahrenheit. Thermometer tastes funny. Suddenly remembers this is a rectal thermometer. Pauses movie, vomits copiously. Tries another of the weirdly flavored potato chips. Vomits copiously again. Ghost girl watches and laughs. Note taken reading, "No change."

24 minutes, 41 seconds: Scientist takes temperature of soil around flowers. Ascends rough stone steps in hillside. At apex, grabs a stone, holds at arms-length over a square hole in the ground and lets it fall into the abyss. Frees part of a painted piece of wood from between stones as Pilgrim women sway in unison behind

her, in what may be the worst choreographed number ever. Passes prominent vertical stone that has lichen growing on it. Fires up generator. Enters house. Puts parts of painted board, which reads as "OVEN", over the mantle. Waits for daily communication on the shortwave. Records plant temperature in journal as 14.4 degrees Celsius with observation "No change". Running out of petrol and tea.

28 minutes, 06 seconds: Critic's temperature measured at 96.3 degrees Celsius. Calls 911, but hangs up immediately after realizing they have confused Fahrenheit with Celsius. Note taken reading, "No change."

30 minutes, 5 seconds: Scientist takes temperature of soil around flowers. Flower seems to lean towards her outstretched hand. Ascends rough stone steps in hillside. At apex, grabs a stone, chucks it into the abyss. Remnants of some sort of former operations (mining?) visible. Wanders around the pier. Passes prominent vertical stone that has lichen growing on it. Fires up generator. Enters house. Waits for daily communication on the shortwave. Records plant temperature in journal as 14.5 degrees Celsius with observation "No change".

34 minutes, 72 seconds: Critic's temperature measured at 96.1 degrees Fahrenheit. Realizes he has suddenly lost ability to accurately record time. Note taken reading, "No change."

39 minutes, 40 seconds: Scientist takes temperature of soil around flowers. Finds a yellow raincoat on the shore. Cleans it. Ghost watches passively from the roof of the house, as ghosts are wont to do. Records plant temperature in journal as 14.5 degrees Celsius with observation "No change".

41 minutes, 523 seconds: Critic's temperature measured at 95.9 degrees Fahrenheit. Scratches nether regions furiously. Realizes it has been days since he showered. Note taken reading, "No change."

43:40 Scientist takes temperature of soil around flowers. Observes lichen growing on a petal. Records plant temperature in journal as 14.7 degrees Celsius with observation "Lichen has appeared on petal of one of the flowers". Takes a bath. Finds lichen growing on scar on abdomen. Generator stops. Ghost watches passively from the roof of the house as she investigates. Scientist lights match. Cursing of darkness assumed.

48 minutes, -08 seconds: Critic's temperature measured at 95.6 degrees Fahrenheit. Furious itching of nether regions reveals lichen growing there. Note taken reading, "No change."

48 minutes, 30 seconds: Scientist takes temperature of soil around flowers. Observes more lichen growing on a petal. On the hilltop, grabs a stone, holes at arms-length over a square hole in the ground and lets it fall into the abyss. Records plant temperature in journal as 14.7 degrees Celsius with observation "The lichen has grown on the flower". More lichen on abdominal scar, too. Nightmare of descending into mine and seeing ghost miners. She stares. They stare back.

50 minutes, 4L seconds: Critic's temperature measured at 95.5 degrees Fahrenheit. Additional growth of crotch lichen. Note taken reading, "No change."

53 minutes, 57 seconds: Male ghost is taking a dump in her bathroom. Ghosts are now shitting in her house. I wonder if name-brand toilet cleaning liquid removes ectoplasm?

Bob minutes, Cheddar seconds: Critic's temperature measured at 95.3 degrees Fahrenheit. Continued furious crotch itching has critic scratching nether regions with uncapped pen tip, resulting in cryptic graffiti on a sensitive area. Note taken reading, "No change."

56 minutes, 10 seconds: Scientist takes temperature of soil around flowers. Observes lichen growing on all the flowers. So far, the most action in this film has involved lichen. Records plant

temperature in journal as 14.9 degrees Celsius with observation "The lichen has spread to all of the flowers". Ghost girls perform some sort of weird song at her house. A helpful male ghost arrives by boat and brings her petrol. He eats a roll she's baked for him. Other ghosts appear in raincoats outside her house. They don't look happy. Perhaps it's because she didn't offer them a roll, too?

56 minutes, 6 seconds, 4 thirds: Critic's temperature measured at 95.2 degrees Fahrenheit. More crotch lichen, and it won't stop itchen'. Critic considers authoring a volume of poetry. Note taken reading, "No change."

1 hour, 14 minutes, 10 seconds: Scientist writes in journal, "The flowers are gone." Montage of images suggest her mind has gone walkies as well. Starts filling all lines of journal with "No change"

4 score, 7 years, 1 hour, 20 minutes, 12 seconds : Critic's temperature measured at 80 degrees Fahrenheit. Observation made of critic, "Deceased". Note taken reading, "No change."

1 hour, 24 minutes, 50 seconds: Footage of slug, which is probably thinking to itself, "Jesus! Even I can move faster than this film!"

Original version posted on 4/24/2023

Evilspeak (1981)

Supernatural forces using modern technology is a concept which rarely works for me. Not sure why as, if I can believe a demon in a movie can communicate through a Ouija board, it isn't much of a leap to have them manipulate computers and cell phones.

In 1981's *Evilspeak*, Clint Howard uses an Apple II to decipher an ancient text he found in the basement of the chapel of the military school he attends. That text was that of Father Esteban (Richard

Moll, Bull from the original *Night Court*), a dark ages heretic banished from Spain and who apparently settled in America. That seems unlikely, but I rolled with it like a twelve-sided die. Anywho, the instructions from the ancient book will resurrect Esteban, who is also Satan. Maybe. It wasn't very clear.

Howard is at the very lowest of the pecking order at the military school he attends. I'm sure that type of school is several circles of hell I'm glad I never experienced, yet the one here seems ridiculous. He's hated equally by students and faculty. The soccer coach proposes the players injure Howard to prevent him from playing again. The school janitor actually tries to *rape* Howard.

Only two people aren't completely repulsive. One is Howard's only friend, who is also the only Black guy at the school. The other is the cook, and I can't tell you how relieved I was when his invitation to Howard to "show him something" was only a dog who had just had puppies. He gives one of the puppies to the kid. Spoiler alert: things will not go well for the puppy.

At first, the computer simply translates text, but it eventually puts a talking face on the screen to address him more directly. The images on the computer screen are obviously hand-drawn animation, as computer technology was far too primitive back then to display something of such resolution. I was somehow willing to suspend my disbelief for this, though I'm unable to do that when a demon face appears on a phone screen in later films.

While largely a picture catering to the lowest common denominator, there is some wit and humor on display. I especially liked a transition where a decapitated head flying off somebody's shoulders in the Middle Ages turns into a soccer ball arcing through the air in the present day.

There are some elements here which I haven't decided are interesting quirks or unnecessary diversions. The school's porny secretary is an expected staple of the genre, but I'm not sure why we see her amused (aroused?) when Howard is receiving a whipping in the adjacent room. Also, I'm unclear as to why Howard suddenly has super-strength in a scene that only required the kind of violence somebody of his build could actually do. Maybe it was explained and I missed it, but I doubt it. Lastly, the ritual requires unholy water, which would be...regular, unblessed water?

Then there's the pigs. Apparently, pigs are raised on the school grounds which has me wondering if they slaughter their own meat. Then there's pigs that inexplicably appear in the house of, and devour, the porny secretary in the shower. Note how Hitchcock used a knife-wielding maniac to commit homicide in a shower instead of using pigs.

The strangest aspect of *Evilspeak* is its structure, in that the summoning isn't successful until ten minutes before the end of the picture, and that's including the credits. The expected plotline would have Howard complete the summoning and become possessed in the first third, with the final third being a battle to rid him of the demon.

Overall, this is a movie largely too conventional to recommend, but quirky enough to be more interesting than I expected. Fans of supernatural horror could do worse, especially since some of the film seems to have its tongue planted in its decapitated-head cheek.

Original version posted on 4/13/2023

Eye of the Devil (1966)

1966's *Eye of the Devil* is a curious film. It eerily seems to anticipate the folk horror genre which would only kick into gear a few years later. It has the feel of Polanski's work around that time, though his only connection to this is Sharon Tate, and he didn't even meet her until the next year. And yet, this film also seems to foretell the coming age of supernatural horror which his *Rosemary's Baby* would greatly influence.

David Niven and Deborah Kerr star as a couple wealthy enough to host a black-tie gathering in London where everybody is thrilled to watch an expert harpist, something I can't imagine unless the performer was Harpo Marx. In the middle of this party, Niven leaves to talk to a visitor who has brought news of the failure of the grape crop at the family's Bordeaux estate. He informs Kerr he must go there immediately, though one wonders exactly what *he* could do in such a situation. Whatever it is going to be, he'll probably need to change out of that tux.

We see him as he drives alone through the village and to the castle that has been in his family for hundreds of years. All along the route he takes, the citizens doff their caps, as if this is still a fiefdom. What is funny is we see many of those same people later when Kerr decides to go there with the children in tow, and everybody is very displeased to see them.

Niven also isn't pleased to see his family arrive, yet he tries to act as normal as possible. Still, he seems to eerily zone out when he drones on about his responsibility to the people, though he is incredibly vague as to exactly what he must do for them. Regardless of what that may be, it is obvious sacrifices must be made.

There are all kinds of intrigue happening around this vast estate. There are secret ceremonies with robed figures. In a painting of Niven's grandfather, one corner shows a group of such figures in a circle around a man, suggesting this ritual goes back an extremely long time. If Kerr is smart, she won't put her trust in anybody. Even the village priest (Donald Pleasance) seems to be hiding something. Also, there's a curious number of British people in this provincial French town, such as John Le Mesurier as the local doctor. I know I would be suspicious if I went to rural France and encountered almost nothing but Brits.

But nothing is as mysterious as two figures in the margins, an alleged brother and sister played by David Hemmings and Sharon Tate. I would say there was something vaguely incestuous about their relationship, except I was never certain if they were exactly human. Whatever they are, I have a feeling they have been there as long as there has been a castle, maybe even longer.

He is an archer who slays a hella lot of pigeons, some of which were magically created by his sister from frogs. Now there's an unusual symbiotic relationship. Hemmings also repeatedly demonstrates to Kerr that he could kill her at any time, and he really really wants to do that. Niven is quick to defend Hemmings's behavior, saying it must have been in jest. That has to be a sign your marriage has some issues.

Tate leaves quite a strong impression here, though her character seems to be inessential to the plot. Instead, her performance is critical for the atmosphere, which is more than half of the viewing experience. Simply put, she is mesmerizing in this film. Speaking of mesmerism, she tries to use that to get Kerr to fall off a rooftop to her death, in one of the film's most powerful scenes. It is a moment which channels something I find hard to put into words, and which makes this rather slight film feel more substantial than it is.

The other real star of the film is the photography, which is crisp black and white. There's an interesting luminosity to the image, as if this was from a silver nitrate print, which I am certain the studio did not do. One image that sticks in my mind is Kerr spying on a secret ceremony behind closed doors, under which the light is so intense that it sears the eyes.

Eye of the Devil is an intriguing, but not very satisfying film, and I say that as somebody who has seen it twice. Fans of folk horror should check it out, as it has a surprisingly similar plot to one of the most famous films of that genre, preceding it by only a few years. Those who are curious about Sharon Tate should seek it out for her unique performance, which hints at directions a longer career might have taken her.

Original version posted on 9/21/2024

Footprints (1975)

Italy's first lunar mission isn't going well. I'd say the first problem is their spaceship is a paper cut-out of the Apollo 11 lunar module. It lands successfully, but something happens to one of the astronauts, rendering them unconscious. Another of the crew is apparently sick of their shit, dragging them away from the lunar module and taking off without them. The abandoned astronaut comes to and is horrified to discover they have been left behind.

And so, there are footprints on the moon, providing one of the titles the 1975 feature *Footprints* was released under. I secretly hoped the title instead was an update of that cliched Christian poem, this time restaging it on the surface of our only satellite. In my imagining of this, the narrator asks why there are only one set of impressions in the dust at one point, and God tells them that's when they couldn't take any more of their whiney ass.

Instead, the opening credit sequence is only a recurring dream Florinda Bolkan has been having. She thinks it may be a scene from a movie she saw as a young girl, one so terrifying she ran out of the theatre prematurely. Bolkan is quite obsessed with this dream and the associated, and possibly false, memory of that film.

It seems to me she has much greater concerns. She has likely lost her job as a translator after failing to show up for three days. While she thought today was Tuesday, it is actually Thursday, and she has no recollection of the days in between. A three-day blackout would have me running to a doctor, but she is instead more obsessed with lesser mysteries such as a single earring and a dress in her apartment, neither of which she remembers.

Another curiosity is in her trash can, a postcard torn into four pieces. The image is of a hotel in Garma, Turkey, a place she swears she has never visited. And yet, she suddenly has vivid memories of what she believes to be elements of that hotel, especially a large stained-glass window with peacock imagery.

The remainder of the film then has Bolkan wandering around Garma, where there are only more mysteries. Various people keep saying they saw her around the area days before she arrived. A young girl played by Nicholetta Elmi tells her they spent a great deal of time together, except the short-haired and brunette Bolkan had long, red hair then and was using a different name.

While this is not a science-fiction picture, time keeps folding back on itself. Cause and effect seem to be reversed sometimes, and past and present get transposed. I doubt what we see bears close scrutiny, but this is definitely more a film about sustaining a mood than having an airtight plot.

That is typical of Giallo, though I will leave it to others to decide whether this is a canonical entry in that sub-genre of thriller. Also typical of Italian cinema, the photography is stunning throughout. I was unable to find an actual Turkish location named Garma in research I did after watching the film; however, wherever this was shot (largely Phaselis, apparently) is so rich in detail that I suspect one could have plunked the camera down at random and obtained some beautiful footage. The hotel is especially stunning, and I found it intriguing the British man working its front desk is how I bet *Last Week Tonight* host John Oliver will look twenty years from now.

Fair warning to those who opt to watch the Italian version instead of the U.S. cut: it keeps jumping between the English dub and Italian with English subtitles. This sometimes happens even in the same conversation, which is surreal. Really, that should enhance the experience of such a movie, which is all about disorienting the viewer, but it is instead quite irritating. In either cut, however, you get to see Klaus Kinski hilariously dubbed in a stock American accent.

I watched *Footprints* as part of the blu-ray boxed set *House of Psychotic Women*. This picture is in good company there, alongside the excellent *Identikit* and the, well, batshit *I Like Bats*. Like those films, this has very solid accompanying special features, most notably an introduction by Kier-La Janisse, whose insights into the film were enlightening, as always.

Original version posted on 10/7/2024

Grave of the Vampire (1972)

When writer and director David Chase discusses his life's accomplishments, I'm sure he talks mostly about *The*

Sopranos. Maybe he occasionally touches on *The Rockford Files* or *Kolchak: The Night Stalker.* But I suspect he rarely, if ever, talks about his first movie screenplay, 1972's *Grave of the Vampire.*

This is an odd movie. In keeping with one of my theories concerning low-budget productions, this plot is weirder than a major studio would crank out for a vampire movie at the time. At least, I'm pretty sure a studio like Universal wouldn't have a vampire rape and impregnate a woman. I didn't say it was a *good* idea, only that it was a novel one.

The baby grows up to become William Smith. This appears to be the first vampire picture he appeared in, though he would dip a toe in the genre repeatedly over his long career, appearing in such doubtlessly classy fare as *The Erotic Rites of Countess Dracula.*

Smith is functional here, but not much more than that. He's a beefy guy who looks like he could be a pro wrestler. Unfortunately, his performance is largely of the caliber I have come to expect from wrestlers who act. His line readings are largely flat and smirky, except for the occasional explosion of rage at moments of high melodrama. For example, imagine a wrestler bellowing, "I'm your *son*, Lockwood!"

For you see, Smith is a half-vampire with daddy issues. Living on blood and uncooked meat, he has tracked dear ol' dad (Michael Pataki) to a university where he teaches a night class on folklore (I guess you gotta go with what you know). Smith is immediately pursued by two fellow students (Anita Jacoby and Ann Arthur) who happen to be roommates. And faster than you can say "threesome", he is bedding Arthur while Jacoby tries to blackmail Pataki into turning her into a vampire. Wait...what?

That development is representative of some of the unexpected twists offered in *Grave of the Vampire.* The movie isn't above average (even for low-budget fare) but it does throw the audience some curveballs. Whether I would recommend a viewing varies wildly depending upon whom I am addressing, but I couldn't help but be charmed somewhat by a film with a line as bizarre as "Why can't dead people eat cake? They're just like us, only crossed over to the other side."

Original version posted on 8/28/2023

Horror Island (1941)

1941's *Horror Island* is the fourth and final film on the third volume of Scream Factor's *Universal Horror* series. All four films in this installment suggest the name of this series is becoming increasingly inaccurate. The first, *Tower of London*, was a straight-up historical drama, though it did have a fair amount of suspense and intrigue. The other three features on the set are comedy-horror, with the emphasis distinctly on the former.

Horror Island is not to be confused with *Whore Island*, a failed reality competition show on Fox I just made up. Like two of the other pictures on this set, it is set in an old, dark mansion on a dark and stormy night. It is a good setting for a gothic horror film, but even better for a parody of one.

Among the characters assembled there are an endlessly scheming sea captain (Dick Foran), his right-hand man and comedic foil (the improbably named Fuzzy Knight, playing a character with the even less likely name of Stuff), a cousin of Foran's who is trying to buy the island Foran inherited from their grandfather, an actual peg-legged sea-faring ne'er-do-well (Leo Carrillo) who has half of a treasure map showing $20 million in gold is hidden somewhere in the mansion on that island, and a cape-clad villain who has the other half of that map (Foy Van Dolsen—"Foy"? Where the hell did people get their names from back then?). Then there's all the characters who paid for the scam "ghost hunt" Foran is working: Peggy Moran, some guy who scans to me as "gay friend" of hers (Lewis Howard), a fussy professor (Hobart Cavanaugh) and a mysterious couple who positively radiate "bad intentions" (Ralf Harolde and Iris Adrian).

That's an overstuffed cast, especially for a film that is only an hour long. Fortunately, their numbers start dwindling almost from the minute they set foot in the mansion on the island Foran inherited from his grandfather. It plays out like a gentle black comedy version of *And Then There Were None*. There's all manner of duplicity, and much discovery of secret passages.

Everybody here is having a good time, and that is infectious. Foran has a casual, smartass demeanor. If this movie had been remade in the 1980's, I could see Bill Murray or Chevy Chase in his role. Foran also has a good rapport with Fuzzy Knight, who is funnier than I expected from somebody with such a weird, vaudevillian handle. Consider this exchange between Foran and Knight: "I thought I told you to get bats." "Where was I gonna get bats? Besides, these pigeons haven't worked in six months." Carillo thoroughly milks his part for the potential to ham it up, and this is the kind of picture that calls for it. Even Howard, who is underused to the extent one wonders why he is even here, gets in a good line when finding a fake skull in his bed: "Hello, Yorrick. Find your own bed."

Horror Island is a trifle, but a mildly enjoyable one. It's the kind of movie where I didn't laugh much while watching it, though I did smile a lot. I would definitely regard this as a comedy and not as a mystery, especially since it doesn't play fair. In one scene, we are shown a character who is alone at the time, acting in a manner for which there is no reason except to deceive the audience. That said, there is an interesting twist roughly halfway through the runtime where a character is killed who I thought would be there at the conclusion. This was an unusual film, to be sure.

Original version posted on 3/27/2024

Hysteria (1997)

1997's *Hysteria* is the kind of movie which I feel justifies my purchases of cheap discs at places like Hamilton Books. If it hadn't been for seeing this blu-ray in one of their monthly drops, I likely never would have been aware of this title. And this is a deeply weird, thought-provoking film I'm glad I didn't miss out on.

I was intrigued mostly because this is the last starring role of Patrick McGoohan. Similar to his role in Cronenberg's *Scanners*, he is a scientist with unorthodox methods, running a secret clinic out of a remote location. In this case, it is a creepy, gothic mansion.

Also like that Cronenberg film, the phenomenon being studied here appears to be along the lines of telepathy. The inmates of this asylum share a hive mind, courtesy of a chip McGoohan has surgically implanted behind the left ear of each. The good doctor has even chipped himself, all the better to fully understand his patients.

The inmates are largely the usual assortment from central casting, with a few notable exceptions. Amanda Plummer steals the show as a master manipulator, maintaining a firm control over the others despite being confined to a wheelchair. Joanne Vannicola plays a physically intense young woman who talks in rhyming verse. There's one guy I couldn't identify from the IMDB listing who acts and talks like he's a character from a 90's side-by-side fighter video game.

Our protagonist is Michael Maloney, playing a psychiatrist who is dismayed at the closure of the mental hospital where he works. As patients are essentially tossed into the street, he laments mental health services only remaining available to the wealthy. I am deeply saddened by how that situation has only become worse in the quarter-century since this movie was released.

Maloney's favorite patient is played by Emmanuelle Vaugier. The exact nature of her mental illness is never revealed, but it apparently has something to do with carnal desires triggering homicidal ones. This is the kind of psychological ailment that seems to impact few people in real life, while a great many have it in those "Skinemax"-type movies like *Color of Night*.

And this is a very horny movie. I wouldn't go so far as to describe it as even softcore porn, though I suspect this unrated film would likely receive a NC-17. What sex is in it isn't strong so much as it is a bit weird, as a chipped Maloney and Vaugier doing the horizontal mambo, which motivates everybody in the hive mind to get frisky. Once again, this seems reminiscent of a Cronenberg film.

Maloney has taken her to McGoohan's asylum because there apparently aren't any other facilities available. Something I had trouble suspending my disbelief over is there were no other options available for Vaugier except a creepy-ass mansion in which a doctor is conducting mysterious experiments. Was the only other available facility Dr. Frank-n-Further's mansion from *The Rocky Horror Picture Show*?

If there's one thing that made me cut the film enough slack to accept this, it is that it has a similar look and vibe as such independent horror movies as *Hellraiser*. I was very surprised it was made in 1997, as every aspect of it would lead me to believe it was made a decade earlier. I know most people wouldn't give a movie more leeway than others just because it had a small budget, was independently produced or was from a particular era, but I try to grade on a curve.

Something else I had to overlook is the nature of the collective consciousness. The specifics of it are left vague, but it appears individuals still have some amount of control over themselves. And yet, when Maloney knees one of the group in the crotch, the others all bend over as well (in one of the film's few moments of intentional humor). But why isn't Maloney also impacted? In an earlier scene, he feels a punch he landed on another guy.

I wouldn't go so far as to say this is a highly intellectual work, but it does have some interesting ideas about identity. I was also surprised by some directions the story takes towards the end. There were some elements of it I could foresee, but a couple of other aspects completely blindsided me.

Hysteria is a pleasant surprise, and I'm interested in exploring the rest of director Rene Daalder's brief oeuvre. It has been a while since I have seen something that felt subversive, maybe even a bit transgressive, and I liked how it cleared out some cobwebs from my mind.

Original version posted on 4/17/2023

I Like Bats (1986)

Like the central character of 1986's *I Like Bats,* I also like those mammals, and feel they are unfairly maligned. Just look at the bodies, sans those leathery wings, and they're a bit like small dogs. The opening credits are superimposed over footage of one eating some sort of fruit, possibly an orange, and it is adorable.

Still, I wouldn't make a ceramic teacup with a bat wing in place of a handle, which is one of the pieces the chief protagonist has made that is for sale in her aunt's shop. This gets the attention of psychiatrist Marek Barbasiewicz, who buys a set which he takes back with him at the clinic he oversees. The artist (Katarzyna Walter) will eventually go to that facility to try to cure her vampirism.

What the doctor doesn't understand is she doesn't just think she is a vampire, but that she really *is* one. We have already seen her claim a few victims, including a serial rapist and murderer, so it seems we could probably do with a few more vampires.

I wouldn't have expected this Polish film to strictly adhere to traditional vampire tropes, and it has some interesting new angles to explore. For one example, she can't be hypnotized. Also, in an unusual twist on these monsters not casting reflections in mirrors, it is discovered she can't be x-rayed.

This film then goes far beyond these twists on vampire lore and has a great many elements that seem to be weird for just weird's sake. Some of these worked better for me than others. Largely, these elements took me out of the viewing experience and kept me at arm's length from fully appreciating it.

Still, some of those moments are mildly humorous, such as a woman in a bar who stands up, lowers her dress and starts dancing topless. I was confused, because this seemed to be a customer who just up and decided to do this on a whim. Then the bartender chastises her for doing this *again*, and this confirms she at least isn't being paid to do this. I chuckled at this bit, though partly out of stunned disbelief

Other moments don't fare as well. There's Jonasz Kofta as Narkoman (I'm imagining a super-anti-hero with that moniker), a junkie at the sanatorium whom we first see painting a self-portrait on a curtain that is several stories high. This facility must have quite an arts and crafts budget. Towards the end of the film, there's another asylum, where the patients are kept in what are essentially kennels, on the beach right at the edge of the ocean. That is absurd and not even the interesting kind of absurdity. It just feels like somebody ran out of ideas.

It's no surprise this is a pretty horny film, though the actual sex here isn't very titillating. Those scenes are largely some sort-porn dalliances between clinic nurses and the endlessly randy groundskeeper. These scenes may not be staged with any degree of taste, but they do actually factor into the plot, even if I only realized that after the film was over.

The best moment in the film is a scene at a masked party. No, it does not turn into something out of *Eyes Wide Shut*. Instead, Barbasiewicz laughs so hard at the vampire mask a novelty-joke-selling asshole is wearing that she accidentally exposes her fangs. Seeing this, the guy has a heart attack.

Aside from the most egregiously weird moments in *I Like Bats*, there were some aspects I couldn't tell were deliberate absurdity or traditional aspects of Polish life of which I am unfamiliar. For example, at the funeral for Barbasiewicz, there are a couple of fish in a large fishbowl placed on top of the coffin. Even the language rings odd to my ears. Spoken at its most slowly, it sounded like a backwards recording. One thing I was still mulling over a day later is a series of streetlights running through a clearing as if they flanked a sidewalk, but there isn't even a worn footpath there. We even see a motorcycle go by it, as if this is a thoroughfare. I was left wondering if Poland had not invented concrete by the time this picture was made.

Original version posted on 6/30/2024

The Leopard Man (1943)

Most horror movies treat murder victims in a trivial way. Consider slasher films, which usually provide little background for those who only seem to exist so they can die horribly.

1943's *The Leopard Man* takes a different, though rather bizarre tact. This is a film where it seems to keep forgetting to follow its leads (Dennis O'Keefe and Jean Brooks), instead constantly diverting its attention to different women who will inevitably turn out to be the next to die.

The primary suspect here is a black leopard. When we first see the cat, it is being walked into the nightclub dressing room of Brooks, courtesy of O'Keefe, her agent. The two have been looking for something to distinguish her act, as she is unable to compete with the Spanish dancer (Margo) practicing in the adjacent room.

There is some humor in this first scene, with Brooks so irritated by the dancer's incessant castanets that she wonders what the appeal is: "My teeth can do the same thing in a cold shower." Then there's this exchange between her and a jealous friend who is always trying to replace her as an act: "I can wear your red dress. It fits me just fine." "I bet someday you'll try on my coffin, and it will fit you just fine." Curiously, we never see Brooks perform, and we never learn exactly what it is she does.

Instead of integrating the cat into her act, O'Keefe merely has Brooks walk the leopard into the club, so as to disrupt Margo's performance. This succeeds, though only momentarily. Margo quickly regains her composure and, clicking her castanets, chases the cat out of the club.

Now there's a ferocious animal on the loose. One would think Margo would the first victim, as a fortune teller lurking in the shadows invites her to choose a card and she draws the ace of spades. But her number isn't up that night.

Instead, she passes by a young woman in an open window (Margaret Landry). This poor kid is forced by her mother to go get corn flour late at night. The film's most horrific moment is when she returns home and bangs on the door to get in. There's a loud thunk as the door buckles inward, a trail of blood seeping under it. Rather strong stuff for 1943.

What is odd is how long that entire sequence takes to play out. I actually forgot about the main characters by the time the focus returns to them. Soon, there is an even longer sequence where we follow a woman who brings roses to the mistress of the house (Tula Parma) for her birthday. Parma takes the roses to the grave of her father and ends up locked inside the cemetery walls, only to become the next victim.

There is much speculation about why a leopard is staying in the town instead of heading for open country. Also, it is curious why it isn't eating those it kills. Hmmm…

The Leopard Man is the work of producer Val Lewton and Jacques Tourneur, who gave us the similarly titled *Cat People*, in addition to *I Walked with a Zombie*. Similar to those pictures, there are some strongly atmospheric moments here, though not as many as I hoped for. There is also one incredibly effective jump scare. But it is telling this film isn't held in as high of regard as those other works. For all these films, the creative team were mandated to create a film that would be appropriate for a predetermined title. This is the first of those films to feel like the material was struggling to rise to that challenge.

Original version posted on 9/24/2024

Messiah of Evil (completed 1971, released 1973)

On rare occasions, I watch a movie that seems to rip off ones that came after it. Such is the case with 1973's *Messiah of Evil*, which somehow has the unique look of 1977's *Suspiria* and elements of 1981's *Dead & Buried*. I seriously doubt either of the later films was influenced by the earlier one. Yet this curious factor alone warrants a viewing from fans of offbeat, low-budget horror from the 70's.

Marianna Hill has come to a small town looking for her missing artist father. Shades of *Dead & Buried* creep in as she encounters the strange, secretive residents of this burg situated on a rocky coast. The first place she stops is a gas station at night where the attendant is firing a revolver into the darkness. When you see something like that, you should only fill up if truly desperate for fuel. Even then, you should opt for self-service.

This scene is barely visible as, unlike most films of this era, the night scenes are truly shot at night instead of using day-for-night. I appreciate that, even if some scenes border on being literally unwatchable. In fact, I'm not sure any scenes inside the town occur in daylight, what with the residents being turned into some sort of nocturnal creature.

Among the few characters Hill encounters are a curious trio of Michael Greer, Joy Bang and Anitra Ford. For a long time, I thought Greer was part of whatever conspiracy is occurring, maybe even the leader of it. He claims to be on some vague mission to "collect stories", though I felt it was never clear exactly what he and his groupies are doing there.

Most of the action takes place in the house of Hill's father. Judging from the murals on the walls, Dad had a screw loose even before his disappearance. Like a proto-Banksy, the walls are covered with stark black-and-white images of people staring back at the viewer.

In the middle of the main room is something that may be a bed or a table or maybe both. Whatever it is, it is suspended from the ceiling by plastic chains. This is where Hill sleeps and I couldn't stop thinking about what a nightmare that would be—sleeping on something that is stiff as a board, that would swing with the slightest movement, while surrounded by faces staring at you from the walls. Strange, but I was never sure if this room was the living room or a bedroom. Maybe it's both?

This is a weird house, and I came to think of it as the main character. And this is where the similarities to *Suspiria* begin. This house isn't just strangely decorated, but it is lit in solid colors, such as a room lit entirely in dark blue, with a bright red corridor in the background. There's even a hidden door in one of the murals, even if you don't have to turn a decorative blue flower (ala *Suspiria*) to access it.

You probably noticed I haven't talked about the plot much and that's because it is a mess. But, like *Suspiria* again, it is an intriguing mess. This is a picture where so much has to be assembled in the viewer's mind that I'm not sure how much of what is on the screen is cohesive.

The main issue is what is happening to the residents. Whatever is transpiring involves creatures in the night that sound like dogs or wolves, though there's no other indications anything like werewolves exist in this world. The creatures we do see are zombie-like and some have ghoulish faces like the undead in *Carnival of Souls*. Curiously, others look normal.

Regardless, they eat raw meat and occasionally devour living people. Still, this doesn't follow the typical zombie formula, in that the eaten do not appear to be converted. Instead, the conversion just seems to happen naturally over time to anybody who stays there long enough.

We see that raw meat consumed in one of the picture's two genuinely scary moments, when one of Greer's hanger-ons follows a stranger into a supermarket in the middle of the night, when it should be closed. First, even though it is standard operating procedure for this genre, I found myself yelling at the screen, "Why are you following a stranger in the middle of the night, who doesn't want anything to do with you, into a store that shouldn't be open?!?". Of course, there wouldn't be a scary scene if she doesn't go inside.

The other big scare is a similar scene, which dispatches the other groupie. She just wants to go to the movies, and you know something is seriously wrong when the marquee is turned off as soon as she enters. As she watches the movie, she doesn't notice people gradually filling the seats behind her. It's a very suspenseful setup and it has a good payoff.

And now a sampling of other random observations I made. There are undertones of Lovecraft, as the populace gathers on the beach at night to await the messianic return of their leader. At one point, a corpse washes up on the shore. It is supposed to be that of Hill's father though she knows those aren't his hands (oh, hi there, *Dead & Buried!*). Also, there's a good synthesizer score with rich analog tones (shalom, *Suspiria!*).

At the risk of overselling it, *Messiah of Evil* is a low-budget mess, but is fascinating to look at and I like its style. Sometimes that's enough. It helps that there are a couple of very well-done scenes of terror. It's odd there are so many better movies I probably won't re-visit, and yet I'm fairly certain I will be checking out this one again.

Original version posted on 6/4/2023

Miss Leslie's Dolls (1973)

It's strange how similar horror and porn can be. I kept thinking about this while watching the 1973 grindhouse horror film *Miss Leslie's Dolls*.

This movie has three college students, one guy and two women, and a young female professor of theirs holing up in a creepy house in the middle of nowhere as a storm rages outside. We quickly establish both young women want the guy, and some of the conversation suggests they wouldn't mind sharing him together. No changes would be necessary to cast the professor as Velma in a porn parody of Scooby Doo, what with her large round glasses, prim demeanor and tight sweater. No points for guessing she's a repressed lesbian.

A great deal of dialogue concerns loosening up and letting go of one's inhibitions. I kept asking my wife, "This is about to turn into porn, right?" And yet, strangely, it never did, only suggesting lesbian sex and a possible threesome. Also, you may have noticed I watched this with my wife. I am the luckiest man on Earth.

But there's one character, the central one, which I haven't mentioned yet. That is Salvador Ugarte as the title character, the least convincing trans person in the history of cinema. I hope I'm not spoiling it for anybody when I say the big twist near the end is the revelation Miss Leslie is a man, but I suspect any toddler could see through this ruse. I was astonished the other characters all fully believe this is a woman. Then again, everybody's acting in this is so bad I wasn't even convinced they believe that.

Compounding the strangeness of this character is a woman's voice is dubbed in for Ugarte's, yet his lips and her voice sync, at best, at random. Any sane filmmaker would have recorded the woman's voice first, but I suspect they did this the other way around. Regardless of how it was done, the poor audio synchronization adds a level of surrealism. Miss Leslie has a black cat that meows a lot, and I wondered if the audio was that of a cat of the opposite gender. It would just seem to round out the general incompetence here.

The plot (though there is not much of it to be found) has Ugarte trying to transfer his spirit to the body of a young woman. He preserves the previous failed attempts in a wax museum of sorts in his house. Each corpse "doll" is in a standing position, and they surround a flame that is somehow always burning. The importance of the flame was lost on me, aside from a general "occult" vibe conveyed by a glowing moon shape suspended in the background.

As the meddling kids in this film believe Ugarte is a woman, it shouldn't be much of a surprise that they also fail to immediately recognize the dolls as preserved corpses. Well, one of the young women does, but the others convince her otherwise. Also, she doesn't try to convince them to leave the house, even after the storm that brought them there has stopped. Myself, I would have wondered how "wax" statutes were holding up so well in constant close proximity to an open flame, but what do I know.

The highlight of the picture for me is the dolls. It is the one element that was genuinely unnerving to me, though I also couldn't stop thinking about The Master's wives in *Manos: The Hands of Fate*. There is a development in the third act involving them which I didn't foresee, and which had the kind of uncanniness other low-budget fare like *Carnival of Souls* sometimes achieved.

Also, the obvious lack of funds and the high grain of the film stock make this a slightly disturbing experience. The closest analogy I can think of is the first time one watches *The Texas Chain Saw Massacre*, and you start to wonder if you are watching a truly dangerous film. I don't want to oversell it, but I found myself nagged by not only the possibility this could suddenly turn into straight-out hardcore pornography, but that it might turn into something far worse.

The movie does try for a bit of sympathy for Miss Leslie, though I don't think anybody would mistake this for an early attempt to portray trans people in a positive way. Miss Leslie is still a homicidal maniac and the trappings of a gender-identity crisis are merely the lazy psychology such films of the time frequently employed to provide motivation.

In the UK, *Miss Leslie's Dolls* was on a double-bill with *The Erotic Adventures of Zorro*. That makes a weird kind of sense, as the bad acting, flat line readings and overall horniness gives the impression this will cross the line into porn at any second. It doesn't do that and, instead, this low-budget, sleazefest ends up being a curiosity: a deeply terrible film where some glimmers of interesting ideas still manage to emerge.

Original version posted on 7/29/2023

The Monster of the Opera (1964)

I love gothic cinema, which I find odd, as it is somehow one of the most loosely defined genres while simultaneously being one of the most restrictive. You must have at least a sprawling old building of some sort, whether it is the baron's castle or a school for girls lorded over by a prim schoolmistress. Other than that, almost anything goes.

The 1964 Italian gothic 1964's *The Monster of the Opera* is set in a monstrous, old opera house that has been purchased by a dance troupe. It is unclear exactly what type of material they do, but it appears to be some sort of avant-garde thing. Before committing to this venture, I wonder if they considered the limited appeal of such material to audiences in rural Italy.

At first, they are oblivious to the vampire (Guiseppe Addobbati) in the basement. Perhaps they should have paid closer attention to Alberto Archetti, as the vampire's Renfield, even if his character's name is really Achille. As he is always trying to undermine his master, I would say he is Addobbati's Achille's heel.

One would think Barbara Hawards, the star of the troupe, would be more in tune to what's going on. She had a prescient dream before coming here, wherein this vampire gets her pinned to the ground with a pitchfork.

This dream is the first scene in the film, and I was completely bewildered while watching it. I was wondering if this guy was a freshly turned vampire and so doesn't know the function of those fangs yet, given he is chasing her with a pitchfork. Also, about that pitchfork: the tines of it are super flimsy, dull at the end and the middle ones are conveniently shorter than the ones on the ends. That way, the longest tines can touch the ground while our heroine is in no way imperiled by the shorter ones that barely touch her midriff.

As ridiculous as this scene may be, I still like the Dutch-angle photography used in the pursuit through some very old architecture. And yet I couldn't stop laughing at the scene, even as she managed to flee in slow-motion. I imagined this as the most surreal old commercial ever: "I dreamed I was running from a vampire in my Maindenform bra…"

Anywho, Archetti keeps trying to get these artists to leave. I liked one line he delivers: "You must leave while the door to the theatre is still open." Even if this movie isn't folk horror, the line made me think of a recurring element of that genre, and that is how people failing to heed such warnings usually pay for their carelessness. I think of it as "the moment of transgression", a point that, like the event horizon of a black hole, one cannot return from.

Myself, I started rooting for the vampire, given how annoying these characters are. Most notable is a woman with a deeply grating laugh that resembles nothing less than that of Woody Woodpecker. And she laughs a lot.

And all the characters are annoying when doing their bizarre dance routines. In one scene, they are supposed to be cleaning the stage area when somebody throws on a record of "The Charleston" and they all start dancing. Curiously, each of them is doing a different dance and I swear not one is doing the Charleston. At the same time, their movements would not succeed in cleaning anything. So, are they cleaning or dancing, since they appear to be doing neither? If this was practice for a routine to be performed, who would possibly be the target audience for this? As far as the quality of the dancing goes, it is almost like watching real people recreate the "Linus & Lucy" moments in *A Charlie Brown Christmas*.

Even more bizarre is a scene there the vampire appears and everybody begins to dance as frantically as possible. Apparently, if anybody stops moving, the vampire will get them. This is a part of vampire lore of which I was previously unaware. That, or the filmmakers were just making stuff up as they went along. This scene has a feel to it like the games little kids play, such as "the floor is lava".

Another bit of vampire lore of which I was previously unaware is you can use fire to scare a vampire to death. You don't even have to touch him with the flames. I'm filing that away for future use, in case I ever encounter bloodsuckers.

Monster of the Opera is, unfortunately, a rather dull film aside from those moments when it is batshit crazy. Most eye-opening is a bit which comes close to becoming a sapphic three-way. Let me tell you, this bit of a tease was far more arousing than some flat-out porn I have seen. It made me recall a bit of stage dressing this bizarre troupe has, which appears to be a brick tower which seems to have problems staying full upright. As this prop appears to be experiencing erectile dysfunction, maybe it needs to be shown that aborted three-way scene.

Original version posted on 2/27/2024

The Night Visitor (1971)

Have you ever watched an Ingmar Bergman movie and wished Max von Sydow would drive an axe into Liv Ullmann's head? If so, what's wrong with you? Regardless, there is a movie for you and your odd fantasies, and that is 1970's *The Night Visitor.*

Filmed in Denmark and Sweden in winter, the film makes great use of a rural house, an ancient fortress of a prison and vast expanses of countryside covered in snow. So, it is basically a Bergman film, but with 100% more axe murders, bludgeonings and strangulations in it.

Max von Sydow is an inmate in that large, ancient prison, serving a life sentence for killing a farmhand working on their property. He has found a way out of his confinement, making nightly trips beyond its walls and returning before anybody notices he's gone.

A police inspector played by Trevor Howard is stupefied by how it appears von Sydow is exacting revenge upon the people who put him in prison, when the fortress appears to be impossible to breach.

At first, I thought there might be a supernatural element to the film, and the killer was somehow mentally projecting himself out of prison and into the external world. Instead, he does physically escape, and the extent of that effort is pretty stunning.

Part of that escape plan involves his nightly chess game with a kindly, old jailer. I wonder if von Sydow was glad to not have to play against Death, as he did in *The Seventh Seal*. At least the stakes have to be lower.

Another part of his convoluted nightly routine involves a rope made up of what has to be every piece of fabric he could get his hands on. One end of this is tied to a long piece of wood. That beam is what secures the rope to the inside of a high opening in a wall. Conveniently, we're not shown how he gets that back *out* of that aperture on the final leg of the return trip.

Curiously, much of the movie is von Sydow running around in the cold while clad only in shoes and underwear. I know revenge is a dish best served cold, but this is ridiculous.

Perhaps the strangest aspect of the film is there is nobody to root for. Our lead is definitely not presented as somebody we want to see succeed. And yet, the people he is killing are all quite nasty as well.

The closest thing to a likeable character among the leads is Howard's detective, but the actor appears to be completely disinterested. One bizarre moment has him surveying some carnage when he says, "I've seen bodies hacked to pieces before, but not like this." As a police captain in a small Scandinavian town, exactly how many dismembered corpses has he seen?

For a film with this much murder in it, you'd think *The Night Visitor* would be more interesting than it is. Given the film is rated PG, the scenes of mayhem end before we see any viscera. And I can't really say it is a psychological drama, as we never really get to know any of the characters. It's a thriller that honestly doesn't have any thrills.

Original version posted on 8/29/2024

Watched on VCI BD-R–yep, a burned disc in packaging bearing the blu-ray logo and shrink-wrapped and everything. A BD-R in full BD clothing. Shame on you, VCI

Nightmare City (1980)

Record Store Day used to be a really big deal to me. I still look forward to each new occurrence, but I no longer camp outside overnight like I used to. For one memorable installment, my brother-in-law was there with me. To pass the time, I brought a portable DVD player and he brought 1980's *Nightmare City*, an Italian zombie movie I had not seen before. I still crack up thinking about all the times the sounds of screaming from the tiny speakers would jar awake those around us. There was a great deal of exasperated people asking, "*what* are you watching?"

Unfortunately, the battery died on the player before the film was half over. I wasn't in any real rush to see it again, but it seemed inevitable I would eventually own the blu-ray of it. That came to pass, and I prepared to laugh at the insanity.

Much of the ironic enjoyment I found in the film in my first partial viewing had to have been due to sleep deprivation. Watching it on a screen roughly five by three inches also probably helped. I remember how much fun it was to shout out who we thought this or that actor most closely resembled. Now having watched it on a bigger screen, the only person I would mistake for anybody is the one military guy who looks like Tommy Lee Jones in the odd frame. And there's Mel Ferrer, who is actually Mel Ferrer but probably wishes he could be mistaken for somebody else.

This is a movie that manages to have a great amount of action on the screen while still being rather dull. There are also many moments of gore that are completely unrealistic looking but still nauseating just because of what they're supposed to be.

There's a glimmer of promise in the very beginning, when an unmarked military plane lands at an airport. Nobody could raise the pilot on the radio as it was touching down. Flight personnel are not visible through the windows of the plane once it has stopped. It brought to mind *The Night Flyer*, a film I really wish I had watched instead of this one.

Armed military personnel surround the aircraft, but their guns are no use against the zombie horde that pours of the plane. One thing that distinguishes this film from its ilk is the undead here are significantly more capable than I have ever seen them before. They can cut people down with machetes or strangle them with chains. I would say they can fire guns with great accuracy, except every firearm here seems to be an Uzi, so all anybody needs to do is just hold the trigger down and spray everybody in the immediate vicinity. Eventually, they're cutting phone lines and manually lowering an elevator full of stuck passengers to the ground floor, courteously delivering a tinned lunch to their fellow zombies.

Having the undead be this intelligent is a huge miscalculation. Since the menace is so well-functioning that they can do everything but talk, why are they the undead to begin with? There is something so simple and effective about the kind introduced by Romero that having them be largely indistinguishable from living (albeit psychotic) people makes the zombie element unnecessary, if not downright laughable.

The nature of the main threat is far (very, very far) from the only ridiculous element. One scene that is hard to forget starts out with too much time spent in a TV studio shoot of a horrible, choreographed routine some spandex-clad dancers are performing to the sounds of the worst kind of generic European disco. Then the zombies kill the dancers but, alas, they do not kill disco as a fad. A particularly gruesome moment has one of the dancers getting her breast sliced off. Note: a zombie *slices* it off.

If a film is going to be this gory, at least the effects should be well-executed. Instead, you have somebody's head exploding like they were that guy in *Scanners*, only for that head to be intact when it hits the floor. One moment that left me slack-jawed involved a character freaking out when she realizes the priest we see in profile is a zombie. Problem is, the half of his face that is disfigured was away from us, but facing her. So, she wasn't freaked out when she can clearly see he's a zombie, but is terrified when he turns to show her the normal side of his face. Even the copious blood everywhere at all times is preposterous fake: watery and bright red as Hawaiian Punch, Mountain Dew Code Red, or any number of things a sane person would eschew in favor of drinking blood.

This is a film that doesn't pull its punches as to which characters it will sacrifice. It would probably help if most of the leads had a lick of sense. One woman seems especially determined to get killed. In the only other moment I found unnerving, a running but unmanned lawnmower creeps across her lawn and she opens the door and steps outside for a closer look. At least she has enough sense to get back inside and lock the door. But then she sees a bloody knife driven into the face of the clay bust she was working on and she does…nothing. There is no payoff to this scene, despite there obviously being a zombie in the house. It also bothered me the knife had fresh blood on it, which seems unlikely, given she seems to live deep in the countryside and by herself.

The nature of the world this movie takes place in suggests this isn't just a different country but a parallel dimension. It is a place where surgeons all know how to expertly throw scalpels, presumably as part of their med school training. Similarly, journalists must have learned axe-throwing as part of their college education. It is also a world where TV monitors explode in flame if thrown at somebody.

I realize there are many people who find much to love in *Nightmare City*, and I'm glad it is preserved on blu-ray for them. As for myself, I watched with greatly diminishing interest until it mercifully ended. Alas, even the conclusion is irritating and an insult to the audience. It pulls the worst kind of twist ending and then follows that with the second-dumbest kind.

Original version posted on 12/8/2024

One Dark Night (1981)

Everything about 1981's *One Dark Night* gave me the impression it would be an R-rated movie, so I was taken aback when I saw it was PG. Turns out the filmmakers were as well, as they thought the movie was gory enough to warrant the more restrictive rating.

Although made the year before *Poltergeist*, it had the misfortune of not being released until after that picture. In addition to having the same MPAA rating, the two have other similarities which led many critics to accuse *One Dark Night* of ripping off a movie whose production started after *Night's* was finished.

This movie would have had a better chance at an R, and a broader audience, if it had any profanity or nudity. Unfortunately for the filmmakers, their primary backer was a Mormon church. I learned this and many other interesting anecdotes in the bonus features on this special edition blu-ray.

What's interesting is this movie is a fully-fledged and effective horror film without the usual trappings of the genre. Meg Tilly stars as an intelligent but unpopular high schooler who agrees to spend the night in a mausoleum as the final initiation rite to join a cool girl clique.

What she doesn't know is the leader of the gang has it out for her because she can't accept Tilly dating her jock ex-boyfriend. She also doesn't know the most recently interred corpse is that of a man with supernatural powers he still possesses after death.

This is "Raymar", and doesn't that name just sound like a bad magician? Early on, we learn he was a "psychic vampire". That phrase amused me to no end when it was used in *Doctor Sleep*, so I laughed out loud hearing it again here.

The movie opens with a team of coroners arriving at the crime scene where Raymar's body is found. There's a closet with female corpses tossed haphazardly in it. It is a sure sign of sloth when somebody is too lazy to hang up their discarded corpses. In an odd decorative touch, he apparently used his telekinetic powers to embed dishes and utensils into the walls. It's like feng shui by way of *Carrie*.

Something I found endearing and goofy is something like five or six coroner vans arrive. How many vehicles does this city's coroner's department have? And they all open their doors in sequence in a neat little bit of choreography. I imagine the coroners practicing this routine when the workload gets light.

The special effects are pretty good. Inevitably, corpses start emerging from their vaults in the mausoleum walls. They levitate instead of walking, and there's a nice touch where we keep seeing the very tips of their toes dragging on the floor as they slide across it.

Perhaps the most spectacular of the effects is Adam West. He's not in zombie makeup or anything, I just mean he is always so stiff and lifeless that it's amazing anybody could convince us he is a living being.

In addition to a large volume of bonus features, the blu-ray comes in a slipcover that gives it the appearance of being a rental VHS. Even the amount of restoration done on the movie is appropriate, as it looks just a bit better than a cleaned-up video image. There doesn't appear to be color-correction, or at least it isn't noticeable. There are even some flecks left in the image. I prefer this to cleaning up a movie so thoroughly that it looks like it was made today.

One Dark Night is surprisingly effective for a PG horror movie. It feels like a *Phantasm* knock-off for those who were too young for that kind of intensity, and it is a good example of why PG-13 would come along in a couple of years.

Original version posted on 5/16/2023

The Outwaters (2022)

The Outwaters is, as of this writing, the latest found footage sensation. It was written by, directed by and starring Robbie Banfitch, with his brother Scott co-starring. Here is how I imagine the conversation went between them as they decided to make this film…

Robbie: "Waaaasuuuuup!"

Scott: " Waaaaasuuuuuuup!"

"Dude, I have this bitchin' idea!"

"Did you just say, 'bitchin'?'"

"Yeah…some middle-aged guy who lost touch with popular culture a couple of decades back is trying to write dialogue for us."

"Ohhh…bogus. Shit, now I'm doing it."

"Don't worry. You know I write dialogue even worse than this guy, so you know we're going to be rolling in the bling. We're going to make a movie"

"Radical! But we don't know shit about making movies. What are we going to do?"

"Haven't you seen *The Blair Witch Project*? It's been like 25 years since that shit and you know that old saying: you can fool all the people all the time."

"YOLO!"

"We'll go on vacation in the desert and just act like all kinds of crazy shit is happening."

"Fuh-shizzle!"

"Yeah, we'll just do shit like act like we can feel the ground vibrating, or hear weird sounds at night, or see some guy in silhouette holding an axe, or pulling extra layers of skin off our real skin, or possibly time traveling, or maybe seeing a demon or aliens or some shit."

"Gnarly! But we don't have any bread—I mean money, so we can't do special effects or shit."

"That's OK. That's why we're going to do what *Blair Witch* did but show even *less*. We'll just run around in the desert at night and everybody will think they're seeing all kinds of shit because all anybody will see is what the flashlights show."

"Where's the beef! But won't people want to know why we're in the desert?"

"That's the best part! I've been trying to get in the jean shorts of this hippie girl who sings, so she'll be in the movie and the idea is we'll be making a music video for her. She has a singing voice like any other woman who can kinda sing, a butterfly tattoo and everything!"

"Dy-no-mite! Is she going to show her tits?"

"Nah, but there's another woman I know who is willing to do that. Maybe smear some fake blood all over them, 'cause you know that's my thing."

"Groovy, man! Hey, wait, wasn't the idea of *Blair Witch* that somebody finds their tapes later? If this is found footage, who finds it?"

"Who cares? We'll just make it look like cops found the memory cards for our cameras and they're watching it. We'll claim it is the raw footage, but insult the audience by having audio and music spanning over some of what would be different recordings"

"Heavens to murgatroyd! But won't the audience notice?"

"That's the *best* best part. Either they'll be too stupid to notice or they'll be too scared to point it out to others because we'll have all these people who immediately defend anything they don't understand!"

The horror...the horror... [the section about horror films]

"That's the cat's meow! Do we have anything we can already use?"

"You know it! We got that stuff I shot at my Mom's when I surprised her by coming home unexpectedly that one time. Then there's that abstract shit I did in my CGI course before I dropped out of film school. *And* there's all that artsy shit I made when I was trying out my new camera. Remember all that stuff I did just pointing the camera down a pipe with a light at the end? We'll use that! We'll use *all* of that! This is like a movie meatloaf and we'll put nothing but bread in it. There's no meat! We can't lose!"

"That's strictly from Dixie! That's a ducky shincracker!"

"We'll be togged to the bricks! We'll hit on all sixes! It's a saltash luck!"

"It'll be a lally-cooler! We'll be a shoddyocracy! We'll be wake snakes!"

"It will be a Banbury story! We'll be chirping merry!"

"A pox on both our houses!

Original version posted on 2/21/2023

Picture Mommy Dead (1966)

One of the most memorable images in 1966's *Picture Mommy Dead* is an unbroken shot of young Susan Gordon running towards the camera as a hawk swoops down on her from behind. I imagine it was easy to act terrified in that scene, and I wondered if she was genuinely scared. I bet there were some interesting conversations with her father later, as he was directing her in that scene.

This is a Bert I. Gordon film, a director famed (so to speak) for such pictures as *Attack of the Puppet People* and *The Beginning of the*

End. Many of his films have received the *Mystery Science Theatre 3000* or Rifftrax treatment. Some of those have been more justified in having jokes made at their expense than others (*Beginning*, which is about giant grasshoppers, is truly dreadful).

I think it would be all too easy to take potshots at *Mommy*. I know my wife and I did while watching it, though we honestly do that to all but a very few pictures. And yet, this was a far more enjoyable and interesting work than anything else I have seen in his oeuvre.

When we first see Susan Gordon, she has been under the care of nuns in what I assume is a psychiatric hospital, especially given a character later snarkily calls the institution "the convent" in a way that he might as well have made finger quotes while doing so. She has been there since her mother (Zsa Zsa Gabor) died in a fire in their Beverly Hills mansion three years earlier.

Now dad Don Ameche has arrived to take her home. Martha Hyer, as his new wife, is also there to welcome her. One can imagine much of the backstory for her relationship with Ameche, as Hyer used to be Gordon's governess.

As the car pulls away, I couldn't help but notice the expression on the face of the nun (Signe Hasso) who walked Gordon out—it is hard to tell if it is pity or relief the girl is going away. Admittedly, something about Gordon feels off from the get-go.

I just happened to see her in 1960's *Tormented* a day or two before watching this for the first time, and it seems she was a better actress when she was only ten or eleven years old. She was good enough then that she even acted outside of her father's work, being especially well-received in the Danny Kaye feature *The Five Pennies*.

She's not a conventionally good actor, but there is still something fascinating in her unusual performance, something off-kilter which makes her compelling to watch. And she is in good company, as every character is some sort of freak.

When the family arrives at the mansion, the person greeting them at the door is Maxwell Reed, who has severe scarring to half of his face. I laughed out loud at the complete lack of tact everybody demonstrates in reaction to his appearance, yet this is more realistic than most movies would allow. His burns were incurred in the fire that took Gabor's life, as he was supposedly trying to extinguish the flames.

Or was he actually after the large diamond necklace Gabor was wearing? That object, where a great number of the gems are arranged in the form of a bird with its wings outspread, is the obsession of many of the characters. Hyer, as the duplicitous gold-digger, seems to want it more than anything. Reed, who is revealed to be just as cold-hearted, has also been looking for it in the house since it mysteriously disappeared following Gabor's death.

That necklace is on Gabor's neck in a large oil portrait with which Gordon becomes obsessed. At one point, the girl scratches at the necklace in the painting hard enough that her fingers leave trails of blood on it, meaning a painting can have craquelure severe enough to cut open skin. I wonder if that's a new way such works can be authenticated.

Everybody seems to have it out for Gordon, who has inherited the family money in a trust fund she cannot access until she turns 25. Ameche has squandered what money he received following his wife's death. He turns to Gordon, to get her approval to sell the contents of the house, and she agrees to that.

She first seeks the council of family lawyer Wendell Corey, here in a weird and funny cameo. He's deeply belligerent, hostile to the entire family and reveling in his repulsion towards them. Well,

I assume that's how he feels, because his dialogue is delivered in long strings of poorly enunciated, Texan-accented syllables. I honestly wonder if this was the inspiration for Mike Judge to create the similarly-voiced character of Boomhauer on *King of the Hill*.

The already-unstable Gordon will lose her inheritance should she die or be permanently committed to a mental facility. The money would then go to Ameche. Upon his demise, it would go to Reed. And Hyer will work whatever angles she can to ensure she ends up in the closest proximity to that money.

The house itself is a pretty strange character. The real mansion used is a startling, if not random, combination of architectural and decorative styles. The hallways are largely painted a uniform, dusty teal. Altogether, the house is so jaw-droppingly ugly that it becomes a strange kind of beautiful. The quality of the video on the Kino Lorber blu-ray on which I watched this presents the surroundings in remarkable detail.

A great deal of intrigue happens in and around that space, some of it deeply ridiculous. In perhaps the most unusual spin on "Chekhov's gun" I have seen to date is "Chekhov's grappling hook", with which a character will meet their end in a manner equally gruesome and improbable.

There aren't any genuine scares here, so much as a general unease which I found intriguing. Especially good is a scene where the dolls and stuffed animals Gordon rediscovers are made increasingly menacing through the use of incrementally shorter edits until the images almost take on a strobing effect.

But the ending of *Picture Mommy Dead* is where it really shines. Gordon's characterization, never fully believable until that point, becomes something transcendent at the conclusion. Whether it is bad acting or a deliberately odd performance, she is perfect in those final moments in a scene that will stick with me for some time. While I sat in stunned silence, the final cuts reverse the sequence of the shots that open the film, revealing Bert I. Gordon to be a better filmmaker than much of his earlier work would lead one to believe. Well played, Bert and Susan.

Original version posted on 8/6/2024

The Possession of Joel Delaney (1972)

It is given that possession movies will be 1) about possession by a demon and 2) centered around the Catholic concepts of such. There will usually be an attempt at an exorcism. So, I was surprised to discover a film about possession that not only was released a year before *The Exorcist*, but which had already broken many of the rules the later film had yet to establish for the genre.

1972's *The Possession of Joel Delaney* has Perry King overtaken by the spirit of a serial killer who was his friend. This was King's movie debut, and he is shockingly young. Something about many of his facial expressions, and especially what he does with his eyes, makes him look uncannily like Elijah Wood at times. Unfortunately, I found King about as believable as I would likely find Wood in this role, which is not at all.

Shirley MacLaine fares better as his sister. There is something a bit creepy between them, as suggested by a scene where they are at a party together and some people there think they are a couple. Also, she seems jealous of his girlfriend.

It isn't surprising that one of the ways we start seeing cracks in King's amiable persona is when he starts asking his sister questions about her sex life. She tries changing the subject by asking him about his recent time spent in Tangiers. He says he met a lot of women like her, and the audience can relate to MacLaine in her failure to understand exactly what he means by that.

Honestly, he seemed to be a bit off even before this, though we see very little of him before he becomes possessed. King seems awfully mousy and pasty to be living in the lower east side. One theme explored by the script is the social and economic divides of New York City, as she seems to never leave her house without wearing a fur coat, while he prefers to live among poor Puerto Ricans. She even asks him, "Why live down there with those people? We all know there's poverty, but you don't have to seek it out." To which he replies, "I think you only see what you want to." Her eyes are about to be seriously opened.

One night, she calls him at his place and all she hears on the other end of the line is primitive percussion that sounds remarkably like the beginning of "Magic Bus" by The Who. This causes her so much worry that she goes to his apartment, only to find him thrashing and screaming as the police drag him away. It turns out he had tried to kill his landlord, and she's baffled as to why he would do that. Apparently, she never met anybody who ever wanted to kill their landlord.

There's a great scene where MacLaine tries in vain to throw her weight around the police station. While she gets her first glimpses of how the other 99% live, her prominent surgeon ex-husband does manage to pull some strings and get her brother transferred to a psychiatric ward.

It is interesting to watch MacLaine as she struggles to understand her brother's sudden issues, an investigation which will introduce her to a community and culture she doesn't understand. Alas, I don't think she made much of an effort to get more involved.

One such moment is an exorcism ritual that is of a religion I did not recognize. At least, I'm certain it isn't traditional Catholicism, and that was interesting. The ritual is done to music playing on a record and I kept wondering what would happen if the ceremony required more time than the length of that side of the disc. That alone shows I probably would handle this ceremony as poorly as she does. As the frustrated priest tells her: "People like yourself, you try to buy God and your mind is closed."

MacLaine needs to find something to resolve King's issues, as he is becoming increasingly unstable. He also has started speaking in fluent Spanish, a language he allegedly did not know previously. To be more specific, King talks in dubbed Spanish that doesn't match his lip movements very well. Oh, and his girlfriend has been found dead, with her head suspended from the ceiling over the rest of her body.

The crime scene is similar to those of three deaths in Spanish Harlem the previous year. It is widely believed those were committed by one Tonio Perez, who happened to be King's best friend. According to Tonio's mother, her son is now dead.

To summarize: we have a person possessed by something other than a demon, and the rituals of an obscure religion are used to try to exorcise that spirit. That is an interesting idea, one that might have improved any of the subpar possession movies in the decades following *The Exorcist*.

Unfortunately, the movie drags out everything waaay too long. It doesn't help that it seems to also believe it is such an *important* film. Worst of all is King's performance, which is never terrible, but which is also never believable. The climax of the film has him jeopardizing MacLaine and her children. He does some appalling things, but I didn't buy him as an intimidating presence and so the scene falls flat.

The Possession of Joel Delaney is interesting in that it somehow subverts cliches that had yet to be established. I was also intrigued by the culture shock experienced by MacLaine. Unfortunately, this slightly pretentious film overstays its welcome.

Original version posted on 1/21/2024

Race with the Devil (1975)

1975's *Race with the Devil* takes place in deeply rural Texas, where a great many of the residents are in a Satanic cult. Heck, maybe *everybody* in the area is in the cabal. And this isn't the modern type of "Satanist" which seems to be a more of a jokey affair meant to get under the skin of particular breeds of conservatives. Instead, these are your dues-paying, "let's occasionally sacrifice a human being" kind of worshippers.

There's a weird code that seems to unite devil-worshipping sects across such pictures, and that is they almost exclusively sacrifice either babies or comely young lasses. This is a movie that opts for the latter, which results in some female nudity I never stop being surprised is in PG-rated movies of that era. I also wondered how often they do these rituals. Regardless of the frequency, I imagine it would be difficult to regularly replenish your supply of attractive, shapely women who are willing to be sacrificed.

A group of four vacationers find themselves pursued by the cult after accidentally witnessing a sacrificial ritual. The remainder of the film has our heroes trying to get to the authorities in Amarillo where they can report the murder. Naturally, they don't just go directly to their destination, because there wouldn't be a movie if they did that. Instead, they make a stopover or two along the way, where it is revealed the cult has a broader reach, and more members, than they anticipated. That baffled me, as the two main elements likely to be the undoing of such a secret society are the extent of its unlawfulness and the number of people involved.

Our protagonists are two couples: Peter Fonda and Lara Parker, and Warren Oates and Loretta Swit. They're on vacation, taking a high-end RV out to the middle of nowhere. They just want to get away from the noise of the city so they can have some peace and quiet they can ruin with their ungodly loud motorbikes.

Curiously, those motorbikes barely factor into the plot. At the beginning of the film, we see a fair amount of Oates's bike dealership and we also see Fonda competitively racing. However, in the pursuit that is the majority of the runtime, the RV is all that is used to evade the bad guys.

And I never thought an RV could be such an action vehicle. This one can go faster than many vehicles smaller than it. It can corner far better than I thought was possible in such an unwieldly monstrosity. Heck, it doesn't roll in some circumstances that flipped what I believed to be more nimble vehicles.

If one can suspend their disbelief enough, the chase scenes are effective and engaging. There are sufficient explosions in one bit to give this the feel of an early made-for-TV *Fury Road*. You even have people leaping onto the RV. Alas, some of those moments are ridiculous, such as the guy who smashes the rear window, only to be pummeled by Fonda wielding what appears to be a vacuum cleaner attachment.

Race with the Devil is enjoyable for the right kind of audience, and in the right frame of mind. It has some exciting and well-executed moments of high pursuit. On the other hand, it also has the villains hiding rattlesnakes in various compartments of the RV, because that's just what Satanists in this caliber of film were always doing at the time.

And these are villains who were daft enough to think nobody would notice their small public library has a curiously large number of books on witchcraft. Then again, our heroes aren't smart enough to question this when Part and Swit steal a couple of books from there. Nor do they question whether it would be a good idea to help themselves to those texts in the midst of the intrigue they find themselves in. As a book collector, I suspect our protagonists aren't being chased because they witnessed a murder. I think the Satanists just wanted their books back.

Original version posted on 9/9/2024

The Return of Dracula (1958)

I love the different ways that some low-budget movies come up with innovative solutions to overcome their lack of funds. One way that can be effective is to have a character imply something is there which we can't see. This is what 1958's *The Return of Dracula* does in some of its best moments.

The heroine of this picture is Norma Eberhardt, who plays an art student who works nights at the old folks' home. It is there she reads a blind woman to sleep. But before the woman nods off, she demands to know, "Who is that at the window?" Eberhardt doesn't see anybody and neither does the viewer. But the suggestion somebody just happens to be outside that window is effectively creepy.

When Dracula comes for her, the blind woman is unable to stop him from attacking. "Open your eyes and look at me," orders Francis Lederer, as The Count. "You can see me if you try. You can see me with your mind." Again, pretty effectively unnerving.

Lederer makes for a very convincing Dracula. The first time we see him, he has attacked a man on a train in Europe. Stealing his victim's identity, Lederer goes to the small California town which was that man's intended destination. There, he is welcomed into the home of the deceased's unsuspecting, distant relations.

I found more in this picture to recommend it than I would have anticipated.

The score is sparse but interesting. "Dies Irae" is used for some scenes. You might remember this from the opening credits of *The Shining*. One of the moments it accompanies here is where a group of men with stakes want to ensure The Count is dead, only to find his resting place empty just as the final rays of the setting sun disappear. I was wondering exactly why they waited to open the tomb until *after* the sun had set. I'm thinking they are fortunate it was empty.

Another piece of music precedes that scene, and I noticed there is a sound in it that was similar to labored breathing. I wondered if a bellows was employed for that. Regardless of the source, it sufficiently sets the stage for the cemetery scene.

The crisp black and white photography is perfect for this type of film. Color is used for only a few frames, and I was pleased by how much this moment caught me off-guard.

The Return of Dracula is slight in both plot and runtime, but I found myself glued to it throughout. Also, I would rather see what a movie with a small budget might do, as opposed to the big-budget ones. No amount of CGI could intrigue me as much as a woman walking alone at night, turning to hear something we don't, and wondering aloud, "What did you say?"

Original version posted on 11/3/2023

Satan's Cheerleaders (1977)

I'm finally starting to notice that books on fringe cinema have resulted in some unfortunate additions to my movie library. For example, reading P.J. Thorndyke's excellent *Satan in the Celluloid: 100 Satanic and Occult Horror Movies of the 1970s* led me to acquire 1977's *Satan's Cheerleaders*.

I likely don't need to go into detail about this film for you to guess how lousy it is, though I will just the same. Even the picture itself seems to know this, as there is some obvious self-awareness. While that doesn't fully excuse it, what is truly baffling is a quick succession of twists near the end that hint at the better film this could have been.

But I'll get to that ending later. First, there's the opening credits, which are effective at establishing the general vibe. The lettering of the titles is in purple and in a font that would otherwise be used only for porn of that era. Those titles are overlaid atop a dark scene of a Satanic ceremony. And, by dark, I don't mean the content. I'm referring to the image. It was so underlit that I couldn't tell what was happening on the screen.

That surprised me, as the director of photography was Dean Cundey, who went on to do stellar work on John Carpenter's best films. I was wondering if an introduction had been made to that director via Debra Hill, the producer of those films, who served here as script supervisor. As always, it is interesting to see where people start out who will go on to far more significant careers.

Fortunately, the scene under those opening credits is probably the only one without decent cinematography, though there is nothing in the course of the runtime I would describe as more than competent. Not that the material really warrants anything special, as this is a film by Greydon Clark.

Through additional glimpses of that ceremony later, we will see everybody there is solidly upper-middle-age, a demographic I don't first think of as being potential Satanists. And yet, they seem to be just that in many such films, including *Rosemary's Baby*, *The Devil's Rain* and *The Sentinel*.

Among the worshippers of the dark one are John Ireland and Yvonne De Carlo, two veteran stars whose professionalism means they deliver unnecessarily good performances. Another of the old followers of old scratch is played by Jack Kruschen, who wants the dark one to punish those who humiliate him. We'll see him working as a school janitor and he's wearing a denim shirt decorated in rhinestones. I imagine Satan is like, "Look, I'll try to help you, but you gotta meet me halfway here."

It is no surprise he spies on cheerleaders while they shower. The song on the soundtrack while watching him watching them is an up-tempo R&B song that is all about "Who you gonna love tonight?" We see him twitching his ass in time to that music he shouldn't be able to hear, in a self-aware moment that suggests there was at least the potential for a smarter film.

That song, and much of the other music in this picture, is all "wacka-wacka" guitar funk, like the kind of music everybody associates with porn of this era, even if they have never seen a clip of the real thing. And that brings to mind one of the most curious aspects of this film: everything from the title on down almost demands this be porn, but this isn't even softcore fare. Instead, it is a curiously chaste affair, with seemingly only a token amount of nudity thrown in. I wasn't surprised to learn after the fact such material has added to make it an R film after it bombed when released as PG. What did surprise me is they didn't go for an R rating (let's face it, a hard R) from the get-go.

Instead, we have that trickle of nudity jarringly contrasting with a film without any blood or profanity. The latter is especially telling in the "aw shucks" performance by Jacqulin Cole. As the cheerleading coach, she is the kind of person who would sooner die than drop an f-bomb.

Her horrible acting only makes her character even more annoying. Every one of her line readings is flat, awkward and delivered in the same manner, regardless of the situation. At one point, she's getting slapped in the face repeatedly by Ireland, and her only response is to whine, "Would you stop it?" in the mildly annoyed way one would get with a sibling engaged in some minor torment they know gets on their nerves. More than a few of her line deliveries feel like the notoriously bad performance of Sally in *A Charlie Brown Christmas*, emerging like this: "Have you gone [awkward pause] completely mad?" So, why is she in this movie? It probably helped that she was married to the director and chief writer.

Faring only slightly better, and to varying extents, are the four cheerleaders of the squad. I was curious why the school only had four football cheerleaders, but maybe that's a normal thing. Then again, there also appear to be no more than four football players, at least at the only practice we see, and I know that isn't right. I was also confused by whether this institution was supposed to be a high school or a college.

Anyway, Kerry Sherman is the best of the lot, which is probably why she seems to have had more of a career than her fellow cheerleaders. Alas, standing out from the crowd is likely what makes Lucifer single her out to rape and possess.

Kruschen is angry because he had abducted the girls in the hope of violating them himself, and then is further outraged when it turns out he has been deceived by the one he worships. In pictures like this, I never cease to be amazed by people worshipping somebody who goes by, among other names, The Great Trickster, only to be shocked when they get double-crossed.

Much that transpires over the course of the runtime is sub-moronic. A typical line of dialogue has a football player remarking of one of the girls: "I can't help it. I'm wild about your backfield in motion." Not that the girls are much more high-minded, such as when one asks what's wrong with Sherman, resulting in this exchange: "She's thinking." "Why would anybody want to do that?" Maybe Sherman was trying to think up a better prank than the boys pull on their coach, where they put a sign saying "BOYS" on the girl's locker room. That the coach falls for this is less of an insult to his intelligence than it is to ours.

What makes *Satan's Cheerleaders* a frustrating watch is that weird series of twist endings I mentioned earlier. These surprises are odd, and I'm pretty sure each is at least partially contradicted by one or more of the others. Still, they hint at something better than anything preceding them. Curiously, the smartest thing in the entire movie is the very last line, when the coach says to Sherman after an impossibly high-scoring game, "Well, I'll be damned." Her quip: "Most likely."

Original version posted on 9/23/2023

Shock Waves (1977)

Zombie Nazis on a ghost ship attack a 70s version of the *Gilligan's Island* passengers and crew. If that sounds promising, then you'll likely have a good time watching 1977's *Shock Waves*.

As Peter Cushing will eventually explain, these zombies are super-soldiers developed by the Nazis. As a sub captain, he had transported the army of the undead around the Atlantic coast, waiting for his side to win the war. Which they didn't, so what is one to do with a boatload of unstoppable, undead killing machines?

One aspect of the film I greatly appreciated is the lack of gore. I realized this only later, when I looked the movie up on IMDB and discovered it is PG. Funny how, just by the nature of the material, I thought this had to have been R or unrated. That it is obviously low-budget only compounds that sensation.

And yet, even without gore, there are some very creepy scenes. Among this picture's best moments are the zombies walking slowly across the ocean floor or rising slowly out of the water. If there is one reason to see this film, it is the moments like this.

Curiously, the film is only 67 minutes long, leading me to suspect this was made solely with the intention of it being at the bottom of a double-, triple-, whatever-, feature playing in drive-ins and grindhouse theaters. I don't have any complaints about the runtime. I believe a movie should only be the length it warrants. That said, there were still moments where you could sense the padding to even get it to this length.

Really, it would have worked better as a short film, though I know those were nearly impossible to see in the era this was made. And this may sound like a dig, though it isn't: it has the feel of a very well-made student film. It is very competently made, but it has that "hey, gang, let's put on a show" vibe to it. Once again, I like such low-budget features and I will cut them more slack than big-budget ones. Also, there's so much grain that this must be a blow-up from 16mm, though some shots look like they might have even been from 8mm.

The cast is largely unknowns and their performances range from fair to above average. None of the non-name actors did anything that made me want to look for other films they appeared in. I didn't even think of these as named characters, but just stereotypes: Pornstache, comic relief guy, and a perpetually bickering couple that seem to be living incarnations of the characters from the terrible comic strip *The Lockhorns*. Oh, and a ship's cook who is like a character out of *Cabin Boy*.

The established actors here are Peter Cushing, John Carradine and Brooke Adams. Cushing's appearance here is little more than a glorified cameo in which he plays the captain of the downed Nazi vessel. He never phones in a performance, and so does a serviceable job here. Inexplicably, Carradine turns in a better performance than in most of the similar roles he also did only for the paycheck. And Brooke Adams is, as always, a joy to watch.

The script is horror boilerplate for the most part, but with some notable lines. One is courtesy of the husband in the bitter middle-aged couple: "I keep asking myself if this is a dream, but then I realized this isn't a dream anybody would believe, so it must be real!"

Taking potshots at this movie would be like kicking a puppy, albeit a living-dead Nazi one. It is slight, but enjoyable. Also, being a PG movie means it is good for younger audiences and those who especially want to avoid gore.

Original version posted on 3/19/2023

Sole Survivor (1984)

Survivor's guilt is good fodder for a horror movie, being used well in fare as diverse as super-low-budget 1962 classic *Carnival of Souls* to 1981's *The Survivor* to the *Final Destination* series of this century. I think it is odd that a shared feeling among many people who survive a traumatic event is they don't believe they deserved to do so.

When we first see Anita Skinner in 1984's *Sole Survivor*, she is sitting upright in a row of commercial airline seats, a stunned expression on her face. Mind you, those seats are not inside a plane but are out in a field amongst the debris of a crash where she is, you guessed it, the sole survivor.

This event had been dreamed in advance by Caren Larkey, playing an actress who gets psychic premonitions. Go figure, Larkey will eventually be in a commercial produced by Skinner. The actress is so unnerved by being around the woman from her dream that she turns what should be a couple of hours' work into a two-day debacle. She walks off set that second day and is fired but, really, anybody causing that extent of problems would have been recast in the first hour of the first day.

Similar to *Carnival of Souls* (of which I am a big fan), Skinner keeps encountering dead people. The first time this happens is at the loading dock of the hospital from which she has just been discharged, where a little girl incongruously appears. In a close-up, we see the girl is dripping wet. While distracted by the girl, Skinner is nearly struck by a large truck that has been silently coasting backwards towards her. Later, we learn a corpse had been missing from the morgue, though only for a half hour. Of course, the body was that of a young drowning victim.

Also like that 1962 film, this is a slow burn, which is telegraphed by the footage that plays out under the opening credits. We see deserted city streets in the middle of the night. There are close-ups on the faces of mannequins in closed shops. The only sign of life will be a bus with Skinner as its only passenger. She is sitting there stoically with a gun on her lap and a fair amount of blood on her white turtleneck. We will come back to that scene near the end of the movie.

Something that really sold me on this film is how Skinner reacts to everything like a normal human being would. I even liked her assessment of her survivor's guilt: "I feel like I'm waiting to be caught." She's closer to the truth than she realizes.

Unfortunately, the dead will also take those close to her if they happen to get in the way. One innocent bystander is a teenager next door, played by Robin Davidson. I liked her character, who is not innocent in all meanings of the word, as she seems to be playing the field with the boys. At one point, Skinner says to her, "I hope I never get hard up enough to go out with one of the guys you bring home", to which she replies, "They're all grey in the dark."

Skinner will eventually strike up a convincing romance with a doctor played by Kurt Johnson. I liked the rapport between them. In general, the dialogue in this film is better than this type of fare requires, and a great deal of those best lines are between these two. Consider this interaction between Skinner and Johnson regarding the coffee commercial she'll be filming: "Nine of ten doctors prefer Roaster's Blend" "I've never heard of it" "Oh, then *you're* that tenth doctor."

I enjoyed *Sole Survivor*, though it largely explores ideas I have seen in a few other movies. It is a fairly intelligent film with a curiously melancholic touch to it. It even has a few genuine surprises. But perhaps the most terrifying aspect of the film is how it shows one horrifically decorated kitchen after another. For those who were born after the 70's, believe me, this is an accurate time capsule of just how hideously most homes were decorated back then.

Original version posted on 8/30/2024

The Strangeness (1985)

I don't understand why so many garbage movies have a cult following, yet it seems everybody feels compelled to dogpile on 1985's *The Strangeness*. This is a very low-budget movie and, while it is by no means a masterpiece, it is a much better film than anybody gives it credit for. Even its creators bash it, apologizing in bonus features for the picture you just watched. This is the only time I can ever recall that happening.

This is the kind of movie where I assume somebody found a location first and then devised a plot around it. In this case, we have an abandoned gold mine, apparently connected to a cave system, being explored by a crew of people with different skills and interests.

The crew is composed of a geologist, an experienced Brit miner, a nerdy writer working on a book about the disaster that closed the mine, the writer's photographer wife and two young freelance miners. The group is led by a middle-aged man from the company that used to work the mine.

There were a couple of other people initially, but they don't last beyond the opening credits. This unfortunate couple goes into the mine only to become an appetizer for the cave monster. But, before that, the guy had found a crude cross in the cave, held aloft by a pile of stones. Of course, he pulls the cross out for no apparent reason. Even if you don't know you're in a movie, it seems to me that removing a cross is always a bad idea.

Things then start out ominously for our main group, as the rope by which they descend into the cave is severed just as the last person literally drops in. It was the nerdy writer, who cries out, "Don't worry—no broken bones." The company man's only funny line in the picture is this retort: "You only fell two feet!" But it turns out the rope didn't just break, it was cut. Perhaps it was prescient that the first person to drop down summoned the others with, "Send down the meat."

These are simple but believable characters, which benefits a cast I assume is largely inexperienced. Still, some of the actors are better than others. And there isn't much depth to these characters, though there are some deviations from stereotypes. I like how the blue-collar guys aren't exactly letches, even if one of them occasionally hits on the photographer. Even the socially awkward writer provides some necessary interpersonal skills to defuse a conflict.

The movie makes good use of the cave, with only the explorers' lights providing the illumination in most scenes. Many of the reviews I have read complained about how the image is too dark in most of the film, but I think this was a good decision. One scene is from the perspective of the only person with a light on at that moment, and I felt like I was watching one of the inspirations for the eventual found footage trend. A great sequence at the end is made more effective by only being lit by the occasional camera flash.

In some scenes, the camera stays wide with most of the screen black, and only a small portion of it lit by the explorers' lights. One very effective shot like this stays black for a second or two after the explorers walk off-screen. That darkness feels very intimidating, solid and lonely. Perhaps the most suspenseful scene is lit by a single flare, which we see sputter out at the conclusion.

Footage of the real cave is mixed in with scenes shot on what is an obvious set. Once again, the way the movie is lit is to its benefit. There were even some moments where I wasn't sure whether what we were seeing was shot on location or on a soundstage. One such moment is creepy and innovative, as the team finds an area with mirrored shards dangling from the ceiling on bits of string. The writer explains the miners started hanging them up to see if anything was approaching from behind.

And now it is finally time to address the Claymation monster in the room. If there is one thing critics consistently ridicule this movie for, it is the stop-motion beast. I love stop-motion animation, so my esteem for a movie automatically goes up a step when the technique is employed. Alas, I also understand why so many found this creature so laugh-out-loud hilarious, as it most closely resembles male genitalia, with the female counterpart as its face. I didn't laugh when I first saw it, but I will say I was stunned. The best I can say is you will never see another film with a monster in it like this one.

I must like *The Strangeness*, as I have seen it twice. If there's one element of it I find bizarre, it isn't the creature—it's how everything about it feels like it was made a decade earlier. Once again, that isn't a fault. I recommend this movie for fans of low-budget cinema which makes the most of its limited means.

Original version posted on 5/20/2023

Sweeny Todd (1936)
The Demon Barber of Fleet Street

It's odd how some very dark moments in history can become popular stories in later eras, the kind of tales told over and over again. In the fourteenth century, a French barber killed his wealthiest customers and stole their money. He then turned their bodies over to the pastry chef next door, who used the corpses as fresh meat for his pies. The tale was adapted into a popular Broadway musical starring Angela Lansbury in the 20th century, and then a Tim Burton movie in the 21st. I expect there will be comedies about the horrors of Jeffrey Dahmer in whatever media we'll have in the 25th century. I kid, of course. The tenor of contemporary comedy is so overly cruel as to leave me surprised we haven't already had a sitcom about him airing on broadcast television.

While the Todd premise is not a story I am particularly enamored with, I was very impressed with Tod Slaughter's 1936 film *Sweeny Todd: The Demon Barber of Fleet Street.* Then again, when you adopt the stage name "Tod Slaughter", it seems inevitable one would eventually star as a murderer named Todd.

The film opens in what was then the present day, and some poor shlub goes into a barbershop for a shave. It is only after the customer is prepped and sitting in a chair that the barber proceeds to wax eloquently about how Todd was the greatest artist of the blade the world had ever known. That's when the customer should be beating a hasty exit. It would be like a leather goods producer waxing fondly on the work of Ed Gein.

Instead, we journey to the past, where Slaughter, as the title character, plies his trade at his shop near the docks. He is way too excited to offer a shave to men fresh off the boat and about to reenter society proper: "Lots of throats! Beautiful throats! Waiting for the touch of the razor." A skeezy guy talking loudly in this manner would seem to be fair warning to not use his services, yet many do, with the wealthiest being "polished off" by him. Nobody is alarmed by how he openly uses that phrase all the time, so I wonder if they thought this was some sort of "happy ending" shave. Also, how does nobody notice so many people are missing, and simply follow the trail of their last known locations back to his establishment?

What is ever more peculiar is, given we're talking about a murderous man who wields a straight razor, his method of extinguishing his customers is bloodless. I assume this is because of the censorship rules at the time. But this picture turns that liability on its head, as Todd literally turns customers on their heads when, with the pull of lever, he upends the unsuspecting out of the chair and into an open trapdoor. Through a basement shared with the bakery next door, he turns the bodies over to Stella Rho who uses them as meat in her wares.

Once again having to circumvent tight film regulations of the time, this feature only makes the vaguest suggestion as to the contents of those pies. Still, it is a strong enough hint that my stomach lurched when the latest young apprentice of Todd (John Singer) sinks his teeth into one, oblivious to the nature of the contents. That Todd gave him a penny to acquire that, and he doubtlessly knows the nature of what is in the pastry, is doubly repellant. Also, I found it interesting nobody seems overly concerned the previous seven orphans brought to Todd for apprenticeships all disappeared, and that is likely an unfortunately accurate element of that period.

But there wouldn't be much of a film here if there weren't additional complications, and that arrives in the form of wealthy shipbuilder D.J. Williams and his comely daughter, played by Eve Lister. Todd has entered into an arrangement to fund the father's latest project, and those terms will put that man's firm into jeopardy, thereby making Williams more receptive to Todd's proposal of marriage to Lister.

Needless to say, Lister isn't receptive to that arrangement. For one thing, she's already in love with a sailor played by Bruce Seton. In a bizarre subplot, Seton will return to England with his own means of support, courtesy of some pearls a man in Africa gave him as he was dying. When I think of potential riches in Africa, I think of diamonds primarily, and maybe gold a distant second, but never pearls. I think it would have been funny if there had been a line stating these beauties were from the continent's legendary pearl mines, just to see if viewers were paying attention.

As tends to happen in my viewing experiences, I found many of the secondary characters to be even more interesting than our leads. Jerry Verno is quite effective as Seton's friend and obligatory comic relief. I liked this exchange between the two friends: "You're a pessimist" "Yes, because you're right. And, no, because I don't know what it means". Even better is the underused Davina Craig, as Verno's girl and Lister's quirky best friend. There's a neat bit towards the beginning where the two couples are basically having the same conversation, and the editing cuts between each of them finishing each other's lines.

There is one line in the film that struck me as funny and that is when a passenger thanks the captain for how quickly a voyage had been *on a sail ship*. I mean, as if the captain could possibly make more wind. All I can think of is the line from *The Princess Bride* that made me laugh the most the last time I saw it: "Is he using the same wind we're using?"

Since watching *Sweeny Todd*, I have read some reviews of it online and am appalled by the general sentiment towards the film. "Creaky" is a noticeably recurring adjective. As for myself, I found it to be surprisingly modern in its tone, despite the vaudevillian trappings. Even Slaughter's wildly over-the-top performance reads like mockery, which suggests to me a genuinely nasty person within the character. Those other reviews lead me to paraphrase that line I liked so much from *The Princess Bride*. Were they watching the same movie I was watching?

Original version posted on 9/16/2024

Sugar Hill (1974)

1974's *Sugar Hill* is a weird beast, a hybrid of zombie, gangster and Blaxploitation genres. It is truly number one in a field of one.

Marki Bey stars as the title character. She's hellbent on revenge for the murder of husband Larry Don Johnson, emphasis on "hell". With the assistance of an old voodoo woman (Zara Cully), she summons Baron Samedi (Don Pedro Colley), who is one of those "king of the underworld" voodoo figures.

He is basically the devil, and Bey offers him her soul in exchange for his help getting satisfaction. Turns out he doesn't deal in souls, and the way he wants satisfaction involves her body. She agrees to an arrangement where she will become another of his deathless brides upon completion of the operation.

The men she seeks to have destroyed are the henchmen of local Mafia kingpin Robert Quarry. This is a man involved with many enterprises. One of those involves a minion going to the docks to collect payment from the poor souls looking to load and unload ships. I was baffled by why anybody would pay to work. For that matter, it seems these guys would earn so little doing such grunt work that I question what the potential take would be for Quarry.

Quarry had Johnson killed because he refused to sign over his successful establishment, Club Haiti, to him. On the night of the murder, four of his thugs appear at the club where Johnson rejects their proposal out of hand. In the parking lot later, the same guys put on stocking masks when they kill him. I found the masks a bizarre touch, as they are wearing the same highly distinctive clothes they were wearing when others might have seen them in the club. One guy (Charles Robinson) is wearing a very loud suit, of which I am betting there has only even been one in existence.

Robinson is the only Black guy in Quarry's operation, and I am surprised he puts up with as much shit as he does. Not only do various people in the organization say the N-word a lot, but he is even made to do such degrading tasks as shining the main man's shoes.

Many of the racial slurs are courtesy of Quarry's mistress, Betty Anne Rees. It is no surprise there will eventually be a huge catfight between her and Bey. It starts with slaps and ends with a bucket of ice dumped over the head of Rees. I was amused by the bartender who provided the ice, as he had been nonchalantly doing various tasks behind the bar while the fight played out. Then he just casually hands the bucket across the bar to Bey.

I'm not big on revenge flicks, but this one is a lot of fun. It helps that much of it is so ridiculous. One scene begins with a disembodied chicken foot hopping around, supposedly on its own. It is a ridiculous idea that should be laughable to anybody, yet it terrifies the guy who is about to die.

What really sells the film is Colley, who plays everything extremely broadly, as befits the material. He looks how Sid Haig might if he was Black. Usually wearing a top hat, his character is even something Haig might play in a Rob Zombie movie.

Speaking of zombies, they're of the very old school variety, the actual Haitian type. A bizarre touch is they have perfectly round, reflective half-spheres over their eyes, as if they have pinballs for eyes. This should be hilarious, but it is surprisingly unnerving.

I love *Sugar Hill*, though I'm aware I am cutting it a great deal of slack. It's fun, it's weird and it is genuinely creepy in a couple of moments. If you can't find anything of value here, you may want to check yourself for a pulse and make sure you're not wearing metallic half-spheres over your eyes.

Original version posted on 11/1/2024

They Have Changed Their Face (1971)

Satire is a funny, delicate thing. It can be sublime on the rare occasion it is done well, but folds like a cheap card table when it isn't. Consumerism is an easy target and is often the subject of such works. The original *Dawn of the Dead* lands solid criticisms of it. 1971's *They Have Change Their Face*, on the other hand, has a reach exceeding its grasp.

The metaphor in this Italian production isn't zombies, but vampires. Adolfo Celi (you know him from *Thunderball*) secretly heads a number of organizations, industries and even government agencies. He regularly hosts meetings with the heads of those enterprises in a conference room in his old mansion deep in the mountains of a remote part of the country. Judging from the faces assembled for one such meeting, he even has control within the Vatican.

I was lost as to what Celi's objectives were. He has a rant about the public not knowing what they want, so he will tell them what they want, but I didn't buy that explanation. Instead, it seemed more like the power he exerts over that public has somehow made him immortal. So, he's a kind of vampire, but the food that is necessary for his survival is nebulous.

It isn't even like he drinks blood. At least, we see him eating food and drinking wine. That "food" is still quite repulsive, as we will see him, his secretary (Geraldine Hooper) and his guest (Giuliano Esperati) eating various forms of goo from compartmentalized plates that are like porcelain versions of old TV dinner trays. The goop they consume is visually distinguished only by color and texture. It's like they have several courses, all of which are that sludge astronauts consume from pouches.

I will concede that was an interesting idea, and I get the intended commentary on processed foods. Most of the other digs at consumerism, however, are a bit too broad, such as the three commercials we see a pretentious filmmaker present for consideration. The first is in the style of Godard, the next Fellini, and the third the Marquis de Sade. Regarding the last of those, I'm pretty sure he never made any films, though doubtlessly would have if he hadn't inconveniently died so long before even still photography was invented.

Anyhoo, de Sade's commercial has topless women bound to a wall in a gothic mansion. An aristocrat comes in and flails them with a whip, though he quickly becomes bored. Looking to inspire him, the women suggest a wonderful new thing only now on the market. It is LSD, now available in regular and family sized bottles. The entire commercial is deliberately over-the-top and might have been funnier in a different film. Also, I don't know how Italian television works, but I couldn't suspend my disbelief enough to think they would ever show a commercial several minutes in length.

What frustrated me is this satire is in the framework of a horror movie with solid potential it then squanders. The plot centers around Esperati, an engineer at one of Celi's auto manufacturers, being sent to the mansion by his boss, a Mr. Harker. Given that name, it shouldn't be much of a surprise Celi's character is named Nosferatu.

On the drive to Celi's estate, Esperati discovers the locals in the nearest village won't go near the old mansion. In stark contrast to the stock company villagers is Francesca Modigliani, a very modern young woman with peculiar fashion sense, as she is topless under a heavy coat she lets hang open. She wants a ride and he is baffled by where she came from. As she cryptically explains, she came from over there and is going in the other direction.

One would think she would play a greater role in the plot but she stays behind in his car he leaves outside the mansion's gates. She will still be there several days later, long after we have realized this film is not set in any kind of reality, not even magic realism.

The creepiest element of the film are the small white cars that endlessly patrol the grounds like guard dogs. They even travel in packs. Unresponsive drivers are behind the wheel of each, clad entirely in white, including their crash helmets. It is an odd and unnerving element, one which hints at the genuinely creepy film this could have been.

There are even aspects of this work that are meant to be both unnerving and satirical, such as the voices coming from the air vents espousing the qualities of whatever product Esperati is interacting with at any given time. When he sits in a chair, the voices deliver a commercial about the quality of that furniture. More disturbingly, they expound upon the joys of a shower while he is actively using it. I'm not sure why the voices come through the air vents, but it could be the little people in the vents in *Don't Be Afraid of the Dark* decided to branch out into advertising.

Unfortunately, *They Have Changed Their Face* could have been an uncanny horror film akin to *Suspiria*, but it wastes that potential on a satire of consumerism painted in strokes too broad to be impactful. Instead of being successful at either one, the elements of each just float out there independently of each other, until each sadly deflates on the screen. To use an analogy from the film, it is a tray of different things kept completely separate from each other, never mixing, and each unsatisfying on its own.

Original version posted on 9/26/2024

Three Cases of Murder (1954)

Some of the most obscure titles in cinematic history have been released on disc, so it makes it even more frustrating when there's one that hasn't been given the DVD or blu-ray treatment yet. I'm hoping what I am about to write will no longer be true at some point in the near future: the best movie I have seen yet to be released on home video is 1954's *Three Cases of Murder*.

This is a solid entry in one of my favorite genres, the horror/supernatural anthology. The British film is largely a showcase for actor Alan Badel, as he is the only person to appear in all three segments. I'm not sure why there is so much focus on this relatively obscure actor, but he does turn in three distinctive performances that are all significantly different from each other.

The first segment is the best and the reason I'll be hounding everybody I know to buy a copy if it ever comes to disc. At an art museum, the meek Hugh Pryse sits in a gallery, enraptured by a painting. Badel appears next to him on the bench and strikes up a conversation about the work. This oddly dressed man encourages the other to look more intently into the image.

Soon, we are seeing the painting straight on and we push into the work, finally going up to the house in the center of it. The front door opens. The transition into the painting is a stunning effect, even today. In fact, I'm not sure how it was done and I have scrutinized this frame-by-frame.

The phrase "dreamlike" is overused, but there isn't a better one to describe the world inside the painting. I don't want to say much about it because I want first-time viewers to experience it for themselves. The tone of this segment has been fantasy up to this point; however, each additional element is creepier than the previous one, until this becomes pure horror.

This mini-masterpiece was directed by Wendy Toye and I want to see more of her work, just because of what she does here. Unfortunately, most of her other directorial efforts seem to be equally difficult to find.

The second segment is a rather straight-forward tale of murder, complete with the surprise comeuppance of the killer. It is the least of the three, yet still far better than the inevitable weak sequence of any other anthology I can think of.

But the third sequence is almost (*almost*) as great as the first. In this, Orson Welles plays a member of Parliament who is subjected to nightmares pushed into his mind by Badel. The dream sequences are inspired, such as one where, in the middle of a Parliamentary session, Welles springs into "A Bicycle Built for Two" against his will and all the other members join in.

Three Cases of Murder can be hard to track down but it is worth the effort. I just hope some day it will be much easier to find.

Original version posted on 2/16/2023

Tombs of the Blind Dead (1972)

Of the many characters and creatures in Peter Jackson's film trilogy of *Lord of the Rings*, my favorite may be the Nazgul, the nine formerly human kings who have been transformed by Sauron into wraiths. When we first see them, they are riding what appear to be undead horses. They are entirely badass, and, in the third film, we see they have an awesome castle that emanates a beautiful dark green glow. I like to ponder what the nine might have done in all that time the one ring wasn't in play and commanding their attention. In my imagination, I picture marathon Scrabble tournaments.

Instead, they may have been occupying graves at a former priory in Spain, popping up from time to time to kill horny young people. At least, what rises out of the ground in Amando de Ossorio's 1972 horror film *Tombs of the Blind Dead* sure look like Nazgul to me. They even ride zombie horses, though they looked like healthy specimens to me. I also was left wondering where on earth the horses stay when they're not needed.

The audience and our heroes (Lone Fleming and César Burner) will eventually learn from a professor (Francisco Sanz) these are the Knights Templar who had a priory which is now those ruins. Not sure why these soldiers of the crusades were engaging in ritual Satanic sacrifices, but that's what we see in a ridiculous flashback to that era.

This is one weird ritual. They secure a woman in the middle of a large room, ride around her on their horses and flail at her with their swords. When it is determined she has been cut enough, they jump off their steeds and suck blood from her wounds. In their present, undead incarnation, they dispense with the ceremony and just get straight to the blood-sucking. Their victims also become undead bloodsuckers, so what we have here is a bizarre combination of zombie and vampire of the likes I'm not sure I've encountered before.

As for the titular visual impairment of these monsters, I also found that a tad confusing. Per the professor's lesson, history documented crows eating the eyes from the corpses of the knights after the pope had them executed by hanging. Well, hey, that's what crows do. Also, it's my understanding the eyes, being the softest tissue in the body, are the first thing to go in the decomposition process. So, wouldn't *all* skeletonized undead persons be the "blind dead"?

Perhaps the cleverest thing this picture does is make the zombie knights find their victims through sound and feel only. Never mind how the inner workings of the ear could still be there after enough time has passed for them to become fully skeletonized. Still, if you're going to roll with a zombie movie, you're going to have to turn part of your brain off and stop scrutinizing everything. Besides, if you don't do that, you'll miss out on a pretty great scene of suspense near the end where somebody realizes their own heartbeat has betrayed their location. This is communicated to us through a great shot that starts wide and then pushes in closer on that person's chest with each...beat...of...their...heart.

I want to circle back to Fleming and Burner, our alleged heroes. He's a total asshat, but she's not completely without blame, either. When we first see them, he's the boyfriend of María Elena Arpón. She sees Fleming, a friend from school with whom we see in a flashback about to get down to some "experimenting". Burner is drooling over Fleming at first sight, and he invites her to join them on a weekend mini-vacation they're about to take. Fleming is very receptive to his advances, until she is damn near straddling him once all three are on the train. Quite rightly, Arpón is pissed about this. Why she didn't leave them at the train station is beyond me. Of course, then there wouldn't be a movie.

Instead, she decides to leap from the train *in transit*, apparently thinking the desolate area with spooky-ass old ruins in the distance would be a good place to bail. Admittedly, this old steam-engine train seems to move about as slowly as those trains they have as attractions at zoos and similar places. One thing I found funny is how the train engineer seems to be a massive jerk, ignoring the emergency stop alarm sounded by Fleming. Later, he will ignore a person lying in a field who appears to be dead or injured. It will turn out he has good reason to not stop the engine. That said, it moves so slowly I doubt there is anything that couldn't overtake it if it had the willpower.

I was hoping Arpón would go on to be the world's first high-fashion hobo. Instead, she walks to the ruins and starts pounding on exterior doors of the various structures, yelling out for anybody who might live there. Now, these are genuinely ancient structures, the vast majority of which are roofless. If somebody was inhabiting such an area, would *you* want to draw their attention? This doesn't stop her from breaking into one of the still-roofed parts and starting a massive fire in the fireplace. The last time I tried to start a fire, I was embarrassed by how inept I was, so I'm hoping I can get her advice for the next time I try to do that.

Come nighttime, the undead crawl out of their tombs and are soon pursuing Arpón. Mind you, they move *very* slowly; however, like the zombies from the original *Night of the Living Dead*, they compensate for this in their numbers. Arpón *almost* gets away, actually riding off on one of their zombie steeds. Just imagine a scene from any of the *LOTR* films if any character had managed to carjack (horsejack?) a Nazgul's mount. That would have been *sooo awesome*.

Instead, she's soon undead herself, and trying to attack Fleming's assistant (Veronica Llimera) at the mannequin factory she owns. Arpón stands stock-still at the end of a long row of mannequins, all of which we see in a lengthy tracking shot. It makes for a great moment of suspense, and is a good jump scare if you're not paying adequate attention.

Curiously, Arpón's corpse is wrapped in a small amount of bandage, as if somebody started to mummify her before losing interest. The naughty bits are all that are concealed, and this is yet another surprising bit of chastity in the type of film that would normally be boobs-a-go-go. There is also a surprising restraint on the gore up until the scene with the knights shown torturing a woman back in medieval times. Then we see her breasts openly displayed until replaced by fake ones we see being sliced open and bleeding. Honestly, the movie was more powerful when it exercised more restraint.

Any concerns for taste and tact and tossed aside in the film's absolute worst scene, where José Thelman rapes Fleming amongst the graves of the templars. There is no reason for this development. Even worse, it scans like this is to "cure" her of the bisexual or lesbian leanings we saw in an earlier flashback.

Thelman, a notorious smuggler, is only there because Burner thought he and Fleming would need a guide who knows the area. The reason for this eludes me, as Burner and Fleming had already been to the ruins once before. Also along on this trip is María Silva, as Thelman's girlfriend. While Fleming is being raped, Burner is making smoochy faces with Silva, which only reinforces how lousy of a human being I thought he was since the first time we saw him.

Even considering the film's downsides, there's no denying the power of the long climactic sequence, which is very well-composed. There are elements of it which were genuinely unnerving, and it may be what puts the movie somewhat hesitantly in the "win" column for me. Overall, it surprised me with good shot composition and photography, as Ossorio would go on to make the inept *The Loreley's Grasp* and *Night of the Sorcerers*.

Tombs of the Blind Dead is clearly the work of somebody operating on a shoestring budget who had access to some key locations. And one has a sacred duty to make a horror film when they have the rights to use a mannequin factory, a steam train operation and some naturally creepy old ruins. I assume the locations drove the writing so as to use each of those, resulting in a fairly weak story, though still one with some very good scenes.

Original version posted on 8/10/2024

Tower of London (1939)

You know you have reached an advanced age when you see somebody in a film getting stretched on a medieval rack and you think about how great your aching back might feel after some time on that. At least, that's what I was thinking when Boris Karloff was subjecting some poor soul to this punishment in 1939's *Tower of London*.

I found this to be an odd film, though mostly because of the expectations I had going in. This was on yet another installment of the *Universal Horrors* blu-ray series. But this is not a horror picture, despite the presence of Karloff. If anything, this is a historical mini-epic.

Set in 1400's England, this film stars Basil Rathbone as a duke who has eyes on the throne. Alas, he has a few people in the line of succession ahead of him. Using a weird diorama of the royal chambers, dolls representing those heirs are literally in line for the throne. I'll admit it is rather creepy watching him remove dolls from the display as he kills each additional person ahead of him. Keep in mind, a couple of those figures are of children. And yet, I was deeply amused to watch our villain play with dolls.

Karloff is his bald, disfigured henchman. I found it interesting that actor has what I consider to be potentially leading man looks, yet he thoroughly transformed himself through horrific makeup throughout his filmography. He has a prosthetic making him appear to have a bum leg, and I am pleased to report I could never quite figure out how they made that work. It is like there's a bend in his leg that couldn't be there.

If there are any horror elements in this, it would be the dungeon where Karloff gleefully plies his trade. This may be the most fully repellant character I have seen him play—the first time one has not had a trace of humanity to let the viewer identify with him. Consider how he begs Rathbone to take him into battle with him: "I have never killed in hot blood before."

That said, Rathbone might be even more intimidating, as he is cold, calculating and ruthless. In one early scene, the queen (Barbara O'Neil) enters a room and her eyes go wide with shock, but we don't know what it is she has seen. The cut reveals it is Rathbone, and all he is doing is standing over her sons while they sleep. There is nothing suspicious in his expression or behavior, but she knows the threat he poses. Hers is a look that speaks volumes.

I was surprised to see Vincent Price cast in a fairly substantial role in a movie this early in his career. In later years, he would have been able to ace the Rathbone role. His youth instead makes him well-suited for playing a decadent coward who is, unfortunately for him, in line for the throne. Price adds some great minor touches to this performance, such as a left eye that starts twitching comically when he becomes overly excited.

But the biggest surprise was how nasty this film is for being released four years after the rollout of the Production Code, as that had hobbled a great many similar productions. I guess what happens here was determined to be acceptable, so long as the events portrayed took place long in the past.

Please indulge me one snarky aside. In an early scene, O'Neil chastises her daughter, but I couldn't understand what she said. I turned on the subtitles and rewatched those few seconds, and the text on the screen actually read: "You can broider your (mumbling) for your doll." This is the first time I have ever seen subtitles fumble.

Tower of London is a good, but not especially noteworthy, film. The strangest thing about it is somebody at Shout Factory thought this was horror. Yes, that aspect is even stranger than the marriage in the film between two children, the boy being so young he lisps when saying, "I will". I'm going to go out on a limb and guess that honeymoon was super uncomfortable for all who were aware of this betrothal.

Original version posted on 2/25/2024

The Tunnel (2011)

The next time you drive over a manhole cover, imagine there is somebody under it and crying out for help, but nobody will hear them over the road noise. That was something that lingered in my mind after seeing 2011 Australian found footage horror film *The Tunnel*. At one point, characters futilely scream up through such a cover, and a cut to a security camera reveals they are under a highway. In another scene, a character can hear subway trains whooshing by on the other side of a wall, but there's no way to break through that wall to reach potential aid.

This picture is filmed almost entirely in abandoned tunnels under Sydney. I'd say that if you know of abandoned tunnels under a metropolis, and they haven't been used in a horror film yet, you have an obligation to utilize them for that purpose. Similar to those under London, large portions were meant to be used as air raid shelters, and so have dormitories, showers, toilets and the like.

A television news crew that has ventured into those tunnels discovers homeless people have been sleeping there. This is in contradiction to government declarations that the area is unpopulated, a claim they have been making to justify their plan to replace the current underground structure with water reclamation tanks.

Bel Deliá is the most recently hired reporter for a major news organization and she needs a big story like this to keep that job. With just a minimal crew (Andy Rodoreda, Steve Davis, Luke Arnold), she will break into the tunnel system one night after failing to get the proper permissions from the government. An attempt to bribe a guard at a subway station also fails. It will eventually be revealed she didn't even tell their boss back at the station what she intended to do, and so it turns out *nobody* knows they are down there.

Despite seeing evidence of homeless having lived down there, they're not finding any of those people. But they will encounter something that is presumably human, though we never get a very good look at it. It is through a night vision camera we see the glowing eyes of Goran D. Kleut, who is billed only as "Stalker", as that's exactly what he does.

An interesting approach to the film is it is not strictly found footage but is instead incorporated into a documentary format in which two of the group that went into the tunnels are being interviewed after the incident. So, we know two people will emerge from this struggle alive, but no bets will be taken on the fate of the other two. It is through those present-day interviews we learn how quickly this mission starts to go off the rails, beginning with the untrustworthy maps they have brought with them: "There were whole sections of tunnel that weren't even on the map."

Another thing said in those interviews nicely covers an aspect of found footage many movies don't sufficiently explain, and that is why every little thing is being filmed. Rodoreda explains he tried to record as much as possible once he started to suspect this will not go well, just for proof he wasn't to blame if he's called on the carpet later.

The first sign something is amiss is when Arnold starts picking up through headphones what sounds like whispering. A little while later, they are recording in a room with a giant metal bell that was to be used as a signal, should that facility be used as an air raid shelter. When Deliá strikes the object, it peaks out the recording levels, so Arnold goes into the next room to mic it from there. This will be the film's first jump scare and it is a doozy.

From here, everything quickly escalates into a frenzy of activity. Most of their gear ends up stolen, leaving them with only the night vision camera, a flashlight and the light on the full-size camera. Rodoreda estimates they have 2-3 hours of battery for the camera light. I can tell you from experience, those never last as long as even your worst-case estimate.

One deeply unnerving scene occurs when the night vision camera is sat down outside a room while the group goes in to survey the carnage they see there. When they emerge again, the camera has been moved. Replaying the footage recorded in that time reveals it had been picked up, and something had recorded them while they were oblivious. Then, in only one frame, we have the most fleeting glimpse of what had picked up the camera.

One scene that seems to be direct lift from *The Blair Witch Project* has Davis turning the camera on Deliá after she reveals nobody knows where they are. He yells at her to keep on getting her "big story" in a way I swear even uses some of the wording from the other picture's "C'mon, Heather, we're making a movie" scene.

The Tunnel is very scary, and one of the better found footage films I have seen. It doesn't reinvent any wheels; however, a feature-length documentary accompanying the movie on a new blu-ray issue details how it became the first crowd-funded movie. As a 90-minute production would be comprised of 135,000 frames, they sold each individual frame of the film for $1 each. I thought that was a brilliant plan, but I pity all those people who just happened to purchase an image of complete darkness or simply indistinct blurs. Naturally, the movie has a great deal of each of those, just given the nature of the work.

Original version posted on 8/16/2024

Vamp (1986)

I'm amazed by how much goodwill I feel towards every person who appeared in the *Pee Wee's Playhouse Christmas Special.* I have always respected Grace Jones, but I definitely became more aware of her from her bizarre appearance there. And you can't have Jones in something without capitalizing on the weirdness she exudes.

1986's *Vamp* puts her to good use as a vampire who strips at a sleazy LA joint. I completely believed her performance as a mute creature with an animal sexuality. The scene where she tears out a victim's jugular is preceded by a suspenseful and sensuous round of her flicking her tongue up and down his torso. Both the moment of foreplay and the instance of horror are equally convincing. Her undergarments in the scene are some sort of metal spirals that look incredibly uncomfortable, yet I wouldn't be surprised if these were her street clothes.

That victim is a college student played by Robert Rusler. He came to the club with his friend (Chris Makepeace) and a guy tagging along only because he owns a car (Gedde Watanabe). Rusler and Makepeace are trying to acquire a stripper for a party thrown by a fraternity in trade for their admission to the house.

The picture opens with an amusing piece that suggests this will be some sort of religious horror film, as robed figures drag the two friends into a church and slip nooses over their heads. Then it is revealed this is a prank that is part of the frat's hazing ritual. This sets the stage for a horror-comedy hybrid ala *Fright Night*, though it isn't very funny or very scary.

If there's one thing it most definitely is, it is very much a product of the 1980's. The sets are incredibly overlit, such as a strip club bright enough to do surgery in—however lacking in hygiene such a place would be. Everywhere else is lit in weird combinations of green and magenta, making for at least one weird looking alleyway. In the climax, we'll discover the world's cleanest sewer system is lit the same way.

A more interesting touch is a headless mannequin, a prop for Jones's stage show that is painted in a style reminiscent of Keith Haring. According to a fascinating making-of that accompanies the film on the Arrow blu-ray, that likely is the work of Haring, as he was part of the entourage the actress brought with her to the shoot. I was a bit dismayed to also learn she demonstrated some diva behavior on the set, including the time the crew waited nine hours for her to show up.

One curious aspect of the film is Jones is barely in it, yet her time on screen is so memorable you'll swear she was in it longer. Another element I found bizarre is most of the leads are rather disposable. I honestly couldn't tell Makepeace and Rusler apart until we were well into the movie. Dedee Pfeiffer is the sweet girl-next-door type working at the club. She looked uncannily like Alison Lohman to me, and she's shockingly oblivious to what is happening behind-the-scenes there. But even more baffling is the local gang (led by Billy Drago) that somehow has failed to notice the large number of vampires on their turf. Still, I believed that more than Rusler giving the beat-down to three of their members.

And this vampire strip club has apparently been operating out of that location for some time. As the club emcee (Sandy Baron) puts it, people go missing all the time and the club makes for the perfect cover: "Nobody tells anybody when they come to a joint like this".

Which leads me to: this is a surprisingly talky movie, and that distinguishes it from similar fare of the time. After Rusler is turned into a vampire, there's an interesting scene where he and Makepeace discuss what being undead is like and whether their friendship can continue after this development.

I seem to have nitpicked *Vamp* to death here, but it was quirky enough that I enjoyed it. At least, I definitely found more to appreciate here than *From Dusk to Dawn*, a film from roughly a decade later that superficially resembles it. Very little works here in a conventional way but, once I turned off my brain, I found myself having a good time.

Original version posted on 1/19/2024

Waxwork (1988)

While watching 1988's *Waxwork*, I couldn't seem to stop thinking about a different movie, that being *Cabin in the Woods*. I think the latter film is truly great. The earlier one, not so much, though there are some interesting similarities.

In both films, a certain number of people must be offered as a sacrifice at some interval. This is per an arrangement made with demonic forces. Also, the deaths occur in various scenarios right out of age-old film clichés. There is even some sort of dimensional/electric barrier between the real world and that of the scenarios. There's a mischievous disembodied hand up to no good. Heck, the first death here happens in a scenario where there is a creepy old cabin.

That happens to Dana Ashbrook, who played Bobby on *Twin Peaks*. I always like seeing him, but it doesn't seem like he ever got much work. It's kind of disorienting to see Deborah Foreman in this, as she looks and acts exactly like Sheryl Lee did when she co-starred with Ashbrook on that show.

The rest of the cast is good as well, with plenty of other surprises. Patrick Macnee of 60's UK TV classic *The Avengers* makes what is basically a glorified cameo. John Rhys-Davies (the *Indiana Jones* series, the *Lord of the Series* series) appears as a werewolf. Zach Galligan is the hero of the picture, and I don't recall previously having seen him in anything except *Gremlins* and its sequel.

But the most welcome surprise for me was David Warner as the owner of the titular waxwork. I always like seeing him as a villain. Hard to believe he was never the antagonist before doing *Time After Time*, seeing as to how effortless this type of role appears to be for him. He's not in this movie much, but he is obviously having a good time when we do get to see him.

Warner's waxwork is operated out of his mansion in a wealthy suburb. And it seems the high school students Warner enticed into seeing his wax museum are *way* too interested in it, with a couple of them even having some knowledge of the history of the art form.

The excessively interested teens get separated and each, in turn, ends up crossing a magical barrier into a real version of different exhibits. So, a display of a werewolf in a cabin leads to Ashbrook stepping across the velvet rope and finding himself battling an actual werewolf.

What had me confused is Ashbrook's corpse *instantly* becomes part of the tableau as soon as he dies. Despite there being the expected pit of boiling wax in the basement, it doesn't seem like any of the victims need to be dipped in it before becoming a wax figure.

One aspect I didn't care for is the movie is very gory, even if the tone is often tongue through rotting cheek. A bit where a guy's leg has been carved up while he's still alive and conscious was too much for me. And yet, almost immediately after that, I laughed hard when a vampire accidentally kills herself by backing into a wall of champagne bottles so hard the tops go through her chest. The bottles even pop open, and champagne shoots out in long arcs across the room.

Probably what I liked best about the picture is how the visual style is tweaked for each exhibit. This especially works in a scene obviously paying homage to *Night of the Living Dead*. In a nice touch, it is filmed in grainy black-and-white using a lot of Dutch angles.

In the end, I wasn't certain whether or not I liked *Waxwork*. It is a bit of a mess, and the plot does not bear close inspection. Also, the gore crossed a line for me, even when I could tell it was being used in an absurd, comedic manner. All that said, I have thought about this picture far more than I expected and I am even curious about the sequel which is packaged in the same blu-ray set.

Original version posted on 8/23/2023

Waxwork II: Lost in Time (1992)

Waxwork surprised me by being better than I anticipated, so I was curious why it only has one sequel. After all, many deeply terrible horror movies have spawned seemingly endless progeny. I don't feel I need to see *Witchcraft* to tell you it isn't worthy of the *sixteen installments* that series has to date.

1992's *Waxwork II: Lost in Time* is a strange animal. Continuing the anthology-like structure of the first film, this one has the same two protagonists jumping around in time.

That central conceit is an interesting idea, but what I found endlessly annoying is they somehow go from one *fictional* world to the other. Our characters end up in what are basically parodies/tributes to *Alien, The Haunting* (spliced with *The Legend of Hell House*), *Frankenstein, Nosferatu, Dr. Jekyll and Mr. Hyde, Dawn of the Dead, Godzilla* and, maybe, *The Princess Bride* (not sure on that last one).

Obviously, director Anthony Hickox has good taste in movies. Unfortunately, all these references simply cutter up the screen. I largely found myself feeling bored, except during a finale that hyperactively bounces across genres.

This sequel picks up exactly where the last left off, with our young lovers fleeing the burning mansion. This time, however, Deborah Foreman has been replaced by Monika Schnarre, an actress who resembles Foreman is no way whatsoever. In addition to being about a foot taller, she doesn't look or sound like the other actress. Also, while Schnarre isn't bad, per se, Foreman is the better performer overall.

Another carryover from the first picture is that mischievous and murderous severed hand which survived the mayhem at the conclusion. When Schnarre returns home, it kills her abusive stepfather in a development that is awfully "handy" (I'll let The Crypt Keeper know his job is safe).

In the resulting trial where she is accused of patricide (step-patricide?), she and boyfriend Zach Galligan decide they need proof such phenomena as killer sentient disembodied hands exist. They are given the opportunity to find such proof, courtesy of exposition provided by Patrick Macnee in a film he made of himself for Galligan and Schnarre to watch after his death. Kind of like a video will.

Speaking of the concept of a "video will", this scene is an example of the many elements of this picture that stuck in my craw to the point where they distracted me from losing myself in the plot. Macnee met Zach not too long before his death in the first movie, so I doubt he had time to film himself, have the film developed and ready to view through a projector he has already set-up.

Macnee will reappear later in a brief scene where he voices a raven. In a moment that seriously knotted by tighty whities, he delivers this fourth-wall break in response to Galligan's exasperation as to *why* he is now a raven: "It's the only way they'd allow me to appear in this one." Also quoth the raven, the reason these jumps through time are into fictional worlds is because they are in "God's Nintendo game." Huh.

If there was one thing I found at fault in the previous film is it crossed my gore tolerance threshold in a couple of scenes. Still, there was a goofy vibe that helped to make those scenes more palatable, so it was a bit like *Evil Dead II* in that regard. So, it wasn't too much of a surprise this one apes *Army of Darkness* by reducing the gore and increasing the comedy. That Bruce Campbell appears in one segment of this only convinces me this was their intention.

He is in a black-and-white segment that riffs on *The Haunting*. If this movie prompts anybody to see that 1964 film, then it will increase my esteem for it. On the other hand, this segment is interspersed with a rip-off of *Alien*. The contrast between these segments is jarring and irritating.

Something else which consistently irritated me is how Galligan and Schnarre have their hair and clothing automatically adjusted in each time jump so as to be appropriate for the era at hand. Still, Galligan is somehow wearing the same t-shirt throughout the feature whenever he isn't wearing a shirt with a collar high enough to obscure it.

I also feel compelled to call out the incongruous music in a medieval-set segment. The music sounds like knock-off Enigma, that group which set Gregorian chants to an electronic dance track. Let's see…when was this movie made? 1992? Yep, that's when that stuff was popular for about a week.

In my review of the first movie, I mentioned the many bizarre parallels I saw to *Cabin in the Woods*. There's a scene in the sequel that is even more uncanny, as we see a room full of objects Macnee collected from the supernatural world. As they examine these artifacts, I kept expecting Galligan or Schnarre to accidentally summon creatures that will kill them. Galligan would not stop playing with a bloody hockey mask, so I was hoping this would unleash "Kevin" from *Woods*, as I always suspected that character is a play on Jason from *Friday the 13th*.

The disembodied hand in both *Waxwork* films also reminded me of *Woods* (particularly the scene where a zombie hand kills Eli Roth). I was irritated when Schnarre disposes of the hand so early in this sequel. In the end, I would have rather watched an entire movie of that hand as it stumbles into one escapade after another.

Original version posted on 9/9/2023

WNUF Halloween Special (2013)

What a strange time we live in, where it seems a great many otherwise sane people are so easily swayed into believing the craziest shit, usually from information posted on social media by somebody they don't even know. I write this as we approach a presidential election which has me filled with outright fear, as it seems the likelihood of roughly half of the US population to believe something is in direct proportion to how disconnected that "fact" is from reality. Right now, many people believe Haitians are eating the pets of the residents of Springfield, Ohio, and I keep waiting for a novelty publication pretending to be a Haitian cookbook but filled with recipes for how prepare cats and dogs for an elegant multi-course dinner.

And yet, you wouldn't be able to successfully pull a stunt today like *The Blair Witch Project* did in 1999, where the filmmakers made it difficult for viewers to shake a nagging suspicion what they were seeing is real. And that's why I suspect 2013's *WNUF Halloween Special* chooses to walk an unusual tightrope of doing a great deal to present itself as a VHS recording of that channel's doomed 1987 special while also sending many signals this never happened. The latter is made apparent by multiple touches of humor throughout, and I'm still on the fence as to how I feel about those.

Even the structure of the work sets up an uncomfortable balance, with the first and last things we hear being a tape being put into, and then taken out of, a VCR. Because of that, we are already one step removed from this being a pure presentation of the material. Compounding this sensation are the occasional fast-forwards through some segments of the program.

The movie has an interesting manner of providing the exposition for the bulk of the program, opening with the news, where anchors Richard Cutting and Leanna Chamish plug the live broadcast to immediately follow. Frank Stewart (Paul Fahrenkopf) will be reporting from the Weber House, where the "Spirit Board Murders" had occurred twenty years earlier.

I thought it was interesting this movie channels some of the "Satanic Panic" vibe of the 80's, with a guy decapitating his parents with an axe because a demon supposedly told him to through a Ouija board. Another callback to the era are elements similar to those godawful Geraldo Rivera specials of the period, as Stewart is accompanied by his walk through the murder house by a psychic couple (Brian St. August and Helenmary Ball) and their cat. They will also be joined by a priest (Robert Long II), who is there in case they need to give the house an exorcism.

Unlike Rivera's notorious broadcast when he opened Al Capone's vault (and I will confess I was one of the dupes who watched that), things will go very badly for the presenter. I'm not sure I was completely sold on how we could possibly be seeing everything that is captured, but there are some genuine, albeit minor, scares.

It is obvious the filmmakers realized audiences are too hardened nowadays to try to pass something like this off as real, and so they take the opportunity to add some humor to the proceedings. Some of these moments are clearly meant to be funny and they often succeed, such as the guy Stewart picks to interview from the crowd outside the house, who is terrified when he discovers a murder happened there. But then there are other times the humor is more subtle, such as an ad for the local arcade claiming the latest hits they have include *Space Paranoids*, which is the fictitious game Jeff Bridges is playing in an early scene in *Tron*. But then another game listed is *George Plimpton's Video Falconry*, which nobody would mistake for a real title, and which takes one out of the experience a bit.

An interesting decision was to play it straight with most of the ads. On a second viewing, I was surprised to find I wish they had taken that approach with more of the material. One ad was for a carpet store, and I could not discern anything of humorous intent in it, and we will even be subjected to it multiple times. More elements such as this would have made the viewing experience more uncanny, even if it would have made it superficially more boring.

I twice enjoyed watching *WNUF Halloween Special*, though I appreciated it more for what it tries to do than the degree to which it actually succeeds. Word of warning to those such as myself who don't care to have animal deaths happen in a film, even if it is offscreen. I'm sure no harm actually came to the real-life cat which supposedly belongs to the psychics. Spoiler alert: even the cat within the film is not eaten by Haitians.

Originally posted on 10/27/2024

Artsy (with a fair dose of fartsy)
The section about the artsy and otherwise undefinable

Anton Corbijn: Inside Out (2012)

I miss those Director Series DVD collections of music videos, where each volume was dedicated to a different visionary. Music video collections met their demise largely because of the advent of YouTube, which is a shame. Not sure why the length of a film warrants whether or not it should also be on physical media. I don't believe I have seen a single music video collection make the leap to blu-ray.

One of those sets was dedicated to the video work of Anton Corbijn. Known instead primarily for his photography, the 2012 documentary *Anton Corbijn: Inside Out* essentially introduces to the public to somebody who is usually behind the camera.

As he explains here, his career started with a passion for music, and he just happened to start taking photos of the bands and artists he liked. Photos of one such band cemented his place in rock history, as his pics of Joy Division are inseparable from that group's mythology.

Then there's his relationship with Depeche Mode, not just photographing them extensively, but directing all their videos for years. Or what about his similar relationship with U2? How about his famous photographs of Nirvana and the video he did for "Heart-Shaped Box"? Then there's photos of Tom Waits, Miles Davis, a young Elvis Costello, Lou Reed with Metallica, R.E.M., Captain Beefheart, Willie Nelson, Nelson Mandella, Mick Jagger (in drag!), Johnny Cash, Peter Gabriel. You get the idea. It would possibly be easier to list the artists he *hasn't* photographed.

In this documentary, we see him conducting a photo shoot with U2. I like that group, but I still think Bono is full of shit. What I found kind of funny is he seems to think the same about himself. He tries explaining Corbijn's technique as "something to do with light and the extinguishing of it", before giving up and chastising the interviewer for bringing up such heady topics before he's had his morning coffee.

Speaking of mornings, a neat little montage in this film shows pics Corbijn has taken at daybreak out the windows of various hotels around the world. In another revealing moment, he comments on the joy of taking a camera somewhere and bringing a piece of that world back into your own.

Corbijn's past is explored, but I never felt like I understood where he came from. His sister explains that, while they came from a large family, it wasn't a very verbal one, and that he grew up lonely and without anybody to talk to. Still, I am always glad when a documentary explores the forces that shaped an artist.

In another revealing moment, he talks about how he was always hiding as a child. I couldn't help but wonder if this tendency towards voyeurism contributed to him having such a great eye for shot composition. That composition skill is demonstrated in a picture taken of Lou Reed and Metallica for their *Lulu* collaboration. They stand at the side of a rusty boat, with a heavy cable hanging across it like a smiling mouth that is both feminine and grotesque. It is definitely a better photo than the album for which it was commissioned.

Bono once said of Corbijn that he is defined by the pictures he takes, that they collectively form an image of himself. I guess any work is inevitably a bit autobiographical, yet I was a bit concerned by some photos he took of himself as various performers. I found it intriguing he posed as Jeff Buckley, Kurt Cobain, John Lennon,

George Harrison and Janis Joplin, but I draw the line at him darkening his skin and imitating Hendrix.

Metallica's James Hetfield sums up Corbijn's work quite well when he says, "He can make anybody look cool. Even us." It is interesting to watch him do his work here, with resulting photos that don't seem possible from a shoot we just witnessed. And yet, I finished this documentary feeling like I still never met the man.

Original version posted on 6/8/2023

Anti-Clock (1979)

The feature-length experimental film *Anti-Clock* starts out promising, as the opening credits are filmed off an extremely staticky monitor. There is a strange beauty in that image distortion, something I imagine wasn't as appreciated in 1979 as it is today. Much of this film by Jane Ardern and Jack Bond seems to be filmed almost as if it foresaw a future nostalgia for what was then the current day.

There's a lot of footage captured from monitors, sometimes showing two monitors at once. One shot even has footage of a monitor playing footage of a monitor. And there's a lot of signal distortion and timecode overlays. Just the lo-fi look of it had me wondering if this was going to feel like a combination of Ballard, Burroughs and early Cronenberg.

To the best I can tell, this picture is a meditation on time and memory; in particular, the subjectivity of both and the unreliability of the latter. At least, that was my main takeaway from the experience. In all honesty, I'm not entirely sure what was the intention of the filmmakers.

I don't want to judge this film too harshly but, for me, it combined the more irritating aspects of experimental filmmaking with the tedium of a long lecture.

Some very heady ideas about time and perception are thrown around here, and I confess most of them were above my pay grade. It probably didn't help most of these highfalutin concepts were dryly delivered in voiceover while images of seemingly little relevance accompanied them. There's lots of looped footage, which is appropriate for the parts about time. There are even moments where video is freeze-framed while a small portion of audio echoes until it diminishes to silence.

A recurring phrase I like in this is: "This is my anxiety survival broadcast." From that statement, I started to wonder if this was a film somebody had to make just to get it out of their head. And yet, I feel frustrated I couldn't grasp what that intention was.

That said, there are many other phrases and concepts I thought were intriguing. Things like: "We are mental snapshots of ourselves." "The infinite sphere of the universe we present to ourselves is constantly changing." And how about "our whole life has been structured by naming and defining our preferences and disinclinations". That last one seems to be analogous to current sentiments regarding labels.

One thing I failed to take notice of was one of those directors, Jack Bond, directed the terrible Pet Shop Boys "movie" *It Couldn't Happen Here*. If I had been aware of that before buying this disc, I probably would have taken a pass.

I honestly didn't notice similarities between the two films, except how both seem obsessed with imagery and concepts that weren't clicking for me. That said, now knowing this connection, I shouldn't have been so surprised at a scene here where dancing dwarves introduce a mind reader in a nightclub act. I also rolled my eyes when the mind reader starts talking about Akashic records, the eternal record of all thoughts. I'm sure Gwyneth Paltrow's site sells some sort of stone to insert into one or more orifices to access those records.

One description I read compared this work to Jean-Luc Godard's *Alphaville*, in that both are avant-garde sci-fi films supposedly set in a future which looks uncannily like the present. While I'm not much of a fan of most of Godard's oeuvre, I am a big fan of that film. Of Arden and Bond's film, not so much.

Original version posted on 6/13/2023

Ass (2504)

This review was beamed directly into my sleeping mind from the year 2505. Apparently, they have yet to build a transmitter strong enough to reach my conscious mind, as most scientific research conducted in the future is dedicated to hair restoration and erectile longevity. When they briefly succeeded in constructing a transmitter of sufficient power, my every waking moment became an endless marathon of the TV show Ow! My Balls! *It was terrifying.*

I donn wanna brag but I apreeshe8 2504's hit movie *Ass* more than mos. My IQ iz almost in 3 digitz—80, maybeez 70. So I enjoy *Ass* on many levelz. Much more levelz than u

Itz OK people laff jus cuz ass fartz. Fartz for 60 mins and also 30 more. Very funny.

It made big moneyz, like jillion zillion dollarz. Winz Oscarz for like best pitshur and best screenplay.

But why ass fart? What is itz motivation? What doez it say bout human condition?

Evbody like *Ass*, so best movie evah. Even people who talk like fagz like *Ass*. Anybody donn like *Ass* mus be tarded and fucked up and shit.

Ne'er mind Prez Commacho order evbody go seez *Ass*. It grate movie gardless. Work on many levelz.

Brought to you by Carl's Jr.

Originally posted on 4/1/2023, which should be a clue. Also, it is helpful if one has seen the movie Idiocracy.

The Body (1970) / Bodysong (2003)

I don't remember recently losing the will to live and yet I willingly watched two feature-length visual poems about the human condition, each of which was scored by members of separate, legendary prog-rock bands. I suspect vastly more people have heard the soundtrack for one or both pictures than have seen the films either score accompanies.

First, there's 1970's *The Body*, as soundtracked by Ron Geesin and Pink Floyd's Roger Waters. Geesin also has a strong connection to that band, as he wrote the orchestral backing for the title track to their album *Atom Heart Mother*.

Tellingly, many of the themes explored here are similar to those found in the band's work at the time, predominately birth and death. I expected this picture to be a documentary about the human body, with some trappings of the era. What I didn't anticipate is it also addresses social and environmental issues, such as pollution, disease and poverty. Also, a large part of it is a visual poem. Parts could even be regarded as music video.

As expected, there is quite a bit of nudity here, but this may be the first movie I have seen that begins with a woman's breast being used for its biological purpose. There will be a lot more nudity after that, and some of it seemingly of a...less than scientific or philosophical nature.

Some of it serves thoughtful sequences, such as a long, winding line of people arranged in order by age, starting with a newborn and ending with a woman of very advanced age.

Then there's the obligatory scenes of childbirth, though these made me think of those early "educational" films that skirted anti-pornography regulations by including such footage alongside that of conception, as if the former justified showing the latter. In an odd moment here, footage of the births is intercut with that of a factory assembly line—an interesting juxtaposition, but I'm unclear as to the intended takeaway.

That same "conception-and-childbirth" logic seems to be applied here, as well, as we see a couple having what I am going to assume is unsimulated sex. I doubt the educational or artistic benefits of showing them 69ing (no joke!). Curiously, this may be among the least sexy footage of intercourse I have ever seen.

Before we see that couple get busy, we see them filmed by a thermal camera, showing the waves of heat radiating from their bodies. There will be similar footage later of somebody exercising, and an old man drinking a cup of tea. I smiled when the old man has a cigarette afterwards and the heat off the match is like a flamethrower enveloping his head. And, when he takes off his hat, I received visual confirmation we lose most of our heat through the tops of our heads.

The framing device for the picture seems prescient, almost foretelling reality television, as groups of robe-clad adults mingle. I found the robes to be laughably pretentious, though a typical touch for the times.

Something I didn't know how to regard is hidden-camera footage of the participants discussing whether they are comfortable with being naked in front of the cameras. So, we are eavesdropping on a conversation where people are voicing their concerns they are being exploited. See how that might be ethically dubious?

And yet, the conversations are often interesting. The scene that most touched me was when a woman who went blind at 16 discusses the paradox of asking people to accept her condition as part of herself, while also wishing she could see again. There's also an interesting insight I hadn't encountered before, as she comes to the realization nobody can ever be cross with her again.

The picture also explores some places most of us are not entirely comfortable looking, such as the lives of disabled children and adults, who are often filmed looking upset. As for myself, an entirely different scene made me squirm, and that is an intimate journey through the digestive system. Great, now I won't be thinking of sex *or* food for some time.

Lastly, some random observations. There's a neat demonstration of a real-life model of an impossible triangle, accomplished through perspective. I also enjoyed the X-ray footage of hands as they play musical instruments, and of the end of a sword as it appears inside a sword-swallower. A brief, interesting segment shows the chemicals that compose the human body, separated into their own containers and presumably in ratios common to the body. On the downside, I'm not sure what was intended, or if I gleaned any insights, from watching from beneath a glass surface as a toddler crawls across, and urinates upon, it.

2003's *Bodysong* is soundtracked by Jonny Greenwood of Radiohead fame. This picture has as many similarities to *The Body* as it has differences, but both are solidly representative of the eras in which they were made. If the earlier picture was the product of the hippie ethos, this one is all cool, intellectual detachment.

The key difference in *Bodysong* is the lack of narration, though there is a more linear structure. That said, this is a series of images upon which the viewer must apply their own meaning and context.

Some of the imagery is obvious, such a long series of babies being born. *Lots* of footage of childbirth. Between these two films, I am well and done with seeing real footage of this, thanks.

Other parts are far more cryptic, such as what must be extremely old footage of a guy on a high wall bouncing an infant from one hand to the other. Wonder what the kid's mother thought of that.

There seems to be a recurring motif of circles, which I found interesting. Towards the beginning, we have enough scenes of people spinning children or dancers around a maypole that this has be intentional. Near the end, there's a montage of people of various cultures around the world drawing patterns that are at least partially circular.

Then there's the sexual imagery which seems to be a requirement of such films. Unlike *The Body*, that content here is *definitely* unsimulated. Funny how I'm not against pornography, but I'm all about context, and I question the use of such explicit material here. That said, there is a pretty funny transition where we go from scenes of people putting in their mouths the male member most resembling a banana to clips of people eating actual bananas.

But that content merely made me uncomfortable. What I really could have done without is the footage of people getting killed. I know this is a documentary (OK, kind of a documentary), but I don't think it is ever appropriate to show a person's final moments in anything that can even roughly be construed as entertainment. That may seem odd coming from somebody who doesn't believe in a higher power or an afterlife, but I simply believe a person's final moments are theirs alone. Seeing somebody die feels like the ultimate violation.

A slate in the end credits, and the chapter menu on the DVD, tells us explicitly what the segments are. My own notes while watching this interpret the sequence as: birth->childhood->young adulthood->thrills->sex->conflict->death->illness->religion->art->the body's ability to make and hear sound->rebellion

Greenwood's score is excellent, as expected. The styles change drastically, and appropriately, to accompany each sequence. Some might raise an eyebrow over the appropriation of some non-western musical elements; however, I have seen in concert Junun, his collaboration with international musicians, and can attest to his obvious love and respect for all musical cultures.

One last random observation I have about this picture concerns a little bit towards the end which intrigued me. I thought we were again seeing footage of an egg being fertilized, but it was actually footage of diseased cells. It was an interesting juxtaposition.

The Body and *Bodysong* are both well-made and thought-provoking. The former is not as much of a mess as I suspected it would be, though it is made almost entirely of tangents. The latter has a more conventional structure, yet it is still a very subjective experience. Both are recommended for more adventurous viewers, though probably not right before you intend to eat or engage in sexy times.

Artsy (with a fair dose of fartsy) [the artsy and otherwise undefinable]

Original version posted on 5/11/2023

David Holzman's Diary (1967)

Some may wonder why the 1967 film *David Holzman's Diary* was canonized into the National Film Registry of the Library of Congress. Criterion also saw fit to include it in its collection, albeit only on laserdisc. Anybody who was confused as to why *Citizen Kane* is ubiquitously considered a great film will surely be downright bewildered as to why this one is regarded almost as highly.

This is a rather dull film. It is sloppily filmed and has long takes in lieu of judicious edits. It largely captures very mundane moments, such as a sped-up series of images of everything the title character watched during hours of television viewing one night, though one might be amused by the nearly subliminal glimpses of *Batman* and *Star Trek*.

It is also an uncomfortable viewing experience, such as when we watch from the perspective of the cameraman stalking a woman on the subway one night. It's just a person at random whom he decides to follow on a whim, but it still recalled for me the horrible serial killer mockumentary *Man Bites Dog*, and I never wanted anything to remind me of *that* film.

The title character isn't a serial killer, and this isn't a horror film, though it is a very early example of a mockumentary. Alas, our hero is a creep who is oblivious to the feelings of others. He is even aware that what he is doing is an act of voyeurism, as he explains to a friend.

Supposedly, his goal is to learn truths about himself by filming his mundane life, citing Godard's maxim that "film is truth 24 times a second." A friend, in perhaps the film's best moment, calls bullshit on the entire exercise, saying, "You're not going to understand it any better by freezing it on celluloid and looking at it over and over again. You have to try to understand it the first time."

But that doesn't stop David from doing things like running off his fashion model girlfriend, as she's uncomfortable with the camera. Although he agreed to stop filming while she's around, he expresses his unhappiness to the camera when he's alone. It is no surprise he thoroughly betrays her trust when he later films her sleeping in the buff, prompting her to storm out of his life. He even films her agent who comes to get her things from his apartment.

She's not the only person he's weirding out. He's creeping *everybody* out, as evidenced by the side-eye and outright glares he gets from total strangers as he films on the sidewalks of New York's upper west side. It doesn't help that he also has his Nagra reel-to-reel strapped to his body and a monstrous lavalier mic hanging around his neck. At one point, he gets a fish-eye lens and walks around on the street while holding the camera over his head pointing downward. You can imagine the looks he gets for doing that.

Modern viewers will likely be thinking of today's culture of social media, selfies and influencers. One might also be reminded of reality shows. There are a shocking number of elements of contemporary society this little no-budget film unfortunately foresaw. I think it is bizarre how, decades before such things as Tik Tok, somebody could so thoroughly capture how repellent an obsession with oneself can be, and yet we reward people for it today.

As I mentioned earlier, this is not a real documentary, though it feels uncomfortably close to being one. The performances may not seem particularly good, but I think it is a testament to the actors in this that they seem to be the actual people they're portraying. If it was easy to act like a real people in a film, then we wouldn't have so many lousy found footage films (and also why the few exemplary ones of that genre are true diamonds in the rough). What is surprising is L.M. Kit Carson, the star of the film, went on to write many screenplays, including that of the remake of Godard's *Breathless*, art-house fave *Paris, Texas* and… *The Texas Chainsaw Massacre 2*?!

By the end of *David Holzman's Diary*, even our central character is sick of himself and this attempt to document his sad life. He even rages, "Why am I sitting here talking to two machines? Why do you make me do things?" As somebody who writes about movies like this for a blog I doubt anybody reads, I'm wondering why I have yet to go off like this towards my blu-ray player and the laptop I'm writing this on.

Original version posted on 11/16/2024

Flaming Ears (1992)

As a middle-aged, suburban, CIS man, I'm probably not going to be the best judge of highly-experimental, post-apocalyptic, super lo-fi, lesbian cinema. Lest you think my description of 1992's *Flaming Ears* is less than objective, this is the description of the movie from the site of its US distributor: "Super-8 DIY filmmaking at its most audacious, Flaming Ears is a pop sci-fi lesbian extravaganza set in the year 2700 in the fictional burned-out city of Asche."

I don't think it will come as a surprise this picture isn't heavy on plot. It is simple in one regard, in that it has few characters and the structure is highly episodic. On the other hand, I wasn't able to match any character to their name and performer until I read the full description on Kino Lorber's site.

When I did that, I was surprised to learn that the nature of those characters is not what I gleaned from watching the film. Instead of relaying what I was told had happened, I will focus on my experience and interpretation.

There are two characters I assume most viewers will remember for the longest time afterwards. One of these is a bald woman in red leather body suit who wanders the city at night, largely eating (fake) rats, snails and the like. The only ornamentation on her costume is a huge on/off switch on the front of her waist, almost like a belt buckle. I never formed an idea of why that element was important; however, as it is front and center in a shot for a long time, something was being communicated of which I was oblivious.

I wondered if this character was supposed to be a devil, and yet she is the kindest person in the film. She shows compassion towards an underground comic artist she finds unconscious in the street. I quickly found myself wondering if one of the picture's ideas is how a person's nature might be the opposite of what most others assume.

This idea was reinforced for me because of the other major character, whom I thought was an angel but who is the nastiest person here. I assume an angel because, when we first see her, she is sitting high up—I thought in the sky, but it may have been a tall building. She leaps down to Earth in a fascinating bit of stop-motion, cut-out animation. Given the descent from a high perch, I interpreted this as an angel falls (jumps?) down from heaven. This would be a bizarre angel, however, as she almost immediately sets fire to a printer's building, and then only after dry humping the corner of a desk.

About that last bit: while I went into this assuming a non-linear narrative, this film is more rambling than I expected. Some of the side trips it takes are more interesting than the main plotline(s). Others are excessively indulgent and/or over-long.

I have no doubt, however, that everything here was the intention of the three (!) directors involved. I don't recall a moment of its 89 minutes that didn't feel like something important to the person putting this material on the screen. Even in its goofiest moments, I was left with the impression this was a deeply personal work. It was often as if an idea went straight from the subconscious to the screen with as little meddling from the conscious mind as possible.

This was an obvious labor of love. It was filmed on Super-8 and I can only assume that was by necessity and not choice. The restoration I watched should have been a mess, as the original elements were lost and all that remains is a 16mm blow-up. And, yet, the images are often beautiful in their own unique way, not dissimilar to how Polaroids have a style and immediacy that transcends technical proficiency.

I mentioned stop-motion earlier, and that is a technique I always love to see used. Another favorite effect of mine put to good use here are miniatures, in particular a lovingly realized cityscape. Almost every establishing or non-actor shot uses stop-motion and miniatures, and this made me smile every time.

There are also jokes scattered throughout. I got some of these, while other moments made me realize there was a bit of intended humor I wasn't comprehending. However, even when there was a joke I knew I was missing, I was grateful for any light-heartedness in what I thought would be a dry, humorless affair.

Those who enjoy exploring the fringes of cinema should take a look at *Flaming Ears*. At 89 minutes, it's a bit much to take in, and my attention did wane occasionally. But I respect any filmmaker who pushes the boundaries of cinema, and I can honestly say I haven't seen, nor ever expect to see, another work quite like this.

Original version posted on 2/19/2023

Nam June Paik: Moon Is the Oldest TV (2023)

Some of the most interesting books on music I have read are about artists or albums I otherwise could not care less about. Some of the most interesting special features I have encountered on blu-rays have accompanied movies I didn't like. And so, I shouldn't have been surprised to find myself intrigued by 2023's documentary *Nam June Paik: Moon Is the Oldest TV,* a profile of an artist whose work I actively dislike.

I encountered some of his work early on in local museums, discovering at a young age how much of a difference there is between pieces that are intriguing and those that are only baffling. I couldn't see an in-road to appreciating these tall humanoid sculptures with television sets embedded in them. I didn't find them whimsical, nor did I detect any intended statement. Encountering his art is one of the few times I have understood the outrage some groups feel when faced with works they don't understand. And yet, I couldn't even be bothered to feel outrage towards what I had seen, and a shrug is probably the last reaction any artist wants to receive.

One of the first statements we hear from the artist in this film is something I locked onto: "I use technology in order to hate it properly." Much like some of the things Warhol said, I wondered if he really thought he was being clever, or if these kinds of potential catchphrases were akin to a stopped clock being right twice a day. Consider: "I'd rather make mistakes for a reason than be successful for no reason." That scans as witty on first read but feels less so upon closer inspection. Regardless, I like the sentiment and the quote.

Again, like Warhol, I was curious as to how much of a genius he really was versus how the public shaped a narrative that built them up as such. Paik originally left his native Korea for Germany to study classical music. Despite apparently having a PhD in pre-renaissance music, we largely see him abusing pianos in various ways, such as smashing a camcorder onto the keys repeatedly. We will repeatedly see him dragging a violin behind him while walking the streets of New York, as if it was a reluctant dog on a leash. Um…genius? Also, it reminded me of the story of poet Gerard de Nerval walking a lobster through the streets of Paris, which I think is funnier.

It was seeing a John Cage performance in Germany that completely changed the direction of his art: "My life started one evening in 1958. 1957 was B.C.: Before Cage." Cage was an artist who believed all sounds were equally beautiful. His audiences may have largely felt otherwise, as indicated by those booing the recital Paik attended.

From there, we encounter a veritable who's who of artists working in the avant-garde at that time. Cage leads to Stockhausen. Paik works with Fluxus, which is an introduction to such artists as Jonas Mekas and Yoko Ono.

Even in this crowd, he finds himself in the lowest castes of artists, having chosen television as his medium. As one talking head here explains, the art world at the time held painters in the highest esteem, while photographers were begrudgingly becoming acceptable. Movies, on the other hand, were considered trash. If the hierarchy of respectable arts was a totem pole, video art would be several feet under the ground.

It came as a surprise to everybody (including, I suspect, the artist) when his *TV Buddha* became a phenomenon. This simple piece has a buddha statuette watching itself on a tv which has a camera behind it pointing at the buddha. The work does have a weird attraction to it, sucking the viewer into a kind of ouroboros, the media snake biting its own tail. It is like a different kind of video feedback loop. In the tradition of Warhol, Paik proceeded to churn out a great number of the pieces for museums and collectors around the world. I guess if you're making a statement about any kind of consumerism, whether it be silk screen reproduction of soup cans or commentary on our obsession over ourselves through media, you might as well make a buck off it. Once again, the ouroboros comes to mind for me.

One element of his work and life I found interesting was his interest in communication and barriers preventing it. Admittedly, television is a medium that has had a huge impact on how we communicate, whether facilitating or complicating it. Paik's work seems to explore both.

The pieces of his shown here I found most fascinating are where he uses large magnets to distort a television picture in unexpected ways. I was less intrigued by his fixation with robots. In the 60's, he built a shambolic thing that he would demonstrate on NYC streets, with all its ramshackle inner workings on display. I assume Beck used to have wet dreams of such a robot. Questionably, Paik used as its "voice" a recording of Kennedy's "ask not what you can do..." speech, despite the assassination of that president being fresh in everyone's minds. Later, he would make many immobile, robot-shaped sculptures with functional TV screens in them, making me wonder if the design of the Teletubbies was somehow a tribute.

Sometimes, he ends up accidentally demonstrating how disastrous technology can be, such as *Good Morning, Mr. Orwell,* a variety show he organized for satellite broadcast around the world on

New Year's Day, 1984. By all accounts, this was a fiasco, and I feel especially bad for the millions of Koreans who were up at 2 am to witness this folly. From the clips we see, it is like bad community television was granted a global audience.

In addition to communication barriers, Paik was intrigued by the physical barriers we put between each other. This was understandable, given the nation of his birth was suddenly divided in two, with a border that is still one of the most heavily secured in the world. It is interesting the first place he lands after Korea is Berlin, which was divided by that famous wall. Both nations also have uncomfortable war-related matters in its recent past to reconcile, with Koreans dealing with the atrocities the Japanese had committed there.

In the end, *Nam June Paik: Moon Is the Oldest TV* did not change my opinion of the artist's oeuvre, but it did give me greater insight into him as a person, and I found him rather fascinating. I still don't believe he was a genius, but why should somebody need to be one to create art? I'm just glad the world has weirdos like him, people who playfully tear down idols and explore new ideas with an almost childlike naivete. It may not result in art I identity with, but it is important it is there, regardless.

Original version posted on 9/27/2024

Samsara (2011)

No matter how much cinema means to a person, there are few films which I believe anybody can say actually changed their life. I would be unlikely to rank 2011's *Samsara* even among my top 100 favorite movies, yet it is the one that had the greatest direct impact on me. Thanks to this picture, my wife and I became vegetarians.

Live chickens get randomly sucked up into a machine. Needless to say, they do not emerge from the other end alive. There was something so cold about this, a literal death machine, that I realized I wanted as little as possible to do with the meat industry going forwards. Unlike hunting, this is completely impersonal. Something about this clean, mechanized and allegedly humane killing just seemed so…inhuman.

That scene isn't representative of most of the picture, a narrative-free affair similar to *Koyaanisqatsi*. I am always a bit surprised that film didn't inspire more like it, but then I'm guessing such films don't equate to big box office. Fortunately, that didn't stop Ron Fricke from taking a 70 millimeter camera to 25 countries over the course of five years, getting truly jaw-dropping footage.

One can appreciate the beauty of the footage at a superficial level. The movie does not force the viewer to come to any conclusions, but it is only natural for one to make connections between the images, as the filmmaker obviously chose these images, and sequenced them in this particular order, for a reason. I largely let the footage just wash over me, but still inevitably came to a couple of conclusions as to what those intentions might be.

I found myself mostly pondering the temporary nature of human existence. We may try to permanently leave our mark on the world, but the vast majority will leave no lasting trace. Very few will leave as long of a legacy as Tutankhamun, and we will see his pristine sarcophagus. We also see the pyramids, but I bet he couldn't have foreseen the shabby apartment buildings within eyesight of them, satellite dishes atop each one.

Largely, even our belongings will be lost to time, such as a house that was doubtlessly once a home, but which is now being overtaken by desert sand. Other structures we see were devastated by water. In one of those, we see several abandoned trophies, things which were doubtlessly of great personal value to a person at one time. Now separated from their owner, they have no meaning whatsoever.

Perhaps our legacy is our trash, and we are leaving behind a great deal of that. One wonders what future archeologists may think when they find our landfills. At the rate we're going, any such scientists may have to be extraterrestrial.

So, there's footage of huge mountains of trash. Similar to that, we get some imagery of some of the weird artificiality of the modern world. A giant, indoor ski slope. Androids that live deep in the uncanny valley. Towering skyscrapers in the desert. Man-made islands.

Some of the more obvious associations are a bit too on the pierced nose. Think that African woman with the giant round things in her huge earlobes is funny? Just wait until the camera is turned back on America, and people who are equally proud of their extensively inked and pierced bodies.

There is one weird misstep in the film, and that is an odd bit of performance art where a man in a business suit sits behind a desk and starts smearing mud on his face. Soon, he is adding paint and all manner of debris to the mess, making himself over as a truly modern primitive. This bit is too showy and too different from the rest of the material to be anything but a distraction.

Despite this misstep, *Samsara* is a film I highly recommend. Even if you have seen similar films, such as the works of Godrey Reggio, this is still a unique experience, though it is often overwhelming. I will admit perhaps it is a tad *too* overwhelming, as I eventually found myself tuning out. By the time we get to footage of a man buried in a coffin shaped like a giant gun, I had become numbed to the imagery.

Original version posted on 10/4/2024

Artsy (with a fair dose of fartsy) [the artsy and otherwise undefinable]

Scala!!! (2023)
Or, the Incredibly Strange Rise and Fall of the World's Wildest Cinema and How It Influenced a Mixed-up Generation of Weirdos and Misfits

Funny how much I miss the repertory cinema that used to be in the city closest to where I live. It has now been 33 years since it projected its last film (*Raging Bull*, and I was one of very few people at that screening). And yet, I actually didn't see many films there while it was in operation. There's even a new cinema operating out of that location today, and I can't imagine going there, either.

What I remember best were the massive black-and-white schedule calendars the theatre gave away. Looking at one of these was always overwhelming, with too much information crammed into the box for any given day. You would pore over these things, as curious and baffling as a route map for a massive public transportation system of a city you've never been to. I knew at least one person who literally wallpapered their bedroom with these movie schedules.

Now having seen the 2023 documentary *Scala!!! Or, the Incredibly Strange Rise and Fall of the World's Wildest Cinema and How It Influenced a Mixed-up Generation of Weirdos and Misfits*, I wonder if the idea of those schedule posters was inspired by the similar ones for London's famous (perhaps more so infamous) Scala Cinema Club. We'll see a fair number of the Scala's version in this film, and I admit theirs were a great deal more colorful and had far greater detail.

The Scala specialized in a wide variety of films that otherwise would have been difficult to see. Among the types of films discussed here are foreign, horror, kung fu and LGBT. Basically, they covered many of the markets underserved by mainstream cinemas. And this was back before most homes had their own

VCRs, and so this was the *only* way to see a great many of these films.

I imagine it was especially difficult to screen such horror films as the original *The Evil Dead* in the UK at that time. The 80's saw the UK media, and many government officials, obsessed with "Video Nasties". I find it hard to fathom, but those who sold or rented videotapes at the time could (and, in one case, did) serve jail time for providing films such as these.

It was noble of the Scala to be one of the few theatres brave enough to screen LGBT cinema. Still, I didn't understand this documentary's obsession with the bathrooms of the theatre and the notorious recreational activities which happened in them. Perhaps it is simply my inability to identify with that culture which is not my own, but I suspect I wouldn't have appreciated all the talk about restroom sex even if I was in that demographic. The result is a great deal of interesting content about movies is relegated to the bonus features.

Many famous actors and filmmakers were regular patrons of the theatre. Some of the many interviewees here went on to careers in film, though largely as character actors known for bit parts. That's probably for the best, as the most famous people rarely make for the best interviews. The lesser-knowns tend to be less candid.

Mary Harron, the eventual director of *American Psycho*, talks about the surreal experience of occasionally dozing during one of the all-night film festivals, only to behold something truly startling on the screen each time she awoke. Comedian Paul Putner, whom I know best from his many put-upon characters on *Little Britain*, shows off his original membership card (and it is nice to see almost everybody interviewed still has theirs). Ralph Brown, best known for playing the drug dealer Danny in *Withnail & I*, worked in the venue's coffee shop and re-sold amphetamines he bought by the garbage-bagful from a dealer he modelled that character upon.

One of the most interesting patrons is somebody we only see in archival footage. Mrs. Reeves is a very stereotypical middle-aged British woman who could have walked right out of an old *Python* sketch. She uses the "royal we" a lot. The gag is she loves violent films and doesn't understand why anybody thinks they would incite others to emulate them. "I don't go out of here wanting to chainsaw somebody."

And yet there were at least two deaths at the venue, though neither was the result of violence (presumably). One person was found unresponsive and slumped over a seat after having a fatal heart attack mid-film. Given some of the fare screened there, that feels almost inevitable. Another incident was a body found on the sidewalk outside which had evidently been a jumper from a high window. That makes 200% more deaths than had happened in my local repertory theatre. Well, at least as far as anybody *knows*.

The theatre also hosted live acts on occasion, such as early shows by Lou Reed and Iggy & The Stooges. Photos taken at those gigs became the cover art for *Transformer* and *Raw Power*, respectively. Other aspects of the music industry represented in this documentary is an original score by Barry Adamson (who is also interviewed), and interviews with The The's Matt Johnson and The Jesus & Mary Chain's Douglas Hart.

There were a few contributing factors to the demise of the Scala. One was their decision to screen *A Clockwork Orange*, despite Kubrick having pulled the film from circulation due to some copycat incidents in the wake of its original release. The theatre could not survive the resulting costly legal battle against Warner Bros. for copyright infringement. But their demise was hastened by the widespread increase in home media following a massive decrease in the cost of videotapes. I find it ironic I watched *Scala!!!* on blu-ray, as there wasn't a way to see it in my country in a cinema.

Original version posted on 5/21/2024

Squaring the Circle (2022)

"Vinyl is the poor man's art collection." This remarkable statement appears to have been coined by Noel Gallagher of Oasis fame, however unlikely it seems to me he could ever come up with anything that clever.

There's a lot of truth in that statement, regardless of who said it first. I know I have been obsessed with album covers as long as I have been collecting vinyl. When I finally had some money, my collection of art books extended this obsession, as I have volumes about Peter Saville (Factory) and Vaughan Oliver (4AD). I can also appreciate, though am not much of a fan of, Roger Dean's fantasy art that accompanies many albums by Yes. But, in my books of album art, the works of the design firm Hipgnosis appear more than any other artist.

Everybody has some familiarity with their work, even if they may not know who the designers are. The prism cover of Pink Floyd's *Dark Side of the Moon*. The pig in the sky over Battersea Power Station on the cover of the same's *Animals*. Naked children crawling on the octagonal rocks of Giant's Causeway in Ireland for Led Zeppelin's *Houses of the Holy*. Peter Gabriel seemingly clawing his way out of one of his album covers.

The core of the firm was Storm Thorgerson and Aubrey Powell, friends since their teenage years, when they would hang out with the people who would eventually become Pink Floyd. Though their firm would eventually have some staffers, the core was primarily Thorgerson and Powell until they added Throbbing Gristle's Peter Christopherson as a partner.

The lineup of musicians sharing reminiscences here is stunning. These include Paul McCartney, David Gilmour, Roger Waters, Nick Mason, Robert Plant, Jimmy Page and…um, Noel Gallagher. Even some fellow cover artists of renown pay tribute, including Roger Dean and Peter Saville.

Every anecdote presented is fascinating. I have always heard it was Syd Barrett who inscribed on a door what would become the firm's name. I was startled to hear so many of the talking heads assembled here attribute that to different people, with each person firmly adamant their version was the correct one.

Regardless of who wrote on the door, that first building was simply where Thorgerson and Powell lived and operated their fledgling business out of. During that time, Roman Polanski filmed *Repulsion* in the same building. Thorgerson helped himself to the camera crew's lighting gear that just happened to be in the hallway after shooting wrapped.

When they finally acquired a stand-alone office, it didn't have a bathroom, so they used the sink for *everything*. At least the former owner of the space let them keep a piano they had left behind. They sold it to a piano store, who moved it out themselves. The sale of the piano enabled Thorgerson and Powell to buy all the camera equipment they needed.

It sounds like they were able to get rid of piano more easily than Powell was able to dispose of a sofa. He chucked it off the roof and smashed a taxi on the street below. There were no repercussions. He relates this story as an example of how lawless London was back then. I don't think I would be able to function in such an environment.

Artsy (with a fair dose of fartsy) (the artsy and otherwise undefinable)

But the best stories are all about the various covers. Such as the small statue McCartney wanted them to put atop Everest and photograph for the cover of *Wings Greatest Hits*. Powell didn't go there, but he did put it atop a mountain in the Alps and snapped the pic. Then McCartney complained about the results, saying the same photo could have been taken in a studio.

Then there's the famous story behind the cover of Pink Floyd's *Animals*, artwork I believe is far greater than the album it accompanies. The inflatable pig got loose, resulting in the temporary stoppage of all air traffic. Eventually, a farmer called to tell them it had landed in his field and was scaring his sheep.

It is also fascinating how so many of the interviewees describe the deceased Thorgerson as the rudest person they'd ever known and yet, somehow, also nicest guy in the world. I love the way Pink Floyd's Nick Mason describes him: "He wouldn't take yes for an answer". And yet, everything I have read in the past about Hipgnosis has been disproportionately about Thorgerson. This time, more of the focus is on Powell. History is told by the survivors, after all.

I loved every minute of *Squaring the Circle* and only wished the blu-ray had included additional interviews as bonus material. At least we have the documentary, with these astonishing testaments capturing the craziness of the rock world at that time. It is good to have these memories preserved when so much else has been lost, such as Plant's copy of the object from the cover of Zeppelin's *Presence*: "It must be somewhere. It's probably a doorstop."

Original version posted on 11/16/2023

Artsy (with a fair dose of fartsy) [the artsy and otherwise undefinable]

Humor is in the elbow of the beholder
The section about comedies

The Adventures of Ichabod and Mr. Toad (1949)

It's weird how many films in the Disney canon are compilations of shorter films. In some of these portmanteaus, the associations between the films will be stronger than in others. It was a trend starting with *Fantasia*, and look at how tenuous the connections are between the pieces of that film.

1949's *The Adventures of Ichabod and Mr. Toad* is one such odd duck. It is jarring to see an adaptation of "The Legend of Sleepy Hollow" alongside an animated segment of only part of *The Wind in the Willows*. So, we have Disney's take on a part of Kenneth Grahame's book that was so light it felt out of place even there, followed by one of the darkest works of the studio's golden years.

Basil Rathbone narrates the Mr. Toad story, which isn't a bad match for the material. Eric Blore voices Toad, bringing the same kind crazed energy and ace comic timing he brought to such movies as *The Lady Eve*. As for the style of the piece, it is closer to something I would expect from Warner Bros than the House the Mouse Built.

I am a pretty big fan of the original book, though curiously really only of one chapter. There's a reason the chapter "The Piper at the Gates of Dawn" inspired Pink Floyd to use it as the title of their debut album.

But that isn't the part of the book adapted here, so we're stuck with the selfish, destructive Toad. He's a constant threat to himself and others, especially once he becomes obsessed with automobiles. When he first sees one, he gets a look like he has suddenly taken strong hallucinogens. Has he been licking one of his toxic cousins from South America?

Then there's the matter of humans and their presence and role in this world. I'm always confused when a movie includes humans and anthropomorphic animals. In *The Great Mouse Detective*, these groups live in parallel worlds that don't seem to intersect. The rat Holmes and Watson, for example, have their own rodent-sized apartment that is in 221 Baker Street. Compare that to *Mr. Toad*, where we have a rat whose house is inexplicably human-sized. This rat also interacts civilly with a human postman. I just never felt like this environment jelled, and I was thinking too much about the rules of it. But I only mull over these things because those rules provide the framework for any drama. Without them, we have no vested interest in the characters, as we don't know the stakes of their various goals and crises.

Anyway, a human judge sends Toad to prison. He escapes, but the ball and chain he's wearing pulls him to the bottom of a lake. It is made to look as if he drowned, though he somehow turns up later. Conveniently, there is no explanation provided for *how* he survived what appeared to be a watery demise.

Bing Crosby narrates the Ichabod Crane half of the picture. His trademark laconic style makes it feel like he is mocking the material at times. And, aside from the weird horror aspects of the tale, Disney has provided much to mock here.

One problem is the titular protagonist. I wouldn't call him a hero. This schoolteacher is shallow, greedy and a glutton. Crosby nicknames the character "Icky" at one point, and that is spot-on.

And yet, he is inexplicably desired by the inordinate number of single moms in this little hamlet. They pay for his services as a music teacher by providing food for his seemingly endless appetite. Given the effect he has on the three women to whom he gives singing lessons, I wonder if there are any other services they provide him.

But Ichabod is obsessed with the same beautiful woman every other guy there is infatuated with, except he is actually smitten with her wealthy father's money. Icky imagines a future with her in which he has a gold tooth. It is touches like this that had me rooting for the town bully who is in competition for her hand.

The best part of either story is the finale to this one, where it becomes genuinely creepy—well, as much as Disney in this era would get. There were many little details I appreciated, such as clouds that look like curved fingers closing in on the moon. Then there's the frog croaking, "Headless horseman. Headless horseman." Top that, Budweiser frogs.

The alleged link between the tales in *The Adventures of Icabod and Mr. Toad* is each is from a great work of literature. Just imagine if they had grabbed any two books at random. Maybe we would see one story from something by Roald Dahl and another from *The 120 Days of Sodom*.

Original version posted on 7/10/2024

After Hours (1985)

It will be difficult to write about 1985's *After Hours* without spoiling anything. By that, I don't just mean ruining the ending for those who haven't seen it yet. I mean *any* of the surprises in it, while are plentiful and begin almost immediately.

The safest summary I can provide is Griffin Dunne plays an office drone who experiences a bizarre night in Soho, stumbling from one unexpected situation to the next. Almost everything he sees, and nearly every person he meets, will tie back to a different event or another person at a later point. If I was to try to diagram all the connections in this film, I would look like the biggest conspiracy nut in the world. It would make your typical JFK assassination obsessive look sane in comparison. Also, if you ever find yourself taking up entire walls with items connected by pushpins and string, you have made some questionable life choices.

It is a testament to everybody involved in the production that it is almost effortless to follow. That said, it is a hair too clever and self-satisfied with its clocklike structure, a Rube Goldberg invention seemingly designed to torture an innocent man so that a capricious deity would be entertained.

Martin Scorsese directs during what was a low point in his career. Despite having *Taxi Driver*, *Mean Streets* and *Raging Bull* under his belt, he was persona non grata in Hollywood following the financial failure of *King of Comedy*. Then his first attempt at *Last Temptation of Christ* fell through just before shooting was about to commence. He needed to make something relatively cheaply and quickly to prove to both the industry and himself that he still had the magic.

This is Scorsese returning to the New York he loves, though this takes place in what was frontier territory at the time. In a bonus interview on the Criterion Collection blu-ray, he talks about how weird it was to film in Soho before gentrification. There weren't any shops. There weren't any bars they could pop into during lulls in filming. Apparently, much of the area didn't have electricity, which boggles my mind, as I can't imagine a part of any modern city where water and power might be scarce. And yet, I believe Flint, Michigan, still has undrinkable water as I write this.

All the action takes place at night, so the area is even more deserted than it would have been during the day. It is into this eerily abandoned world that a speed demon cab driver deposits Dunne. The $20 bill Dunne was going to use to pay for his fare blew out the window as the cab zigzagged through traffic in undercranked shots.

As a result of this, our protagonist doesn't have sufficient money to get home. Even taking the subway is out of the question, as the change he has would have purchased a token only up until a couple of hours ago, as the rate just went up to $1.50. In case you haven't guessed it already, these efforts could be described as Kafkaesque. It also feels a bit like a Beckett play.

Except Beckett was never this funny. Perhaps the biggest surprise is Scorsese would make a movie this funny, even if it is all dark humor. I would be hard-pressed to explain why some things in this made me laugh. Many of these moments are from the cracks that start to appear in Dunne's polite demeanor. It isn't too far from a couple of movies John Cleese made following his Python years, where his innate British civility seems to handicap his characters as they face increasingly absurd situations.

To try to give a sensation of the movie's bizarre humor and disorienting nature, allow me to list a few of its elements, all of which factor to some degree in the plot. Plaster-of-Paris paperweights that look like a bagel and cream cheese. A crude drawing on a bathroom wall of a man with a shark biting down on his erect member. A bed surrounded by rattraps, each illuminated by a tiny spotlight. A life-size paper mâché sculpture of a cowering, shrieking man. A bar where the price of admittance is to either have, or be willing to receive, a mohawk haircut. A Mr. Softee ice cream truck slowly leading a mob of flashlight-wielding vigilantes. Arrow signs helpfully directing people to a dead body. I was reminded somewhat of those 90's point-and-click adventure games where the player encountered various bizarre scenarios through which they had to navigate.

While all of these play into the storyline, I suspect one's tolerance for this weirdness will vary for each viewer. I can fully understand one person hating this movie with a passion, while another will have found their new favorite film. I was somewhere past the middle, towards loving it but finding myself an arm's length from it at all times. It was all a bit too artificial for my tastes.

One aspect I don't think anybody could argue is the quality of the cast. Among those appearing with Dunne are Teri Garr, Rosanne Arquette, John Heard, Verna Bloom, Catherine O'Hara, Linda Fiorentino and Dick Miller. There's even Cheech and Chong as thieves who are *very* central to the plot. Who would have thought this comedy duo would be in a Scorsese picture?

Of those actors, the most noteworthy is O'Hara. What distinguishes her performance is she does many of the same things that would be for laughs in other films, but which are quite menacing here. It is an interesting demonstration of how context is everything.

After Hours is an anomaly in Scorsese's career. Heck, it is almost entirely unique among movies, period. There is so much content here, and it is so open to analysis and interpretation, I suspect it could serve as a kind of Rorschach test for each viewer.

Original version posted on 1/25/2024

Bandits (2001)

I have seen many movies where the actors appear to be having a miserable time and so I had trouble connecting with the feature. 2001's heist comedy *Bandits* has the exact opposite problem: the actors appear to be having a great time, to the extent it is like watching a party to which the audience wasn't invited.

It's interesting the lead here is Bruce Willis, as he also starred in *Hudson Hawk*, one of the few movies I have seen with this same problem. There, he and Danny Aiello did a song and dance number during a heist, and the two seemed so pleased with themselves and each other that I wondered if they even cared whether the cameras were rolling.

Willis co-stars with Billy Bob Thornton and Kate Blanchett in *Bandits* and a quick check of IMDB shows the cross-pollination of these three between various projects. With that, it isn't surprising they have great repartee here. I suspect they were given considerable latitude to improvise, as some scenes run much longer than necessary.

It's like director Barry Levinson couldn't bear to part with any of the resulting dialogue. I was surprised the director of *Rain Man* would consider helming a heist comedy like this. Then again, that Oscar-winning picture was more than a decade in the rearview mirror at that point. Also, he directed *Good Morning, Vietnam,* where the endless improvisations of Robin Williams was a boost to both of their careers.

In keeping with long-standing film traditions, our bank-robbing leads have mismatched personalities. Willis's character is all things manly: impulsive, with a brute physicality, and always ready with a quip. Thornton plays a sensitive hypochondriac, whose long list of fears includes antique furniture. At one point, he is driving while listening to a medical encyclopedia as a book on tape. I don't know if there ever was such a thing, but I found this very clever and funny.

This is a movie that hits the ground running. There isn't much exposition or character development before Willis and Thornton escape prison when the former unexpectedly steals a cement truck, drives it through some woods and finally through a series of backyards, annihilating one fence after another. The aerial shot of this is one of the funniest moments in the movie.

And there is a lot to laugh at in this. Possibly the best moment is completely at random, as Thornton startles himself awake crying, "BEAVERS AND DUCKS!" The first time we saw this, my wife laughed harder than I think I have ever seen her laugh before. She's in good company, as William Jackson Harper singled out this scene in an installment of the AV Club's "11 Questions" feature.

Even with such moments that are clearly meant to be humorous, I found myself a bit unnerved by some other scenes early in the runtime. Before we get any real insights into the characters of Willis and Thornton, they park a stolen car in a random open house garage. They then creep inside where they interrupt two teens who are dangerously close to getting horizontal. It is hard to read Willis's expression, but I found my skin crawling.

Fortunately, nothing disturbing happens in the time these men are in the house. However, at one point, the boy finds a shotgun in a closet and points it at Willis. I wondered if this was going to turn out like a similar scene in *Funny Games*. It doesn't, but it made me wonder why the boy didn't use that time going through the closet to call the police instead. Then I remember: oh yeah, teenage boys.

Willis and Thornton next pick up Troy Garity, whose goal in life is to become a movie stuntman. We first see him in a solid bit where squibs all over his body fail to go off, only to explode when he least expects it. Seeing this, I immediately thought of Chekhov's Gun, even if the gun in this case is curiously non-existent. Chekhov's Squibs just doesn't have the same ring to it.

With Garity as the getaway driver, Willis and Thornton come up with a novel idea for robbing banks. The night before the intended robbery, they invade the house of that bank's manager, hold them and their family hostage and then go with them to the bank the next morning. Even before the bank is open for customers, the manager has opened the vault, and the robbers have left with the money.

This led to another of those uncomfortable moments for me. The first time the robbers commit one of these home invasions, the wife of the bank manager won't stop crying. I had a hard time finding the humor in that. I mean, imagine the thinking behind this: "It's funny because she thinks they might all get killed! HAHAHAHAHA!"

As the number of successful robberies increases, they become media darlings. They become dubbed "The Sleepover Bandits", which my mind kept twisting into The Wet Bandits.

Parallel to this, we see Cate Blanchett as a lonely woman looking for excitement. When we first see her, she is preparing an elaborate meal while dancing energetically. I've never before seen anybody who enjoys cutting up vegetables as much as I do, but I definitely don't dance around with flailing knives while doing it.

At the end of all this, her husband says he forgot to tell her he has a business dinner he needs to attend that night. While I will admit this is jerky, I suspect I would have invented an excuse not to eat with her after watching this spectacle.

Blanchett tears off in her car, driving recklessly and at random. Thornton happens to be fleeing police on foot at that time. He runs out into the road to hijack her vehicle but she hits him with her car. She tries to drive him to a hospital but it isn't long before Thornton, terrified by her erratic driving and behavior, tries to jump out of the moving vehicle.

Still, she takes him to a scheduled meetup with Willis and Garity at a secluded cabin. Seeing the opportunity for adventure, and showing an immediate spark with Willis, she basically forces them to take her along as a hostage. Before long, she is alternately making time with Willis or Thornton.

This development is one of the most surprising in the picture, as she refuses to commit to either man. As she puts it, between the manly bravado of Willis and the sensitivity of Thornton, they together make the perfect man. The details of this arrangement are left to the imagination, as this is a PG-13 film.

Unfortunately, the movie shifts down a couple of gears as the three try to figure out this relationship, resulting in long turgid stretches. It is as if the picture wanted to be a wild comedy completely disassociated from reality while also being a drama exploring the complexities of this romantic entanglement. Maybe a better film could have handled this more deftly, but I can't imagine it.

Fortunately, at least half of the movie is deeply humorous. One example: when Blanchett and Thornton first arrive at that remote cabin, they see a man on fire running through the woods, which turns out to be Garity trying out another stunt. This surreal moment made me laugh long and hard, just from the absurdity of it.

I know I will watch *Bandits* again at some point in the future, if only to see all the great little bits of humor in it. In that viewing, I hope it becomes a more cohesive experience for me. As it is, this is almost like somebody took all the best bits from a sketch comedy show that was originally unrelated sequences and then stuck those elements anywhere they could in the plotline of a more serious film.

Original version posted on 10/11/2023

The Big Bus (1976)

Mad Magazine was a big thing for me when I was the right age for it. I especially liked the movie parodies, even if I had yet to see most of the films they skewered.

I find it funny the first movie to carry the magazine's brand, *Up the Academy*, was correctly identified as garbage by its target audience (including yours truly) just from the advertisements. Somebody had already beaten them to the punch by four years with the movie they should have made, and that is 1976's *The Big Bus*.

In an odd inversion of cause and effect, this feels like a movie adaptation of a *Mad* parody. But this isn't just a parody of one movie, this is a gentle takedown of the entire 70's disaster movie craze that was getting long in the tooth at this point. Other films are obvious influences, including *Zero Hour!*, which would be directly parodied four years later in *Airplane!*

The titular bus is a double-decker, double-length monstrosity. It is also nuclear-powered, with a rocket thruster on the back. It is as bizarre and over-the-top as the double-width train on NBC's legendary dud *Supertrain*.

The vehicle makes its first appearance at a press conference. For this, a group of approximately two dozen journalists get on a shuttle bus, which travels but a few yards to pick up a couple of company spokespeople. Then it circles back to where it started and everybody disembarks. If you can find some degree of amusement in that concept, this may be the movie for you. If not, then this is going to be like an interminable bus trip where you're seated next to somebody who won't shut up.

Joseph Bologna will be captain of the bus for its inaugural non-stop voyage from New York to Denver. Why not all the way to the west coast? Again, this is indicative of the off-beat humor of the film. As for myself, I think it would be even funnier if it went from one unimportant place to another, like Poughkeepsie to Tulsa (no offense to either place, as I live in flyover territory myself).

Driving the vehicle is supposed to restore Bologna to his former glory. When we first see him, he ventures into a bus driver's bar called "The Bus Stop". Almost all the patrons are hostile towards him because of a bus crash where he resorted to cannibalism to survive. It is widely believed he consumed more than 100 people, but he claims he only ate a single foot, and even that was by accident.

I thought that was a pretty funny joke, though I didn't realize that was referencing something in popular culture at the time. A big movie of the same year had been *Survive!*, about a real-life airplane crash in the Andes where the survivors had to resort to cannibalism. The 1993 movie *Alive* concerns the same incident.

In a resulting bar fight, only John Beck comes to his defense, breaking a tall milk carton in two and waving it around like a broken bottle. The bartender: "Look out! He's got a broken milk carton!". Bologna will go on to ask Beck to be his co-driver, a decision he will almost immediately come to regret.

As you may have guessed by now, the comedy is very hit or miss. Some of the supporting cast is rather impressive, including Stockard Channing, Ned Beatty and José Ferrer. Ruth Gordon is here but little used, and not well-used when she does make an appearance. Not to knock the rest of the cast, but most of them are primarily from television: Bob Dishy, Larry Hagman, Richard Mulligan and Howard Hesseman. That was an indicator of low quality in the 70's and 80's, as people usually didn't pay for a movie so they could see performers they could see at home.

Unbeknownst at first to anybody on the bus, there is a conspiracy to sabotage the vehicle. This is masterminded by oil baron Ferrer, as played from within an iron lung. I didn't find that funny, but I was amused by the paintings on the walls surrounding it, each of which captures a different 70's disaster. One is of The Hindenburg, another is of a skyscraper on fire, etc.

Curiously, the hit ratio for the gags gets lower for me once we get to the bus journey itself. I understand all the passengers are stereotypes from the kinds of films being parodied, but that in itself isn't especially humorous to me.

And yet, I found many of the most outlandish features of the vehicles to be among the best jokes. I laughed an embarrassingly long time when they test the automated tire replacement system, as the tire explodes off a wheel and a new one slides into place. Similarly, the self-washing system made me smile. It has tall brushes of the kind found in any automatic car wash, except these emerge from a recessed area and roll down the sides of the bus on a track system.

Also, the bus has a pool, albeit one that is ridiculously small. But I didn't find that anywhere near as funny as the single lane bowling alley, which becomes as troublesome as most people assume having one in a moving vehicle might be.

The film builds to a final set piece that is visually impressive, though I didn't find it particularly engaging. At one point, the bus is ready to fall off a cliff, precariously balanced at its central point. There is also a pickup truck embedded into the side of the bus. Don't ask.

It is almost impossible to say whether I would recommend *The Big Bus* to anybody, even among the people I know best. Some of the physical comedy that didn't work for me may be endlessly funny to somebody else. I prefer such scenes as the one where Bologna speaks openly at the grave of his deceased father, only for the cliché to be upended when he realizes there is a different person talking to every tombstone around him. Basically, I don't think everything will click for anybody but, hopefully, every viewer will find at least one solid belly laugh. Not unlike any road vehicle, your mileage may vary.

Original version posted on 2/4/2024

Bugsy Malone (1976)

I have long been aware of 1976's all-kids gangster musical *Bugsy Malone* and now, having finally seen it, I just have a few lingering questions. One of these is "What the fuck?". Another question is "What the fuck?". OK, I have a long list of questions and they're all "What the fuck?"

But, really, why was this movie made and who is it for? This is such a bizarre and unappealing concept. And yet, if you're the kind of person who wants to see little boys as gangsters, and girls as gangsters' molls and chorus line dancers, then I guess this is for you. I assume you will one day be on the national sex offenders registry, if you're not already.

I know I tend to overthink movies I'm watching, but I just couldn't lose myself in something I had so many nagging questions about. For example, what are the rules of the world in which this takes place? I'm guessing that, if this was the real world, the kids would all be in the age range of elementary up through junior high school.

So…where do the kids come from? Scott Baio, as the title character, mentions his parents. Are they somewhere else and they sent him here after he was a toddler? For the love of all that's good and holy, please don't tell me the kids here are the offspring of other kids.

There's a scene that bothered me more than it should where a girl opens a window and yells for everybody outside to keep the noise down, and there's the sound of a baby crying from behind her. Is *she* supposed to be the mother of that baby?! I have read some contemporaneous reviews of this picture and I have yet to find one where anybody is asking questions like these.

Let's assume the kids are sent from someplace else to here. Where do they go when they age out of the acceptable range?

Which leads me to the especially strange rule of this world, that being you are apparently dead if you get "creamed". This can happen via pie or a bizarre machine gun that shots crème puffs. I never bought into this conceit. At the end, the movie doesn't either, as everybody in a speakeasy is covered in whipped crème, and yet they all start singing an upbeat Paul Williams song and all is forgiven. So, are these supposed to be zombie children having a sing-a-long?

All the music here is courtesy of Williams and, while I don't always like his work, you gotta give the man props for his innate composition ability. The numbers here aren't bad, but also are not a type of music I care for. I'll concede the last number I mentioned is especially strong and wouldn't have been out of place in *The Muppet Movie*, for which he also did the score. All that said, there's a number towards the middle that employs many 70's affectations and it is horrible and out-of-place.

The child actors mostly range from barely serviceable to better-than-average. No surprise Jodie Foster is already on an entirely different plane than anybody else here, even at such an early age. It is a tad eerie how fully she is "Jodie Foster" at this point. It's almost as if they shrunk an adult version of her back to pre-teen size. Even the second-best actors in this had yet to learn the kind of nuances with which she shades her expressions and line deliveries.

The director of this was Alan Parker, who would go on to make *Pink Floyd The Wall*, which is somehow less crazy than this G-rated mess. I don't know what he or anybody else hoped to accomplish here, but my skin crawled the entire time I watched this. Odd that never happened watching that later film, even with all of its intentionally disturbing imagery.

Original version posted on 4/4/2023

Brain Donors (1992)

We will never see the likes of the Marx Brothers again, and woe to those who try to be them. On the other hand, we'll never see the likes of them again and so we'll never see a new Marx Brothers film. It was in that frame of mind that I approached 1992's *Brain Donors*.

At least the characters aren't named Groucho, Chico and Harpo. Eyebrow-raising casting has John Turturro, Bob Nelson and Mel Smith, respectively, in roles analogous to those characters, even if they aren't exact copies.

Turturro hews the closest to the obvious inspiration for his character. No knock on Turturro's abilities, and I have seen him in comedies before, but I went in expecting him to fail as a parallel-universe Groucho. To my surprise, he brings the required manic energy. Then there's his line deliveries, which are spot-on, even if few of the lines would have been worthy of the original Groucho. Fortunately, he doesn't do any of the trademark shticks, such as rampant eyebrow-wriggling, that would have pushed his characterization into parody.

Similarly, Bob Nelson's performance has many of the elements that bring to mind Harpo, though with some noticeable differences, the most notable being he talks. But he does have a trench coat, and it is from the pockets of this he can extract a seemingly endless number of unlikely items. I do not recall having seen Nelson in anything before, but he fares the best of the cast. Part of that may be due to him getting the lion's share of the most absurd material.

The Marx Brothers films often seemed to struggle to find the best uses for Chico. Curiously, *Brain Donors* has the same problem with Mel Smith as the surrogate for that character. Smith is far from being the straight man here, but he is rarely given any business that does more than augment what Turturro or Nelson are doing.

Similar to the characters being approximations of three of the Marx Brothers (there's no dopple-Zeppo here), the plot is clearly an homage to *A Night at the Opera*, but with some key differences. The most noticeable of these is ballet being the form of high art skewered this time. It's interesting how little impact this change has, and it made me realize the Marx Brothers's film could have been about either art form with next to no alterations.

There are many deliberate similarities to the earlier picture, some of which work better than others. The film opens with Nelson waking up in the morning and destroying an alarm clock with a giant mallet, recalling a toss-off Harpo bit in *Opera*. There's also some business with a contract which, while funny, could never hope to equal the justly famous "Sanity clause" bit this intends to mirror. There's even Nancy Marchand as a surrogate for the wealthy dowager character Margaret Dumont made famous in multiple Marx features. The group even helps a couple of young, struggling and love-struck artists (Spike Alexander and Juliana Donald), who are just as thinly drawn as Kitty Carlisle and Allan Jones when Groucho and the gang came to their aid.

If there are any quotable lines in this, they would be among Turturro's, though few would resonate outside of context. Probably my favorite that would work is his complaint when he and Nelson are seated at the ballet: "These seats are terrible! They're facing the stage." I also took note of this line: "Someday you'll have my children. They're out in the car, if you want them."

Everything in the plot builds up to the debut performance of the ballet, which is gleefully subverted in many ways. Some of the gags are of very base humor, such as Nelson dropping a whoopee cushion into the back of the villainous star dancer's (George De La Pena) tights. Others are like outtakes from the legendary Looney Tunes short *What's Opera, Doc?*, such as when Nelson wears a duck costume while Turturro and Smith pose as duck hunters.

Speaking of ducks, *Brain Donors* opens with an extensive Will Vinton sequence which, while well-done, feels a bit out of place. The most curious aspect of this animation is the frequent appearance of a duck, which might have made more sense if the film had kept the original title of *Lame Ducks*. Then again, neither title suits the film well, and its initial title recalls *Duck Soup* for a picture that mostly apes *A Night at the Opera*. And yet, that opening sequence might have had the strongest moment of association to the Marx Brothers for me, as it had me already asking, "Why a duck?"

Original version posted on 11/18/2024

Canadian Bacon (1995)

I have only vacationed in Canada once, taking a brief road trip to Toronto by way of Windsor. We had apparently picked the wrong time to do this, with the country's relations with the US at an ebb as result of a trade dispute. Having always heard how polite Canucks are, I was stunned by how rude everybody was to us. Some people went out of their way to be rude, which I rarely encounter, even here in the colonies. I started wondering if I had somehow driven to France.

At least the states hadn't started an all-out war on the great white north, which is what drives the plot of 1995 comedy *Canadian Bacon*. Alan Alda is a peace-loving US president whose policies have resulted in the closure of a arms manufacturer that employs most of the residents of Niagara Falls. Having run out of enemies, he and his cabinet decide to stage a phony war with Canada just to give the economy and Alda's poll numbers a boost. So glad this movie is satire, as the US would *never* invade a country under false pretenses. *cough*

Things are going well for the bogus war except for the heroics of the Niagara Falls sheriff, played by John Candy in his last role. The economy in his town is so bad that he and his deputy (played by Rhea Perlman in one of the few times I have seen her without husband Danny Devito) try to fish the corpses of jumpers out of the water. They get $50 a corpse, but only $25 if they successfully discourage a potential suicide, so they are always at the base of the falls' observation platform yelling, "JUMP! JUMP!"

In the beginning, we see one such attempted suicide, in an inspired performance from Kevin J. O'Connor. This is an actor that tends to play unbalanced personalities. Here, he reminded me of Bill the Cat from the comic strip *Bloom County*, though I'd be hard-pressed to explain why. We first see him trying to drive his sad little car off the observation deck of the falls, except parts keep falling out of it along the way. The front bumper barely nudges the railing as it coasts to a stop. The determined O'Connor had wrapped himself up in duct tape, so he wriggles out of the car and tries to jump the railing, only for a loose end of tape to get caught on it, leaving him suspended like a human yo-yo.

O'Connor is a friend of Candy and Perlman so, together with Bill Nunn, they band together to fight the imagined Canadian menace. First, they accidentally foil the destruction of the power plant, as attempted by US operatives posing as a Canuck strike force. Next, they sneak across the water to that other country to commit the highest offense of that land: littering. They manage to escape while two Mounties civilly discuss whether the warning one of them had given was grammatically correct. Our heroes fail to notice they left Perlman behind, where she will embark on a second storyline where she essentially turns into Rambo and becomes obsessed with destroying the CN Tower.

Worried the fake war with Canada might escalate into a real one, the US military tries to stop these assorted nutjobs from causing further damage. One bit I liked involves the Omega Force, which appears to be the country's most elite fighting squad. I laughed hard when one of the White House staffers points out Geneva Convention forbids the Omega Force from being used against Caucasians.

It is moments like that which show this is a film by Michael Moore. This movie is worth seeing not just because it is John Candy's last role, but because it is Moore's only non-documentary film. Many of his sensibilities are present, though the humor is far gentler than that in his other works.

Much of the humor is at the expense of the US, though always in contrast to Canada. There's this exchange when Candy and company invade the country: "Are you sure we're in Canada?" "Do you smell anything? No? Then we're in Canada!". Then there's their effortless ability to overtake a power station there: "There's not a locked door in the whole country."

Some very welcome cameos round out the experience. Steven Wright appears as a Mountie chief in the laconic style for which he's known. Dan Ackroyd has a great bit as a motorcycle cop who pulls over a vehicle covered in anti-Canadian slogans and makes Candy add French translations to them, so as to observe the country's dual-language regulations.

Canadian Bacon deserves to have a larger audience than it has so far. I wouldn't say it warrants a cult following, but it is much funnier than its reputation (or lack thereof) would have me believe.

Original version posted on 7/15/2023

Cluny Brown (1946)

My dad was a plumber, so one might think I would have a greater affinity for that work than I do. Unfortunately, I dread the possibility of any issues arising which require such skills and loathe having to use them.

Jennifer Jones, as the titular character in Ernst Lubitsch's 1946 screwball comedy *Cluny Brown*, obviously enjoys plumbing far more than I could ever hope to. I think she enjoys it more than anybody in the history of the trade, as she is blissed-out with a post-coital glow after unclogging a drain. Unfortunately for her, a woman having a passion for such manual labor was greatly frowned upon in 1938's London.

We first see Jones plumbing at the apartment of Reginald Gardner. He had tried to summon plumber Billy Bevan on a Sunday to clear his blocked kitchen sink, as guests for a cocktail party were arriving shortly. The belligerent plumber refuses, unaware his enthusiastic niece will go instead.

Gardner is appalled when she arrives, and still so even after she successfully dispels the clog. Charles Boyer, as a visitor to the man's apartment, is very intrigued by this unusual plumber who has such enthusiasm. He also obviously enjoyed watching her roll down her stockings before getting down to work.

Her uncle is far less thrilled about what has happened, appearing later at Gardner's apartment to find her lying down on a sofa, completely relaxed and stretched out in a manner suggesting she had cleaned out a different type of pipe altogether. Then he's even more upset when he learns the only service she supplied was of the plumbing trade. He's also likely feeling a bit of umbrage regarding the martini she had in celebration afterwards.

And so, he sends her off to be a parlor maid at the estate of the wealthy and titled Reginald Owen and Margaret Bannerman and their son Peter Lawford. It is there, and in the nearby town, the various characters converge and have a great many strange and hilarious misunderstandings of the type for which director Ernst Lubitsch was justifiably famous.

Lawford, a young idealist alarmed by the rise of the Nazis in Germany, has invited Boyer's exiled Czech professor to stay with them. A distraction for Lawford's attentions is wealthy socialite Helen Walker, who has been playing with his heart, as well as those of other men. I think every male character aside from the butler comments upon how well she sits a horse, which made me wonder if that is really a euphemism for another activity they can imagine wherein she straddles something else.

The other romance is a repressed attraction between Boyer and Jones. The only reason for their inability to express their feelings is to keep the plot going. With an apparent lack of interest from Boyer, she responds positively to the affections of town pharmacist (Richard Haydn). His is a completely repulsive character, with an even worse mother (Una O'Connor). Haydn likes to keep customers waiting, which sets up a great gag where Boyer opens the shop door each time he walks by, summoning the increasingly outraged pharmacist to find a store empty of customers. I could watch an entire film of just this gag repeated ad nauseum.

Typical of comedies, and the screwball sub-genre in particular, reaction shots get the majority of the biggest laughs here. It helps that, the straighter the straight man or woman, the funnier those become. And the heads of the household (Sara Allgood and Ernest Cossart) are so stiff-backed as to be two Margaret Dumonts, the "wealthy dowager" archetype so perfectly realized in the Marx Brothers films. The very best scene has them overhearing Jones talking to Boyer after he has left her room, something which is already a compromising situation. Just imagine how they react to this without any other context: "I can't thank you enough. I feel so much better. How lucky we met in that flat. I wish I were back there right now. I wish I could roll up my sleeves and roll down my stockings and loosen the joint. Just bang, bang, bang."

Also typical of Lubitsch films, the dialogue is consistently razor-sharp and often hilarious. Even relatively minor characters, such as Walker's droll social butterfly, get choice lines, such as her intentional obliviousness at Lawford's claim they had a huge fight the prior evening: "If we ever do have a row, tell me about it, so we can have a long chat about it." O'Connor's character also has perfect dialogue, even if she never says a word. Instead, the pharmacist's mother communicates a great deal using just grunts, huffs and snorts.

The performances are very solid all around. Jones seems to have an endless supply of energy throughout the runtime, and her joy is infectious. One odd element of her character is her enthusiasm for everything and not just plumbing. How she could be intrigued by Haydn's mundane interests, such as playing the harmonium, is beyond me. Boyer has never been funnier, and it is enjoyable to see him play something a bit different from his usual schtick, the kind of thing for which he was the inspiration for Pepe Le Pew. Peter Lawford appears to be the least confident of the cast, but he is awfully young here. I can't help but wonder how he eventually became a member of Sinatra's Rat Pack. At least he has a genuine British accent, whereas Jones doesn't have one at all. On the other hand, it is just as well the Tulsa-born Jones didn't attempt one.

I had a great time watching *Cluny Brown*, though it is not even among my top favorites of the director's oeuvre. That said, I can't imagine anybody seeing this and not laughing at least once. There is a recurring line here, a shared joke between Boyer and Jones about feeding squirrels to the nuts instead of nuts to the squirrels. If somebody doesn't like this movie then I'd say nuts to them.

Original version posted on 12/26/2024

The Court Jester (1955)

Pushing yourself outside your comfort zone can be beneficial. I have always said how much I hate musicals. But, the more I thought about it, I realized I not only liked some movies with numerous musical sequences (i.e. the Marx Brothers' Universal films) but I even liked some musical numbers, such as "On The Atchison, Topeka And The Santa Fe" from *The Harvey Girls*.

With that, I went into 1955's *The Court Jester* fully knowing it was a musical comedy. What I didn't expect was action, intrigue and wildly inventive wordplay. This is a very smart movie full of energy and stylized chaos. Once again, like the Marx Brothers.

The gleeful subversion starts with the opening credits sequence, where Danny Kaye is dressed in traditional jester garb. He is on a stage and it is obvious he is going to be addressing the audience directly. These are not promising signs. That said, once the credits really begin, the lyrics to the title song comment on the various job titles and names on the screen, as well as the general absurdity of its premise. Kaye even gets nudged around the screen by blocks of text, with one pushing him flat to the ground as it flies in. This does a good job of establishing a tone of irreverence.

Once the main plot is underway, we quickly establish the various gears which will drive a complex plot that is deceptively simple in appearance. *The Court Jester* makes it effortless to follow the intertwined threads of a king worried about an heir to the throne who has escaped the king's campaign of infanticide (shades of Moses—odd for a such a light-hearted film), the rebellious Black Fox (shades of Robin Hood) who has an army of bandits to protect the prodigal infant, the theatrical clown (Kaye) who aspires to fight in the rebel army, the female captain of the guard (Glynis Johns) of the Fox's army going undercover to become the king's right-hand wench (not my word choice, folks), the plotting of the king's duplicitous henchman (Basil Rathbone, an expert swordsman in real life), and the attempts of the king's daughter (Angela Lansbury!) to avoid an arranged marriage to Robert Middleton. Whew!

Humor is in the elbow of the beholder [the section about comedies]

The main plotline kicks into gear when the Black Fox devises a plan which requires getting one of their people inside the castle in order to safely put the infant on the throne. Serendipitously, the rogue army encounters the new court jester en route to the castle. David Carradine makes a brief appearance as that jester, and I have to admit I was disappointed we never see the Wolfman clowning it up for the king.

Once Kaye is in place as a bogus jester, he is hypnotized by Lansbury's handmaiden (or whatever they were called in ye olde make-believe medieval times). Her only objective was to make him fall in love with Lansbury but, unwittingly, she also fills him with unearned confidence that makes him believe he is an expert swordsman and general all-around badass. It only takes a snap of the fingers to toggle the transition from man to mouse and back again, leaving a dumbfounded Kaye in the middle of seducing the king's daughter or embroiled in political subterfuge, but without any idea how he got there. It's a great conceit, used frequently, and always to good effect.

One of the best recurring bits is some outlandishly convoluted wordplay. Let's see if I can remember the most famous example correctly: "the poison pill is in the vessel with the pestle, but the chalice from the palace is the brew that is true". My tongue got tied just trying to remember that as I was typing it.

I am generally less inclined to appreciate choreography than I am a musical number, but I was actually impressed by some of it here. To be honest, it is largely atypical of what I have come to expect from musicals and is instead more like fight choreography. One astonishing sequence has Kaye, disguised as the Black Fox, replicating into doubles, triples and quadruples of himself. Then one of the four of him (wow—that was a strange thing to write) cuts the other three in half with one horizontal sweep of a sword, revealing what appeared to be three full-height masked doppelgangers are actually six midgets. It is a stunning effect, and even more impressive when one considers no CGI could have been used.

I have never seen Kaye in a movie before and I was greatly impressed. The rest of the cast is solid as well, though I don't feel like singling out all of them here. One person I will call out is Angela Lansbury who, as the king's daughter, is dependable as ever. But even though she was roughly the right age for this character, it is still always jarring to see her when she was young. I suspect that, even if she never went on to star on *Murder She Wrote* in her most famous role, it still would be impossible to see her at an early age and not picture her as a senior citizen. Something always seemed grandmotherly about her. Heck, she was cast as Laurence Harvey's mother in *The Manchurian Candidate* when she was only *three years* his elder, yet nobody blinked an eye.

I highly recommend *The Court Jester* and I know I will watch it again at some point. I doubt I can resist the allure of a movie with lines like "A jester unemployed is nobody's fool".

Original version posted on 1/7/2023

Fatal Instinct (1993)

The early 90's were a frustrating time to be in your late teens. As if the 80's weren't oversexed enough with all those horny comedies, you had the 90's ramping things up to a fever pitch with the epidemic of erotic thrillers that were the rage at the time.

The genre was ripe for the kind of parody Mel Brooks or Abrahams and the Zuckers might do. Instead, former Brooks co-performer Carl Reiner helms 1993's *Fatal Instinct*, a work which may not reach the heights of the best material of those other filmmakers, but which I still found to have many laugh-out-loud moments.

Many films of the era are skewered, most notably *Basic Instinct* and *Fatal Attraction,* hence the portmanteau comprising the title. Many of the jokes either reference films I haven't seen or take potshots at some of the genre's conventions. Many films of the first era of noir (or at least their trappings) are also fair game, such as a character saying, "That's the postman. He always rings twice."—not that I found that line particularly funny.

Far better is a recurring gag where Sean Young, as an obvious surrogate for Sharon Stone, keeps getting things stuck to the soles of her stilettos. Over the course of the film, these items will include a gum wrapper, the empty bag of some sort of junk food, toilet paper, a pop can and a car floormat. I was watching closely for the next of those moments, hoping an impossibly great number of exceptionally large objects would be stuck to the underside of those shoes, as if this was the game *Katamari Damacy.*

Young does very well with this material. I keep forgetting how good she is in comedies, especially parodies. How could I forget how great she was in *Young Doctors in Love?* It is interesting how she always comes across as intelligent, but she never seems to be above the material. I like to think she has a healthy sense of humor about herself.

The object of her affection is Armand Assante, in the Michael Douglas role. I'm not sure I have seen him in anything previously, but he fares pretty well here. He takes the same approach Leslie Neilsen did in films like *The Naked Gun,* by playing the character completely straight. In what I thought was a clever innovation, Assante plays a cop…who is *also* a defense attorney.

Humor is in the elbow of the beholder [the section about comedies]

Young is joined by another femme fatale in this film, with Kate Nelligan playing Assante's wife. She's cheating on him with Christopher McDonald, a mechanic who has spent weeks on end unsuccessfully repairing her car at their house. I don't know what world this takes place in, but I want to live in a place where mechanics do house calls.

Sherilynn Fenn is the third female lead (and, let's face it, the types of films parodied here are all about the ladies) as Assante's excessively loyal secretary. I still have a huge crush on Fenn just from her being on *Twin Peaks* but…ugh…as much as I hate to say it, much of her performance here is too self-aware. I didn't believe her much, and that is in a role where the character is meant to be a shallow stereotype.

Still, she's pretty funny in some moments as the straight woman where everything else around her is bizarre. Probably the best bit she is in is a montage of trying on hats, each of which is more insane than the last, until she finally settles on a helmet flanked by beer cans and the large letters on it proclaiming her to be a "BEER BIMBO". Also in that scene is James Remar in a riff on the Mitchum/DeNiro character from the *Cape Fear* of your choice. He may be watching from a distance inside the store, but he's soon swept into the spirit of the thing and trying on a succession of frilly chapeaus. What I found strange is Van Morrison's "Brown-Eyed Girl" plays under the scene, though Fenn has blue eyes.

Something I learned after the fact is the original title of the picture was to be *Triple Indemnity*, which shows the writer has a decent knowledge of noir. The insurance policy bit here made me smile. For it to pay off, Assante must be shot while on a northbound train, and drown in a freshwater stream.

Of course, if you're going to primarily parody erotic thrillers of the time, it is mandatory you have ridiculously convoluted sex scenes. There's only one, but it is a doozy, as Young and Assante somehow couple while rolling down a flight of stairs, and then packed together in a normal household refrigerator. At one point, they are in the missionary position, except Young is balancing plates spinning on the ends of sticks in each hand, and even one somehow supported by a foot.

Some equally strange moments send up smoking, a staple of noirs of both eras. When we see a cigarette pack, the brands are Black Lung Lights or Fatal 100's. There's a really bizarre scene with Nelligan and McDonald have a post-coital smoke and neither has their cigarette lit. McDonald even proceeds to "blow" non-existent smoke rings. I didn't find it funny, but I can honestly say that's another thing I've never seen before.

And there is still more here I have never seen before. Off the top of my head, there's the criminal who is always wearing a stocking mask, including while trying to eat a snow cone or chew gum. In court, his wife and kids are also similarly masked. There's a car chase involving bumper cars, one of which turns out to have a functioning airbag built in. A clandestine conversation in Yiddish in a public park is understood by the man on the bench across from the speakers, as he has been reading the subtitles. There's a car with a working household ceiling fan in it. There's a fairly well-done animatronic skunk riding a roller coaster with Sean Young.

Fatal Instinct was pummeled by critics at the time, and I think unfairly so. Alas, it isn't exactly comedy gold either. It throws so much on the screen that I don't see how anybody can't find at least one thing to laugh at. As for myself, I laughed a great deal, though I realized there were far more misses than hits. All that said, I gotta like a movie that repeatedly has saxophone on the soundtrack, only for it to be revealed Clarence Clemmons is playing the instrument nearby. At times, it is a smart-dumb film and, at other times, merely dumb-dumb. I suspect a statement made by Assante could be applied to film overall: "I don't look as dumb as I am."

Original version posted on 7/27/2024

The Galloping Major (1951)

I'm not up to it anymore, but I have camped out on sidewalks overnight for many of the past years' Record Store Days. In 1951's *The Galloping Major*, Basil Radford is much older than I am now, and yet he should have camped out overnight at a horse auction that is essential to the plot. Instead, newspaper reporters intent on interviewing him inadvertently prevent him from getting there in time, which leads to him mistakenly buying the wrong horse.

The problem is he hasn't just likely wasted his own money. He obtained the money by selling shares in the horse to the community.

Father's Folly, the horse which is purchased mistakenly, is skittish and hard to control. He is especially startled when aircraft fly overhead, prompting him to jump a barricade. The owners were about to sell him, until the jockey convinces them they have a potential Grand National winner on their hands. Instead of a runner, they unintentionally acquired a jumper.

One unexpected party who becomes a key figure in this endeavor is Hugh Griffith as a bill collector who we first see ready to repossess all of Radford's property. They bond over horses— Radford, because he loves the animals, and Griffith, because he loves a flutter. And, by using the word "flutter", I realize I have seen way too many British films.

Anywho, I like how Radford invites the other man to stay with his family and he's just there for the rest of the film. I also like how flustered Griffith gets when he is made treasurer of the group who owns the horse, stammering, "I'd be very honored to have the honor to be honored in this way…"

A young Janette Scott is Radford's daughter and she is given quite a bit to do here. It is she who provides the inspiration for selling shares in a racehorse, following the model of a syndicate she is in with some other girls. They collectively own a bicycle, with each getting it for one month. I hope for her sake that's a small group, lest she see that bicycle only every so many years.

Scott was a confident actor even at that young age. If there is a misstep with her character, it is her tendency to misspell things, and those errors are 2 cute by haf: "plaice" instead of "place" and "ergent" for "urgent". Her lines, at least, are far more intelligent than the mind that would write in such a way. I found it especially amusing when she rages against the tortures she is subjected to at the beauty parlor: "I wish I could be ugly and be a man and drive a bus." Fortunately for the UK movie industry, she would instead grow up to be an attractive and accomplished actress.

The horse is put to good use here. Its owners can't afford to train him in a real facility, so a public park is put to use for that purpose. Scott fails to properly secure the stable the night before the Grand National, leading to the horse going on a walking tour of the town. I swear he showed a genuine curiosity in some of these moments, like he was really taking in the sights.

He will eventually wander onto a film studio's property, and I hoped we would have a scene not unlike the mayhem created by Pee-Wee Herman on the Warners' lot in *Pee-Wee's Big Adventure*. Alas, nothing as crazy as that happens, though he does get airbrushed to a different color as he was not the horse one film director was expecting.

The third act is all fast-paced mayhem, and it earns it. Various parties have to find the horse, convince the studio to surrender it and then get it to Liverpool in time for the race. Although largely rear-projection and stock footage, the event is quite exciting. The finale of it is quite a surprise, with moments that had me laughing harder than at any other point during the runtime.

The Galloping Major is rather a slight film, even for this kind of thing. It isn't a product of Ealing Studios, but fans of their output will find much here to be in a similar vein. I know I only laughed a few times, but my pained facial muscles tell me I must have smiled throughout my viewing of it.

Original version posted on 3/17/2024

Ghostbusters (2016)

Is it possible to write anything resembling an objective critique of the 2016 reboot of *Ghostbusters*? For one thing, it isn't even sure what its name is, with the single-word title in an isolated credit towards the beginning, while the end credits declare its full title to be *Ghostbusters: Answer the Call*. Both titles are used in seemingly interchangeable ways on the case of the blu-ray disc.

I didn't bother watching the film until seven years after it was released. The only reason I had not until then was a near total disinterest in anything related to the series aside from the first film. I only watched *Ghostbusters: Afterlife* to prepare to see *Ghostbusters: Frozen Empire*, and I only was seeing the latter because my wife and I were taking my Ghostbusters mega-fan brother-in-law to see it.

Those two more recent films seem to be part of a concerted effort to purge the 2016 film from the public consciousness. Admittedly, the film was a minor financial success in its original run, but the most enduring aspect of its legacy is how thoroughly it polarized audiences.

There was a curious amount of outrage from overwhelmingly male fans over this reboot, seemingly all of which concerned the idea of four women as the leads. Then again, I was confused as to why the reboot took that particular tack. Simply doing a gender flip feels like a lazy attempt at reinvention, not to mention a tad patronizing. But then, if one doesn't slavishly praise the movie, there are many people who get defensive, as if any criticism leveled towards it must be due to that gender-flip and, by extension of that, an attack on women in general.

So, back to my original point, how does one set aside the drama outside the film so that it may be scrutinized entirely on its own merits? Probably the first thing that helps me in this effort is that, aside from the 1984 original, I completely give rats ass about this property.

Now then, cutting directly to the chase: is it any good? My opinion is that only the original release is superior.

One way it is better than *Ghostbusters II* is it actually takes the story in fresh directions. And it is better than either of the subsequent sequels in that it isn't burdened by the expectations of the massive glut of fan service which hobbled those films. Don't even get me started on the two different animated series or the video games…

What I found odd about my enjoyment of this feature is I have seen three of the leads in other films before and never found them to be especially funny. Of those, I have found Kristen Wiig to fare best in other works because she has the most versatility. She's wisely cast here as the straight woman (and I'm not talking about sexuality, thank you very much) to Melissa McCarthy and Kate McKinnon. The latter is given way too much latitude to literally bounce all over the place, though I still laughed hard at some of her character's more audacious moments. There was a bit, however, where she dances to DeBarge's "Rhythm of the Night" which, if I'm being tactful, I can only say I endured.

Go figure, the film's secret weapon is a Black woman, Leslie Jones, not unlike how the original's actual best performance is delivered by its sole Black actor, Ernie Hudson. Admittedly, her character (like Hudson's, honestly) is largely written to be not specific to any race. And yet, one of the biggest laughs this film got from me is when she tries stagediving at a heavy metal show and she hits the floor hard when the audience members part like the Red Sea. "I don't know if that was a race thing or a lady thing, but I'm mad as hell right now." Just one more line I loved from this character: when Jones is asked if she knows what something unusual she's seen is called: "If I knew what it was called, I wouldn't say it was a weird staticky thing."

In fact, not only is the dialogue of that character largely not race-specific, the overwhelming majority of the lines of any character are not gender-specific. So, you have a film whose main gimmick is the previously male leads are all now female, but those characters could have easily been performed by men after only a few edits (the script, that is, and not the men). The only things that came to mind that would be sacrificed are a couple of gross gags involving the female body, and I wouldn't have missed those if they had been removed.

Even if the cast had been kept male, you could probably even keep Chris Hemsworth as their exceptionally dim-witted receptionist. Wiig seems to be the only one interested in him romantically (which leads to some pretty cute moments of her crushing on him, actually). So, if she had been male, then we could have had the first gay Ghostbuster and guess how well *that* would have gone over with the crowd that was outraged over the casting.

Humor is in the elbow of the beholder [the section about comedies]

His character is more stupid than humanly possible while still being able to eat, dress himself and get around the city without assistance. The jokes concerning his stupidity are completely unbelievable, though often hilarious. My favorite moment was when he shows some proposed logos he has created for this enterprise. One is of a hot dog and, below it, a house. Hemsworth explains a ghost is holding the hot dog, because how else would the food be floating in the air? I smiled just writing that line in this piece.

There are two versions of the film on the disc I watched and so I opted for the longer cut. It is definitely too long, though I suspect much of what I enjoyed so much is only in this extended version. I also suspect the theatrical version would feel just as long, but I don't intend to find out for certain. When I inevitably watch this again, it will be the extended cut I will be revisiting.

One curious aspect of the blu-ray presentation I assume is true of both versions is some of the effects extend into the mattes above and below the widescreen image. This daft and pointless move took me out of the film as immediately and thoroughly as any fourth-wall break, and it is a gimmick I hope to never see repeated.

In the end, the women of 2016's *Ghostbusters* (or whatever you intend to call it) made a highly entertaining film, much more so than either of the two course-corrections that followed it. Alas, they also made a movie that has many of the worst traits of the series and the genre in general: it is too long, too loud, and has a final battle that wears down the viewer until they are apathetic. So, in one way, a weird kind of equality has been achieved, though one I don't think should necessarily be celebrated. And yet, this much-maligned film manages to one-up many of its peers.

Original version posted on 5/22/2024

Hey There, It's Yogi Bear (1964)

When I was a kid, I had a yellow teddy bear named Boo-Boo. I'm not sure why I named it that, as I don't remember ever watching *Yogi Bear*, where Boo-Boo was the sidekick to the titular character. Still, I was curious when Warner Archive released a disc of 1964 movie *Hey There, It's Yogi Bear*. I thought watching it might jog some memories.

Look, can I go ahead and mention something that bothers me about this feature? It's that title. It's just so strangely bland. It's why *Triumph of the Will* isn't titled *Hey There, It's Hitler!*

I wondered how a movie could be made with Yogi as the main character for 90 minutes. In 2010, he became fully realized via CGI in *Yogi Bear*. I don't know what circumstances could force me to see that movie, but I believe I can accurately gauge its quality, regardless.

Instead, this 1964 film is likely the best that could be done with this character and his few shticks. The humor is of the kind I think most people familiar with Hanna Barbera cartoons will expect. I don't recall even chuckling once, but I did smile quite a bit. Anybody who watches this now will be doing so for the nostalgia factor and not because they think it's going to be gut-bustingly hilarious.

Tellingly, the three act structure of this feels like three half-hour episodes strung together. There are the typical shenanigans in Jellystone National Park, then there's an escape from a low-rent circus, before everything ends in a big finale in the city.

In that first act, spring has arrived and the bears are coming out of hibernation. This has definitely awakened something in Cindy Bear, who decides she is going to get her freak on, and Yogi will be the bear for the job. Yogi, on the other hand, demonstrates that fear of commitment all males of that era seemed to have in movies and on TV. Boo-Boo is nothing more that the straight man to Yogi's antics.

Those antics, as always, are centered around food. Yogi's attempts to acquire this include shooting an arrow through a restaurant, accumulating items on it along the way, until it lodges into a tree on the opposite side. As Yogi says of the food-laden arrow: "Shish-ka-Boo, Bob-Bob! I mean, shish-ka-bob, Boo-Boo!" That line is a fair example of the humor here.

The impetus for the characters leaving the park is a ruse Yogi pulls when he suddenly finds himself slated to go to the San Diego Zoo, and he instead deceives another bear into putting the tag around his own neck. The tag reads, "one bear destination San Diego Zoo", and I spent a weird amount of time pondering that. If somebody sees the tag, wouldn't it be obvious the wearer is a bear or not? And why "one bear"? If they have two bears, do they put one of these tags on each, or somehow put a necklace around the necks of both, with a single tag reading, "two bears"?

I likely found myself musing upon such petty things because there isn't much that happens here. Technically, there is continual action, but it isn't for much of a purpose.

Consider the second act, where Cindy, thinking Yogi was sent to the zoo, tries to go there as well, only to be sent to the St. Louis Zoo. She escapes the train but is captured by a traveling circus and forced to become their main (only?) attraction. Yogi tries, and fails, to rescue her. In the end, Boo-Boo saves them both.

Somehow, the circus seems an appropriate setting for any Hanna Barbera cartoon. The outfit here, Chizzling Brothers, is on its last legs, which makes it like almost any other circus I think of. Yeah, there's Cirque de Soleil nowadays, but I'm thinking of the old-school kind that always felt slightly dangerous because you could tell how shady these things were.

Anyway, that second act felt like the most pointless element in the movie because it is only a set up for the inevitable rescue to happen. Unlike the plotless antics of the first act, how this is going to end is such a foregone conclusion that one might as well advance a few chapters to after they've successfully escaped. What, did you really think they were going to become bear-skin rugs or something?

The trio is pursued by a sheriff through the rural countryside and there are some amusing moments in that. I especially liked the tricks Yogi pulls to evade hound dogs. Still, I could have done without the scene where they float down a river on a barn door (don't ask) and imagine they're on a gondola in Venice.

That bizarre setup is merely the ruse to shoehorn in another song. This time, it's the deeply terrible "Ven-E, Ven-O, Ven-A". James Darren sings this and, although I don't know who that is, Boo-Boo tells the singing Yogi, "Hey, you sound just like James Darren!" I wonder if Mr. Darren was ever a big cheese, but I'm too lazy to find out.

The other songs in the film are better than that, but nothing threatens to become an earworm. The title song was written by David Gates, presumably the same guy who went on to front 70s soft-rock behemoth Bread.

Most viewers are probably curious first and foremost about the quality of the animation. It is definitely better than what one would expect from the studio's television fare, but it doesn't exactly have the visual splendor of Disney in its best years, either. Backgrounds are especially detailed in some scenes, though I wouldn't say masterfully. Myself, I would have been happier with backgrounds that were more along the lines of the abstractions of mid-century animation. One imagines what UPA would have done if they had produced the film.

The only extra on the disc is an episode of the TV show. In it, it's Yogi's birthday and preparations are being made for a surprise event for him to be broadcast live on television. It's all just an excuse to have related characters from other Hanna Barbara cartoons appear as guests, and only to promote their own shows. I didn't find much of merit in this, though it was interesting to see in contrast to the film. Also, I was surprised one of the guests wasn't Muttley, as the circus in the movie has a dog with a similarly wheezy laugh.

Hey There, It's Mahatma Gandhi...I mean, *Yogi Bear*, is a slight entertainment. I honestly can't imagine any children today warming to it. It exists purely for nostalgia, and I am so grateful to Warner Archive for making such films available on disc. I doubt such features would ever appear on blu-ray otherwise and, typical of their work, they do the usual fantastic job of remastering the video and audio.

Original version posted on 12/25/2023

Hobson's Choice (1954)

Among the more famous of the many renown album covers in Bob Dylan's catalog is that of *The Freewheelin' Bob Dylan*. It shows Dylan and a woman talking towards the camera, her arm looped through his and hugging it tight. There's a huge, genuine smile on her face. I challenge any guy who has seen that, regardless of their preferences, and not wanted the moment the photo captures. That is the feeling throughout 1954's astonishing comedy *Hobson's Choice*, though my analogy might need the genders reversed.

This is a film set in the era of Dickens, though it felt rather outside of any specific timeframe, aside from sometime in the late 19th century. That there are only a few horse-drawn carriages shown goes some ways to generating that feeling of timelessness. Still, it is a time when shops would have a giant symbol of their wares hanging outside for the benefit of those who can't read.

It was also a time when women had few options. Brenda de Banzie is a woman with a strong mind for business, being the true brains behind father Charles Laughton's shoe shop. Her two younger sisters (Prunella Scales and Daphne Anderson) work alongside her on the display floor. All three long to marry, but Laughton knows de Banzie is too important to his store to let her go. As for the other two, their prospects are jeopardized by him being too cheap to pay dowries.

John Mills is the illiterate shoemaker working in the basement below, creating the actual product. After a wealthy woman (Helen Haye) seeks him out specifically for the quality of his craftsmanship, de Banzie sees an opportunity. She decides Mills is going to marry her and they will start their own shop together courtesy of a loan she's sure they can obtain from Haye. As she puts it to him, "You're a business idea in the shape of a man."

It is uncertain which prospect Mills is more terrified by: the wrath of Laughton when he ends his employment or the prospect of marriage. In the brief period of wooing before the nuptial, the two sit on a park bench facing a polluted river, which isn't a great portent. He tells her he can't marry because he does not love her. She says that's OK, because she has enough love for both of them.

Humor is in the elbow of the beholder [the section about comedies]

There's also the small obstacle of his current courtship of Dorothy Gordon, the daughter of his landlady (Madge Brindley) in a very poor section of town. De Banzie goes there to explain the change of plans, which does not go over well. I love how, while Mills is standing outside and hearing the confrontation, he sees a Salvation Army band marching towards him holding aloft a banner reading "BEWARE THE WRATH TO COME". Then, in a beautiful moment, we watch Mills's face as he feels a newfound pride and strength resulting from the high praises sung by his new fiancée. As they walk away afterwards, she tells him he will never have to go back there again, and his gradual smile is truly heartwarming to see.

Still, there is Laughton to contend with, though he is doing a stellar job handicapping himself through his addiction to drink. He holds court with his cronies each day at a pub named Moonrakers. I only learned after the fact that is slang for "fool", which is appropriate. It also foreshadows a great solo scene for Laughton, where he tries to catch the moon's reflection in various puddles in the street. With his soft, fleshy features, he's like a drunken toddler as he stumbles around.

What's interesting is he is top-billed though he is far from the star of this feature. Mills is second-billed and, though he has far more screen time than the other actor, de Banzie is the undisputed top attraction. Her performance is brilliant, and that is among a very stacked cast. There's not a miscast performer, and every characterization is pitch perfect. Also notable is a very young Scales, whom I know best as Sybil in *Fawlty Towers*. It is interesting how she already has many of the same mannerisms and expressions she would use later in that legendary sitcom.

Nothing about this film is flashy, but it is brilliant, nonetheless, and it feels as if it was no effort to make. Every shot and transition uses only whatever composition or technique is appropriate. Laughton's signature "moon chase" scene has gorgeous photography, which seems odd to say of a cobblestone street which is an obvious set. A great transition occurs after the wedding of de Banzie and Mills, where the couple is showered with flower petals, and a crossfade seems to impossibly follow that same shower of petals across town to their basement apartment.

Similarly, the script is perfect and every line crackles with electricity. And yet, curiously, this isn't a very quotable film. I can't imagine dropping any lines from it in conversation. This isn't *This Is Spinal Tap* or *Withnail & I.* Of course, unlike those films, nobody would recognize the source if I did.

I wish instead I could somehow quote subtle facial expressions, because that is where *Hobson's Choice* especially shines. One of the great treasures of cinema are the many instances of Mills gradually realizing he has the potential to be something far beyond his dreams, and it is all because of his new bride. And then there's the look she gives him when he stands up to even her. Her moist eyes as she steps up to him are full of pride, and I bet that guy felt like Dylan on the cover of that album.

Original version posted on 11/11/2024

Ladies Who Do (1963)

In 2012, some of the confetti used in the Macy's Thanksgiving Day parade was discovered to be shredded internal files of the Nassau County Police Department. Intact strips of paper included names, address, phone numbers and social security numbers of officers, including some who were working undercover.

While we know the importance of internal documents today, I was stunned to see this used as the main plot device of a movie from 1963. In *Ladies Who Do*, four cleaning women discover the value of documents recovered from trash cans in the offices they clean. They use this information to their financial advantage in an attempt to save their neighborhood from demolition.

Peggy Mount is the leader of the charwomen, to use the British parlance. Nobody notices her pocketing a barely-smoked cigar from one of the bins. She wraps it for safekeeping in a random scrap of paper and gifts this to one of her residential customers, Robert Morley. He has a knowledge of business and finance, but I suspect he fell on hard times because of a gambling addiction and perhaps even the application of some unorthodox accounting practices.

That random bit of paper enclosing the cigar gives him the insider knowledge to make a killing on a stock transaction. This gives him the idea of working together with Mount and other chars to get more such data from trash. Although this alone is illegal, there are still certain moral bounds to the operation, with Mount insisting only that which has been trashed can be used.

I noticed she still takes some liberties with her own restrictions, eventually listening to an answering machine recording. She also tries reading info on Harry J. Corbett's blotter. One of the best gags in the film has her supervisor entering the room at that time, and Mount improvising by pretending to use this large pad to smash a fly against a mirror.

Corbett is the villain of this piece, the developer who wants to demolish the neighborhood of her and her friends. I like how the script even affords him some nuance, as he tells Mount of his humble origins as the son of a char. Still, his familiarity with their class and their struggles does not provide the insight for him to understand the offense they take at his offer of alternative accommodation.

This is a hilarious and thoughtful movie that touches on many heavy themes, but never with a heavy hand. There's the class struggle between the working-class cleaning women vs. their upper-class superiors. There's women vs. men. There's rampant capitalism vs. human needs. There's even one of my favorite staples of film: the natural leader who emerges unexpectedly.

Ladies Who Do juggles so many themes, characters and plot elements, yet watching it is as easy as breathing. And it should be taken as a warning, even today, that what you think of as disposable, whether corporate information or your lowest-paid workers, might just be your undoing if not treated properly. Just ask the Nassau County Police Department.

Original version posted on 1/28/2023

The Love God? (1969)

1969's *The Love God?* is the only one of the five films on Shout Factory's Don Knotts collection that is rated higher than a G. I was very surprised to see it is rated PG-13. Now, having watched it, I'm even more surprised it is rated higher than a PG. Typical of the other films in this collection, this is sitcom-level humor. But even the strongest of this material (even the word "strong" is quite an overstatement) is pitched at the level of such shows roughly a decade later. It's no surprise Knotts played a character on *Three's Company*, because this material would have fit in there.

This time, he's the publisher of the very unpopular *Peacock Magazine*, which is about birds of the feathered variety. He's such a fan of our avian friends that he has the ability to imitate the calls of a great many kinds of them. We first see him doing this accompanied by music at a fundraiser, ending his performance with a hilariously enthusiastic impersonation of an eagle, complete with wild arm flapping. There will also be a hilarious callback to this bit towards the end of the film.

That fundraiser generates $47,000 shy of what it will take save the publication. Swooping in to supposedly save the day is Edmund O'Brien, publisher of girly mag *Nude & Naughty*, that seems to have none of the former and only a touch of the latter. He has lost his fourth-class mail permit, and Knotts has one. Now he can continue publishing Knotts's magazine but featuring a different kind of "bird", as that was a popular slang word for comely young women back in the 60's. The magazine doesn't even have to change its slogan of being the finest bird magazine in the world.

Our lead is oblivious to what has been happening, as O'Brien sent him out of the country on a wild goose chase. Well, it's not a goose exactly. I can't remember the name of the rare bird Knotts is dispatched to get a photo of, but there's a great bit where the bird he thinks he's been luring is just another enthusiast using the same call. In the meantime, he's unaware of an international manhunt for him the FBI has initiated. That they did this for obscenity charges, let alone for a magazine so tame the Amish might possibly not take offense, seems ludicrous.

That's just the setup for a rather complicated plot which involves a great many more key players than I would expect for such fare. There's B.S. Pully as a superficially reformed gangster now heading a network of companies, who will forcefully take over publishing operations from O'Brien. He puts Anne Francis in charge of the reformatted magazine that will combine sex and classiness, in what is obviously a riff on *Playboy*. She has the world's top photographers do pictorials of the world's most beautiful women, which means the magazine's former staple, O'Brien's wife Maureen Arthur, is out of a job. And back at home, there's the ridiculously naïve and optimistic Maggie Peterson as a woman madly in love with Knotts and waiting for him to propose marriage.

Once Knotts has been apprehended by the authorities, he stands trial for obscenity. A famous attorney played by James Gregory defends him, but only because he turns it into a very public freedom of speech case. Even in his defense of his client, he portrays him as a man with insatiable lusts and bedroom eyes. Just the idea of anybody describing our lead as having bedroom eyes is a hilarious concept. But this change in public perception leads to seemingly every woman now regarding him as a ladies man.

Francis realizes that persona is critical to the success of the magazine and so uses Knotts in a way that maximizes the potential for him to be its mascot. She puts him up in the ugliest penthouse I think I've ever seen, where his wait staff is four women in French maid outfits. There are four additional young women who are the "Peacock Pussycats", who will accompany him to all public appearances. And Knotts will be dressed in a jaw-dropping series of deliriously bad clothing combinations of the likes not even Prince could pull off.

That wardrobe is meant to be laughably bad and is a good example of the satire of various trends and social mores. It may take only the gentlest of pokes at its subjects, but they are more spot-on than many potshots made at the same things by films that are far more acerbic. Some of those targets here include the sexual revolution, college protests, fashion and the public's fickle nature.

I liked many of the characters. Francis has some agency at first, until she finds herself inexplicably enchanted by Knotts. Can't she be the editor of a high-end skin mag and a woman, too? It made me wonder how Christine Heffner felt when she took over operations of the Playboy empire from her dad. But I found Pully, though he's not in the movie for long, to be the most interesting character. He's forever trying to better himself, and delights in demonstrating his enhanced vocabulary by using the new word he learns each day.

Unfortunately, all good will I felt towards him dissolved when he repeatedly threatens Francis if she becomes interested in any other man than him. The movie also regards Peterson in a strange way, openly mocking the innocence of her character, while that of Knotts is celebrated in the end. Still, I enjoyed a recurring gag where she sits on the front porch of the house the same night week after week, expecting our hero to follow through on his promise yet again to propose marriage to her there. At one point, she's out there in the snow as Christmas music plays on the soundtrack. But I was baffled by a pointless bit where Knotts actually socks her in the jaw, ostensibly to keep her from getting hurt by Pully and his goons. That doesn't scan well, regardless of his intentions.

The Love God? is an odd movie. It likely would have been my favorite of the films Knotts starred in for Universal, if not for some curious missteps it makes along the way. That's a shame, because this overall gentle film makes some surprisingly trenchant insights into the sexual revolution and other trends of the late 1960's. Apparently, the film touched a nerve with some audiences who blanched at the idea of a Knotts film with even extremely mild innuendo, and some theatres reportedly wouldn't even screen it. How I would love to time travel some of those people to the present day, so I could see how quickly they would have an aneurysm.

Original version posted on 10/23/2024

The Major and the Minor (1942)

I have seen many comedies where I found myself unable to laugh because the characters are too stupid to be believable. I realize people in comedies rarely act like real human beings—that is part of the reason why those are comedies. But the premise of a picture, and the world it builds, sets the bounds in which those characters can operate. That said, some plots are so preposterous that I find it impossible to suspend my disbelief enough to accept them.

This is why I'm amazed I enjoy 1942's *The Major and the Minor* as much as I do. It is a deeply funny movie, but everything is hung on the concept of a 30-something Ginger Rogers passing herself off as an eleven-year-old ("I turn twelve next week"). While the actress's small stature helps to sell this ruse, such elements as the lines on her neck betray her age.

The only reason she is doing this is because she didn't have enough money for the adult fare from New York back to her hometown in rural Indiana. In the train station, she alters her outfit to be more like that of a child. I like how she made what I can only assume are colorful striped socks (this is a black and white film, after all) out of the arms of a sweater. To complete the ensemble, she steals a balloon from a distracted girl.

Two conductors appear to be the only adults on the train who are suspicious of her, and they become determined to trick her into revealing she's an adult. One of the best laughs in the film is when one of them asks why she's so tall and she replies she is of Swedish stock. One of the men challenges her to say something in Swedish, and she replies in her best Garbo impersonation, "I vant to be alone…"

Humor is in the elbow of the beholder [the section about comedies]

It is while fleeing those conductors that she ends up hiding in the compartment of Ray Milland. He is the major of the title, and the head of a military school. Something that boggles my mind is he insists she spend the night on the spare bunk he has. His intentions are entirely honest, yet I can't imagine the scandal, if not actual prison time, this would result in today.

Instead, the potentially bigger scandal is if it is discovered Rogers is of legal age. That is what his fiancée (Rita Johnson) and her father / his boss (Edward Fielding) correctly assumed at first. There is a long setup to my favorite gag in the film, so I won't go into that here, but the first time they see Rogers is through the window into the train compartment where she and Milland are doubled over laughing, apparently at the expense of Johnson and Fielding.

Realizing his career and potential marriage are at stake, Milland convinces Rogers to come with him back to the academy so she can help clear his name and restore him into the good graces of his fiancée and her father. That the other adults so readily believe Rogers is a prepubescent girl is up to the viewer to decide whether or not they will accept this conceit.

My favorite character in the picture is the only one to see right through this ruse. Diana Lynn is Johnson's young sister and roommate for Rogers while she's on the campus. Only somebody closer to the age Rogers is pretending to be can see the artificiality: "Oh, get up and stop that baby talk." Being the only person Rogers can be herself around, Lynn is the only one she treats like an equal. The scenes between the two aren't funny, but they're among the best in the movie and I wish there were more of them. Lynn is so good here, and at such an early age, that I find it hard to believe she would be subjected to the endless inanities of *Bedtime for Bozo* just a decade later.

I wasn't surprised every other character here of Lynn's age is convinced by Rogers's act, as they are all boys, and at a military school, to boot. All 300-plus cadets are eager to pass the time with her. We will see a few of them try their awkward demonstration of alleged legendary military tactical maneuvers, when they have different maneuvers in mind. These scenes don't play very well today. Some might say those were more innocent times, but I don't think there is anything innocent about these moments of attempted assault. It is especially weird that Rogers is fending off advances from boys she conceivably could have conceived, given the age differences.

One of these boys happens to have Robert Benchley as his father. In the opening scene, we'll see the history she has with his character, as she fends off his advances when she comes to his apartment in her employment as a "hair treatment and scalp massage specialist". If such an operation sounds like a front for prostitution, I suspect that is what it really was, though nobody informed Rogers, who has sunk what little money she had into the tools of the trade. I'm always pleased to see the Algonquin Round Table wit in a film, and he is great here in basically an extended cameo as a cad: "Why don't you get out of that wet coat and into a dry martini. I'd offer you a gin and tonic, but I have yet to think of a joke for that." Her cover will be at risk of being blown when there is a big cotillion at the academy, which will draw in the cadet's parents for the weekend.

The dramatic tension is a curious series of delicate trusses. Rogers is clearly interested in Milland, so it seems like she has nothing to lose by revealing her true nature. Her goal is to not disrupt his engagement to Johnson, but that woman honestly doesn't seem very interested in him. She keeps interceding to prevent his transfer to active service, despite that being what he most wants to do. Heck, even her younger sister better knows what Milland wants, and she's rooting for Rogers to deep six that engagement. But, curiously, if Rogers succeeds in doing that, and helps Milland get into active duty, he'll be kept far apart from her. Hell, maybe *permanently* away from her, given this was wartime.

In the penultimate scene of *The Major and the Minor*, we will see Rogers with her mother who, surprisingly, is played by her real-life mom. Then, Rogers makes herself up to impersonate her mother. She is about as unconvincing playing somebody almost twice her age as she was playing somebody less than half of it. And yet, this film is enjoyable enough that I am willing to overlook this or, to put it more accurately, to overlook how all the other characters bar one believes it.

Original version posted on 8/3/2024

Making Mr. Right (1987)

In a perfect world, Ann Magnuson would have had a long career of leading roles in movies while attracting a growing cult following for her musical endeavors. Alas, neither of these things happened, though not for lack of trying. I challenge anybody to see 1987's *Making Mr. Right* and not wonder why they haven't seen her in more things.

Prior to the first time I watched this movie back in the 1990's, I was mostly aware of her as the vocalist for the band Bongwater, which paired her with studio wiz Kramer as they mostly did deeply weird covers of songs from the first psychedelic era. I think the title of the track "Dazed and Chinese" will tell you exactly what it sounds like.

Up until seeing this film, I only knew she had an amazing voice. Turns out she has stellar acting chops as well, though there haven't been many opportunities to see her beyond some supporting roles.

She is well-served by director Susan Seidelman, whose previous film was *Desperately Seeking Susan*. No knock on Madonna, but Magnuson could act circles around her. She could probably act all kinds of complex patterns around that other singer, of designs that are usually only achieved using a Spirograph.

I imagine it is especially difficult to hold your ground when your co-star is John Malkovich. He doesn't do many comedies, but his performance here makes me wish he would do more of them. Here, he plays a brilliant but socially awkward scientist who creates an extremely lifelike robot modelled after himself. This humanoid is to helm a spacecraft to be sent on a one-way trip to explore the cosmos.

Things go haywire when the robot gradually falls in love with Magnuson, who is running the public relations campaign for the cybernetics firm. A solid setup for comedy is created when she tries to make her philandering former boyfriend jealous by pretending the scientist is in love with her. An even better one has the android sneaking out of the facility and getting in various mishaps.

Curiously, the funniest scene involves the escaped cyborg and Laurie Metcalf, who thinks she is on a date with its creator. I felt terrible for Metcalf's lovelorn character, who endures many humiliations from the oblivious robot, but I didn't feel so bad that it prevented me from laughing. At one point, Malkovich seems to be eating one of every item on a restaurant's entire menu. "I usually don't get foods with so many colors." He starts covering everything in ketchup, and this inadvertently includes Metcalf.

Another shocking and hilarious scene involves Glenne Headly as Magnuson's best friend, who makes a disastrous attempt to seduce somebody she does not realize is an artificial man. That scenario ends up with Malkovich literally ass-backwards. An interesting bit of behind-the-scenes trivia: she was Malkovich's real-life wife at the time.

Other actors also fare well here, though few roles are anywhere near as substantial as those of the two leads. Magnuson's sister is played by Susan Berman, who is preparing for a wedding to which their mother (Polly Bergen) vocally disapproves. I think it's funny how shocking Berman's blue hair must have been at the time, when nobody would blink if they saw it today.

Also, it is interesting how these three look like they really could be related, something you rarely see on the big screen or TV. The similarity makes their rapport seem even more natural. Consider this exchange between Berman and Bergen about the former's hairy armpits: "Shaving armpits is such a bourgeois concept." "*Marriage* is a bourgeois concept."

I enjoy *Making Mr. Right* more each time I see it, and I think I've seen it three times now. There is an additional element to this that may appeal more to some viewers than it did to me, and that is people with a strong nostalgia for the 80's will find much to gush over. And yet, the movie, with all of its retrofuturism and Florida Art Deco architecture, is nostalgic for earlier eras itself. So, I recommend this for those who are nostalgic for the nostalgia of an earlier era.

Original version posted on 2/24/2024

The Man Who Wasn't There 3D (1983)

The Man Who Wasn't There is a 1983 3D comedy with a very apt title. It stars Steve Guttenberg, an actor who is consistently in deeply bland roles—incredibly inoffensive nobodies whose favorite color is probably beige.

I saw a lot of beige while watching this, or at least varying degrees of some sort of weird monochrome with varying amounts of colors somewhere between light brown and light pink. Sometimes, there would be an especially strong blue or red, which is jarring. The reason for this is because I watched this as an anaglyphic 3D presentation on Kino Lorber's new blu-ray issue. That is the kind you watch through glasses with red and blue lenses. Needless to say, colors have to be limited or else those color filters would wreak havoc with the image. You end up with this weird color scheme that reminds me of those old two-strip Technicolor films.

What is odd is how there are so few effects that realize the potential of the gimmick. Instead, one is left with the bizarre experience of seeing largely unremarkable objects appear to jut out from the screen. I was so irritated by the mundane objects and dull scenes we witnessed that I started sarcastically yelling out what we were seeing *in 3D!!!* "A common handrail...*in 3D!!!*" "An unremarkable meeting of four old men around a small table...*in 3D!!!*" "Steve Guttenberg's bare ass...*in 3D!!!*"

To that last statement, there is a shocking amount of nudity in this movie—a solidly R film with humor at a pre-pubescent level. That's not the only incongruity here, in a picture that plays like a combination of *The Man Who Knew Too Much*, *Porky's* and *Memoirs of an Invisible Man*. Oh, and in 3D, of course.

Guttenberg is a low-level US diplomat whom we first see working the second room at an event, one where the representatives of lesser countries not worthy of the primary room are given far less preferential treatment. I'll concede that is an interesting idea, except it is very poorly executed. The extent to which this is explored here is limited to a food fight between broad ethnic stereotypes. The worst of these (and the only character from this scene who will appear again later) is Charlie Brill, playing an ethnic character of indeterminate origin. It's the kind of shtick Peter Sellers used to do, and this guy isn't Peter Sellers.

Inexplicably, Guttenberg, while working this event, is late for his own wedding to Morgan Most. It is completely unbelievable somebody would be at work while everybody at their wedding was just waiting for them to appear. And it is that type of illogic which kneecaps every single setup in this film. Jokes only work if the premise on which they hang adhere to some degree of believability. It would also help if a single joke was funny.

Soon, he is stripped down to his boxer shorts in front of the wedding party (don't ask) and locked in a hotel room. It is then a double-agent for the bad guys enters the room, though our hero can't see him, as this agent is invisible. We only know roughly where the guy is because he is carrying something that looks like a miniature version of one of those deadly spheres from *Phantasm*. That is only the container for several vials of what looks like windshield-washing fluid, which is the serum that renders consumers of it invisible.

Then a group of characters who are very unlikely to be together bursts into the room. There's a guy in a business suit, a Native American in painter's overalls, a George Romero impersonator and the world's least believable punk rocker. Way to blend in, guys, especially in Washington D.C.

Our protagonist escapes with the sphere and is soon using those vials when needed. Being invisible should lead to all kinds of clever scenes, but this film caters to the lowest common denominator, with him doing such things as sneaking into the showers at a girl's school. There was a lot of this kind of crap in the 80's, and other constants of that era which haven't aged well include homophobic slurs and jokes. There's even a joke about women drivers. I'm just surprised there isn't a joke about airline food.

The effects should really be the star in a movie like this, but they are so-so. Much of the invisibility is accomplished through chroma keying. As much as I hate how prevalent CGI has been in the cinema of this century, I have to admit this particular niche genre is where that technology shines. Before that, you had such lousy moments as a bit here where a drinking glass is suspended by very obvious wires that are even more conspicuous in 3D.

Another element of this particular niche of sci-fi/horror I find grating is how becoming transparent apparently motivates people to start talking to themselves ad nauseum. We see a window raise and we hear the invisible person doing that say something like, "Guess I'll try to sneak out this way". Well, no shit. We don't think the window just raised itself. We don't think there's now ghosts in the world of this film. It's a movie that thinks its audience is deeply stupid, and it might be correct in that assumption.

When it isn't insulting the audience's intelligence, it is often confusing them. The identity of the main villain has been concealed until a moment that should be shocking but is instead stupefying in that it doesn't make any sense. I suspect it is impossible for this person to have filled that role, but I don't care to scrutinize the film to find out.

Even more bizarre is a concluding scene, where Guttenberg and Lisa Langois are invisible and getting married at a ceremony where everybody else, including the priest, are blindfolded. This scene makes less than no sense, to the extent it becomes a tad creepy, like we are seeing an outtake from *Midsommar* by way of *Eyes Wide Shut*. The people at the wedding have to know who is tying the knot. What explanation was provided to those guests that they allowed themselves to be blindfolded? For that matter, why are the bride and groom invisible? Then the potion wears off, the happy couple are standing there naked, and everybody takes off their blindfolds anyway. What prompted people to take a peek? Did they *hear* those two resume visibility?

But perhaps the most inane scene in *The Man Who Wasn't There* has Langois making out with an invisible Guttenberg. I found it impossible to not see this as basically what is really happening: a woman is weirdly contorting herself and thrusting her tongue around in the air. It is no surprise she will also get naked, making this an uncomfortable scene of what appears to be an elaborate act of autoeroticism. I felt embarrassed watching this. The titular man may or may not have been there, but I know I wish I hadn't.

Original version posted on 8/21/2024

The Missionary (1982)

When a movie shows prostitutes of 19th century London's seediest neighborhoods, I imagine them marketing their wares as if they are vendors at a baseball game: "Get your hot seh-fuh-lisss heeer-yuh! HOT syphilis!"

In 1982's *The Missionary* Michael Palin plays the title role, a seemingly decent man who has faithfully served the Church no matter where they send him in the world. In the opening credits sequence, we see him happily teaching, doctoring and mingling with members of an African tribe. Despite having seen so much of the world through his profession, he remains curiously naïve.

Perhaps this is why his next assignment upon returning to England is to start a mission in the poorest area of London, to minister to "fallen women". There's a pretty funny bit where his privileged fiancée keeps asking for clarification, yet never grasps what this really means: "Are they having knee problems? Are their legs broken?"

Not sure why these two were engaged to begin with. He has been in Africa the past ten years, sending her endless letters and postcards the entire time. She doesn't seem to comprehend the sentiments expressed in those, yet she has an intricate filing system and knows the ID, date and location of each item. This felt a bit like the jokes in Terry Gilliam's *Brazil*, with all the cryptically named forms everybody in it has to file. She also is bewildered as to why there needs to be a mission in their home country: "But everyone's English in England..."

Palin's co-star is a lusty baroness played by Maggie Smith. Since I always think of Smith as being roughly 80 years old, it felt very strange to put the word "lusty" in that previous sentence. And yet, she wants Palin's holy body before she'll convince her husband to pony up the dough for the mission.

Her husband is played by Trevor Howard, who earned a lifetime of goodwill from me for his performance in *The Third Man*, my favorite movie. Apparently, the actor was drunk and belligerent during the production of this film and would die only a year later. That's a shame, because he's a hoot in this as a crazy old ex-army official. When Palin tells him the mission is for the underprivileged, he barks, "Underprivileged? Not familiar with the term!"

Denholm Elliott, excellent as always, takes Palin on a visit to the area where the mission is to be established. He tries to introduce Palin to a prostitute and she tells him there's no discounts for bishops. Bonzo Dog Doo Dah Band singer Neil Innes makes a cameo in this bar as a singer who takes a flying chair to the face, which made me laugh embarrassingly hard.

Once the mission is established, the fallen women fall hard for the missionary. Palin finds himself balancing the needs of his lusty wards, his frustrated fiancée, his sponsor and the Church.

This is a movie that is cleverer than it is funny, and it may not be for everybody. In fact, I'm not entirely sure *who* it is for, but I just happened to enjoy it.

I enjoyed some sequences which intentionally took a long time to play out, most notably a scene where Michael Horden, as a senile butler, leads Palin all through a mansion without ever seeming to find their destination. This reminded me of a similar scene in Jacques Tati's *Playtime* in which we watch his Hulot character walk down a very long hallway before tripping at the end of it.

Given how dry most of the humor is in this picture, it was jarring to have occasional moments of farce, such as a brief shot of runners on a beach as accompanied by the *Chariots of Fire* theme played on bagpipes.

One thing that is consistent throughout is gorgeous cinematography. Many of the shots look like paintings from that era come to life.

Those who are interested, and own a region-free player, are encouraged to seek out the Powerhouse/Indicator region B blu-ray. It has a great many special features, including extensive interviews with Palin and Smith.

This film was produced by Handmade Films, the company founded by George Harrison originally to fund *Monty Python's Life of Brian*. As the man himself once put it, all he wanted to do was see the Python film so, by ponying up the dough to finish that production, he bought the most expensive movie ticket of all time. Then the production company just kept making films. *The Missionary* fits in well in that catalog of charmingly offbeat pictures.

Humor is in the elbow of the beholder [the section about comedies]

Original version posted on 5/9/2023

Moving Violations (1985)

It is awfully sad when a film cast as its lead somebody only because they are the relative of a famous actor. Consider the pathetic *Operation Kid Brother* from 1967, which is one of the very few pictures to star Sean Connery's younger brother, Neil. I thought about that feature a great many times while watching 1985's *Moving Violations*, which stars John Murray (brother of Bill) and James Keach (brother of Stacy).

Murray doesn't fail horribly, but it is like getting Jim Belushi in a movie when you thought his brother John was in it. This is a performance that perfectly illustrates the difference between somebody playing a smartass you're rooting for, versus the kind of smartass you want to see get his comeuppance.

His nemesis is a draconian traffic officer played by Keach. He fares better than Murray but then, as in most comedies, the straight man tends to get most of the laughs. He also somehow maintains some sort of dignity when subjected to such humiliations as pissing his pants or running through the streets of L.A. while in bondage wear.

I feel I need to bring up something I otherwise might not be able to work in, and that is the great pains it goes through to present the illusion it takes place somewhere other than Los Angeles, when that is unmistakably where it was shot. Heck, the film is even shy about which *state* it is in, as all signage declares this to be "Birch County". Despite the name, this must be more than a mere county, as it appears on license plates where the state name would normally be located.

Keach and fellow officer (and love interest) Lisa Hart Carroll gleefully issue citations for assorted vehicular shenanigans. A judge played by Sally Kellerman then suspends the licenses of everybody in the ragtag group of various oddballs who were cited for traffic violations. They are all sentenced to traffic school for a week. Those who fail the class will have their driving privileges permanently revoked and their vehicles sold at auction.

That seemed a bit extreme to me, but Kellerman's reason for this is because she is taking a big cut of those sales. Seems to me somebody would have noticed this but, hey, this is an 80's comedy in the mold of *Police Academy*. I'm not sure I continued watching that series past the second installment, but I remember the first one had some solid laughs in it. Similar to that film, I laughed at least a half dozen times in this and was immediately embarrassed after most of those occasions.

As much as I disliked Murray in this, the first time I laughed was when he accidentally hands Keach a different item than the driver's license he was told to surrender: "Oh, that's my membership card for the Communist party. I only joined for the softball team."

Most of the humor is sight gags that trying to describe in writing would be an exercise in futility. And yet, I will try to convey the humor in a gag where a runaway bowling ball takes out of group of people waiting for the bus. Each person actually flies into the air on collision, while we hear the sound of a ball plowing through pins. The incident that landed Brian Backer in court is too complicated to describe, but he is telling the truth when he says, "I hit a casket with a puppet stage. What am I doing here?" What is even weirder is Nadine Van der Velde attending the traffic school, as she is an underage driver using a fake ID. Since the only info the cops have on her is inaccurate, why go through this ruse? It's like doing somebody else's jail sentence.

Like so many comedies of the 80's, this has many elements which carbon date it to that decade. First, it is completely sex-obsessed, including a sex scene in a zero-gravity chamber where hair still conveniently observes the laws of gravity. The obligatory obscure celebrity cameo is courtesy of Clara Peller, likely at roughly 14 minutes and 58 seconds of the 15 minutes of fame she earned from doing those Wendy's "Where's the beef?" commercials. Lastly, the music is terrible, particularly a strange bastardization of James Brown's "I Feel Good" by somebody who must deeply hate that song.

I enjoyed *Moving Violations* more than I thought possible, though I would be hard-pressed to recommend this to anybody. The worst aspect of the film is its star, such as when he declares, "Driver, take me to the nearest nuclear power plant. My pants are full of uranium." Everybody laughs, and I had no idea why. On the other hand, there were little moments with minor characters that made me laugh, such as using a legally blind old woman as a lookout: "Did you see anybody?" "I don't know."

Original version posted on 7/12/2024

A New Leaf (1971)

Comedy and film legend Elaine May first achieved fame as half of a comedic duo she formed with future *The Graduate* director Mike Nichols. Later, she was one of Hollywood's most sought-after script doctors. She has also directed four feature films to date, writing three of those. One of those films completely astonished me, and it sure as hell wasn't *Ishtar*.

That would be 1971's *A New Leaf*, her directorial debut. It is believed to be the first time a woman wrote, directed and co-starred in a film for a major studio. And it is amazing anybody could so thoroughly knock it out of the park with their first film. This black comedy feels like the wheels could come off at any minute, but I was as spellbound to see if May could pull it off as I was to see if lead Walter Matthau could achieve his nefarious goals.

Matthau is a New York City playboy who has completely squandered a substantial trust fund. His lawyer (William Redfield), has been informing his client for years of his inevitable, impending penury. In a great scene, Redfield seems to channel the mannerisms of May's former comedic partner as he becomes increasingly exasperated in his attempts to explain this. All Matthau is concerned about is a check he wrote for $6000 that has bounced. Redfield tries to explain that, not only is he lacking the funds to cover that check, but the lawyer even covered a previous bounced check for $550 by using his own money.

As just one small example of the brilliant dialogue in this script, I submit the following:

"I have you given you $550 of my own money for only one reason: disliking you as intensely as I do, I wanted to be certain that when I looked back upon your financial downfall, I could absolve myself completely of any responsibility for it." This doesn't result in any gratitude from his client: "I don't suppose you'd care to give me an additional $6000 and insure yourself against guilt permanently?"

Now that the penny has dropped that Matthau has no more pennies to drop, he confides his crisis to his loyal butler, played by George Rose. This is an excellent small part in a film overflowing with them. Rose proposes his employer marry into wealth, not just for Matthau's continued financial security, but his own, as well. As Rose explains it, so few find it necessary to retain a gentleman's gentleman. Rose champions his boss as somebody who upholds traditions long since ended even before the man was born. Matthau agrees to this plan but does not reveal an additional twist he has in mind, and that is to murder his new bride once inheritance is secured.

We only see one of Matthau's aborted attempts at wooing, and that is of a needy, middle-aged woman played by Renée Taylor. Her dialogue seems to be lifted entirely from self-help books of the era. Professing her need to be loved, she is about to undo her bikini top when her suitor bolts. In what I like to think was an improvised line, he barks, "No! Don't let them out!"

A better target presents itself to him at a tea party. When we first see May, she is simply in the background, with no effort made to focus our attention on her. And yet, she is still somebody the eye gravitates towards as Matthau and Graham Jarvis have a conversation in the foreground. Completely lost in thought, she seems to be facially reacting to whatever is on her mind. It is already fascinating to watch her.

May will drop her teacup, with the host accepting the first occurrence, but weirdly going into a tizzy when it happens a second time. May becomes intrigued by Matthau when he intervenes, dumping the contents of his own cup onto the rug, and delivering this speech to their host: "I have seen many examples of perversion in my time, but your erotic obsession with your carpet is probably the most grotesque and, certainly, the most boring I have ever encountered."

Desperate for financial rescue, Matthau reels in this fish, even if he is repulsed and confused by her. He finds himself cutting price tags off the clothes she's wearing. He expresses despair at the messiness of her eating, telling Rose she has to be vacuumed after every meal. He finds her interests dull, as they seem to consist entirely of the study of ferns and her desire to find a previously undiscovered variety. Her taste in wine is unique, as she fails to convince Matthau of the appeal of her favorite alcoholic beverage,

Mogen-David extra-heavy malaga wine with soda water and lime juice. Every part of that concoction cracks me up, but I seemed to laugh consistently at the "extra-heavy".

Matthau will make some sacrifices in marrying her. The moment of proposal is quite painful, as he accidentally drives a knee into broken glass while doing so. Even in this moment, he retains composure, rejecting her concerns for his well-being: "Kneeling on glass is my favorite pastime. Keeps me from slouching."

It's also goodbye to his bachelor pad. He and Rose move into her family mansion. Matthau proceeds to throw out the corrupt and shifty house staff which was installed there by her equally corrupt lawyer, played by Jack Weston.

In a surprise development, Matthau develops a series of skills of which he was hitherto unaware. He brings in competent staff, manages the house and even investigates her tax returns. In the course of plotting to murder a wealthy woman he married, he accidentally becomes a better and more thoroughly realized person. Could he possibly experience a change of heart by the time the end credits roll?

Admittedly, those credits seem to be a bit long in arriving, with the runtime coming in around 15 minutes shy of two hours. What I find baffling is May's original cut was much longer, at three hours. No comedy should be three hours long, and *It's a Mad Mad Mad Mad World* only confirms that. Although the excised footage has long since disappeared, we know some excised subplots would have taken the film into far darker territory, which feels like a betrayal of what remains for us to see today, a return to the screwball greats of the 1930's and 40's.

Similar to those classics, there are a great many bit parts in this picture. In addition to the actors I have already singled out, there are some great turns by James Coco and Doris Roberts. I never thought I would ever say Coco was underused in anything, but he is pitch-perfect as Matthau's wealthy uncle. When we first see him, he is laughing hysterically, the camera close on his wide-open mouth as it seems to be ready to chomp down on Matthau's head that is far in the background.

I have seen *A New Leaf* twice, finding it enjoyable the first time and falling completely in love with it the second. It is a very smart and deeply funny film, but still one with a weirdly lumbering structure that may bewilder viewers who are less forgiving of something that doesn't follow the usual series of beats. From what I learned about her on the commentary and special features on this blu-ray, that might have also been a fair description of May herself: a brilliant and funny person who was determined to follow her own course, but who apparently rubbed some people the wrong way.

Original version posted on 10/28/2024

A Night at the Opera (1935)

It has only been in the past five years or so that I have truly come to appreciate the Marx Brothers, but I can still recall many of the reasons why, even if I didn't actively dislike them, I was confused by why they are so legendary. With this in mind, I have decided to present 1935's *A Night at the Opera* in a manner meant to appeal to the unconverted. Really, given all the existing essays, books and videos about even this one film, I doubt anything new can be said about it.

So, let's start with some of the hurdles I had to overcome in order to appreciate their work.

First, even for somebody who watches a lot of cinema from nearly a hundred years ago, I still had trouble understanding much of what they said. It didn't help that prints of their work were in poor condition before pristine restorations were performed in this century. While the audio is now significantly clearer than before, it still helps to train one's ear by watching other films from this era.

Even then, you'll need to be receptive to the peculiar "Mid-Atlantic Drawl" that was the accent used by most actors in the first era of talking pictures. I've never had any trouble understanding it, but then I also never had any problems reading cursive writing, so maybe I just have an old soul.

Another technical hurdle is the odd pacing and editing. There are frequently pauses after humorous lines, and these were intentionally timed so audience laughter would not step on the next line. But, if you're not laughing, these moments will seem awkward and weird.

Modern viewers may also be confused by the numerous jump cuts. There are a couple of reasons for those. In even their initial release, these films were meant to maximize the potential for laughs, so some rather artless excisions may have resulted from that process. For films made during or before 1935, however, there likely will also be censors' cuts made per the Production Code in the years following. Since re-release prints of such films are largely all that remain, we will only ever have these truncated versions, as studios used to destroy the parts they took out. I have to stop myself before I think too much about such facts, as I will get pointlessly worked up.

Lastly, there's the nature of the Brothers themselves, who will seem very strange for the uninitiated.

Groucho has a "mustache" that is obviously black face paint. There's an amazing bit in *Duck Soup* where two of the other Marxes find in his bedroom a jar of that paint, and each makes themselves over to look like him, which means Groucho himself (in the world of the film, no less) is wearing a fake mustache. It is a moment so meta that I'm amazed the movie doesn't collapse in on itself into a point of singularity.

Then there's Chico, which everybody is always shocked to learn is pronounced "Chick-O". Even more astonishingly, that is because the ladies used to throw themselves at him. He's an odd character, with an "Eye-tal-yan" accent so preposterous that it goes so far beyond being offensive until it becomes acceptable. It is simply too ridiculous of a caricature to cause any affront.

Lastly, there's Harpo, a mute in a fright wig, usually wearing a trench coat from which any number of unlikely objects might be retrieved from its magically bottomless pockets. Honestly, I was weirded out and even a bit scared of him the first couple of times I tried to watch one of their pictures. He is Exhibit A for silence being intimidating, which is why I suspect most people don't like mimes.

Actually, there's one more "lastly" beyond that lastly, and that is Zeppo. This poor guy—he didn't really have any kind of shtick, so he was the straight man. But since these films usually pit the brothers against everybody else, everybody but the main three are the straight men, rendering him a surplus good. He bowed out of the group after *Duck Soup*.

He wasn't even the best straight man they had, and that person is really a straight woman. Margaret Dumont is the textbook definition of the "wealthy dowager" stereotype. She was a great foil for Groucho, who often said the actress was so straight in real life that she never got his jokes. Not only is that insulting to her intelligence, but that is flat-out wrong. In the first scene of *A*

Night at the Opera, you can see her trying not to crack up, and it is a beautiful moment. She is widely, and correctly, regarded as the fifth Marx Brother.

If there is one scene I think would be a great introduction for the uninitiated to their work, it is the stateroom scene here. The setup is Groucho has been given a very small room on an ocean liner. Opening his steamer truck, he discovers he has three stowaways. It would be hard enough to get four people, the trunk and the bed in that room, but Groucho gleefully lets anybody and everybody in, until there's also three waiters with overflowing trays of food, two service men there to fix a pipe, two cleaning women and a woman who asks to use the telephone. The resulting churning mass of humanity has reduced me to tears of laughter every time I've seen it. I'm smiling just thinking about it as I write. My favorite moment is when there's a knock on the door and a woman asks Groucho if he would like a manicure. With a sarcastic enthusiasm that would be a clear inspiration for Bugs Bunny, he says, "No! Come on in!"

The Brothers are like a hurricane, often causing havoc in any situation they are remotely proximate to. At first, I didn't understand this and often felt they were pointlessly harassing innocent bystanders. Then I apparently had some manner of surgery I can't remember where the stick was removed from my ass, and I started finding these shenanigans endlessly hilarious. Really, there's no good reason for them to swap an orchestra's operatic score with sheet music for "Take Me Out to the Ball Game", but I love it that they do. That Groucho is immediately hawking peanuts to the opera attendees makes a weird kind of sense.

Their work prior to this feature was all chaos and usually dressed in the thinnest semblance of a plot. *Opera* would be the first of their films where they actually are in the assistance of others, and it makes for a more solid viewing experience, though also more conventional. This time they are helping young star-crossed singers who aspire to become opera stars (Allan Jones and Kitty Carlisle, the latter being somebody who really could sing opera). The two leads are quite bland, but you wouldn't expect anybody who could possibly upstage the real stars.

Another standard of their movies is a piano scene for Chico and a harp scene for...wait for it...Harpo. Each has their own fascinating self-taught approach to their respective instruments. For the longest time, I was tempted to fast-forward through these numbers, but I now find them deeply satisfying. Chico has a peculiar manner of "shooting" the keys, occasionally pointing a finger like a pistol and striking a key almost faster than the camera can capture. An even greater joy is Harpo at his instrument. He is fully in his element, despite his method apparently being completely unorthodox. In his autobiography, he writes about wanting to learn how to play it correctly, but one master after another he hired told him to not change a thing.

There are many Marx Brothers films I would recommend as a starting point for newcomers, and *A Night at the Opera* is way up there on that list. Even then, you may need to see a couple of their films to know whether or not they're right for you. I remember when I couldn't appreciate them, and that just makes me all the more grateful that I can now.

Original version posted on 11/19/2024

A bonus feature on the Warner Archive blu-ray is an Academy Award winning short by Robert Benchley, of Algonquin Roundtable fame. Harpo was also part of that group of wits, treasured because the others wouldn't stop talking and they were so glad to finally have a listener.

Humor is in the elbow of the beholder [the section about comedies]

Strange Brew (1983)

I keep thinking the comedies of the 80's were all oversexed, but then I forgot about such glorious outliers as *Pee-Wee's Big Adventure*, which seemed to subvert every expectation one might have for a comedy from a major studio at the time. Almost as audacious, but not quite as good, is 1983's *Strange Brew*.

This brings *SCTV's* Bob and Doug McKenzie (Rick Moranis and Dave Thomas) to the big screen, in what would be their only feature film as these characters. On that show, their shtick was riffing on Canadian stereotypes, in the context of them hosting a public access show called *The Great White North*. Their world boils down to beer, donuts, beer, hockey and beer.

Obviously, a feature film would have to expand beyond that conceit, so the movie we're watching initially proves to be a movie within the movie, and even that has a movie within that: an extremely amateurish post-apocalyptic sci-fi made by the brothers, set "ten years after world war four" (fortunately, that film is *not* their take on *A Boy and His Dog*). We then see the outraged audience watching that film storm out of the theater. The brothers escape through the theater's emergency exit where they encounter in the alleyway a guy with two crying children. As the father tells them: "They've been saving their allowance for weeks to see this movie. What am I supposed to tell them? *What am I supposed to tell them?!*"

With this business out of the way, we're on to the movie proper. I would have expected everything here to be sketch-based without any overall plot. Instead, we get the McKenzies stumbling into employment at the Elsinore brewery and finding themselves in a bizarre conspiracy. To think their journey begins with them trying to scam free beer by claiming they found a mouse in a bottle of beer. A great touch is the mouse in the bottle Thomas uses as evidence is *alive*. I love how none of the characters seem to notice this. As for myself, I wondered how the filmmakers got the live mouse through the tiny neck of the bottle.

Something is obviously amiss at the brewery. Just it being immediately adjacent to a mental institution arouses suspicions. That the place is almost bereft of workers is even more bizarre. Aside from Bob and Doug on mouse-monitoring duty alongside the conveyor belt, the only other employees seemingly doing any work directly related to beer production are Angus MacInnes and Douglas Campbell.

I should make that "non-evil beer production", because some others at the facility are involved in a nefarious plot to add a drug to the product which will give them full control of its consumers. Max von Sydow makes a surprising appearance as the diabolical mastermind behind the plot. Brian McConnachie is his technician who seems to do all the actual labor involved in implementing that plan, such as subjecting inmates of the asylum to the tainted beer and monitoring the results. Paul Dooley plays a schemey but deeply stupid middle management type who was involved in the death of his brother, the founder of the brewery, and is now trying to wrest control of Elsinore from his niece (Lynne Griffin). I suspect Dooley is regarded as so incompetent as to not even be trusted to commit the murder he set out to do: "He was already dead when I killed him!"

The test done on the inmates to ensure they can be controlled is unusual. The loonies (and, by that, I mean the crazies from next door and not the Canadian currency) are kitted out in hockey gear that looks closer to that of the Storm Troopers from *Star Wars*. That makes for a bizarre meta moment when MacInnes is wearing that gear, because he was Gold Leader in that film.

Vastly more important than the plot is the question of whether the picture is funny. As always, humor is even more in the eye of the beholder than beauty, but I found this film to be hilarious. Most of the humor comes from interactions more than anything else. I love a line, supposedly improvised, when Moranis says to Griffin, "I'd kiss you if I didn't have puke breath." Moranis also has a weird aside about the synthesizer used to control the drugged inmates, "Hey, look, this piano has a computer." There are weird little visual bits, like an arcade game titled "Galactic Border Patrol". There are even a couple of shock moments, such as the brothers catching their parents in bed, with Moranis being the mom and Thomas the dad.

One moment recalls the wry breaking of film boundaries done so perfectly in *Big Adventure*. Doug is driving a van and Bob is in the passenger seat. Bob asks Doug if he's ever noticed how, in movies, somebody who is driving will often turn to the other person and carry on a long conversation without watching the road. Doug then folds his arms across his chest, turns his head towards his brother and proceeds to do exactly that. There's also an unusual spin on the MGM logo at the beginning, with the lion belching.

There are some elements of the film that were simply odd. The computer discs that control the evil operation at the brewery are unlike any other media I have seen, something like the old 5 ¼" floppies, but with rounded corners. Not sure why I am unable to stop thinking about those, but that's just my nature. Another element I can't seem to stop thinking about is a brief bit where the McKenzie's dog drops one of those discs off the roof of their house so that a police detective will find it. In a deeply uncanny moment that goes by in a blink, the dog then rolls back up the roof of the house and over the edge. I keep waiting for that to creep into my nightmares.

While *Strange Brew* plays some with the structure of comedy, it isn't an anarchic as I want it to be. But what truly matters is whether it succeeds as a comedy and, to me, it is deeply funny. Still, I couldn't help being mildly annoyed it could not sidestep one trapping of the era: a deeply horrible title credits song some executive obviously thought had potential to be a hit single.

Original version posted on 7/8/2024

Swing Vote (2008)

The past few years have seen polling workers and the vote tabulation process subjected to extreme scrutiny, with officials and even low-level workers facing intimidation and death threats. In 2008's *Swing Vote*, young teen Madeline Carroll is so upset deadbeat dad Kevin Costner has failed to show up at the polling station that she forges his signature in the ledger of the sleeping monitor. She has just put the card in the electronic voting machine when a cleaning woman accidentally knocks loose the power cable. Because of this, no vote is recorded. Just imagine how insane the furor would be today if this happened.

What is really unfortunate is this particular presidential election is a dead tie. Neither incumbent Kelsey Grammer nor opponent Dennis Hopper has enough electoral college votes, and the popular vote in New Mexico is split evenly until the vote it appears Costner was going to cast is resolved. He is given ten days to recast his ballot. The candidates move their operations close to him, each desperate to curry his favor. An ensuing media circus descends upon the small town where Costner lives.

That town is Texico, New Mexico, a natural rhyme that just begs to become a couplet in a song. The perfect person to do that would be Willie Nelson, who is in this eclectic cast. Alas, he doesn't do that in his brief appearance here.

The large and rather unusual cast also includes Paula Patton as the TV reporter who breaks the story, Nathan Lane as Hopper's campaign manager, Stanley Tucci in that same capacity for Grammer, George Lopez as Patton's boss at a small station, Judge Reinhold as one of Costner's two best friends and Mare Winningham as our protagonist's estranged wife. In addition to Nelson, another key cameo is Richard Petty, who shows up at Costner's trailer in his race car and offers the man the opportunity to take it out for a drive.

That is the ideal bribe for the type of person Costner plays here. Regardless of what one may think of the actor, he knows a particular type of low-income American laborer. Although his "Bud" character here is a buffoon who drinks too much and can't hold a job, he is still likeable. Even better, he will gradually experience a great deal of personal growth by the time the end credits roll.

That growth is largely courtesy of Carroll, whom we first see waking her dad in the morning and getting him ready for his job at the egg packaging plant. She's even packed his lunch, and he complains about it being egg salad again. She reminds him he needs to vote today. She also needs him to sign a school assignment where she was supposed to get his political opinions but instead wisely filled it out on her own.

At school, Patton and a cameraman are filming Carroll and other students reading these essays, which means it must have been an exceptionally slow news day, even for rural New Mexico. When it is discovered the election hinges on one errored ballot that needs to be recast, she follows the clues to Costner. Lopez is thrilled, saying, in what I like to think was an ad lib, "I'm so excited, I got my accent back!"

The film's second act is its strongest, with increasingly ridiculous and desperate efforts of both candidates to secure that vote. My favorite bit was Grammer's anti-environment Republican suddenly announcing Costner's favorite fishing spot on the Pecos River will become a nature preserve, making previously protesting Sierra Club members in attendance cheer while Grammer's supporters next to them start booing. The reactionary responses to Costner's every whim will have Hopper also doing a 180 on a couple of his policies, making ads against immigration and abortion. The latter is the film's most audacious and hilarious moment, as Hopper's commercial has him walking around a playground where there are children playing. To illustrate a point about children who would not exist if they had been aborted, the tots explode one-by-one into colorful puffs of smoke.

Despite many funny moments and lines in the film (and there are a great many), it does touch on several issues, some of which are even more relevant today than they were at the time. Costner expresses fear of not being able to afford insurance and that immigrants will steal his job. No matter how one feels about those topics, one can see how they would be a concern to somebody in his position.

The many speaking parts in this film are perfectly cast, except for Patton, who I never really believed as her TV reporter. Part of that may be how her character, despite being important to the advancement of the plot, is given relatively little to do. She expresses scruples early on that no aspiring journalist would pretend to have. Towards the end, it seems she is falling for Costner, but this seems unmotivated.

The best performances are Costner and Carroll. There's a child-like joy to the sudden attention he's receiving, such as a bit where they are in a limo, watching live TV of a helicopter shot of their vehicle in transit. He amuses himself by poking his hand out the window and watching it appear instantaneously on TV. Despite his energetic performance, Costner is often at risk of being upstaged by Carroll, who takes the opposite approach. She doesn't even have to deliver a line most times to get a laugh. Her obvious disdain for the phoniness surrounding her speaks for itself.

Also impressive are Grammer and Hopper. I would have thought the idea of Hopper as a potential president laughable before seeing this, but he definitely sells it in one of his most restrained performances. I liked how the script doesn't portray either as a buffoon, but each as a person who once had ideals that were slowly whittled away by the endless compromises necessary for a political career.

In the end, our hero will arrange a debate where, as he puts it: "Tonight, a below-average man is going to choose between two exceptional men." The questions will all come from the voluminous mail he has received, recalling the courtroom scene of *Miracle on 34th Street*.

And this film recalls much older cinema in regards to both humor and drama. It often feels downright "Capra-esque" as it recalls such Frank Capra works as *Mr. Smith Goes to Washington*. While that director's works were widely derided as "Capra-corn", *Swing Vote* wisely avoids cheap sentiment for most of its runtime (though it does come close to that on occasion).

I won't give away the ending, but I will say it completely sticks the landing. And yet, my wife and I had a nagging thought as the end credits rolled. There was a line of Carroll's earlier that social services will take her from Costner if he gets *another* felony. Were felons allowed to vote in New Mexico in 2008?

Original version posted on 11/24/2024

The Twonky (1953)

In 1953, the movie studios were terrified by the threat television posed to their livelihoods. I have seen many films from that era that took satirical jabs at the medium, but that year's *The Twonky* is the first time I have seen an actual TV set as the villain.

Hans Conried is perfectly cast as the lead here. Between this, and the even more bizarre *The 5,000 Fingers of Dr. T*, he seems to have been the go-to person for a particular breed of weird cinema at that time.

When the film begins, he is receiving a long list of last-minute reminders from his wife (Janet Warren). She's rushing off to stay with her sister, who is soon to give birth. Warren has gifted him a television so that he won't be lonely. In a good example of the quirky humor of this picture, he tells her, "by the time you get back, I promise you I'll know all the latest wrestling holds." Her list of to-dos and to-don't's include him wearing a hat if he goes into the dining room, as the ceiling plaster is falling.

But the television is not what it appears. In lieu of showing programs, it can shoot a laser beam from its screen, which it uses for all kinds of mayhem. At first, it is simply insistent on lighting his cigarettes. For some reason, it also wants to zap into shrapnel any coffee cup he holds. And yet, it puts his cleaned dishes back in the cupboard. It can even zap people in the head, making them change their minds. In one very funny scene, it has inexplicably made Conried's college professor deviate from his planned speech to instead detail the plot of a steamy romance novel.

It can even literally make money, though those bills will later draw attention from the police for being counterfeit. Still, that doesn't stop Edwin Max's hilariously dim TV shop delivery and repair guy from scooping up the bills from the living room floor. That the bills are laid out in a neat grid in front of the TV would likely give me pause, but not Max. Never mind it seems odd he believes he is entitled to what one would assume is Conried's money, regardless of the bizarre manner in which he appears to have stored it. The way Max goes after the cash despite all this has me convinced he would have eaten food right off the floor displayed in the same manner.

One way this film is different from how most others would handle the subject is this otherworldly appliance does not hesitate to flex its powers in front of others besides our protagonist. Especially curious is William H. Lynn, as Conried's friend and coach of the university's long-losing football team. He's the one that bestows the designation of the title upon the set: "I had Twonkies when I was a child. A Twonky is something you do not know what it is."

The coach is a fascinating character, and possibly the real star of the show. He is a running tap of non-sequiturs, sharing such bizarre insights as: "In 1906, I personally lifted 500 pounds...and two French women." Maybe that's how he made this memorable connection to French-fried potatoes: "Women—they confuse me. All my life, when I think about them, I think of French-fried potatoes". Wait, is Billy Bob Thornton's obsession with French fries in *Sling Blade* a sexual metaphor?

Unusual beverages also have a slight recurring theme in the film, what with coach whipping up his own concoction that is yogurt, molasses, grapes (which he crushed with his feet in his basement), Tabasco sauce and a dash of Benzine. The last must have been a thing at the time, as Max has a curious idea of what the kids were drinking then: "They mix Benzine and that uranium stuff and they call it a cocktail."

We never learn for certain the true nature of the Twonky, though it seemingly admits to being a robot. Maybe it traveled from the future, as speculated by the coach, but for what purpose? It seems to exist only to torment Conried. It is very determined to not be removed from the house, yet it never seems to have an apparent greater goal. It even does things to get the professor in trouble with his school and with the law, which seems contrary to it keeping its hooks into its alleged owner. One particularly surprising ruse, given how uptight audiences were at that time, is it calls a phone switchboard to try to solicit a prostitute for Conried.

When faced with a great enough threat, the Twonky will use its ray to zap the person unconscious. This seems to happen to roughly 70% of all people who set foot in the house, which will eventually be a surprisingly large number. When a zapped person comes to, they inevitably say in a stunned manner, "I…have…no…complaints. I…am…going…home."

That is pretty creepy. Actually, despite the sitcom-level humor of the material, the picture overall scanned as a horror film to me. The inane soundtrack reinforced that "offness" in my esteem. Then there's the Twonky's "walk", which is basically puppet legs that clearly are not what is really advancing it forward. Watching that thing move around the house is far creepier than any of those stupid things walking up walls and around on ceilings in too many horror films from this century.

My only complaint about *The Twonky* is the way I watched it, and that was a rip likely done from a VHS tape. The image had a high amount of artifacting, which was distracting at times. We have so many films that are nowhere near as good as this one, but which have had multiple releases on various disc formats already. It is astonishing this hasn't even been released on DVD yet, and I wish somebody would rectify that.

Original version posted on 9/5/2024

Will Success Spoil Rock Hunter? (1957)

Short answer: yes.

I suspect the general impression most people have of 1950's America is it was hopelessly naïve. Although I wasn't there to experience it myself, I know there had to be a lot more going on with most people than obsessively looking out for an imagined communist menace while cruising in a monstrous car, sipping on a malted at the soda shop or watching a movie at the drive-in.

Looking at some of the studio releases of 1957, however, shows signs of the coming cynicism of the next decade. That year saw the release of such pictures as *Sweet Smell of Success, A Face In the Crowd* and *12 Angry Men.* In a similar, but more lighthearted vein, is *Will Success Spoil Rock Hunter?*

Tony Randall stars as an advertising man, one of five non-blue-collar jobs it seems a man in the movies of the late 50's and early 60's could have. If movies are to be believed, half of adult men were architects or working in advertising. The rest were scientists, commercial pilots or in the armed forces, if I recall correctly.

The big (only?) client for Randall's firm is Stay-Put Lipstick. This account is going to move to another firm if he can't come up with a stellar campaign. The revolutionary idea he comes up with is to hire the most famous actress in the world (Jayne Mansfield) to be their spokesperson. Yep—that's his whole idea, and everybody thinks he's brilliant for coming up with it. Never mind *how* they are going to convince her to work for them.

I'm indifferent towards Mansfield, but this is a good role for her. In a lesser film, her character would have been a brainless bimbo. Here, she is quite savvy about how to manipulate the media to her advantage. Some of the movie's satirical points along these lines could be applied to today's culture of media influencers. Still, Mansfield tends to say things incorrectly, and often humorously, such as this statement about men: "I can pick them up and I can pick them down."

Mansfield just happens to have fled Hollywood for New York City to try to make her himbo of a boyfriend jealous (Mickey Hargitay—yep, the father of *Law & Order: SVU*'s Mariska Hargitay, whose mom is Mansfield, by the way). In her hotel room, she's on the phone with Hargitay, teasing him about another man in her life, though one doesn't exist in reality.

Fortune smiles on Randall when he goes to that hotel room to propose his sponsor's offer to Mansfield. She has a whole other kind of proposal in mind after she gets him on the phone to play the role of her new boyfriend. Having successfully made Hargitay jealous, Mansfield also manages to whip up a media frenzy with the announcement of her new romance. As thanks, she agrees to be the spokesperson for Stay-Put.

In addition to the media manipulation aspects of this picture, there is much that is still relevant in the skewering of the advertising industry. Even meaningless industry double-speak is mocked as Henry Jones, playing Randall's boss, blathers such inanities as the spokesperson idea being "The greatest thing since chlorophyll".

This is about the thousandth film I have seen where I wanted to spend more time with minor characters like Jones than with the stars. Betsy Drake left quite an impression as Randall's long-suffering secretary and girlfriend (a fairly typical arrangement in 1950's films). Joan Blondell steals every scene she's in as Mansfield's secretary and all-around right-hand woman. She has an especially great spiel about a milkman who is the great lost love of her life. In her grief, she follows this up with an interesting bit where she starts to pour a shot of booze and a tall glass of seltzer, but some complicated maneuvering leads to her downing a tall glass of booze and a shot of seltzer.

But the centerpiece of the picture is a moment of physical comedy where Mansfield puts Randall in one of Hargitay's suit jackets, in addition to lifts to make him taller. The result is Randall looks more than a bit like David Byrne in the famous big suit, as he stomps around like a cross between a giant toddler and Frankenstein. The punchline arrives when he goes to Drake's apartment like this and finds her in the dark, face and palms down on the floor and elbows in the air. Turns out she fell asleep while doing push-ups. Still struggling with his bizarre costuming, Randall puts her to bed, where she ends up lying on her back with her hands and arms still locked in place like she's doing "jazz hands".

Will Success Spoil Rock Hunter? is gently subversive, even from the opening credits, where Randall accompanies the 20th Century Fox logo to say he is contractually obligated to do so. The credits then play out over parodies of advertisements of various product types. This sets the tone for the rest of the movie, a light comedy that throws some gentle stabs at aspects of fame and advertising that are still relevant today.

Original version posted on 7/13/2023

You Never Can Tell (1951)

I think it is strange so many people seem to believe animals have souls and that there is a Heaven for them. Does that apply to anything that has lived? Will there be spiders in animal heaven? In that case, I have sent a great many to their heavenly reward. What about plants? They were all alive at some point, even if they don't have consciousness.

1951's *You Never Can Tell* has all manner of animals that have shuffled off their mortal coil gathered around a mystical watering hole. A lion rules over this layover to their final destination, a bestial purgatory named with the portmanteau of Beastitory. This is animism taken to a weird extreme. Also, it is presented only as a negative image, which is creepy as fuck.

The lion that rules over Beastitory looks especially menacing in such imagery. He listens to the plea of King, a recently deceased German Shepherd, who asks to be sent back to Earth to solve the mystery of his own murder. You see, he had inherited millions from the deceased owner of the legendary Polly Cracker Company (motto: "Everybody wants a Polly cracker"). Now that he has been poisoned, his former owner's secretary (Peggy Dow) is next in line for the windfall. Unfortunately for her, she's accused of poisoning King.

The dog is granted a brief return to the terrestrial world to clear Dow's name and finger the true killer. And he will have actual fingers to do that, as he is brought back in the form of a private investigator played by Dick Powell. Assisting him will be a former racehorse, now reincarnated as his partner at the firm (Joyce Holden).

I thought it was interesting they are set up in an office, complete with the name of Powell's character on the window. That name is "Rex Shepherd", because the lion-God-of-animals apparently has a sense of humor. I wondered what the other tenants in the building thought when there was suddenly, and I suspect instantaneously, a new business adjacent to their own. As we later discover, Animal God didn't think to put any case files in the filing cabinet.

There are many funny moments involving Powell and Holden engaging in behaviors that only made sense in their previous incarnations. Powell is constantly snacking from a bag of kibble, and I wondered what his now-human digestive system will think of that. Holden uses a feedbag as a purse, and she keeps a ready supply of hay in it for snacking. And here I thought Powell had some interesting gastrointestinal phenomena to look forward to.

She also always wears a hat with wings situated in it in a way that makes it appear she has horse ears protruding through the brim. Also, she can still run as fast as a horse, chasing down a city bus that is going 40 miles an hour. How is that even possible with human bones, muscles and tendons?

Lastly, the characters who were animals still have any physical infirmities they had in their previous form, such as Powell still having the bad knee he had as a canine. That strikes me as very strange, as human knees are nothing like dog knees.

An even weirder concept the film lightly touches on is that of "humanimals", or fellow humans who were once dogs, in particular. I don't remember this idea being formally brought up in dialogue, and only Holden can identify these people. And the generations of offspring from that humanimal are also identifiable as such.

You Never Can Tell requires the viewer to set aside their disbelief so far that it might as well be buried like a dog bone. For those who can, this is a light, though still rather odd, comedy with shades of darkness. After all, you have somebody who murdered a dog to get their hands on a fortune. Perhaps even stranger, you have a man who was reincarnated from a dog express carnal desires for Dow, who used to be his master. That presents some uncomfortable issues, though I can't blame him. I would likely also dry-hump Dow's legs.

Original version posted on 9/29/2024

You don't want no drama

except this is the section about dramatic movies

Atlantic City (1980)

There's a large sign on a building that could either be in the process of being remodeled or prepared for demolition. Given what we have seen so far of the titular *Atlantic City* in this 1980 film, good money would be on the latter. The sign reads "Atlantic City you're back on the map. Again". First, there's the wording, which implies the city is actually looking forward to its *second* recovery. Then there's the suggestion this town is on a map of places sane people might want to go.

It is obvious Atlantic City, the place, is not going to achieve its goals of rehabilitation. Like attracts like, and the denizens we see are all has-beens and never-wills who can't escape this black hole. It's like a movie populated with characters from Steely Dan songs.

The two main characters are played by Burt Lancaster, an elderly man who was allegedly a major player decades prior, and Susan Sarandon, as his next-door neighbor who has aspirations of becoming a blackjack dealer. At first, there isn't any interaction between them. The closest they get is when he secretly watches her every night as she stands at her kitchen window, dousing herself in lemon juice to wash away the smell of the oysters she spends all day shucking at a casino.

These are the small lives of people in limbo, just waiting for anything to happen. Anything arrives in the form of a husband Sarandon discarded, and he has brought along her pregnant sister. We can assume the backstory.

Robert Joy plays the soon-to-be-ex-husband, and it's a shame he isn't in more of the film. He brings a considerable amount of skeezy, schemey energy to the proceedings, as well as a large quantity of stolen cocaine that drives the plot. Another character I wish was in the movie longer tells Joy "You look like a fire sale" and "You look like a training poster for the NARC squad."

The final scene in which Joy appears is when he attempts to flee a thug by climbing the levels of a parking structure with moving platforms. As the levels pass by one another, this proves to be another game of chance in a town fueled by gambling. Except the stakes are the highest possible this time, and he's going to lose.

Because of this, Lancaster ends up the recipient of the cocaine, and he uses some of the resulting proceeds to make arrangements to send Joy's remains back to his hometown. Sarandon believes Lancaster is using his own money. Things will get more complicated when she discovers the money he's spending is really hers.

Atlantic City feels very real and natural. It isn't like we're watching a documentary, but it has that sensation of heightened reality the best movies have. Nobody does anything that isn't in keeping with what we have seen of their characters. Also, no character ever suddenly possesses any knowledge or skills without explanation.

Atlantic City of 1980, the place, looks like the realm of losers, a place where dreams go to die. Almost miraculously, *Atlantic City*, the 1980 film about such losers, is a winner.

Original version posted on 2/14/2023

American Buffalo (1996)

"That dyke cocksucker." This curious statement is just one of many made by Dustin Hoffman as part of the verbal diarrhea he spews throughout 1996's *American Buffalo*.

This is a movie adaptation of the famous David Mamet play. As always, his dialogue has a certain profane spark to it which you will either find intriguing or highly off-putting. There's also the slightly stilted way his characters phrase things. For me, his scripts read not like how people talk in reality, but instead uncannily convey an aspect of real conversation I can't seem to put my finger on. It's like how a great impersonation is never something anybody would mistake for the original. Instead, a successful impersonation only channels one or two elements that are unique to the subject at hand.

The stage play is barely opened up for the movie adaptation, though this didn't feel airless to me. It all takes place in a large shop Dennis Franz owns in a rundown part of an unidentified city. His establishment is filled with disorganized junk. I have read a couple of reviews where critics expressed disbelief such a store could exist. I can confirm they do, and in great numbers. I almost feel like I somehow have been in the exact store Franz owns here. And, every time I wander into such a place, I wonder who would ever set foot in there and, if they did, what they hoped to find. I usually find myself at a loss as to what brought *me* into the store.

In addition to Hoffman and Franz, the only character wandering in and out and around the shop is Sean Nelson as a kid who clearly idolizes Franz. I'm not sure why he does exactly. He also respects Hoffman, though obviously not as much. Nelson basically hangs around the shop a lot, listening to the ramblings of two men old enough to be his father and who have clearly done little of note in their lives. Mostly, Nelson runs errands, such as getting bacon for Hoffman from the nearby diner, which the older man disposes of in a way that is weird, funny and which I like to think was improvised.

The film also makes Nelson a bit of an enigma for most of the runtime. The kid appears dedicated to Franz, but I noticed something early on that suggested he may be pocketing some of the money the older man gives him for diner runs. There will also be the titular, and highly valuable, nickel which Franz believes a customer stole from his shop. Eventually, Nelson happens to have a buffalo nickel he tries to sell to Franz. Is the kid trying to sell back to Franz a nickel he stole from him?

What drives the plot is Franz's idea to break into the apartment of the guy he believes stole from him and get the nickel back. But not anything by the band Nickelback, as nobody wants that. Hoffman connives his way into this operation, but insists Nelson not be part of it. That Franz even humors the idea of Hoffman providing assistance shows a serious lapse in judgement. Then again, this is a man who runs a store that seems to serve no conventional purpose.

But Franz does have enough sense to bring in another person, one who is described as being highly competent. We only have the assessments of our three leads to go on, as the mysterious Fletcher is essentially the Godot of this piece, somebody the others talk about all the time but who never makes an appearance.

That is, unless Fletcher is one of the people we see in extreme close-ups in footage of a poker game which is interspersed in the opening credits. Really, is there anything more essentially Mamet than a poker game? One of the players is only seen by her long fingernails, so I assume this is the equally absent "Ruthie" whom Hoffman so memorably described in my opening sentence.

The performances are largely top-notch, as one would expect, and which is necessary for a movie with only three roles. Franz especially excels in his performance, and his increasing exasperation at Hoffman's seeming inability to stop talking made me laugh a great deal more than I expected from this film.

As for Hoffman, he plays things a bit too broadly, though it is hard to deny the power of his performance. He is a whirling dervish of nervous energy and profanity. I think a new source of alternative clean energy could be Hoffman's insecurity. I can imagine entire cities powered for years from it. He's like if Ratso Rizzo somehow lived on to see middle age and evolved into something even *less* appealing.

American Buffalo is not the best presentation I have seen of Mamet's work, but it is intense and intriguing. It is also far funnier than I expected, but I think that has to do with how I regarded some of Hoffman's more outrageous statements and Franz's irritation towards him. Really, an equally valid reaction would be to not laugh at all. Regardless, I recommend the film to those who might be interested.

Original version posted on 2/8/2024

Bad Day at Black Rock (1955)

Never underestimate a one-armed man. For example, nobody believed Richard Kimble in *The Fugitive* when he tries to convince them such a man murdered his wife. I'm not exactly sure what the singularly limbed guy in *Twin Peaks* is all about, but he's pretty creepy.

Ernest Borgnine is a thug in a very small desert town, and he unwisely picks a fight with a one-armed Spencer Tracy in

1955's *Bad Day at Black Rock*. Tracy had lost his arm serving in WWII, and he appears to damn near crush the bigger man's windpipe with a single karate chop. Still, Borgnine will get up three more times and try to take him on. The last attempt is after extricating himself from a screen door Tracy tossed him through.

Tracy is treated in a hostile manner by all but a couple of the denizens of the titular town. Everybody is collectively hiding something, and worried he will get to the root of that mystery. Heck, the telegraph operator is downright apoplectic nobody let him know the train was going to be stopping there to let Tracy off, as no other train had done so in the past four years. In a telling exchange with the conductor as he stepped off the train, Tracy says, "I won't be here long" and the other man replies, "In a place like this, it could be a lifetime." The poor welcome he'll receive suggests he just might end up there permanently, though only briefly among the living.

At the hotel, the visitor insists on being given a room, despite the protests of proprietor John Ericson. All the rooms are empty, which makes any arguments against Tracy renting one all the more baffling. And yet, I was even more confused by why this town even has a functioning hotel, given the trains never stop there.

Some others who are less than helpful include Borgnine and Lee Marvin as local muscle. The former is especially terrifying as he obviously enjoys inflicting pain on others. And, as the second paragraph in this essay details, he thinks it is fair to pick a fight with a physically impaired man a couple of decades his senior.

But there are a couple of characters who, while not excessively helpful, are at least sympathetic to Tracy's plight. Dean Jagger is a disgraced sheriff who finds solace in the bottle but obviously still feels conflicted by an internal sense of right and wrong. Walter Brennan is the town doctor, in what is pretty much the Walter Brennan role. I was fascinated by an odd line he says when asked how he regards the present situation, that he looks at it "with the innocence of a fresh-laid egg." Lastly, I was surprised to see Anne Francis in a minor role as the owner of the gas station.

Everybody is subservient in varying degrees to Robert Ryan, playing the kind of sociopath he excelled at. I never stop being amazed at how often he played such monsters in features, and so convincingly, as everything I have read has described him as a kind and generous soul in real life.

This picture was filmed in Cinemascope, and it makes great use of it. Some scenes that might otherwise feel a bit too stagy are improved by distributing non-key characters to the edges of the frame. It somehow makes those moments feel more natural. The widescreen image makes an impression from the first frames of the opening credits, as it manages to capture in profile the entirety of a passenger train as it tears through the desert.

Perhaps the strangest aspect of this film is Tracy likely wouldn't be so dogged in his investigation if everybody hadn't been so antagonistic. Of course, if everybody acted nonchalant, there wouldn't be a movie.

The central mystery of this picture is not too hard to figure out, but it is deliberately concealed to an extent that revealing more feels like a spoiler. And yet, when we learn what has transpired, it is even more baffling to me why everybody has chosen to be under Ryan's thumb. What I will say, however, because it is a great line, is what is being covered up occurred after the responsible parties became "patriotically drunk".

In the end, *Bad Day in Black Rock* feels similar to *High Noon*, with only one man willing to stand up to an evil the rest of a town will not fight. I would say I'm not completely sold on the idea of a town, even one as small as this, completely acquiescing to the will of one person, except recent history has shown how some entire countries are all too happy to do so. What is even weirder to me is, whether in this movie or in real life, the one the people will sacrifice everything for is somebody who doesn't have any of their interests in mind.

Original version posted on 9/22/2024

Clash By Night (1952)

Although I have never been much of a fan of Marilyn Monroe, I suspect it is only because I haven't seen enough movies she was in. She has that quality which is most difficult to describe, that star power which makes a viewer pay attention to what she is doing whenever she is on screen, regardless of the other actors in the same shot.

She's a minor character in 1952's *Clash by Night*, but she steals every scene she's in and seemingly with little effort. That's pretty good when you sometimes have to hold your own against Barbara Stanwyck. Here, Monroe plays the fiancée of Stanwyck's brother, played by Keith Andes. It is pretty strange to see Monroe cast as a shlub gutting fish all day at a cannery. That she is believable in these moments is a testament to her oft-derided acting ability.

Stanwyck has returned to this seaside shithole after failing to make it big in the outside world on her terms: "Home is where you come when you run out of places." This is after marrying a rich man and then quickly becoming widowed. She received a nice inheritance, only for the other heirs to successfully challenge it in court.

One person who is thrilled to see her back is Paul Doulgas, a boat captain with a big, open heart and who has always been smitten with her. Her successfully woos her, and they eventually marry and have a baby together. Admittedly, Stanwyck has set the bar rather low: "I want a man to give me confidence. Somebody to beat off the world before it swallows you up." She commits to Douglas, though she had warned him he's too nice and she'll ruin him. That's partly true—she'll have help from some others in that effort.

Also in their house is Silvio Minciotti as Douglas's father and J. Carrol Naish as his uncle. Naish has a particularly juicy role as a vile shit-stirrer who is always looking to plant seeds of discord, even when it has no direct benefit to himself. Needless to say, he will be a catalyst in Douglas's eventual downfall.

Almost as vile is Robert Ryan as the alleged best friend of Douglas. Ryan always radiates a thinly-veiled hostility in his performances, and he is especially sinister here.

From the moment Douglas introduces him to Stanwyck, he is a threat to their relationship. This, despite Ryan already being married to a burlesque dancer. He is also such an unrepentant misogynist that he says of his spouse he wants "to stick her full of pins just to see if blood runs out." Another charming bon mot is "Haven't you ever wanted to cut up a beautiful dame?" It's no surprise he's also a racist, and we'll be treated to his shockingly crude impersonation of a Chinese person.

These are not the only repellent men in this film. There is also an undercurrent of a threat throughout Adres's performance. In one disturbing scene, he "playfully" strangles girlfriend Monroe with a towel, as if such a thing can be done in such a lighthearted manner. I was very happy when she responds by slugging him in the kisser.

Overall, this is a darker film than I expected, even for one directed by Fritz Lang. There are mentions of news stories where dead bodies were found nearby, including one of a days-old infant. Curiously, these elements do not factor in the overall plot, but they still establish an air of lingering dread.

The cynical nature of the material is not surprising when one realizes the script is from Clifford Odets, the scribe of *Sweet Smell of Success*. Similar to that film, the dialogue is clever almost to a fault, though not as memorable as that of the other film. Characters here keep saying, "Go away, dust", which I doubt was ever a popular phrase anywhere at any point in the past.

The finale of *Clash by Night* has Douglas as a cuck amok, snapping from the various pressures put upon him by almost every other character. His rage is believable and understandable, even if the developments and characters in this picture are not entirely realistic. I mildly recommend this film, despite it being a curious work that never feels quite settled or sure of itself.

Original version posted on 5/9/2024

Comfort and Joy (1984)

Bill Forsyth makes interesting movies. I doubt I would be able to tell a picture is one of his without knowing that in advance, but the ones I have seen so far have a humanity to them I greatly appreciate. There's also a quirkiness that goes beyond expected human behavior but never crosses into anything cartoonish. The closest analogy I can think of is the work of Aki Kaurismaki, though that director's films definitely cross farther into the realm of the absurd.

Consider 1984's *Comfort and Joy* where a Glasgow radio DJ (Bill Paterson) becomes the mediator in a turf war between rival ice cream vendors. He gets caught up in this intrigue only because he was instantly smitten with a woman he sees in one of the trucks while it's in transit. He follows the vehicle until it stops, which scans as a tad creepy and stalkery.

Almost as soon as he has a cone from the vendor, a car roars up and three men in balaclavas get out of it and start smashing up the ice cream truck. One of the thugs recognizes the DJ and asks him for his autograph, as his mother is a huge fan. Thus, poor Paterson is roped into a bizarre gang rivalry.

But then the guy was already unmoored and looking for a purpose after separating from long-time girlfriend, Maddy (Eleanor David). Personally, I think he was better off without a kleptomaniac who is best described by the word formed by the first three letters of her name. I'm hoping the sex had been great at least.

The scene where she decides to leave him is shockingly abrupt. The couple is relaxing in their apartment, when she gets up and starts gathering various items. When he asks what she's doing, she casually replies, "I'm leaving and I'm just getting some things together. I meant to say this ages ago".

Paterson is a nice enough guy that he even helps to move the furniture out. In the end, everything is gone. As he tells a visiting friend, "She took everything but the mortgage. That was mine."

Perhaps he is flexible to a fault, which is how he gets involved in this bizarre feud centered around ice cream. He complies when told by thugs he needs to follow their ice cream truck to another location. I wouldn't have done that.

The feud becomes almost a parody of the various Mafia films we have all seen. A meeting with one of the factions is held in a sad little booth in a corner shop. Instead of eating meticulously prepared foods of their former homeland, these men in suits and overcoats are dining on packaged snack cakes as if these are equivocal.

Not sure why they don't just eat their product instead, as each gang touts their frozen goods as being superior to all others. Both gangs keep giving Paterson containers of their goods, to the extent I lost count of how many he receives. Sorry, but I need to correct myself, as he insists on paying for that first container he receives while touring a production facility. I was amused the kingpin of that operation gives him change.

The manufacturing scenes mirror an amusing bit that runs under the opening credits. It is Christmastime, and children are watching a department store window display of animatronic elves making treats. The various expressions on the kids' faces are amusing, especially one girl whose bemused look conveys she is less than impressed.

I'm not sure my words here will convince anybody to see *Comfort and Joy*, which is a shame, as it is such an enjoyable film. Without any real violence in it, it sold me on the idea there could be a turf war for any business, even ice cream. At the same time, the movie realizes the absurdity of this and has fun with the concept, while never crossing the line into farce. Recommended.

Original version posted on 12/16/2023

The Cook, The Thief, His Wife and Her Lover (1989)

What is one to do when a monster enters their lives, running roughshod over everything without ever being kept in check?

When we first see Michael Gambon in 1989's notorious *The Cook, The Thief, His Wife and Her Lover*, this gangster has a chef stripped naked while he and his thugs force-feed the poor man dog shit. If you're already thinking this may not be the movie for you, then you may be right. But then you would be missing out on a strangely beautiful, painterly film that is as stirring emotionally as it is visually.

One aspect of this which will stick with me is it is a long movie. I'm not referring to the runtime, which is of appropriate length, but instead to the expanse most of the set occupies horizontally. With the exception of a couple of key scenes near the end, the drama takes place entirely within a long strip that begins with a parking lot and goes through a massive kitchen and cavernous dining area before terminating at what may be the most spacious restroom I have seen.

I was using words like "painterly" and "staged" intentionally, as this is a deliberately artificial environment. The dining area is saturated in a lurid red and dominated by a reproduction of a Flemish Baroque painting showing wealthy men dressed in the finery of that era. Not by coincidence, Gambon and his mob are dressed in a similar manner the first time we see them. Even the first shot reveals the set to be a giant stage, and the picture is bookended by the parting and closing of theatrical curtains.

I'm not sure if it is because of, or despite of, this high theatricality, but the drama seriously got under my skin. Gambon's behavior is consistently, deeply repellent and yet it is, unfortunately, within the realm of the believable. Even if we hadn't witnessed some of that behavior, it is obvious from his wife's (Helen Mirren) resigned demeanor that life with him is hell. Seeing a bookish man (Alan Howard) dining at a nearby table over consecutive nights, she sees the opportunity for escape, however brief.

Their dalliances are initially in the restaurant's bathroom. There's a genuine sensuality and delicacy to their first encounter, even if it is in a bathroom stall. I wasn't sure if they had even exchanged any words prior to this moment. Naturally, a man like Gambon's character would have no hesitation in storming into the ladies', which he does. Disaster is averted, but not before he delivers this appalling line to Mirren, whom he believes is alone in that stall: "Are you playing with yourself? You're not allowed to do that. That's my property."

Before long, the chef (Richard Bohringer) arranges for them to have trysts in various parts of the kitchen. He seems to genuinely like these secret lovers, though I suspected he also enjoyed having some measure of revenge against the boor who is holding his restaurant hostage night after night. Gambon had even gone as far as to impose a huge neon sign for the exterior, changing the establishment's name to the surnames of himself and the chef.

There are some interesting observations here about the relationship between sex and eating. We will see different characters consuming the same food but with different reactions. I find it interesting how the mouth tastes the food, but it is the brain that appreciates it (or not, in the case of Gambon and his thugs). Then there's sex, where people may use the same body parts with each other, but the act is passionate and beautiful between Mirren and Howard, while Gambon reduces it to nothing more than animals rutting. Bohringer even has the interesting observation that "Eating black food is like consuming death" and are not orgasms often described as "the little death"?

That association between food and death foretells an audacious finale. I'm sure many viewers will find that moment excessively ridiculous, repulsive or both. And it is both, while also being the perfect conclusion. In a concise and shocking moment, *The Cook, The Thief, His Wife and Her Lover* finds a way to deal with the monster at the heart of the story, and in a way that is as perfect as it is unique.

Original version posted on 12/5/2023

Cooley High (1975)

Hard to believe there was a time when one could load their movie soundtrack with an album's worth of prime Motown sides from the 60's for a pittance. And yet, that's what happened with *Cooley High* when it was in production in 1974. People may think tastes change faster now, but the present can't complete with how radically different urban culture was between 1964, when the movie takes place, and 1974. By that time, what was devastatingly hip music in the recent past was now so passe as to be sold like Motown was having a fire sale.

This is an American International Pictures release. Although that studio raked in the dough around that time for their blaxploitation flicks, *Cooley High* has none of the trappings of that genre. There are no monsters, guns, pimps or prostitutes. Nobody does any martial arts. This is just a movie about a group of high school seniors in 1964's Cabrini Green.

This movie is unique in so many ways that it is difficult to summarize all of them here. It is a comedy-drama in that it is almost all comedy up to a certain point near the middle, only to become solidly drama in the second half. It shows how people can be happy and fulfilled even when they are, by most people's definition, poor. And it is somehow light-hearted and good-natured, even when these guys joyride in a stolen car (admittedly, they weren't the ones who stole it), drink or smoke dope.

The center of the group is Preach (Glynn Turman) and Cochise (Lawrence Hilton-Jacobs). These two *own* these roles, but what is surprising is how good the rest of the cast is when, aside from a teacher played by Garrett Morris, everybody else is an amateur who actually lived in that neighborhood at the time.

What most intrigues me about this picture is how this group of friends could seem so real. The camaraderie and rapport are so natural that I wish I had ever had friends like these. I know I can't imagine what it is like to be Black, impoverished or living in the Civil Rights era, let alone all three, but there's still something magical captured here which I have never experienced personally. I would even settle for being Pooter–poor, lowly *Pooter*, for chrissakes!

The screenplay is by Eric Monte, writing from his own recollections. I have never seen an interview with Monte, but it is easy to imagine him as Preach, the bookish guy who, according to text at the end, went on to become a successful Hollywood screenwriter. Indeed, Monte was already established at the time this film was made, having been one of the creators of TV's *Good Times*.

In a bizarre twist, those Motown tracks I mentioned in the opening paragraph prevented this picture from having a legitimate release on videotape. Basically, nobody at the time of its production could foresee the coming home video revolution, so the soundtrack rights were only negotiated for the theatrical release. Ironic that the film which turned those old tunes into gold again was the overwhelmingly White *The Big Chill*.

I find it disappointing the most frequent description applied to *Cooley High* is "a Black *American Graffiti*". Such labels do a disservice to both movies. Maybe I am delusional, but I identified far more with *Cooley High* than I ever did Lucas's film. This is a great movie to revisit, to spend a bit of time with some old friends I never had.

Original version posted on 5/17/2023

The Damned Don't Cry (1950)

Despite my best intentions, I am still always comparing Joan Crawford to Bette Davis when I see the former in a picture. That isn't fair to her, and there are definitely movies where she is better suited to a role than Davis would have been. A great example of such is 1950's *The Damned Don't Cry*.

Crawford plays almost two distinct characters here, though they are the same person at different points in time. The earliest we see of her is when she is a wife of a poor oil well worker. Together, they have a young son who wants nothing more than a bicycle. The father is furious when he learns Crawford managed to get one for the lad. Something I think is intriguing is we don't know *how* she paid for it, and I felt there was a suggestion it was obtained in trade. Maybe that's what he's really upset about. She tries to placate him by saying, "All the other kids in the neighborhood have them", and he replies, "I don't care if they have zeppelins". Now *that* I want to see!

The family lives with the husband's parents in what may be the most depressing house I have seen in any movie. It looks like it is maintained in the best manner possible on the inside, but that doesn't matter when the house is literally surrounded by derricks. It reminded me of nothing less than the house of the girl's parents in *Eraserhead*, and I imagine those people moving in right after these current occupants have moved on.

In a moment that lays it on a hair too thick, the adorable little scamp is riding his bike that same day when he is struck dead by a car. Somehow, I doubt they will be able to get that bike restored to a good enough condition that it will be accepted for a return. The idea of consolation from the others in the household is to tell her it was God's will. I was stunned by her response: "He was six years old. I don't believe God works like that."

That isn't such a shocking statement today, but that would have been regardless as blasphemous by many in that unenlightened age. Nope, wait, society is possibly even more stupid now, so it is likely *more* people would be offended by that statement now.

She flees to the big city but, without any marketable skills, she will have to rely on *something* else to make a living. Things start out innocently enough. Crawford is asked to model some dresses, but then the owner of the operation asks her to join him and another model in "entertaining" some clients that night. I assume nothing too scandalous happens that first night; however, when she's exiting the car at the end of the evening, she says, "I feel like something that's been on sale at a bargain basement". The other model gives Crawford her "cut", and it is fascinating to see the slowly dawning realization there's more specialized services to be expected eventually.

Crawford becomes very worldly in short order. The final transformation of this character is completely believable, even if we don't see the intermediate steps to get there. I also believed the combination of luck, skill and intuition that leads to her becoming the arm candy of a gangster (David Brian). She accomplishes this through helping a bookish accountant (Kent Smith) improve his financial standing by applying his trade to criminal enterprises.

Brian is trying to apply contemporary business principles to organized crime. Some of the old school gangsters aren't having that, especially Steve Cochran. Brian sends Crawford to California to get some inside information through the seduction of Cochran. She's not thrilled by this request: "You want me to ingratiate myself to this rotten thug? Is that all I've meant to you? Just another investment?" Brian will come to regret asking her to do this, as she falls in love with Cochran. From there, the movie does what noir movies do.

You don't want no drama [except this is the section about dramatic movies]

An aspect of this picture I found fascinating is how convincing Crawford is throughout, despite being clearly too old. And yet I believed her at each step of her transformation from kind-hearted mother to world-weary moll.

I also felt the three male co-stars hold their own against her, and I suspect that was never easy to do. Smith wisely underplays as the humble everyman, ordering a chicken salad sandwich at a high-end club. Brian is interesting as a gangster with aspirations. As he explains it to Crawford, what she called a flowerpot is really an Etruscan vase, and it is a whole other thing to be able to appreciate it. Lastly, Cochran excels at playing a complete sleaze, but a charming one regardless.

There is much to recommend *The Damned Don't Cry*. Crawford really shines in this film. The black-and-white photography is fantastic. It is a tad more melodrama than it is noir, but I couldn't care less when characters are shrieking dialogue this good at each other.

Original version posted on 7/14/2024

Day of the Locust (1975)

I don't know if audiences of the 1970's were clamoring for films set four decades prior, but the studios delivered a ton of them. Paramount, especially, seemed to have a hard-on for making films set in the 1930's, among them *Paper Moon, Lady Sings the Blues* and *The Last Tycoon*. Well, it worked with *Chinatown*, so I can understand wanting to see if that mine might yield any more gold.

1975's *Day of the Locust* would not be such a film, seemingly as predestined to fail as its miserable characters. This adaptation of the Nathanael West novel is as nihilistic as *They Shoot Horses, Don't They?*, though it didn't pack as strong of a punch for me. Like that film, it will culminate in a devastating climax which feels inevitable. With that in mind, this essay will concern the entire film, so I'll warn you now: there will be a great many spoilers.

It has been long enough since I read West's novel that I can't say how closely this hews to the source material. It is certain the film adds more material, just by it being a 2 ½ hour adaptation of a rather slim text.

What I remember most vividly from the book is how it rambled. It is far more a character study than a plot-oriented work. If there is one central character, it is that played by Karen Black as a vapid, aspiring star who, at best, occasionally gets work as an extra.

She and her father (Burgess Meredith) occupy an apartment in the same complex as William Atherton, playing a Yale grad employed as an art director at Paramount. Their flirtation is equally shallow on both sides: he likes her looks and she is always looking to worm her way into a film. This is her idea of letting him down gently: "I could only let a really rich man love me. I could only love someone criminally handsome."

Black's role is interesting because the character intentionally doesn't have any depth. She has no backstory and there is no reason for us to root for her to succeed. That isn't bad writing, but a deliberate and brave choice. Her dream is to be a movie star, though seemingly without reason. Near the end of the runtime, she tells Atherton he just doesn't understand her, but we don't, either.

Also involved with Black is Donald Sutherland as a character named Homer Simpson. Curiously, he doesn't enter the film until nearly an hour in, and that is when Meredith, peddling a kind of snake oil door-to-door, collapses in his living room. When Black arrives to take her father home, the shy and awkward Sutherland is instantly smitten. She will move in with him following the death of her father, and they will have a sexless relationship based on security and him buying her everything she wants.

Among the interesting minor characters is Billy Barty, as a deeply repellent person I couldn't quite get a read on. He drinks a lot and is always looking to screw. Following the death of Meredith, he proclaims, "I'm gonna go get laid…for Harry!" An honorary lay—that's a kind of tribute I was not aware of previously. This role is different from anything I have seen him do before, as I never expected to hear the actor casually drop the n-word.

The remaining residents of note in the complex include a mother who is forever grooming her nightmare offspring to be a child star. I thought the brat was a girl, and was surprised it was Jackie Earle Haley in a curly blond wig, shorts and frilly socks. This monster is forever tap-dancing from one place to another, snarling and spewing pure venom. He especially seems to have it in for Sutherland's timid accountant, pushing him until the man stomps the boy to death in the street. It is a testament to Sutherland's performance that I can understand why he does this.

Haley's shtick of sarcastically singing and crudely parodying celebrities (we first see him doing a grotesque Mae West) is similar to Meredith's performance. The older man is a former vaudevillian furious to be reduced to selling crap. I mentioned how the film rambles, and the weirdest tangent is an extended bit where we follow him on his rounds. His desperate need to play the clown fails to mask his seething hatred. I also detected the faintest suggestion of incest in his relationship with his daughter, but I suspect I am reading too much into that. Honestly, it is hard to guess how much evil a man is capable of once you've seen him doing his old shtick, though wearing makeup, and attired in a manner, which makes him look like the world's oldest Droog.

Sex hangs in the air throughout this picture, yet there is nothing titillating. Atherton, at the invitation of a producer (Richard Dysart), goes to a brothel (ran by Natalie Schafer–Lovey Howell from *Gilligan's Island*!) where he joins in watching a stag film with a bunch of older, wealthy people. It seemed about as awkward as I imagine it would be. While there, he sees Black's best friend (Lelia Goldoni) working as "entertainment". It is inevitable Black will eventually follow her into this line of work.

It seems neither Atherton nor Sutherland ever get to make time with Black, as she is too preoccupied in that regard with a couple of rough guys played by Bo Hopkins and Pepe Serna. I think a telling metaphor is both guys have cockfighting roosters, and Black is fascinated by their cocks. She will eventually move these two into Sutherland's garage "until they can get back on their feet". One night, the accountant becomes a peeping tom at his own house as he watches in horror from outside a window as these two, Black and almost everybody else in the movie, proceed to trash his place.

The film is big on scenes of destruction, as if no aspect of Hollywood can keep from imploding. Earlier, there was an amazing scene where the set for the film on which Atherton was working collapses. That the film was about Napoleon's battle at Waterloo seems to foretell even the movie within this movie cannot succeed. This sequence is spectacular, starting with an actor or two falling through the floor, culminating with entire sections falling a couple of stories. A nice touch is famed director/producer William Castle playing the director of this fiasco, in what was his final appearance on screen.

But these scenes have nothing on the violent riot that is the film's climax. Sutherland had killed Haley within a block of a red-carpet movie premiere in progress, and the mob that was there to stargaze ends up tearing him apart. From there, cars are overturned, shop windows are smashed, and things are suggested that I am glad we don't have to see in detail. Atherton, in the midst of the chaos, imagines faces in the mob turning into what look like crude, featureless black-and-white illustrations. This was so similar to what Alan Parker did in the "Another Brick In The Wall" sequence of *The Wall* that I wondered if this was an influence on him.

Hollywood has always secretly loved films that take its own livelihood to task. But this film isn't like similar, earlier efforts such as 1952's *The Bad and the Beautiful*. *Day of the Locust* is genuinely hostile, and that's why industry veterans such as Sidney Lumet called out director John Schlesinger for "shitting where he eats." It is a weird, sprawling beast of the kind the major studios would stop taking risks on by the end of the 70's. In a way, its messiness conveys the insanity and instability of the lives of its characters. It is a vortex of cruelty that has to destroy Sutherland, a normally gentle man who must be pushed to his breaking point. To do otherwise, or to make a tidier film, would be a betrayal.

Original version posted on 5/27/2024

Dead Again (1991)

The IMDB listing for 1991's *Dead Again* puts it in the genres of crime, drama, mystery and thriller. The one it leaves out is comedy, which is how I will remember this feature. It is so slyly a comedy that not even the film itself might realize it is one.

I will concede one problem I faced is my difficulty taking Kenneth Branagh seriously, and he both stars and directs here. His co-star is Emma Thompson, his wife at the time. I have enjoyed performances by them in some movies or shows but, in general, I find both too self-aware in their acting. They remind me of the irritating drama kids in high school who were always desperate for the spotlight. Today, he is a Knight and she is a Dame of the British Empire, which feels fitting somehow.

This movie finds the couple in interwoven timelines alternating between events in 1949 and those in the then-present of 1990. In the past, he was a famous conductor sent to the electric chair after being convicted for stabbing her to death with a pair of scissors. I guess the last thing he conducted in that life was a great deal of electricity. In the present, he's a private eye trying to help her, an amnesiac, recover her memory.

In the past, the couple lived in a mansion that, decades later, is transformed into an orphanage. The plot thread set in the present begins with her scaling a wall and sneaking into that institution one night. Any person with even the most remote connection to reality would be calling the cops on her but, no, the head of the orphanage calls in Branagh's P.I. instead.

Even this early in the runtime, I started wondering if this was meant to be a parody of this kind of thriller that was so popular around that time. The lead priest barks orders so angrily, he might as well be literally foaming at the mouth. While he's doing that, Thompson is in the courtyard, looking at a soccer ball in her hands with a level of confusion suggesting she might be an alien. I laughed hard at the matching cut showing a concerned nun and a ragtag bunch of orphans who just want their ball back.

Further suggesting this is a comedy is a supporting performance by Robin Williams. Yes, he has been in serious films, but he is given way too much latitude in doing his trademark motormouth shtick. His character is a former psychiatrist who is now stocking shelves in a small, ethnic grocery of some sort. In his few moments here, he is allowed to ramble on and on, largely about such topics as past lives and karmic retribution. I guess it is beliefs in things like that which started his downfall. His character is angry, but the performance is largely "angry funny", as was the rage at the time (so to speak). At one point, Williams calls Branagh a dumb dick, and I wondered if he knew the cameras were rolling.

The central conceit of the plot is whether the Branagh and Thompson in the present are reincarnations of that earlier couple and, if so, will one of them murder the other. I don't believe in reincarnation, though I will accept it in the world of a given movie. Even then, I doubted these two in the present would look exactly like their past selves unless they were in fact blood relations of those people.

Helping these two get in touch with their previous selves is Derek Jacobi, as a hypnotist who abuses his abilities to get inside information on antiques he might acquire for his store. Wayne Knight is interesting as a friend of Branagh's who is eager to assist in the investigation. I almost would have rather seen a film about these supporting characters than I would of the leads.

But then we would have missed a finale so over-the-top, so deliriously batshit, that it confirmed my suspicions this is a secret satire of the genre. Much of this will take place in an apartment where a character is supposedly so obsessed with that murder in 1949 that all of the artwork there incorporates scissor imagery into them. There's Dali's famous melting clocks, except it is now melting scissors. There's Michaelangelo's God reaching out to the hand of man, except this time it is to pass the shears. You can probably imagine what happens with the Mona Lisa. Really, there is no way this could have been intended to be taken seriously.

You don't want no drama [except this is the section about dramatic movies]

And still I have yet to mention the worst performance here. I did not believe one millisecond of Andy Garcia's portrayal as a writer and rogue with designs on the newlywed Thompson back in the 1949 storyline. But Garcia does get the one genuine and clearly intentional laugh in this picture when his elderly, post-tracheotomy iteration permanently puts Branagh off cigarettes when he smokes one through the hole in his throat.

Perhaps the most genuine surprise in *Dead Again* is an architectural cameo, courtesy of North Hollywood's High Tower Court. This distinctive neighborhood, nestled high in the hills, is accessible via an elevator in a curiously isolated tower. It was prominently featured in Altman's *The Long Goodbye*, which was a slyly skewed reassessment of the private detective trope. *Dead Again* may be a similarly dry parody of the genre. If not, then it is a deeply terrible film.

Original version posted on 5/1/2024

Elmer Gantry (1960)

Circuses, carnival attractions, revivals. I'm starting to think one should avoid all enterprises held in tents.

1960's *Elmer Gantry* stars Burt Lancaster as the title character, a smooth-talking travelling salesman who schmoozes his way into the organization of a popular tent revival. The star of the revival is Sister Sharon Falconer, as played by Jean Simmons. She's the perfect foil for him: pure of intent, but whip-smart.

And yet, like every other woman in this movie, she isn't immune to his charms. There is a palpable sexual tension between these two, and I was surprised by how much of this movie seems to be about the similarity between religious ecstasy and sexual ecstasy. As Shirley Jones, playing a prostitute from his past which will come back to haunt him, says, "He rammed the fear of God into me so fast I never heard the old man's footsteps!" Pretty surprising stuff for a movie from 1960.

Another surprising aspect of this picture, given its vintage, is how it portrays organized religion as being obsessed with money. When Lancaster connives to have a revival outside a major city, this leads the revival committee to become mired in heated, petty bickering about funding. I marveled at the idea of tent revivals having a board like that of a major corporation.

I assume it is elements like this that led the producers to add a bizarre disclaimer to the beginning. At some length, it seems to defend revivalism while condemning certain aspects of it, but also defending anybody's choice to worship as they please. In the end, it urges you not to show it to impressionable children. 'Cause those kids, y'know…always dying to watch 2 ½ hour cynical dramas about religion and how it can exploit the masses.

Lancaster justly won the Oscar for Best Actor for his performance here. He is intense, as I have come to expect from every movie I have seen him in. Copiously sweating, cords standing out in his neck—how did he not have a heart attack every couple of years?

I find it interesting his character treats commerce, religion and lust so similarly as to erase the barriers between them. When we first meet him, he goes from telling dirty jokes in a bar to soliciting money from the patrons for the Salvation Army. His pitch includes a bizarre statement about how Jesus would have been the best All-American quarterback of all time. He thanks the Lord for closing a sale for him. Then he takes a street walker (well, stool-sitter in this scene) back to his place.

Jean Simmons more than holds her own here, and I am surprised she didn't take home a Best Actress statuette for this. Shirley

Jones, on the other hand, *did* take home Best Actress in a Supporting Role, though I found her a bit too over-the-top as a conniving lady of the evening. In my rather prurient assessment of her performance, I was mostly aware the future matriarch of the Partridge family had a chassis built for some serious oscillation.

By the end, there are some interesting themes explored. Things like the hollowness of revenge. Then there's a point explicitly conveyed by a character, "The mob don't like their gods to be human".

That is in regard to the first revival after the public turns on them, a surprisingly jarring scene which should have been the ending. That said, the major event in which the movie does end is also shocking.

And now the usual random observations. Did there used to be radio stations that played burlesque music all the time? I'm imaging a station identification like, "You're listening to WSKN— The Skank." A disgraced Jean Simmons sitting in a darkened office where a combination of graffiti and light shining through a window makes the words "REPENT SHARON" appear on the wall behind her.

I don't think it is a great movie, but *Elmer Gantry* is a unique and memorable one. It is a bit too tawdry, and goes into histrionics too frequently, to succeed entirely for me. But I do admire the subjects it dared to approach, especially for its time. Highly recommended.

Original version posted on 5/13/2023

Housekeeping (1987)

It is just after dawn, but before anybody is on the streets of a very small town. Despite the absence of cars, a vehicle slowly comes to complete stop at any intersection and signals they are turning right.

We're not even out of the opening credits and we already know something about the driver. Here is somebody who always follows the rules, even if nobody is around to notice whether or not they do so.

Such is the subtlety of *Housekeeping*, an amazing 1987 film which has never been promoted much. I watched it on an import blu-ray, only because I was intrigued by a cover that misled me into thinking this would be a zany comedy.

Though it has some laughs, this isn't primarily a comedy. It also has an amazing character played by Christine Lahti who could very well be described as "zany", though there is also an underlying melancholy there.

Lahti is the sister of the woman we saw driving in the opening credits—a woman who kills herself in as orderly a manner as she was driving and likely as orderly a manner as she lived her entire life. Left behind are two daughters for whom no other relations can be found except Lahti, who reluctantly accepts the role of surrogate mom.

The daughters are played by Sara Walker and Andrea Burchill. I don't believe I have seen either in anything else. Here, they turn in what are among the best performances I have ever seen from teen actors.

Turns out Lahti has been living rough and riding the rails for years. She has a great deal of difficulty settling down, though her love for her nieces is obviously strong.

Housekeeping communicates this, and much else, largely through fleeting glances and tiny mannerisms. The dialogue is good throughout, but much more is happening in unspoken ways.

This movie is a minor miracle—a film so free of pretentions that it sneaks up on you without you realizing how great it is. It has been a year since I watched it, and I'm still chewing on it.

Near the end, a character in narration says, "And that was the end of housekeeping". I love that line, as it is as if the character is both commenting wryly on what is happening on the screen and also providing a meta-commentary that the movie is over.

And yet the movie still goes on for just a bit after that. I can't remember if there was any more narration after that line, but I hope there wasn't. It wouldn't make or break the moment, but it would make even more special a final image that is among the most beautiful I have seen in a film.

Original version posted on 1/31/2023

Identikit (a.k.a. The Driver's Seat) (1974)

In her prime, Elizabeth Taylor had more influence than almost any other actress in Hollywood. I greatly admire her for some of the bizarre roles she chose at that time, including such curiosities as *Reflections in a Golden Eye* and *Boom!*, two movies I first learned about from the book *The Worst Movies of All Time*. I found merit in both those films, though I will concede neither makes it easy for the audience to appreciate them.

1974's *Identikit* (a.k.a. *The Driver's Seat*) is another such movie, yet another daring choice that would have dimmed the star of a lesser performer. This deeply odd film has her playing a disturbed, volatile character who suddenly goes to southern Italy. Her reasons for going there are far from immediately obvious.

Her behavior is unusual from the first moment we see her in a dress shop. Admittedly, it is a strange dress shop, with seemingly no clothes except for the garish outfit she tries on. The rest of the space seems to be occupied by bare mannequins with silver foil wrapped around their heads. Maybe this store just sells one outfit, but one that is *really* expensive.

The dress is unique, I can say that for certain. It is so gaudy that it is kind of stunning in its own way. It would definitely take a confident person to wear it. As her landlady asks her when she's wearing it later: "Where are you going dressed like that? To join the circus?" Taylor almost didn't buy the dress after discovering it was stain-resistant. Seems like an odd thing to go into such a tirade over, yet this will factor into the plot eventually. Also, the pattern and color combination on it is crazy enough that it would take some significant contamination for anything to show up.

Everything about Taylor's journey will be odd. At the airport, an elderly woman asks her for advice on which of two books to buy: "Which do you think will be exciting…more sadomasochistic?" Things get even stranger on the flight. The guy seated to her right (Maxence Mailfort) suddenly gets up and changes seats as the plane is taking off. On the other side of her is Ian Bannen, played an obnoxious lech who is very insistent he is her type. He also talks at length about being on a macrobiotic diet. He claims the rules of that diet require him to have an orgasm once a day. I have my doubts about that.

From here the film will repeatedly flash forward to the police interrogating different characters Taylor had encountered at one point. Mailfort will be shown the most, largely getting grilled about why he changed seats so abruptly. There are other characters, such as a woman who had seen Taylor at the post office, saying, "It's like something came out of her. A latent force that all women have."

And yet we still don't know at this point why the police are interested in her. Maybe she's a suspect in some of the terrorism that seems to be a constant concern. Especially memorable is a long row of soldiers armed with rifles at the airport—an image which immediately brought to my mind *Children of Men*. I guess you need that kind of security when you have incidents like the man who runs through the airport past Taylor with the police in hot pursuit. He snags a child as a hostage before being shot to death by the cops.

Taylor seems to be a magnet for weirdness in this picture. Perhaps the biggest surprise is Andy Warhol in an extended cameo. It is interesting to see him playing somebody other than himself, though the role isn't much of a stretch, admittedly. There's an old woman (Mona Washbourne) Taylor goes shopping with who first appears to have died while in the bathroom, when she really just fell asleep on the can. I wish I could relax like that.

Taylor's performance is mercurial, vague and fascinating. The script gives her many great lines full of melancholy, such as, "I'm feeling homesick for my loneliness. I want to go home so I can feel my loneliness." There's also this: "There's so much confusion. I left part of myself at home. The rest of myself will be arriving shortly."

It is especially curious how she keeps parting with things, such as her passport, which Washbourne watches her shove between the seat cushions of their taxi. At one point, she carelessly tosses her house keys into shrubbery without breaking stride.

If my description of *Identikit* may seem frustratingly vague, then I have accurately conveyed some of the experience of watching this. And yet, the film will conclude with an ending that makes sense given what we have seen. In retrospect, it is inevitable it would arrive at this conclusion. But more than plot, this is a film more concerned with sustaining a certain mood.

Original version posted on 6/8/2024

If Footmen Tire You, What Will Horses Do? (1971)

Having survived the first half, the "sleaze" half, of Indicator's Ormond family box set, we now progress to the faith-based films family patriarch Ron would focus on exclusively for the rest of his life. For a while after that, his son Tim would take the reins for a few more such features.

This abrupt change in the nature of their work was the result of Ron and his wife, June, surviving *two* plane crashes. I gotta admit—I can understand why their takeaway from that experience was to serve a higher power. And yet these religious pictures are as insane as their grindhouse fare. It takes some disturbed minds to come up with some of this material.

None of these films were ever shown in a real movie theatre, as prints were only available for rental to churches. I was raised in a Southern Baptist church where what was taught is largely in line with the propaganda in these films. Yet, curiously, I had never seen any of these before buying this box set.

One thing I remember from my Sunday School days was how much my teachers hated Communism. Strangely enough, they also hated vegetarians. To the best I can recall, the rationale for that was people who don't eat animals are disobeying God giving man dominion over them. Anywho, one concept repeatedly shoved down our throats was: Vegetarianism leads to Atheism, leading to Communism. Hmmm…come to think of it, I am a vegetarian and an atheist, but I still find much to like in Capitalism. It means people have money to waste on books of movie reviews by anonymous authors of no renown.

But nobody hates Communists more than preacher Estus Pirkle. He claims (alongside imagery of such scenarios) an impending invasion will happen "within the next 24 months". How does that work, Estus? Does the clock reset with each new viewer of the movie, or weren't you concerned about what people watching more than two years later might think? Obviously, he's not Nostradamus.

But his visions are about as crazy as that seer's. Estus foresees Communists riding on horseback, enslaving people and killing anybody who claims to be a Christian. I'm not sure why the Russkies are on horseback. I like to think they crossed the ocean from Cuba while mounted on steeds that were swimming with snorkels in their mouths.

Anywho, the children will be forced to work 16-18 hour days on collective farms and still have to go to school. I guess they sleep during school. And that's when soldiers aren't puncturing kid's eardrums with bamboo sticks, as we see in one scene.

Like a punchline to a gag, we see the child afterwards and it is made to look as if the soldier shoved one piece of bamboo into one ear and *through the kid's head* and out the other ear. I guess that'll learn 'em. I was reminded of the *New Yorker* cartoon where a fencer has decapitated their opponent while crying, "En garde!"

I think it says something about the creative minds behind this film that they would come up with something like this. It doesn't seem to me to be any different than their last sleaze picture, *The Exotic One*, where a guy is beaten to death with his own severed arm.

There's another bit that wouldn't be out of place in a Hershel Gordon Lewis film, where a father is executed in a way that makes his own sons responsible for his death. This guy is suspended over upturned pitchforks by a rope hanging over a high tree branch. At the other end of that rope are the young boys struggling to keep dad from getting skewered. I fail to see the point of this, as there is only one way this is eventually going to end up. It's like those old video games which didn't have an ending, so the goal was just to play for as long as you could.

If Footmen Tire You will be a shock for anybody who did not grow up in the kind of environment I did. It is the product of sick minds and makes as little sense as its title. And yet, this picture feels eerily reminiscent of the earlier "sleaze" films of the Ormonds. This reinforces what I have long suspected: sin and religion are opposite sides of the same coin, and it is a very thin coin.

Original version posted on 11/2/2023

Images (1972)

Cathryn Harrison must have had a curious upbringing. In her teenage years, she starred in two deeply weird movies: Louis Malle's *Black Moon* and Robert Altman's *Images*. She was also in the Donovan-starring *The Pied Piper*, which had to be the most traumatic of those films to make. At least, it is the most traumatic to watch and, believe me, those other two are *truly, deeply* weird.

In 1972's *Images*, she plays what seems to be the young doppelganger of Susannah York. Whatever she may appear to be, she is definitely the daughter of Marcel Bozzuffi, one of two men with whom York has had an affair in the past. The other man is Hugh Millais.

Both men, and her husband (Rene Auberjonois), seem to be constantly underfoot at her country home deep in rural Ireland. This is especially remarkable, in that Millais is dead and so is only in York's imagination. A bigger threat is Bozzuffi, who is constantly pawing her every time her husband has his back turned. Still, the man brought Harrison with him, so York at least has a kindred spirit around.

York's character has never had children, and there seems to be ample, contradictory evidence as to whether or not she wanted them. And yet, here is Harrison, apparently as the daughter she never had. Together, they go for walks and work on a jigsaw puzzle that nobody can seem to solve, but which is obviously a picture of the house they're in.

When that puzzle is finished, it turns out not just to be a picture of that house, but it also includes a tiger and a unicorn. I'm not sure about the tiger, but the unicorn is in a story York's character has been writing and thinking about throughout the film. In a weird meta moment, it is revealed at the end this text is from a book the real-life actress wrote.

The meta nature of the film extends to the names of the main characters. Cathryn Harrison's is named Susannah, while Susanna York plays Cathryn. And get a load of the men who are her various lovers: Rene Auberjonois plays Hugh, Marcel Bozzuffi is Rene and Hugh Millais stars as Marcel. I'm not sure if there's any depth beyond that, but it intrigues me.

Another seemingly meta aspect is how various objects tend to reflect York's fragmenting identity, as there are many deliberate close-ups on objects that distort light, such as crystal wind chimes or her husband's reading glasses. Mirrors are an overused metaphor in cinema for the splitting of a personality, but almost every mirror in this film curiously is of the antique type that has a product advertisement partly obscuring the surface. So, when looking into the mirror, it's hard to get a decent reflection. Then there's a still camera which always seems to be pointed at York when she's near, as if the actress cannot get away from it. Not sure if that's a commentary on the sensation of being a film star, but it feels like one.

Speaking of split personalities, we will see various iterations of York observing other incarnations from a distance. She'll watch from a hilltop as, in the distance, another version of herself is driving the car up to her house. And we're increasingly uncertain as to whether what she is experiencing is real or imagined. In many scenes, Bozzuffi will be tormenting her, except nobody but York can see him, as he died years before.

Altman has said he was heavily influenced by Bergman's *Persona* when making this film. I can understand that, though I enjoyed this far more than the Swedish master's movie. Though both are rather airless affairs, there was nonetheless a moment here where I laughed long and hard, as York flees in terror from a small, happy dog. Even the music accompanying this bit, worthy of *Psycho*, compounded for me the hilarity of the situation, whether or not that was Altman's intention. Speaking of humor, there are the lame jokes her husband is always telling, until his last one seems to foretell the coming breakdown of reality: "How can you tell the difference between a rabbit? None. They're both the same."

The jigsaw puzzle is an interesting metaphor for the plot, which is full of ambiguities, complications and seeming contradictions. Similarly, the puzzle is remarked upon as seemingly not having all the necessary pieces and may even be missing some. At the end of the film, I wasn't sure if all the pieces of it fit together in the end, but it was an interesting puzzle, regardless. I believe I could have just as easily been frustrated by this work as I just happened to instead be enthralled. A few decades before studio A24 was established, Altman had already made the best film of the type they specialize in.

Original version posted on 7/6/2024

Inserts (1975)

In the first few years of the MPAA's rating system, an X didn't have the stigma that eventually led to it becoming equated with pornography. Many serious films were initially given that rating, only to be re-rated as R later, such as *Midnight Cowboy, A Clockwork Orange* and *Medium Cool*. It isn't often movies from that era get re-rated to receive the modern-day equivalent of X, the NC-17. When that happens, you know you are going to see something special.

Such is the case of 1975's *Inserts*, a little remembered film starring Richard Dreyfuss, Jessica Harper, Bob Hoskins, Veronica Cartwright and Stephen Davies. That's it—that's the *entire* cast.

It is surprising this picture did not appear to impact the career arc of Dreyfuss at all, as this was between *Jaws* and *Close Encounters*. I think it is interesting audiences still accepted him, and producers still came calling, after appearing here as an alcoholic, impotent director who has been reduced to making a porno in his home.

Although the particulars are never given, his character was a legend in the silent movie era but was unable to transition to talkies. His friend, and star of his latest picture, is played by Veronica Cartwright. She is a junkie and former star who is another victim of the advent of sound. We also do not know for certain why she fell from grace, but her grating, baby-doll voice is a likely culprit.

I like seeing Cartwright in films, though she is often the most frightened and hysterical of the cast in anything in which she appears. One thing I always like about those performances is she seems to be the audience surrogate, the only person who completely locks up when facing a xenomorph or hordes of pod people. But I have never seen her before as she is here. I don't just mean how little clothing she wears for much of her screen time, but how she is such an outgoing sex object in this picture.

Her costar in the film-within-this-film is Stephen Davies, condescending dubbed "Rex, the Wonder Dog". I found it interesting how Cartwright's character would usually be described as a bimbo, yet there is a lot more going on upstairs than she was likely ever given credit for. On the other hand, Davies is definitely a "himbo"—an endlessly scheming dimwit who will never make it past any of the many casting couches he is doomed to briefly occupy.

Dreyfuss seems to think the porno he is directing is more sophisticated than other such pictures, but the scene we watch him film is violent and disturbing. Apparently channeling his impotence into rage, he encourages Davies to hit Cartwright and then strangle her with his ascot. Cartwright's subtly shifting expressions are a marvel in this bit, as we can tell she is wondering just how dark this is going to get. I'm sure her character was wondering if this was still acting, or if this could possibly become a snuff film.

Everybody is so caught up in the moment they fail to notice the arrival of Hoskins, their producer. He has cash for Davis and smack for Cartwright. He has also brought along Harper, his squeeze who wants to get into the movie business. She has a lot of questions for Dreyfuss and the, uh, consummate scene shows how far she will go to get that knowledge.

It is odd how many legitimate movies that push the envelope for sexual content are usually the least sexy films imaginable. This one may have even more sexual content than David Cronenberg's *Crash*, and yet somehow manages to be even *less* sexy. Perhaps the most intimate moment is when Dreyfuss helps Cartwright shoot up, tying up her arm with a necktie. At least that moment is tender. She's even shy about the track marks and raised veins in her elbow, while having no insecurities about baring it all.

The one thing I didn't expect is how funny this picture is. There aren't any lines I can think of to present here that would make sense without providing a glut of context. This is the kind of humor which is closer to wit. There's an especially good scene between Hoskins and Davies with some great comic moments in it. The timing of these two performers is perfect.

I hate it when people use phrases like what I'm about to say, but the living room in Dreyfuss's mansion is like a sixth character. There are open bottles all over the place, and I'm not sure he ever takes a drink from the same one twice. The cigarette burns all over the white piano seem to tell a story all their own. As if being a discarded relic from the silent era isn't bad enough, he's the last holdout on his block in a neighborhood soon to be razed to make way for an interstate. Progress, in multiple forms, is destroying his life.

I have always heard the Hollywood studio system of the 70s was the heyday of the mavericks. *Inserts* is a stellar example of the kinds of risks the major studios were willing to take at that time, and probably the last time they would.

Original version posted on 6/2/2023

You don't want no drama [except this is the section about dramatic movies]

Ladies and Gentlemen, The Fabulous Stains (1982)

It is hard to believe The Go-Gos were originally an important group on the LA punk scene. Not to slight that group's pop turn once they signed to a major label, but it is astonishing to consider where they began. 1982's *Ladies and Gentlemen, The Fabulous Stains* follows the quick rise, and even faster fall, of an all-girl group which roughly follows that same career trajectory.

A fifteen-year-old Diane Lane fronts the titular Stains. The movie starts with a *60 Minutes* type program where she is being interviewed as a follow-up to an earlier, wildly popular segment wherein she quit her fast-food job on-air. Another fake news show will be used as a framing device through the rest of the film, providing a sort of narration or Greek chorus. I thought it odd this is a *local* news program with a correspondent who follows the band's progress around the country, but I enjoyed the movie enough to put it out of mind.

Lane's bandmates are her sister and a cousin, played by Marin Kanter and Laura Dern, respectively. I don't know which one, Lane or Dern, was weirder to see so young and made up as a punk rocker.

The band they initially support on their rise to fame are The Looters. This is a fake band in a major studio (Paramount) production, so it is shocking how good they are. But then this is a fake band with some serious credentials, as it is composed of Sex Pistols Steve Jones and Paul Cook, with Paul Simonon of The Clash on bass and Ray Winstone on vocals. And I already think I need to walk back my earlier statement about how strange it is to see Lane and Dern in this—they can't hold a candle to how weird it is to see the Winstone, the future star of *Sexy Beast,* so young, thin and full of righteous anger.

I don't think it is spoiling anything to say the band's meteoric rise has a corresponding, precipitous fall. For that matter, why do we even have the term "meteoric rise"? Since when do meteors fall *up*?

There is much in this movie to recommend it. Probably the best aspect of the picture is everything has a ring of truth to it. Yet this is still a movie, and it adheres to certain conventions, but so much of it feels like an approximation of the trials many artists have been through (perhaps even an amalgamation of the experiences of numerous artists). I was not surprised to later learn it is a favorite movie of many real-life rockers.

Unreleased theatrically in its own time, *Ladies and Gentlemen, The Fabulous Stains* gained a cult following over the decades through late-late-night cable airings and multiple-generation tape copies. Somehow, it feels appropriate that is how this highly recommended movie has left its legacy.

Original version posted on 1/4/2023

The Little Girl Who Lives Down the Lane (1976)

You can learn the weirdest things in movies. For example, the ending of 1976's *The Little Girl Who Lives Down the Lane* teaches one should never enter a staring contest against Jodie Foster. Not only will you lose, but you run the risk of your eyeballs drying out and the shards falling out of the sockets.

I thought this while watching her in an unbroken take over which the end credits roll. She shows a startling amount of control for being only thirteen years old. Then again, she had already demonstrated a maturity well beyond her years in films like *Taxi Driver* and *Bugsy Malone*, other movies she made *that same year*.

Foster plays her age as a girl who seems to live in a rented house without any adults. When people ask to see her father, she always has a cover story—usually that he is working in the study and can't be disturbed. She goes around town getting money at the bank from her father's account and buying groceries. It's like she's a real-world realization of a *Peanuts* character, fully functioning in a world where parents exist but we never see them.

It shouldn't be any surprise, but she, indeed, lives on her own. While her father was dying, they prepared for her to live on her own until she was of legal age. Her mother is still alive, to the best either of them knows, and the dying father is worried she will reemerge following his death, but only to claim his estate.

I think this is a fascinating premise. Foster's character is whip-smart, but you know it is impossible for anybody to sustain such a ruse for five years.

A particular problem is her nosy landlady (Alexis Smith). Given her hatred of outsiders, her sense that something is amiss is like blood to a shark. The scenes where she verbally spars with Foster are among the best in the film.

What is especially telling is when she asks if her son has dropped in on Foster. At this point, we have already been introduced to him, as played by Martin Sheen in a deeply creepy performance— intense, jumpy and predatory. Similar to his mother, he also suspects Foster is living on her own, and he wants to exploit that for his own skeezy goal.

Another key figure in the plot is a teen boy played by Scott Jacoby. His character will become a love interest for Foster after he helps her cover up an accidental death which occurs in the house. I guess strong relationships are built on shared experiences. And yet, there is some good rapport between them, including a moment that felt ad-libbed. There's also a small bit

You don't want no drama [except this is the section about dramatic movies]

I'm sure was scripted, but felt natural, where she sees him struggling to cut his lamb chop, so she picks up hers and starts eating it with her fingers.

This is the second time I have seen this picture, and I came away with a better impression of Jacoby this time. In that first viewing, I thought he was creepy—nowhere near as disturbing as Sheen, but something still seemed off about him. Maybe it's because, when we first encounter him, he is wearing a cape and top hat, as he is on his way to do a magic show. Or maybe it's because he played the title character in *Bad Ronald*, where he hides in the walls of a house and spies on the girls who live there.

Something that likely didn't paint him in a favorable light is the movie's one major misstep, a sex scene between Foster and Jacoby. While the sex was consensual, the scene is unnecessary. Compounding the unease surrounding this scene is a body double used for a naked Foster. So, we now have a disturbing and unnecessary scene where the filmmakers found it necessary to show what is intended to be a naked thirteen-year-old girl, and it is obvious an adult woman was used as the double (Foster's real-life older sister!?). This is the kind of thing a lot of movies from the 70's need to answer for, and it feels like an extension of the environment which initially condoned Roman Polanski's behavior.

Aside from this, which I consider to be a near-fatal flaw, *The Little Girl Who Lives Down the Lane* is a fascinating thriller. Despite being essentially a one-room play, it is tightly plotted and every performance here is intriguing. I think the highest praise I can give this is that I meant to only skim this movie in order to write this piece and instead found myself watching it again in its entirety.

Original version posted on 5/2/2023

A Lion Is in the Streets (1953)

The opening credits of 1953's *A Lion Is in the Streets* play out on top of footage of a lion at the Lincoln Memorial. It walks back and forth in front of it, occasionally stretching up towards it and roaring. I wondered how they got the lion to do this. More than that, I wondered *why* they did this. I'm sure it is a metaphor for something, likely something about politics, but I was confused as to exactly what it was supposed to convey. And yet I don't think I was as confused as this movie.

It takes place in the rural south, where James Cagney plays a peddler whose smooth talk can convince people to do his bidding. He convinces the local schoolmarm (Barbara Hale) to marry him. He convinces the congregants of the local church to renovate his house. If his powers of persuasion are so strong, I wonder why he was not in a more financially rewarding form of employment than travelling salesman.

Already, I had a hard time swallowing the "aw-shuckness" of this whole endeavor. Hollywood has consistently portrayed the poverty-stricken of the rural south in a patronizing manner, and this is no exception. Even worse, there's an outright dishonesty on display, such as the "JIST MARRIED" sign on the back of the peddler's caravan. You just know his wife, who is a teacher, would correct that.

And things get even worse when Anne Francis enters the plot as a scheming bayou hussy who always had designs on Cagney. Furious he has tied the knot, she flails at him, yelling that he always promised her he would wait. She even tries to feed Hale to a gator. Surprisingly, the fake gator isn't too bad of a creature effect for a film of this vintage.

Since Francis and Cagney will eventually have an affair, I found myself wondering if their relationship was entirely legitimate before she became of age. But that would make the peddler a pedophile, and I just can't think of a portmanteau which does that justice. Pedoler? Peddlerphile?

The action really kicks into gear when Cagney takes on a conglomerate of cotton gins that had been using dodgy weights to shortchange farmers. Larry Keating, as the head of the syndicate, sues Cagney, claiming he has been falsely accused.

There's a tense scene where one such corrupt facility foils a trap laid by Cagney, correctly assessing the amount of cotton a farmer (John McIntire) brings in. But our protagonist notices the weights are brand new and a search finds the fraudulent ones that had been used every previous time.

Thugs shoot McIntire to keep him from testifying in court. Cagney convinces the dying man to testify in court instead of gently slipping away courtesy of a morphine shot a doctor mercifully offers. As if that isn't audacious enough, he convinces a judge to hold a spur-of-the-moment hearing. McIntire still dies in the courtroom before he can say anything, and Cagney uses this moment to whip the mob into a frenzy.

Cagney will channel this populism into a campaign to elect him governor. But that can only be accomplished with the assistance of Onslow Stevens, a puppet master with a goal in mind Cagney can't foresee. In the end, Cagney will be a pawn in a game he realizes only too late he is part of. Still, he gladly shook the devil's hand at every step of the way.

This movie tries to do many things and fails at all of them. I understand Cagney's character is supposed to be a "man of the people" who simply connives or bullies others into doing what he wants. But he should be charismatic to be able to do that, and that didn't come across to me. The character Francis plays should generate friction between the married couple, but their affair is carried out without Hale even finding out, so there aren't any repercussions. There's simply no reason for Francis to still be in the picture after her unsuccessful attempt to kill Hale.

Even the political perspective of the film is wobbly, as it seems to switch alliances constantly. I'm all for objectivity, but there's a noticeable lack of commitment here. Without some sort of center, the whole thing just falls apart.

The very last shot of *A Lion Is in the Streets* brings us full circle to the opening credit images, except the lion collapses at the foot of the memorial. This was so daft and unexpected that I was literally in tears from laughing so hard. It may have been the perfect image to summarize a picture so confused that it dies on the screen. There weren't any close-ups of the lion but, if there were, I hoped we would see it was toothless. That would have been an even better metaphor.

Original version posted on 1/7/2024

Lust, Caution (2007)

As I write this, I have just finished being devastated by 2007's *Lust, Caution*. This is a 2 ½ hour picture set in Japanese-occupied WWII China, with dialogue in Chinese. And, oh yes, it's NC-17. Honestly, it might as well be NC-40, because this picture is too sophisticated for those who are just looking for wank fodder.

Unlike most movies that have carried this, the most restrictive of ratings, to date, here is a picture made on an astonishingly big budget. You can clearly see that money on the screen, as entire period streets (complete with an ancient streetcar) are recreated. Top-tier CGI extends the city beyond the edges of the street. All of this is done tastefully, immersing the viewer in this world.

This is an epic movie in time, spanning four years, and space, taking place in Hong Kong and Shanghai. What is impressive is this remains an intimate work even within that scope. This isn't a film of epic battles. Instead, this is all about small glances and conversations where what isn't said is as important as what is. As a key character here observes, small talk is a rare moment to be treasured.

Tang Wei makes her feature debut as young actress recruited in a plot to assassinate a high-level official in the collaborative government. That official is played by Tony Leung Chiu-wai, an intimidating figure of few words and in complete control of himself and the others in his circle. I have no doubt this character is very effective at torturing those he interrogates. Wei has her work cut out for her in trying to seduce him.

And yet she is up to the challenge. Her approach succeeds where previous operatives failed, and DAMN does she ever snag him. Not much in the way of sex happens until about one-and-a-half hours in but, when it does start, the movie earns its NC-17 rating. That said, if you came to this for entirely prurient reasons, you will likely be disappointed.

The rather strong sex scenes here are less about what is happening physically than it is the millions of tiny assessments and transactions in their glances. In this time of war, this is yet another battlefield to navigate. You can see each of them appraising the other, wondering if they can truly and completely surrender themselves. And, even if can do so, should they?

Bear with me while I quickly touch on a few random aspects I took away from this experience. In a time jump backwards four years, Wei is walking on a stage, gently touching the branches of artificial trees, when she is recruited by her fellow actors for the mission. I like the symbolism of her transition from acting on stage to acting on the largest and most dangerous of stages. Also, while the picture is seriously lacking in comic moments, there is a nice bit where two of the actors fail miserably shooting at bottles until one is shattered almost by accident: "One bottle assassinated!"

Lust, Caution is an extraordinary film, and I especially liked how it immersed me in a time and place with which I wasn't previously familiar. I even came away with a deeper understanding of how significantly different the various dialects of Chinese can be—apparently almost like different languages. And yet, more than the cultural differences, this picture is more concerned about the similarities of people around the world. Whether it is body language or the language of love, *Lust, Caution* is mostly about things which require no subtitles.

Original version posted on 4/3/2023

Man on a Swing (1974)

I'm just going to come right out and say something: Joel Grey is a creepy motherfucker. He's perfectly cast in 1974's *Man on a Swing*, where he plays an alleged clairvoyant who insists on helping the police investigate the murder of a young woman. He may or may not have such powers, he may or not be the killer, or he might be involved in this killing in some other regard.

Supposedly based on a true story, this is a film that maintains a curious feeling of unease and uncertainty throughout its runtime. Things never fully gel, and I don't believe it is a spoiler to say things remain largely unsettled when the end credits roll. This may irritate some viewers, but I found this resulted in a more memorable and intriguing work than what would have likely resulted from a more straight-forward approach.

Cliff Robertson plays the police chief on the case. The strangled body of Dianne Hull had been found in the passenger floorboard of her Volkswagen Beetle. Her panties and shorts had been lowered, but no penetration had occurred. There also did not appear to have been a struggle. There is a high concentration of carbon monoxide in her blood, suggesting she had been in a garage while a car was running. Robertson is especially intrigued by a spot of blood on her right breast.

So far, this is a fairly straight-forward police procedural. The opening credits are displayed over footage of a police car on its way to the crime scene, where Hull's bug sits sadly isolated from other cars in a grocery store parking lot. We stay with Robertson and the officers as they work their way backwards from Hull's friend who found her body, to a clerk who remembers selling the victim a hibachi, to interviewing a woman who had been assaulted in that same parking lot a year before. Her assailant (Christopher Allport) has just been released from prison, so he is brought in for questioning.

The investigation seems to be heading for the cold case file, with the list of suspects drying up. There is also a lack of fingerprints on the vehicle, except for those of a careless officer at the crime scene (Peter Masterson). This is the point where Grey shoves his way into the investigation.

To say he chews the scenery doesn't do his performance justice. In fact, he does everything *but* literally chew on it. Instead, he throws himself against it as if he's magnetized and everything around him is iron. He smashes things while more or less dry-humping a table. He foams at the mouth at one point. It's no wonder the guy is so thin, given the workout he puts himself through here. I got tired just watching him.

Robertson's terse performance stands out in sharp relief. He is as intense as Grey, only his is one of internalized, smoldering intensity. One of the few times in the film he opens up to anybody is to his wife (Dorothy Tristan). I believed these characters, separately and together, and I enjoyed their banter. It is obvious she doesn't enjoy him discussing the case at home, but things are taken to a whole other level when Grey shows up when she's home alone in one notably creepy scene. As she lays down the law for her husband: "I will not have suspects in my home." But then there's lighter moments such as when Robertson asks his pregnant wife her thoughts on clairvoyants: "Is my opinion worth anything? After all, I believed in my diaphragm."

But the main relationship here is between Robertson and Grey, as the chief finds the man's antics and vagueness increasingly irritating. Grey agrees to participate in a test of his powers, but his rate of success is less than that of even blind chance. After freezing him out of the investigation, Robertson gets vaguely threatening mail and phone calls to the house. All the while, Grey bears an almost mockingly innocent expression which scans as smugness, making him very punchable. You just know Robertson wants to do that in some moments, yet never succumbs to that urge.

The poster for *Man on a Swing* asks of Grey's character, "Clairvoyant. Occultist. Murderer. Which?" While the picture barely touches upon the second of those, it teases us as to whether he is the first, and to what extent. The film concludes while still on the fence as to whether he is the third, or if he is culpable to some undetermined extent. It remains vague, which will understandably frustrate some viewers. As for myself, I found it an intriguing unsolved riddle which I enjoyed considering for some time after.

Original version posted on 6/4/2024

The Master (2012)

I was reminded of *Infinite Jest*[1] the entire time I watched 2012's *The Master*[2]. Both works are way too long and pretentious. This Paul Thomas Anderson[3] film stars Philip Seymour Hoffman[4] and Joaquin Phoenix[5].

[1] You know, the 1996 David Foster Wallace novel[1.i], roughly a third of which is in the endnotes[1.ii].

[1.i] Didn't Paul Thomas Anderson also direct a movie of *Infinite Jest?*[1.i.a]

[1.i.a] You're thinking of *Inherent Vice,* which was written by Thomas Pynchon, so kind of the same thing while not being the same thing at all.

[1.ii] Yep, I actually read the goddamn thing. I found more of interest in it than I did, say, *Ulysses,* though I can't imagine anything would make me read it a second time.

[2] Goddamnit, I thought this was going to be a movie about the leader of the cult in *Manos: The Hands of Death.* Nope, this is all a veiled history of the early days of L. Ron Hubbard's founding of Scientology[2.i].

[2.i] There are all kinds of weird regarding the movie's faux religion, The Cause[2.i.a]. What stuck with me is our Hubbard surrogate giving a wedding toast about lassoing a dragon. Did he get that from *Valley of Gwangi*, and just substituted a dragon for a dinosaur?[2.i.b]

[2.i.a] Like what is going on with a blackboard with words like "coitus" and "douche" on it as a woman in front of the blackboard supposedly relates experiences from before her birth?

[2.i.b] I may be an atheist, but I am willing to consider a Harryhausen-based religion.

[3] A character in this stomps a jailhouse toilet to pieces. I couldn't help but be reminded of the scene in Anderson's *Punch-Drunk Love* where Sandler destroys a restaurant bathroom. This would be a strange recurring theme to have through one's film career[3.i].

[3.i] At least that recurring theme isn't one of the first images in this picture. We see a group of bored sailors on a Pacific island in WWII, and one way they find to pass the time is to make a sand woman to simulate (?) sex with[3.i.a].

[3.i.a] So I wasn't surprised when the next stop after the war is a mental hospital, where our protagonist sees explicit sexual imagery in every card in a Rorschach test[†].

[†] Actually, the first one looked like Batman to me. How couldn't it look like that to the future Joker?

[§] "Get Thee Behind Me, Satan" What a weird-ass song. And kudos for finding the hidden footnote!

[4] So weird he's dead, isn't it? I keep forgetting that until I see yet another movie he was in.

[5] For a change, I didn't believe Phoenix's character was a real person here[5.i.] Every second felt like I was watching a performance[5.ii]. Unnatural.

[5.i] Talking out of only the left side of his mouth while squinting his right eye. Is he secretly supposed to be Popeye?

[5.ii] Phoenix is supposedly a method actor[5.ii.a], which has me even more weirded out by the scene where he may be boning a sand-woman[5.ii.b]

[5.ii.a] So did he actually drink ship fuel, which is apparently something sailors desperate to get drunk have actually done?

[5.ii.b] Then there's the scene where we see him jerking off into the ocean. Thank all the gods that was shot from behind.

Original version posted on 7/24/2023

The Music of Chance (1992)

David Lynch has repeatedly said he is more interested in questions than answers. 1992's *The Music of Chance* isn't a Lynch picture; however, it has an intriguing premise which left a few threads unresolved at the end.

But this is the rare kind of movie where I accepted the lack of complete closure. I feel it was appropriate for a work with such a bizarre premise.

The movie starts with Mandy Patinkin driving down a country lane when he sees a figure stumbling by the side of the road. This will turn out to be James Spader, who accepts the offer of a ride.

He has a very curious story, claiming to have been ahead in a high stakes poker game when robbers made off with the proceeds. Supposedly, he was ahead by roughly ten grand when the robbery occurred, and two players who especially took a fleecing accuse Spader of staging the heist himself. Those men, the cryptically named Misters Flower and Stone, have invited Spader to their mansion for a three-man game, should he be able to raise ten grand for the pot.

If this sounds like the plot for a Mamet film, then you have a good idea of what it is aiming for. It isn't as good as, say, *House of Games*, but it holds its own and will turn out to be a distinctly unique experience. Similar to a lot of Mamet's work, the dialogue is often profane and feels like violence even when no physical violence is being shown.

I find it difficult to say much about the plot without giving away potential clues for the directions it takes. At the same time, I have to relate enough of it to convince you to see it. And you should see this film.

Basically, Spader is being set up by Flower and Stone, and Patinkin fronts him the necessary funds. Exactly why Patinkin does this is curious, especially when a career poker player is a compulsive liar by definition. Plus, Spader is wearing a shirt covered in tiny symbols that I swear is the Wingdings font or something very similar to it. That may not be a sign of a deceptive nature, but it definitely suggests insanity.

And yet, Spader proves his mettle in a long round of games against Patinkin, who claims the pants have been beaten off him. Fortunately, that isn't literal, unless he was wearing one pair of pants over another, which gives me an idea in case I ever have to play strip poker.

In the mansion where the poker rematch will happen, Flower and Stone reveal a room containing a town in miniature, a "City of the World" that supposedly shows key moments in the life of Willy Stone (Joel Grey). Tellingly, many of the moments captured in miniature show crime doesn't pay, whether it's as simple and humorous as a burglar slipping on a banana peel or more sinister ones, such as a man being executed by firing squad.

Patinkin enquires about an undeveloped area of this microcosm, and it is explained to him that part of this will be a miniature of the house they are in, replete with a reproduction of the "City of the World" with them looking at it. I bet Escher would have creamed his shorts over the idea of such an endless regression.

Needless to say, the poker game ends with Spader and Patinkin deeply in debt to these two sinister old men. Charles Durning, as Mr. Flower, especially oozes menace in the poker sequences. He has a line I keep chewing on, concerning numbers having souls and how they must be treated as individuals. Prime numbers, in particular, are ones that refuse to cooperate. Grey, on the other hand, just radiates potential serial killer vibes which, to be honest, is how I think of him in everything I have seen so far. Yes, I am including *Remo Williams: The Adventure Begins* in that.

It is arranged that Patinkin and Spader will repay their debt by building a long stone wall on the property. It is estimated that, at $10 an hour, they can complete the work and repay the debt in 50 days. The wall will serve no purpose other than being a monument to itself. The two can stay in a trailer that, tellingly, is already on the site.

I knew of this premise going in and thought it sounded too strange for me to suspend disbelief. But I can happily report it feels like a natural development in the world of this film. It is also no surprise to see Grey building a replica wall in miniature in "The City of the World" in parallel with construction of the actual wall.

That's about all I feel I can say without giving too much away. As I said at the start, not everything will be resolved, but I believe that is true to the nature of the movie. Recommended for everybody.

Original version posted on 4/30/2023

Nineteen Eighty-Four (1954)

I was a weird kid.

I don't know why my elementary school had a copy of George Orwell's *1984* in its library but, when I first saw it there, I knew I had to read this enigmatic paperback. Not sure why such a book was expected to appeal to kids in the first through fifth grades, but it got my attention when I was in the fourth grade. Can't say I understood all of it at the time, but I read every word.

Not long after that, I fell in love with Terry Gilliam's dystopian nightmare *Brazil*, not knowing the working title had been (appropriately) *1984 ½*.

So, I have a pretty long history with this work. I even have a soft spot for 1984's movie of *1984*, though I am disappointed every time I see it.

But the first adaptation of the book was for BBC television back in 1954. When I learned it stars Peter Cushing, Donald Pleasance and Andre Morell, I decided it is *on*.

Like most British TV of that era, the production was a live shoot. If there was enough money, there might be filmed inserts. The benefit to the technical crew is these provided time to move cameras and change sets while also giving the actors time to prepare for the next scene. Those filmed sequences look great on blu-ray. Unfortunately, the live portions were captured for posterity via a kinetoscope, which uses a film camera pointed at a monitor. This technique is as dodgy as it sounds it would be.

The original broadcast caused a firestorm of controversy in its time, and I can see why. In fact, once one sets aside the artificiality of the often-crude sets, it still packs a wallop today. Actually, the inexpensive sets are likely one of the reasons *1984* was deemed suitable for a TV adaptation in the first place.

Something about this TV version of *1984* feels truer to the source material than the later film. The script was penned by Nigel Kneale, a highly regarded scribe of such other monumental BBC works as the *Quatermass* series. As expected, his script fully channels the bleak despair of Orwell's text.

As for the cast, everybody is in top form here, and that is even more considerable when one takes into account all of this was done live. Cushing, in particular, turns in one of the best performances of a career that has so many highlights. His Wilson Smith is on screen for the vast majority of the runtime, and the scenes where he is tortured are somewhat difficult to watch.

In any form, *1984* has become only more relevant over time. Unfortunately, we live in an age where only recently a president forbade the Center for Disease Control from using certain words, making it nearly impossible for scientists to discuss a pandemic. And, at one time, we would have laughed at the idea of a machine that automatically writes pornographic books, yet we now have artificial intelligence programs producing images from movies that never existed.

All I feel I can do is encourage people to remain critical and keep reading works like *1984* and think about how it might reflect the world of today. Failing that, at least you could watch this stellar BBC adaptation, which hasn't lost its punch nearly 70 years later.

Original version posted on 3/5/2023

No Highway in the Sky (1951)

I'm trying to write this essay while still reeling from this movie. I wouldn't go so far as to say it feels like I walked away from a plane crash but, well, I'm not sure what to say right now.

I went into this with zero expectations. I didn't even know what it was about. The sum total of what I knew going in was this stars James Stewart and Marlene Dietrich. I didn't even know the movie reteamed Stewart with *Harvey* director Henry Koster, a fact which makes this endeavor even more bizarre.

You see, *No Highway in the Sky* isn't a comedy, though it does have some sparkling dialogue that made me laugh only because I'm predisposed to doing so and I tend to react that way when something pleasantly surprises me.

This movie is far closer to straight drama than *Harvey*, but it sure seems to have trouble deciding which drama it wants to be.

Things start out promisingly enough, as we see Stewart as a stereotypical, absent-minded genius engineer who is subjecting the tail section of one of his employer's planes to a stress test. Stewart is convinced the tail will fall off the plane after it is subjected to 1440 hours of vibrations. Strangely enough, he seems to think this will happen at *exactly* 1440 hours of testing. Those are some bizarre expectations to apply to an estimate. That, and the model of aircraft is named The Reindeer, which seems to imply everybody at this company is loopy to begin with.

Stewart's home life is what one would expect from what we see up to that point: he is prone to walking into the wrong house, he doesn't know where anything is, and books occupy every chair and flat surface. A young Janette Scott plays his daughter, and she's highly intelligent, wise beyond her years, and exceptionally low-key without being aloof. I liked the interaction between Stewart and Scott. I probably would have been happy if the rest of the movie was just us hanging around with them in their disheveled house.

Inevitably, Stewart winds up on a flight and no points for guessing

- The plane is a Reindeer
- It has logged 1422 hours in the air

Bum bum BUM BUM BUUUUUUUUUUM

Now, I know the engineer is supposed to be a head-in-the-clouds kind of guy, but it seems he would at least bother to check what kind of plane he was going to board. He doesn't even notice the plane's unique styling, and he had to cross the tarmac to get to it. This is one seriously cool, but weird, looking craft: it is like one of those art deco trains from the golden age of travel, but with wings.

Once the flight is well underway, Stewart learns he is on a Reindeer and how many hours it has logged. He channels some Shatner-having-seen-a-gremlin-on-the-wing hysteria, which has the expected results. What I didn't expect is something he will do to the plane which, HOLY SHIT, is unprecedented and definitely the reason to see this movie.

I should say a couple more things about the flight, because this is where two key characters are introduced. Marlene Dietrich plays a movie star whom Stewart tries to advise how to best survive a plane crash. She is weirdly shoe-horned into this movie, as if she was contracted to do a movie and they had to find something for

You don't want no drama [except this is the section about dramatic movies]

her to do. The always excellent Glynis Johns gets the superior role, as a steward who is conflicted as to whether or not she believes Stewart's claims. Johns does so much with her eyes and subtle changes of expression, and the camera wisely stays on her even during some scenes with Stewart or Dietrich.

So, I can't say much more about the movie without giving anything away except the third act is a pretty significant deviation from what preceded it. It becomes more conventional, leans into the melodrama and becomes an altogether less satisfying affair. I had such high hopes for this movie, but I guess that tail eventually had to fall off.

Original version posted on 1/15/2023

Obsession (1949)

I find it odd I wasn't weirded out by Robert Newton keeping Phil Brown chained for weeks on end in an abandoned building. What I did find unnerving was the white circle on the floor he had put down in advance to mark the farthest Brown can get from the wall. Not exactly sure why, but I was reminded of *Silence of the Lambs* and the woman kept captive in Buffalo Bill's basement, even if she was in a pit. And yet, like that film, a captive will manage to get hold of their captor's dog.

1949 UK thriller *Obsession* is limited in how gruesome it might get, if only because of the era in which it was released. On the other hand, this being a British film, it wouldn't be as handicapped as an American film would have been, due to the restrictions of the Production Code.

If this film had been made in the US, I would be surprised if it had the second bathtub in the room where Newton keeps Brown chained. Each day, when Newton brings sandwiches and a thermos of martinis to his captive, he also dons thick rubber gloves and empties the contents of a hot water bottle into that tub. With all the time Brown has to ponder his situation, I'm amazed he hasn't realized that tub is how his captor intends to dispose of any remains.

The offense Brown has committed was to be the lover of Newton's wife, played by Sally Gray. The lovers may assert it was a harmless little flirtation, except Newton is finally taking extreme measures after a long series of infidelities. "I decided what to do with the next one even before you met my wife."

Newton caught them about to make time in his house when they thought he was away on a trip. They claim to have been at a concert, which Newton says was an impossibility, as it had suddenly been cancelled at the last minute. They fall for his bluff, with Gray not thinking to check his story until after the cat is out of the bag.

I thought it was interesting how coolly Gray exits the room and heads to her bedroom after Newton displays a gun and announces his intention to kill Brown. But the husband is not going to kill him then and there, hence the room he prepared in that abandoned building.

And that is where Newton takes Brown at gunpoint. Even if one is under duress, a lesson all should take away from this film is never go to a second location with somebody who says they are going to kill you. Better to die quickly right there and then instead of possibly experiencing a prolonged torment somewhere else. Plus, the odds are in your favor that person could be bluffing.

Not that Newton is bluffing this time. For a while, I thought his intention was simply to drive the other man crazy, as the captivity goes on for weeks. Brown repeatedly expresses doubts he will be murdered, despite constant reassurances from Newton that is the end goal. At least the condemned man keeps a sense of humor, quipping after such a provocation: "Probably by boring me to death."

On the case is Naunton Wayne as a slyly mischievous imp of a Scotland Yard supervisor. His crafty performance is a joy to watch, and not that different from what Peter Falk would eventually do on *Columbo*. Like an episode of that show, Newton will make the mistake of underestimating the inspector. He also unwisely snaps at Wayne in such moments as when the man drops in on Newton while he's preoccupied with his large model train setup. You know, when you are a model railroad enthusiast, you're kinda begging to be a cuckold.

Obsession is an extremely solid, though not great, thriller. It is twisty without being excessively convoluted, clever without calling attention to itself. There are good performances all around, especially that of the dog I mentioned in the opening paragraph. That is one smart pooch and, in a humorous touch, he will even have his own circle on the floor marking the extent of his range.

Original version posted on 10/18/2024

Pretty Poison (1968)

Anthony Perkins may have been typecast because of the success of *Psycho*, but it's only because playing disturbed persons seemed to come so naturally to him. I don't know what the man was like in real life—maybe he was as sweet and kind as Boris Karloff or

Peter Cushing. But you can't deny Perkins brings an edgy energy to every one of his roles.

Such is the case with 1968's *Pretty Poison*. Here, he plays a man recently released from a mental hospital. It will be a ways into the runtime before it is revealed what he did to be confined there and, even then, the full extent of the story is only gradually disclosed.

The one thing that is established immediately is his tendency to tell falsehoods. It is hard to tell if he is a compulsive liar or if he is genuinely delusional. Maybe he is a bit of both. It is a fine line he will walk throughout the picture.

We see only glimpses of disparate elements he will eventually weave into larger false narratives. Admittedly, even some of those individual elements are bizarre.

I thought he was employed at a lumber mill, yet his job has him doing quality control, monitoring small brown bottles as they go down a conveyor belt. What exactly is being bottled? Whatever it is, Perkins has decided it will play an important role in the narrative being pieced together in his mind. Thick, red, liquid waste of some sort is being discharged by his employer into the adjacent lake, and he will obsess over that as well.

A disparate piece in the puzzle will be Tuesday Weld, playing a high school student he first observes in a color guard practice. I have always found that high school activity, with its fake rifles, to be deeply bizarre. And what is a "color guard", anyway? Is to protect a color or is it to offer protection from a color? If it is the former, I'm guessing the color is white, because I've only seen Caucasians do this shit.

Perkins eventually draws Weld into his world of fantasy, as he has apparently convinced her he is a covert CIA agent investigating the mysterious output of his employer. That may seem unbelievable, but there is far more to Weld's character than her pretty, blonde façade reveals. Even the questions she asks him early on about his alleged CIA work are not what I would have expected, and these are early hints of something off-kilter.

Even before it is revealed she is the more dangerous of the two, everything about her scanned as a tad creepy to me. She's all too happy to take pills from Perkins, a strange man she only recently met. She also has a telling comment about sex, saying, "When grown-ups do it, it's kind of dirty. That's cause there's nobody to punish them."

Perkins and Weld are both fascinating to watch in this. Perkins doesn't even have to say anything to be unnerving, as he seems to travel exclusively by running from one place to another as if his life depended on it.

I am so surprised I had never heard of *Pretty Poison* before, and this is a movie that deserves to be better known. It packs a punch today, so I can't imagine what audiences thought of it upon its original release in 1968.

Original version posted on 7/19/2023

R.P.M. (1970)

Remember that movie they were making in *The Exorcist*, the one about protestors on a college campus? I couldn't stop thinking about that while watching Stanley Kramer's 1970 feature *R.P.M.*, an equally over-earnest and deeply unhip affair on the same subject.

We're not even through the opening credits when the first misstep happens. I know they couldn't possibly license a Dylan song for this, but did they have to go with Melanie? "Brand New Key"

Melanie? I know she performed at Woodstock, but I still never would have chosen her to be the "voice of revolution". Karen Carpenter may have been a bolder choice.

Anthony Quinn plays a liberal professor who is the only college president the students will accept after they oust the old one. No surprise, but the students turn on him when he is unable to push through all of their demands. To be fair, Quinn plays his actual age and it often comes up in dialogue.

His co-star is Ann-Margret. I have seen her do well in other movies, so I am confused by how she barely phones it in here. She is Quinn's lover and former student. She doesn't exactly look too old to be in this May/December romance, but she acts like it, slinking around in a manner that is less "free-love hippy" and more "Vegas sexy". It rings as false as every one of her line readings, all of which she delivers with dead eyes. It is a singularly bad performance.

As for the dialogue, most of it is stock slogans peppered with cries like "right on!" Though stilted, some of the dialogue still has some snap to it, such as this exchange: "I remember him. He was black!" "George, he still is"

R.P.M. is a movie with its heart in the right place, but it misses the mark. On the surface, it demonstrates an intention to spark dialogue between generations, races and income brackets. It is an exploration of what happens when the anti-establishment becomes the establishment. Unfortunately, it ends up feeling like another lecture about these kids nowadays.

Original version posted on 4/20/2023

Rain (1932)

The "pre-code" era of cinema began roughly with the advent of talkies. It is more certain when it ended, as that was the introduction of the Hayes Code in 1934. I have not seen many of the key films of that period, but I occasionally find one that is truly shocking when compared to the sanitized fare of the first couple of decades following the adoption of the code.

The one that has most stunned me so far is 1932's *Rain*. This was originally a hit Broadway play named after Sadie Thompson, its main character. It had also been made into a movie in the silent era. But it took the advent of sound to maximize the potential of this story of a battle of wills between a missionary and a "fallen" woman.

Joan Crawford plays Sadie, a prostitute from San Francisco who was facing a three-year prison term. I think it's interesting we don't know exactly why she was convicted.

We are introduced to her, and most of the other main characters, on a boat docking at Pago Pago. Crawford's first appearance here is one of the most impressive introductions I have seen in cinema history. We first get a close-up on each of four sailors interrupted in mid-conversation as they suddenly look to their left. The next series of shots has her curiously compartmentalized. We see a woman's hand against one side of a doorframe, several jangly bracelets on her wrist. Next, the other hand on the opposite side of the doorway. Then one ankle and then the other.

Then, at last, Crawford's face as I have never seen it before. It isn't just that she's so much younger here than in the other movies I have seen her in, it's the lively, knowing expression of a woman who enjoys life. It is safe to say she has "known" many men in the Biblical sense.

Speaking of the Bible, the ship she's arrived on has some fellow passengers who are going to cause trouble for her. There are two married couples, and all four of these people are missionaries. The most alarming of these is Walter Houston as man with rock-solid convictions which cannot be changed. Beulah Bondi plays his wife in what may be one of the most joyless performances I have seen.

All these people are going to be stuck on the island for at least two weeks while the ship deals with a potential cholera outbreak among its crew. They find rooms in an inn operated by Guy Kibbee, who seems to be the hub of all commerce on the island.

He's married to a native woman with whom he has many children, and I was very surprised Bondi did not feel compelled to comment on that. Also, I would be *very* surprised if she and Huston had any children, as that would mean they have had sex at least once.

But Bondi has the most to say about Crawford. That she and her husband are portrayed as intensely unlikeable tells us this is a pre-code film. Starting in 1924, it would be forbidden to portray representatives of Christianity in a negative light. Of course, any other religion would be fair game for mockery.

I was surprised by how good Houston is as her husband and fellow missionary. I always think of him as a cad (and father of another legendary cad, John Houston), who brought a telling orneriness to roles like Old Scratch in *The Devil and Daniel Webster*. He brings that same energy here to his portrayal of an obstinate, holier-than-thou jerk.

Despite strong performances from all the leads, the material feels a bit thin. Also, despite the excellent production values, this rarely feels like anything more than a stage play opened up for the big screen.

Speaking of those production values, this film looks astonishing, especially in the restoration on VCI's blu-ray. Of particular note are the advanced shot compositions, editing and camera movements, like a film made decades later. Probably the showiest and most astonishing shot has the camera stay face-on a ship captain as he walks completely around a table.

The movie begins with gorgeous visual poetry, as we see scattered raindrops pelting a variety of surfaces, such as sand and a pool of still water. As the rain increases, the cuts get progressively shorter, establishing a building tempo which culminates in a deluge. After a couple of scenes, the rain subsides and we see roughly the same sequence again, but with the tempo slowing until the downpour subsides.

This type of imagery is more reminiscent of the best pictures of the silent era. One aspect of this which could only have been possible as of a couple of years prior is the excellent dialogue, most of which is given to Crawford. On booze: "I was born hooched." On boredom: "There's so much time on this island, people ought to bottle it up and send it where they need some." For some reason, I really liked a moment that felt potentially ad-libbed, when she sees her high-heeled shoes are ruined by mud: "Farewell, my pretty ones."

That's as much as I care to say about *Rain*, though there is far more of merit there than I wrote about here. I'm not sure it is a great movie, but it has so much to offer that I recommend it to everybody. There's stellar camera work and brilliant dialogue. Best of all, it has Joan Crawford in the kind of role I'm not sure she ever attempted again, and she obviously relishes every minute of it.

Original version posted on 9/24/2023

The Rainbow Boys (1973)

Donald Pleasance has ruined his pants, which I guess was bound to happen soon or later, because they appear to be decades old. Don Calfa has the solution, an item he once bought at Macy's bargain basement. Soon, Pleasance is dressed in the most spectacularly weird fashion: Depression-era newsboy from the waist-up while, from the waist-down, it's white bell-bottoms covered in stars and smiley faces. It isn't like there are any clothing retailers nearby, as he, Calfa and Kate Reid are deep in the Canadian Rockies, looking for gold in 1973's *The Rainbow Boys*.

This trio is looking for a gold mine Pleasance supposedly inherited from his father. Whether or not the mine will be there is something I will not reveal, as it is as likely to be there as not. He has a tendency to tell rambling stories which might be knowing fabrications, inventions of a fractured mind, or a combination of the two. This is a guy we hear talking about German bombers in WWII dropping land mines, and how one was stuck in a tree in his yard.

Still, this mission provides something that had been missing in the lives of Pleasance, Reid and Calfa. We never learn much about them, but they all seem to be scarred from various things in their past. Calfa was apparently in prison, though we don't know why. Reid was likely married for only a brief time and is still bitter and cynical. We're never even fully certain what has reduced Pleasance to this bizarre assortment of personality quirks, complete with an apparently mild touch of Tourette's.

Despite some of the dialogue rather mildly addressing adult themes, the three leads are like children. Each is impulsive and prone to extreme mood changes. Calfa is like a kid who is excited by pictures of naked women without fully understanding why he finds himself aroused. Reid is so cantankerous as to seem to be channeling Lucy from *Peanuts*. Pleasance is extremely proud of a house he built entirely by himself from items salvaged from the river, though the result puts the "shack" in "ramshackle". It's like he built a kid's treehouse, except on the ground. Even their mission of going to get gold feels naïve, as their enthusiasm for this seemed to me like little kids looking for pirate treasure.

A fourth character is Calfa's unusual means of transportation, a shamble that is almost a physical representation of the mess that is Pleasance's mind. This trike is obviously a custom-made job, a hybrid of a motorcycle, the bench seat of a sedan, two car tires and God only knows what else. It seems to have a max cruising speed of less than 25 MPH, and it's a wonder it will stay together even at those speeds. Supposedly, he drove all the way from NYC on it.

Still, it will carry them up steep, winding, dirt roads into the mountains. Alas, the wheels will come off the film when the wheels come off the trike. I was surprised to find myself gut-punched by the moment it rolls off the road and shatters into a great many pieces after a long fall.

It is at this point the picture continues in the same manner as before, except it becomes more wearing than charming. In a way, it's a bit like how I feel about exuberant children: amusing for an hour or so, then deeply tiring afterwards. I stopped caring whether they would strike gold or even find the mine. I just wanted it to end.

The Rainbow Boys is in the general wheelhouse of the works of Jim Jarmusch, whose oeuvre I don't care much for, and Aki Kaurismaki, whose films I love. I really wanted to like it more than I did, this oddly compelling film that is as jumbled but endearing as its leads and, especially, that trike.

Original version posted on 11/5/2024

Remember the Night (1939)

It may appear I am excessively harsh to most movies I write about, but I really try to find something positive to say about each. Then there's movies I fall in love with, and I *really* can't seem to shut up about those. Such is the case with 1939's *Remember the Night*.

I liked Barbara Stanwyck in this as a repeat offender shoplifter. I even liked the hat she wears for the longest time, until a cow eats it. I liked Willard Robertson as her attorney, who passionately presents an insane defense in court. I liked Fred MacMurray as the prosecuting attorney who can't bear the thought of her spending Christmas behind bars. I liked Tom Kennedy, as Fat Mike, the bails bondsman. I liked Fred Toones as MacMurray's right-hand man, who goes above and beyond the call of the duty when managing his boss's apartment and life. I liked MacMurray's family back home in Indiana, including Beulah Bondi, Elizabeth Patterson and Sterling Holloway, though the last of those may have laid on the "aw shucks" shtick just a little too thickly. Then again, that guy was the voice of Winnie the Pooh, so what do I know.

The film begins with Stanwyck stealing a large, jeweled bracelet. Robertson's defense for her in court posits his client was helpless to keep from absconding with it because she had been hypnotized. This results in some great reaction shots around the room, most notably from the incredulous Stanwyck. MacMurray later asks her why they didn't try for the kleptomania angle, to which she replies, "To be a kleptomaniac, you can't try to fence anything afterwards, lest you lose your amateur status." Almost all the dialogue has that spark to it.

Despite being patently ridiculous, it is obvious these arguments are going to sway the jury. But MacMurray has a powerful trump card to play: the court psychologist is already away for the holidays, so he argues the trial be put on hold until his return at the start of the next year. This means Stanwyck will be spending Christmas in jail, which should be the title of a Tom Waits song if it isn't already.

MacMurray can't bear to do this, so he asks Fat Mike to post bail for her. Little does he realize, the bail bondman will deposit her at MacMurray's apartment, where he is bewildered as to what to do with her. He tries to make nice but, as Stanwyck observes, "One of these days, one of you boys is going to start this scene different, and one of us girls is going to drop dead from surprise."

But Toones already senses a potential romance between MacMurray and Stanwyck and so brings them each a scotch and soda. I like how this guy knows what his boss wants even before the man himself knows it.

This was the first of four movies starring our leads, and we see here how quickly they developed a rapport. The Preston Sturges script is fantastic, and it is amazing to hear such unrealistic banter roll out so naturally from the mouths of our stars. Even some characters on the margins get snappy lines: "Conviction of a first-time offender at Christmastime is tougher than tiger meat." I don't care to know how MacMurray's assistant at work knows that.

When MacMurray and Stanwyck discover they are fellow Hoosiers, the plot turns into a road trip, as they go to see their respective mothers for the holidays. I especially like the bit where the car crashes through a farmer's fence in Pennsylvania. Stanwyck had distracted MacMurray by yelling what seems to be an impossibility: "LOOK OUT! THERE'S AN ELEPHANT!", which turns out to be a disused harvester shrouded in cloth. This is all a setup for them to be arrested for trespassing the next morning, a turn of events which has a great payoff. Their escape involves some impromptu arson, so they get out of the state fast.

The next stop for these low-key fugitives is her mother's house. The movie wisely eschews music for the entirety of this scene where we meet a cold, bitter woman. Her assessment of her daughter is "good riddance to bad rubbish." I love this sharp exchange between MacMurray and Stanwyck's mother: "It's been very interesting meeting you Mrs..." "The name does not concern you." "It certainly does not."

An entirely different type of family greets the couple at his mother's house. I best remember Bondi as a bitterly Puritanical missionary in *Rain*, so it was a relief to see her play such a warm character here. Stanwyck gets a taste of how life might have been different for her if she had been raised by better people. There's a hint it might not even be too late for her to change her life now.

I don't want to say more about this picture because I don't want to spoil the wealth of pleasant little surprises in it. So many moments in this are like small presents waiting to be unwrapped. And then it puts a big bow around the entire package when it completely sticks the landing. The ending may not leave all viewers happy, but it is the right ending, the true ending, and the one the audience deserves.

For a film set entirely around the winter holidays, *Remember the Night* felt less like a Christmas film than every other such picture I can think of, and I mean that as a compliment. I would consider it to be a Christmas movie as little as I would *Die Hard* or *Brazil*. It is exceptionally smart and funny, and can be watched at any time of year. It is also genuinely heart-warming and poignant and so, despite starring Stanwyck and MacMurray, it isn't *Double Indemnity at the North Pole*.

Original version posted on 12/11/2023

The Running Man (1963)

One of my favorite meals I can remember was at a suburban Thai restaurant where the power was out at the time. Their stove used gas, so they could still cook. As long as you had cash, they would serve you. The front and back doors were propped open, so a light breeze wound through the space. The only light in the place was what little reflected off the blacktop and cars outside. It is hard to explain exactly how this moment felt, but it seemed we were outside of time and place, briefly occupying somewhere "other." Not somewhere outside the US, but somehow outside of everything.

I mention this because there is a beautiful scene in 1963's *The Running Man* where the three main characters (Laurence Harvey, Lee Remick and Alan Bates) have a casual conversation at night in the plaza outside a shabby hotel in Spain. This scene has a similar vibe to it, a feeling we are outside of time and space. I suspect most people would find this scene unnecessary, but it was the soul of the movie for me.

Harvey plays a man who fakes his death in a glider crash. I was surprised a glider was used and not a plane. Maybe gliding was a popular trend at the time this movie was made. All I know is I heartily agree with a statement about the hobby that some guy makes at the airport Harvey departs from: "It is dead set against our materialistic civilization. You can't imagine anybody doing it for money."

I'd say that is the truth, unless your goal is to commit insurance fraud, like Harvey is doing. After his funeral, he sneaks back into his apartment to have a brief liaison with his co-conspirator and wife, played by Remick. Their conversation is interrupted when a representative from the insurer (played by Bates) stops by.

The insurance company doesn't investigate further, and Remick stays behind for a while to collect the payout while her husband sneaks off to France. He conveniently adopts a new identity when an Australian sheep farmer he meets in a bar accidentally leaves his passport behind.

Remick is less than thrilled with this new persona once she catches up with him. It doesn't help he has been staying in a mansion as the guest of a woman who obviously has designs on him. Even worse, he has become a boor and does bourgeois things like belittling waiters. Hey, I think I have a new word: "boorgeois".

The action then moves to Spain, which is where Bates catches Remick at a table at an outdoor café. He just happened to miss the departing Harvey by seconds. Bates says he is on holiday, but is he really? What if it is just a ruse to investigate the claim?

If Bates isn't still working the case, it is odd how many insightful questions he asks. Much of what he says is highly ambiguous, and Bates delivers the best performance here, in a role that walks a razor-thin line.

About those questions, the script is full of clever lines. Possibly a hair too clever, but it is how I wish people talked in real life. "How many sheep do you have?" "I don't know. I only count them when I'm trying to go to sleep." Remick, in particular, gets some of the more interesting lines, such as this still-relevant observation: "Why do people always get so angry in cars?" Or how she demurs when Bates says he has something he has to tell her: "Whenever somebody says 'I've got something I just have to say', I don't know, but I never want to hear it."

That dialogue isn't quite on par with director Carol Reed's most famous movie, *The Third Man*, which just happens to be my favorite film of all time. Still, there's enough of that magic in *The Running Man* to be of interest to fans of that picture, as well as other thrillers. There may not be enough action to satisfy some people, but this is a good movie for those who can see the beauty in small moments and in lines of the type you wish you had ever thought to say.

Original version posted on 6/26/2023

The Shop at Sly Corner (1947)

Seldom have I been rooting for the bad guys as much as I did while watching 1947's *The Shop at Sly Corner*. I also cannot recall ever wanting to see one character kill another as much I did here.

The two I wanted to get away with everything are Oscar Homolka and Manning Whiley. Homolka is an escaped fugitive from another country. Now in his advanced years, he has a fairly prestigious antiques store. He also buys stolen goods provided by Whiley. These two are such gentleman criminals that, when Homolka decides to stop doing business in purloined goods, he pays the other man far more than what the most recent batch of items was worth.

The antiques dealer has done well enough for himself that he can send his daughter (Muriel Pavlow) to professional violin instruction. There's an odd tangent related to that where Homolka criticizes that instructor for "teaching [his] daughter to be a woman." Ew. And then nothing more is ever said about that.

Her fiancée is a naval officer played by Derek Farr. He has returned from his most recent tour of duty with, as Homolka puts it, "Presents you brought for me to buy." Among these are darts with tips coated with curare. They might as well be coated in foreshadowing. Something that amazes me is those are apparently going to be put on sale with the poison still on them. Seems to me that is a lawsuit just begging to happen.

Another man with designs on Pavlow is Kenneth Griffith, an especially nasty character who works in the shop. He'll do things like aggressively get a low price for an item an old woman desperately needs to sell, something of her mother's which she has had her entire life. Griffith overhears a compromising conversation between Homolka and Whiley and uses it to blackmail the former. And, like most blackmailers, he never stops making demands. And so, I was yelling at the screen for the kindly Homolka to dispose of Griffith.

The photography does not call attention to itself, so it is easy to overlook some rather complicated camera moves employed in a couple of moments. The first scene has the camera track through one room and around the corner into the next. The very last thing we see in the film is an astonishing crane shot which pushes in from the back of a theatre and ends on a bouquet held by Pavlow. This is not unlike a similar, and rightly legendary, moment in Hitchcock's *Notorious* the prior year where the camera pushes in from a couple of stories up until it ends on a close-up of a key in Ingrid Bergman's hand. Such set-ups would have been time-consuming and costly, and so were interesting decisions for a rather modest picture. That these techniques don't call attention to themselves means they are used appropriately.

The performances are excellent all around. Homolka, in particular, is a joy to watch. I could watch his easy banter with such actors as Whiley even if there wasn't a plot. Pavlow and Farr deliver solid supporting performances, though I didn't detect the strong chemistry they had behind the scenes, where they fell in love and soon married for life. Griffith, who I am used to seeing cast as an unassuming everyman, is terrific as the villain. I can even cut him some slack for playing a little too broadly here.

I don't want to say anything more about *The Shop at Sly Corner*, as there is much for noir fans to enjoy in this rather unassuming film. Heck, there is much for movie fans, period, to appreciate.

Original version posted on 10/5/2024

Storm Warning (1950)

I just finished watching 1951's *Storm Warning,* and I'm feeling a little punch drunk.

Ginger Rogers plays a fashion model. In a deceptively benign opening scene, she's on a bus with her travelling companion, a co-worker who has a crush on her. There's a cute exchange between them, and an exposition dump where we learn she is getting off at the next stop to drop in on her sister she hasn't seen in a long time.

It's late at night when she disembarks. She immediately encounters hostile locals, such as a cab driver sitting at the counter of the hamburger stand who won't take her fare. She runs back to the bus station as it turns off its lights. Behind her, the lights of the hamburger stand go out. Soon, she is walking down the street as other businesses start turning off their signs. I'm not sure if this is noir or horror. Noirror, maybe?

At the end of the block, she is about to cross in front of the police station when its lights go out. Fortunately, she pauses at the corner just as there is a commotion. A group of Klan members rush out from the side of the station, beating and shoving a prisoner. When he tries to run off, one of the Klansmen shoots him in the back twice. In shock, some of the hooded figures unmask themselves, revealing one of them to be Steve Cochran.

Rogers retreats into a doorway while the killers ensure their victim is dead. When they depart, she delicately steps into the light, only for the lights to come back on in the station as an officer opens a window and looks outside. In a panic, Rogers runs across the street and down an alleyway in a silhouette so perfect as to recall similarly composed shots in *The Third Man*.

She catches up to her sister (Doris Day) while she is at her job serving drinks at the bowling alley. It is strange to see Day so young. Rogers looks like she could be her mother. This made me realize how awesome it is a movie of that era has a woman of her age as the lead.

Rogers owns this movie and is especially strong in the scene where Day brings her home…where it is revealed Cochran is the husband, of course. Not realizing Rogers saw him kill a man, Coogan is confused by her speechless, seething hatred towards him. I thought the rest of the runtime would be a cat-and-mouse game between the two, but she accuses him of murder within minutes of him showing up.

Instead, the movie recenters around Ronald Reagan's district attorney and the case he has been building against the local Klan chapter. Reagan correctly surmises from the time Rogers's luggage was checked in at the depot that she had to have witnessed the murder. What the plot will hinge on is whether she will testify against her brother-in-law or if she will lie on the stand to save the man Day loves.

I'm not sure I have seen Reagan in anything before. I have always seen him labelled as a hack who never graduated from B-movies. His performance here is rock-solid, but maybe this film is an outlier in an otherwise lackluster career.

Sadly, the movie is still rather prescient, even if the Klan isn't the threat it used to be. The local businessmen and politicians are more worried about the court case's potential damage to the town's economy and image than they are about a man being murdered in cold blood. They are especially appalled this had to happen the week before Christmas. As Reagan drolly retorts, "So, a week after Christmas would have been alright."

Another prescient moment is when a radio reporter is insulted and threatened by people outside the courthouse—people who despise outsiders, the media and, most of all, national news reporters. It breaks my heart that so little could have changed since 1951. I'm just surprised the crowd is this picture doesn't chant "FAKE NEWS!"

The element of *Storm Warning* that will stick with me is it has some jarring shifts in tone. Among the genres it dabbles in to varying extents are noir, earnest social drama, soap opera, courtroom drama, and the kind of overheated fare Tennessee Williams used to pen. And that is no way a dig at the picture. All I am saying is it kept me on my toes the entire time.

Original version posted on 6/25/2023

Testament (1983)

I must have some sort of obsession with dramas about the survivors of nuclear war. God knows I have seen enough of them. Most of these movies were made in the 1980's, which makes sense. Prince's "1999" captured the prevailing feeling of the time, that we could be annihilated in an instant.

When most people think of such pictures, I'm betting they first think of *The Day After*, the miniseries that traumatized a nation. Watching that today shows it has lost much of its power as, however good its intentions might have been, it is pure shlock.

But there is another, and far lesser-known, movie that still packs a devastating punch. It also was originally intended to be a TV movie until the studio realized how great it was and gave it a theatrical release. That movie is *Testament*, and it is going to hand your ass to you.

The minor miracle this film performs is that it keeps everything small-scale. It is focused on one unremarkable family living in a cookie-cutter subdivision in California. We hardly get to know these people before the bombs hit.

Even then, the only special effect is a blinding light through the living room windows. The filmmakers didn't even stoop to using that stock footage of atomic bomb tests we have all seen a hundred times over.

This isn't a movie about huge numbers of casualties. This isn't a post-apocalyptic adventure where people go feral and tribal. Instead, this is only about one family and the slow, horrible fade to death that awaits each one of its members.

The performances in this are astonishing, in that it feels like we are seeing real people. Some people may dismiss such natural performances as lazy. I counter it is easy to perform a role like one is wearing a costume, as opposed to just some everyday nobody. Basically, there is nothing less natural than trying to act naturally (regardless of what Ringo sings in that song from *Rubber Soul*).

The movie centers around Jane Alexander as the mother, and she was rightly nominated for Best Actress for this. William Devane plays the father, and the last time we see him is when he leaves for

You don't want no drama [except this is the section about dramatic movies]

work. We never even find out what happened to him, which gives an idea of how this film operates.

Curiously, two performers who give less than stellar performances are a very young Kevin Costner and Rebecca DeMornay, and that is only because I perceived them as being "in character" and thus a tad artificial. Lukas Haas plays the youngest in the family, demonstrating early on why he has had a long career in film.

In its own way, *Testament* is a beautiful film and I hope I have the courage to watch it again someday. For now, it was so effective that I find it hard to even think about it. I feel like I briefly met real people, only to watch them die.

And yet the movie has a message of optimism for us, the ones who can still avoid a nuclear war. The message isn't even ham-fisted—it is just floated out there near the end of the film. To paraphrase this message, I want to conclude this piece by saying we need to create a world worthy of its children.

Original version posted on 5/11/2023

Thunder on the Hill (1951)

In movies, people are always taking sanctuary in churches, monasteries and convents, but I do not recall ever hearing about somebody doing this in real life. This is what residents of a flooded town do in 1951's *Thunder on the Hill* as they seek shelter in a hilltop convent. As for me, I wasn't taken in when I charged into a church shouting "SANCTUARY!" like I was the hunchback of Notre Dame. How could I know I would be disrupting a wedding?

One of the arrivals is Ann Blyth, playing a woman convicted of murdering her brother. She was in transit to her execution by hanging when washed-out roads forced this layover. Despite Blyth's belligerent manner, head nun Claudette Colbert comes to believe she is innocent.

Colbert has a great role here: a highly intelligent and resourceful manager of a large building and those who do their work in it. She's the kind of person who keeps her head in a crisis. I was reminded of Deborah Kerr's role in *Black Narcissus*. And, if you don't know that movie, stop reading and watch that immediately. I'll still be here when you get back.

I watched this picture as part of one of the sets in Kino Lorber's excellent *Dark Side of Cinema* noir collection. I am glad I got to see this picture, though I wouldn't label it as noir. Instead, this is solidly melodrama, as one would expect from Douglas Sirk, the go-to director of "women's pictures" in that era.

Colbert and Blyth both turn in solid performances and are supported by a decent cast. Connie Gilchrist is particularly noteworthy as Colbert's enthusiastic second-in-command, the kind of person who finds joy in work. She especially cherishes old newspapers, probably having more uses for them than even the cleverest homeless person. This actually figures into the plot, as she helps Colbert research the history of Blyth's case via newspapers she used for shelf liners. A nice touch is how they work backwards chronologically through the course of the investigation, finding each previous edition of the newspaper according to the order of the projects Gilchrist had worked on.

A decent but less convincing performance is delivered by Michael Pate as a person of diminished mental capabilities except for when the script needs him to be smarter. He's kind of the Forest Gump of the picture. You know, he's dense as the bogs surrounding the convent, yet is the only person able to retrieve a boat. Then he demonstrates frankly unbelievable metal powers when he decides to destroy the boat after it is used, so nobody can easily transport a potentially innocent woman to be hanged.

Still, I couldn't help but enjoy his interactions with other characters, especially Gilchrist, who gently chastises his sloppy eating with, "Put the food in your mouth not your mouth in the food." I think I saw that on a sign once at a Golden Corral.

I wasn't able to fully suspend my disbelief while watching *Thunder on the Hill*, but I enjoyed it, regardless. In a way, it is like the title, as thunder cannot actually strike anything, despite what AC/DC says.

Original version posted on 7/1/2023

Thursday's Child (1943)

A twelve-year-old girl is in a waiting room. A man walks past her, does a double-take and orders her to stand up. He also demands she turn around. Has the proper reaction to this ever *not* been to knee the jerk in the balls and run?

Sally Ann Howes plays Fennis Wilson, a girl destined to star in a movie even though she doesn't want to be actress. As she tries to explain to a persistent director: "I have other plans." "What plans?" "Secret plans."

She is very direct and plain speaking—perhaps too direct for people in an enterprise rooted in deception. That guy who first saw her is irritated she won't answer his many questions with the kinds of answers he expects from people seeking film work. "Are you dumb or trying to be funny?" Her reply: "Neither."

This is 1943's *Thursday's Child*, a UK Pathé drama-comedy (roughly 75% the former) about this sincere young girl who refuses to be compromised by the studio system. I guess Hollywood isn't the only place that loves to make movies about itself.

Fennis refuses to have her brown locks dyed. She won't let the studio change her last name. She didn't even want to be in the movie. So why was the studio so insistent she be a star, anyways?

It was her older sister that was at the studio auditioning in vain when Fennis was discovered. In what would be a bitter rivalry in a lesser picture, the relationship between these sisters is more subtle and complicated here. The older sister *is* jealous, but she tries to temper it, and you can see her straining to do so.

There's a nice scene I like between these two characters in the older sister's bedroom late at night. Fennis eats some sandwiches while talking to her and says, "I wonder why things taste extra delicious after midnight." I like that. And it's true.

The greater conflict is between the stern father (Wilfrid Lawson) and each of his children. He demands his son continue the family business. He refuses to let the older sister appear even as an extra in the picture Fennis is starring in. And he threatens to pull Fennis from the movie if it goes to her head.

Go figure—her father is a chemist (pharmacist, for those of us in the colonies) and a stern control freak. So, he's basically the same father as the one in *Pink String and Sealing Wax*, which also starred…Sally Ann Howes. What is this, the Old British Comedy Cinematic Universe?

Original version posted on 6/3/2023

Times Square (1980)

I thought about music the entire time I watched 1983's *Times Square*, and it wasn't just because of a killer soundtrack, with music by (among others) Roxy Music, Joe Jackson, The Ramones, Talking Heads, The Pretenders and XTC. It even has Lou Reed's "Walk on the Wild Side". The soundtrack alone is an embarrassment of riches.

This is a rare instance of a movie being worthy of such a collection. In general, the quality of movies from that era were inversely proportionate to that of their soundtrack. That it was produced by Robert Stigwood especially gave me pause. After all, this was the man responsible for the movie *Sgt. Pepper's Lonely Hearts Club Band,* starring the Bee Gees and Peter Frampton as the title characters. Turns out I worried unnecessarily, as it was a blast to watch.

It starts with Robin Johnson wandering New York City streets at night with all her meager possessions in tow. One of those items is her guitar and small amp. In an alley, she starts playing along to "Same Old Scene" by Roxy Music, which is on the *film* soundtrack. Outside of musicals, I've never seen a character performing to music that isn't in the environment of the scene we're watching. My word-a-day calendar tells me the word I'm looking for is "non-diegetic", and I bet I'll be using that again in a few sentences.

Johnson looks more than a little bit like David Johansen if he was a young woman. She even has a similar voice and mannerisms. I wasn't surprised they duetted on a song on the soundtrack (though not appearing on-screen together).

A random act of destruction leads to her arrest (the latest in a long series of them), but the first place she is offloaded is a mental hospital. Her roommate will be Trini Alvarado, playing the deeply repressed daughter of a city commissioner. There is obviously nothing wrong with Alvarado except she has a father that won't listen to her.

Peter Coffield plays that commissioner, a bureaucrat staging an intense campaign to clean up Times Square. Dude, were you the person behind the eventual Disneyfication of the place in real life? You asshole! For most of the movie, he is more concerned about his image than his daughter, even when she and Johnson escape the asylum and go into hiding.

The friendship between the girls happens fast but in believable steps. I especially like the scene where Johnson runs around the hospital, blaring "I Wanna Be Sedated" on her boombox. Not only is that the perfect use for that song in a film, but I loved the use of diegetic music for it. See, I just *knew* I'd get to use that word again!

Stealing an ambulance and driving the wrong way down one-way streets, Johnson is a whirling dervish—a true force of nature that sweeps Alvarado up in its wake. They become a young queer Bonnie and Clyde, even if their attempts at significant crimes like robbery fail hilariously.

About that last statement: I may be a hetero CIS middle-aged male, but I think I can safely say these two are definitely in a romantic relationship, even if they never share a single kiss on-screen. In a telling moment before settling down to play house in an abandoned waterfront warehouse, they become blood sisters by pressing their nicked wrists together and yelling out each other's names as loud as they can.

Tim Curry is actually the headliner of the picture, but he is definitely a secondary character. Playing a DJ operating out of a station overlooking the titular area, he becomes fascinated by the girls and their antics. His role here reminded me a bit of Cleavon Little's DJ in *Vanishing Point*, as he reads letters from them on the air and even acts as a sort of intermediary between them and the outside world. A line I love from one of those letters is, "I am not kidnapped. I am me-napped."

Things seem to get wobbly near the middle of the runtime and I started worrying it might go straight off the rails. Fortunately, it doesn't, but I was wondering what tone the movie was employing as Johnson's behavior becomes increasingly erratic and destructive. I'm going to assume that tone was pure objectivity, and without judgment, once the girls start doing things like dropping TVs off of rooftops. Nobody gets hurt, but somebody could have just as easily been.

All of the characters grow some with their experiences in the course of the film. Even the father gains new facets, as he tries to converse with his daughter when possible, instead of simply demanding she come home. He will track her down to a club where she has been employed as a dancer, and his approach is respectful. The moment where Alvarado transforms from being cripplingly bashful to letting herself go on stage is beautiful. Johnson also learns to let her defenses down a bit and even writes a pretty good punk song.

There will be another punk song later and, if there is an elephant in the room regarding this movie, that would be this track. It has a chorus with two racial slurs, as well as a homophobic one, and it is probably the only aspect of this production more shocking today than when it was released. Around the same time, Patti Smith had a song with the N-word in the title (and repeated ad nauseum in the lyrics), so I can see what they were aiming for— even if I cringed to the extent of near physical pain the entire time.

Instead of the paragraph of random musings I usually indulge in at this point, how about some more of my favorite quotes? "Out of the frying pan and into the fire is where you go when you don't want to be eaten for dinner." "I'm brave, you're pretty. I'm a fuckin' freak of nature."

Despite its moments of ugliness, or perhaps because of them, *Times Square* turned out to be far more beautiful experience than I anticipated. Although the relationship between our heroines is too intense to last, I had a blast spending some time with two such high-spirited young women, so alive and so in love.

Original version posted on 3/21/2023

The Unguarded Moment (1956)

There was a term I kept trying to recall while watching 1956's *The Unguarded Moment*. I looked it up afterwards and discovered it was "cognitive dissonance". Basically, this means holding two contrasting beliefs in one's mind at the same time, usually leading to irritation. It seems to me a couple of characters in this movie demonstrate this cognitive disparity, and it led me to feel agitated.

This is the first serious drama Esther Williams made after spending years trying to escape a box the studio system put her in. For the longest time, she starred in movies where her swimming expertise was employed for complex choreographed musical numbers, all done in and around bodies of water. I'll confess I have yet to see any of those movies, but that's a novelty I imagine wears thin pretty fast. So, I was glad she had an opportunity to show what she could do outside of that context.

And she is very good in this. If there is a reason to see this picture, it is for her performance. And that is remarkable, as she had to overcome some strange dialogue in an awkward script.

She plays a high school teacher who goes on the warpath when she receives anonymous lewd notes from a student. She even calls the author's bluff and goes to an empty locker room that night for a proposed tryst. While I admire her confidence, this is a very questionable move. Worse, she becomes mousy and placating when she finds herself cornered in the dark room by an assailant keeping a flashlight on her.

She flees before getting raped. Once on the street, she is apprehended by the police and taken to the station, where they do a breathalyzer on her. Wow, those are some priorities. Then she is loudly interrogated by a police lieutenant (George Nader) in a room where other officers are within earshot. I was surprised by the lack of courtesy he demonstrates by having a sensitive conversation openly in a room with others in it.

I'm not even sure exactly what the police think happened. I suspected the officers who brought her in thought she was a prostitute. I don't know if it was mentioned in any dialogue, but I don't think anybody bothered to check out the locker room where she was assaulted. And Nader gets short with her because she isn't forthcoming with any information. But who would when there's others in the room?

She has other another reason for not wanting to press charges or give any information, and that is because, as she puts it later, "That is a high school boy, not a criminal." And there's some of that cognitive dissonance I mentioned. A student first bothers her with suggestive notes and then tries to rape her when she confronts him in that locker room, but she believes he should be cut some slack because he's a student. Never mind he can still be a threat not only to her but also to other women. And not just as rapist—he may also be a murderer. Oh, and I failed to mention he's *eighteen*. Old enough to be tried as an adult makes him no longer a kid in my book.

John Saxon plays the disturbed, um, lad. This is the youngest I have seen him in anything before, and he looks significantly different than he would in the later films I know him from. The movie provides a psychological reason for Saxon's behavior towards women via a couple of uncomfortable conversations with his dad, played by Edward Andrews.

Dad is extremely bitter about his wife having left him years before. I suspected he actually killed her, and then I was surprised that is an avenue the movie doesn't explore. One really odd rule Andrews has is he refuses to let Saxon date. The film's creepiest moment is when he informs his son how seriously he will enforce that: "If you knock down what I've spent years building up, I'll break every bone in your body".

More cognitive dissonance comes courtesy of the school principal, played by Les Tremayne. For some reason, Williams goes to him to report Saxon, when she didn't say anything to the police. The principal's behavior is about as questionable as that of the police. He just summons the student to his office, so he, Saxon and Williams can have an uncomfortable conversation. Even though Tremayne believes Williams, he refuses to do anything about Saxon, as he is the star of the football team.

But, really, shouldn't this be a police matter? Why doesn't Williams talk to them instead of her boss? And I wanted to jump into the screen and punch Tremayne when, at a football game where Saxon makes a great play, he turns to Williams, laughs and says, "And that's the boy you wanted me to discipline!"

The most confusing thinking on display here is how the script regards women. It has one cautious foot in an era that is more progressive than the times, and the other firmly in the kitchen, where it expects women to be. Williams gets a lot of flack from seemingly every guy in the movie. I lost count of how many times one asks her if she's miss or missus, or if she has a boyfriend. I was glad when she, rightfully, is angered by all this focus on her relationship status. And yet, she is charmed when Nader comments on her abilities in her kitchen. Then there's Tremayne, right after he says that shitty thing to her at the game, going on to say how happy he is to see her there with Nader. Really, fuck these people.

I won't ruin the ending of *The Unguarded Moment*, except to say I thought it was preposterous, unnecessary and completely unbelievable. One thing that shouldn't surprise anybody is she settles down with Nader. I wonder if he will let her keep teaching? I have the nagging feeling he won't, and that she will be OK with that. Strange how this movie has as its central figure a stronger female character than most films of the time, yet it doesn't seem to know what to do with her. At least the change in genres was a new opportunity for its lead, for Williams to escape from the weird cinema ghetto she was trapped in before.

Original version posted on 2/10/2024

Valley Girl (1983)

Funny how perspective can change so much over time. In 1983's *Valley Girl*, a hot mom played by Lee Purcell puts the moves on a high school boy who's interested in her daughter. The scene is kind of funny, as she quotes lines from *The Graduate* and he has no idea what she's talking about. You can tell he's trying to leave gracefully.

I know that, if I had seen this when I was younger, I would have been going, "Dude! Go for it!" Now I see something like this and I'm appalled any adult would want to socialize with a high school student, let alone try to sex them up.

Overall, this is a sweet little romantic comedy, as well as a time capsule of the early 80s. Nicholas Cage plays a guy from the wrong side of the tracks who falls in love with a well-to-do popular girl played by Deborah Foreman. A telling moment has them hanging off each other while a marquee behind them advertises Romeo & Juliet. I guess this movie is a bit like that, only with 100% fewer suicides.

This movie was directed by Martha Coolidge, and it is refreshing to see a movie of that era directed by a woman. Also, I was surprised it was directed by a woman, given the extent of boobage on display. One of the top-billed actresses is Elizabeth (E.G.) Daily, who was Dottie in *Pee Wee's Big Adventure*. Odd, but I was seriously uncomfortable seeing Daily topless, and she does so for longer than I ever would have expected.

I don't know anything about Coolidge, but I have no doubts she was familiar with the punk and alternative scene in LA at the time. Maybe it was studio interference, but I was surprised the "crazy" club Cage and his best friend (Cameron Dye) take Foreman and her friend to has The Plimsouls as the house band. No knock on this group, but it isn't like they went to go see L.A. punk legends X. The Plimsouls do their signature tune, "A Million Miles Away" twice. Funny, but I was thinking the movie was starting to tread water when that song suddenly started up that second time. I found myself overwhelmed by déjà vu.

You don't want no drama (except this is the section about dramatic movies)

Speaking of the soundtrack, it is very solid. In addition to The Plimsouls, there's choice tracks by Psychedelic Furs, Modern English, Men At Work and Sparks. There are also some one-hit-wonders like "Johnny, Are You Queer?" by Josie Cotton and "Jukebox (Don't Put Another Dime)" by The Flirts, and now I can't get that latter track out of my goddamn head.

I was wondering how that Josie Cotton track might be regarded nowadays and that started me thinking about how some elements of this movie haven't aged well. Some of these may have been off-putting even then. My biggest grievance is how Cage hides in the shower during a party he just got thrown out of, waiting for Foreman to appear so they can talk. Hiding in the bathroom while different people come and go, doing their thing, oblivious to the fact he's there—really?!

I'm not sure if it was the director's intention, but an ending with Cage and Foreman in the back of a limo seemed awfully similar to the final shot of *The Graduate*. At least the tone of *Valley Girl* is more upbeat at the end than the one for that film. And I found this 80's teen comedy more enjoyable than, and free from the pretentions of, that earlier picture. But where this really shines is the soundtrack. As Cage jokes to Foreman's friend, when she is too scared to get out of the car at the "punk" club, "If they attack the car, save the radio." Amen, brother.

Original version posted on 5/29/2023

Without rhyme or reason

(well, frequently rhyming, but rarely employing reason)
Musicals, and movies about music

23 Seconds to Eternity (2023)

WTF, KLF?

I admit I purchased the blu-ray of 2023's KLF film *23 Seconds to Eternity* knowing little about the musical group, except they were legendary pranksters of a sort. What intrigued me most about them is they once burned a million pounds of their money as a performance piece. Aside from that, all I know about them is they released some techno music that didn't leave much of an impression on me, regardless of the names they released it under, among those being The Timelords, The Justified Ancients of the Mu Mus ("The JAMs") or The KLF.

Regardless of the name, they were only ever Bill Drummond and Jimmy Cauty. Their first hit was "Doctorin' The Tardis", putting the *Doctor Who* theme to an electronic beat, and incorporating chants of "Doctor WHO-OOO" in the manner of Gary Glitter's "Rock and Roll Part 2". The result is the most entertaining of their endeavors and it is well served by the accompanying video, wherein an American police cruiser pursues charmingly goofy homemade Daleks. There's even a shot where you can see under one of the Daleks, the feet of the actor inside clearly visible as he scootches it along.

That video is the first item in this alleged movie. I use that qualifier because this is absolutely not a film. It is basically the collected visual works of the duo, all but two of which are music videos. Aside from a sentence or two of text on the screen between the films, there is no additional information. For any context, one is required to read the accompanying booklet or watch the special features on the disc.

While I was amused by the "Doctorin' the Tardis" video, the worst video on blu-ray follows immediately after. *The White Room* is a road movie, only in that there are two guys in a car and we see them driving…a *lot*. Although the soundtrack is little more than one song after another, I wouldn't even describe this as a long-form music video.

And yet, "long" is the operative word here. At roughly 50 minutes in length, it feels like this takes longer to watch than it did to film. And the filming must have been extensive and expensive. The car from the previous video (which the booklet informs me was dubbed "Ford Timelord") goes through London streets at night, through deserts in the daylight and even into an area deep in snow. But, without a destination, it doesn't actually go anywhere. *Two-Lane Blacktop* feels heavily plotted in comparison and had a more satisfying resolution.

Even having said that, I will concede the footage is often beautiful. But this suffers from the same problem anybody's vacation videos have: these are inherently of the most interest only to those who made them and unlikely to have much appeal to others. It's like the filmmakers here were so in love with the images that they couldn't bring themselves to cut anything. And, without a plot, there isn't a yardstick by which one can judge what is essential or not. Maybe it is all necessary, but it just as easily might be all filler. All I know is the last time I was so bored watching beautiful imagery was when watching something by Antonioni. And this ain't Antonioni…

As if adding insult to injury, the next piece is a music video where the footage from the unreleased *The White Room* finally found a home. Really, they could have just put the longer piece on the disc as bonus content and just left the music video in the program. Even then, it is amazing how tedious the footage is even when condensed to only about five minutes.

Next up is my second-most favorite part, a trilogy of videos they did as a combination of stage performance and some rather endearing landscape miniatures. I especially liked the model Ford Timelord we see from behind as it flies through a miniature futuristic city. Really, I don't have more to say about these three thematically-linked videos. The songs didn't really click with me, the stage performance is appropriately bombastic and the miniatures were cute. I don't have any notes.

Then they just had to thoroughly deep six any goodwill they had earned from me. We now get to another long-form music video, *The Rites of Mu*. We know we're in deep trouble right from the opening credits; namely, we're watching a *music video* with opening credits. One of those credits says "Narration by Martin Sheen". My first thought was, "Martin Sheen, really?", when I have should have been wondering why a music video has narration. Then there was an attribution for the people who created the film's wicker man. I was waiting for a credit for "moose trained to mix concrete and sign complicated insurance forms by…"

The production is a curious mix of crappy amateur filmmaking interspersed with moments of truly top-notch photography. Seriously, some isolated moments of this are truly gorgeous. Unfortunately, like *The White Room*, it was so much effort for so little return. It is stylized like folk horror, which had me intrigued. My hopes gradually diminished to nothing as the payoff for a great deal of nothing is a wicker man supposedly combusting from the combined concentration of the gathered robed figures. And that lead-up takes…way…too…long…to…play…out.

Speaking of which, let's speed things up here. Let's see…there's a music video where they block off a road and Drummond barks the names of northern locales into a CB handset. Huh. They do a video with Tammy Wynette, and I was surprised to see how game she was for that. There's a very cinematic video where they use Pinewood's largest studio to show them sailing a full-sized Viking boat, ostensibly to conquer America (spoiler alert, they failed to conquer the charts in the colonies).

The collection ends fittingly, but in a clip that still takes too damn long to play out. In what appears to be a demolition derby, Drummond and Cauty destroy Ford Timelord. Congratulations on killing the thing that has the most personality of any element or individual from your assorted films.

The final statement on the screen before the end credits roll is "The KLF have left the entertainment industry." That would suggest they had been entertainers at some point, which I find highly debatable.

I'm not sure what the "23 seconds" of the title pertains to, but watching this felt a lot closer to eternity. This was a long, miserable experience, with very few bright points along the way. Couldn't we at least watch them torch that million pounds? My net worth is nowhere near that. By duping people like me into buying this disc, do they think I also have money to burn?

Original version posted on 11/12/2023

23rd Century Giants (2021)

Since the 1990's, I have been a fan of The Residents, a group whose best-known attribute is their anonymity. The group had their own record label, Ralph (as in the slang for vomiting), on which they had off-beat artists who likely would have been unable to find a home elsewhere.

The best known of these acts that weren't The Residents were Renaldo and The Loaf, a British duo who initially specialized in music that challenged even most Residents fans. And The Residents have made some…challenging music, to put it diplomatically.

Prior to watching this documentary about Renaldo and The Loaf, my only knowledge of them was through their early music, particularly debut album *Songs for Swinging Larvae*. Their work didn't click with me then, but I liked this film so much that I am seriously considering revisiting it.

As for my initial exposure to their music, that was courtesy of a video made for a medley of tracks (I'm not ready to use the word "songs") from that album. That short film is greatly unnerving, even today. I can't imagine what it would have been like to see it unexpectedly on a late-night program in the 80's like *Night Flight*. Without any conventionally objectionable content, the *Songs* clip still leaves one with the feeling you have seen something that shouldn't have been broadcast.

That clip was directed by Graeme Whifler, who had also created the legendary early music videos for The Residents, which shows how much the group and their label loved these like-minded iconoclasts from across the pond. And let's just take a quick look at what else Whifler has done and…WTF, he wrote *Dr. Giggles*?!?

Anywho, Renaldo is Brian Poole and David Janssen is The Loaf, and this documentary details their working relationship through five decades. For the first couple of decades, they didn't hang out together except to make music. After three formal albums were released (in addition to a great number of self-released cassettes), life got in the way and they followed their separate pursuits after losing interest in recording. It doesn't appear to be an acrimonious split–they just didn't have much in common except for the music.

These two are far different from what I suspect most people would imagine from their oeuvre. I know I wouldn't have expected them to be soft-spoken, thoughtful and conservatively dressed. They even held down prestigious jobs for a long time. Poole was an architect and Janssen was a pathologist.

One of my favorite aspects of this documentary is seeing how, after a couple of decades pass without keeping in touch, Poole and Janssen reconnect. They not only perform live for the second time ever and record a new album, but they discover a friendship that exists beyond their creative output. Or, as Janssen puts it (if I remember correctly), "The music used to fuel the friendship, but now the friendship fuels the music".

I watched this on blu-ray, and I highly recommend those who are curious take the leap and watch it on that format, as there is a wealth of bonus material. I wish some of the extended interviews had been included in the movie proper; however, these being relegated to the bonus content results in a very lean feature.

I don't know if a reappraisal of their music will make me a fan, but I thoroughly enjoyed this time spent with Poole, Janssen and their fans. I feel *23rd Century Giants* is one of those rare music documentaries that isn't simply fan service. Instead, it shines a light on an obscure niche of music which only a handful have experienced and introduces us to the fascinating people who made it.

Original version posted on 2/2/2023

Bluebeard's Castle (1963)

The folk tale of Bluebeard is at least 400 years old. I am amazed it has persisted in the public consciousness to this day, as it is a very simple, and rather repulsive, story. It has been made into a movie many times over. There is not enough material to warrant the length of a feature film, so each version I have seen had to stretch the plot so thin as to nearly break.

Having now seen 1963's adaptation *Bluebeard's Castle*, I realize opera is the ideal medium for telling that tale. I have attended many operas over the years and, during those performances, I often found my mind wandering without ever losing the plot. It is almost like meditating.

My appreciation of opera is limited to only a few works, all of which are classics. I doubt anything will surpass the staging of Verdi's *The Masked Ball* which was my introduction. Conversely, *Nixon in China* was so interminable that I suspect I may be in the audience watching it still, and only hallucinating everything I think has happened since then.

Though quite modern in all regards, *Castle* is far less like *Nixon*, in that it is as enjoyable as the works of Verdi. When I say "modern", I mean that in relative terms, as it was composed by Bartók in 1911. Given the source material, it is no surprise it is a somber work, though only an hour long. The material is made even weightier through a libretto by Béla Balázs that makes this more of a journey into the title character's psyche than a literal series of discoveries in the castle's rooms.

This work was not well-received in its own time, and it was rarely performed in the decades that followed. Because of that, this 1963 presentation for German television is the ideal way to stage this unusual opera which only has two performers.

Norman Foster assumes the title role, and his acting and bass-baritone are equally flawless. In his crude leather jacket (think early Vikings), I believed this was a man capable of killing each woman he loves. Foster believed so much in the project that he was the one to initiate it. I feel a bit bad he was a producer, as all things opera famously fail to recoup their investment, and this was no exception.

But it is Ana Raquel Satre as Judith, his latest wife and consequent victim, who steals the show. That is surprising for a retelling of a story that is traditionally deeply misogynist at the surface. Despite her inevitable fate, it somehow feels she has achieved a strange sort of victory in the end. At least, she is the one who has dignity at the conclusion, unlike Bluebeard, who has to live with his ever-deepening shame. Judith has succeeded in plumbing the psyche of her husband, even if it is to her detriment.

I wouldn't call what happens to Judith a spoiler since, once again, this story is an archetype that is nearly half a millennium old. Very curiously, the BFI seems to think otherwise, as the first line in the accompanying booklet is a spoiler alert. If there is anybody willing to read that booklet who doesn't know this story, then I have a great joke for them about a chicken and its motivations for traversing a motorway.

The design of this production is astonishing. Each of the castle's rooms Judith enters are parts of her husband's subconscious. The first couple are the most intimidating and these, one with torture devices and the next with weapons, reflect the harsh exterior he uses to keep her and others at arm's length.

These objects are covered in blood, conveyed by bathing the set in red light, but she brings daylight, and corresponding yellow light, into these dark corners. With that, she proceeds to additional rooms, though she seems pretty beaten down by the time there's only a couple of rooms remaining. Her spirits may have been broken by his room full of original *Star Wars* action figures unopened in their original packaging. Sorry, I was just seeing if you were still paying attention.

Vivid colors are used throughout, and the visual elements are curiously vague. It is like somebody took one of those super-artsy, abstract classical album covers of the 1950's and somehow rendered it in three dimensions. It is particularly unnerving to see objects that just barely resemble the mutilated bodies of the past wives. The lighting on these is deep teal, only reinforcing the weirdness. But what I may have liked most in the visuals were the seven doorways that resembled nothing other than tombstones, and seriously ancient ones at that. They are covered in what appear to be runes.

It was no surprise to me this was directed by Michael Powell, who had previously brought the epic opera *Tales of Hoffman* to the big screen. While that film is astonishing, I will concede it is extremely long and not something I would recommend to those unfamiliar with opera. Instead, this hour-long work would be a far better introduction.

I watched *Bluebeard's Castle* in an astonishingly pristine presentation on a BFI blu-ray. In addition to the film, there are a couple of welcome supplements, such as a documentary on the background of both the original work and Powell's adaptation. There is an option to watch the film with the libretto sung in English. Though I welcome that option, I recommend watching this in the original German. I don't know what it is, but opera always seems a bit daft when not sung in one of the older European languages. While *Nixon in China* would have been crap in any language, it might have been improved if I hadn't known what they were singing about.

Original version posted on 12/10/2023

Catch Us If You Can (1965)

"It's completely deserted. It smells of dead holidays." This isn't the kind of dialogue I expected in 1965's *Catch Us If You Can*. By all logic, this should have been a retread of *A Hard Day's Night*, except this picture stars The Dave Clark Five instead of The Beatles.

Mind you, the movie starts out in the vein of that film, with Clark and the other four all shown living together in a decommissioned church. Their unconventional home is full of all kinds of wacky elements, like a shower that has an inflatable raft as its base. What is odd is the members of The Dave Clark Five don't play a band of musicians here. Instead, they're a group of stuntmen. That is a bizarre choice, even if Clark really did work in that capacity in many films prior to this one.

This gang appears in commercials and billboards as part of a mod ad campaign for the meat council. The real star of the ads is Barbara Ferris. Surprisingly, she is the real star of this movie as well. How odd a real-life band doesn't play one in their own movie and aren't even the stars of it. Not only that, but every person from the group, bar Clark, will be jettisoned as soon as possible.

Honestly, this works in the film's favor, taking something that should have been a quick cash-in and instead producing something more distinctive. A tinge of melancholy creeps in around the end of the first act and builds over the rest of the runtime until it overwhelms the picture.

Honestly, I would have been surprised if the picture didn't take a left turn at some point, as it was helmed by John Boorman. Everybody has to start somewhere, and you know the guy whose later career is defined by such films as *Deliverance* and *Excalibur* will deviate from the expectations one might have for a film like this.

Stealing a car from a commercial shoot, Clark and Ferris try to get to an old holiday resort island she's interested in buying. The journey is far from straight-forward and plagued by strange detours. Also, the movie takes place in winter, so the scenery is starkly beautiful at best, though one could just as accurately describe it as bleak.

The first place they stop at is what appears to be a town that wasn't rebuilt following the war. In one building, they find proto-hippies that are so bored with pot that they are looking for heroin. Ever notice how movies starring The Beatles never have a plot point where a character tries to score some horse?

Then it turns out this abandoned town is a training ground for the military. There are live rounds being fired and explosions everywhere, one of which takes out their purloined car.

Now without transportation, our unlucky couple takes to hitching a ride. They get picked up by an older couple (Robin Bailey and Yootha Joyce) who take them back to their home. To my surprise, this couple swings less in the sense of the 1960's and more in the vein of 1970's suburbia and notorious "key parties". Neither Clark nor Ferris succumbs to the advances made towards them.

Actually, Bailey is very meek and seems embarrassed to be put in the position of trying to seduce the younger woman. He instead seems intent on sharing with Ferris the joy he takes in his collection of old media. She's bored at first, but then she becomes intrigued by these moments preserved from the past, as if in amber. The performers on old phonographs, captured in their prime, are singing better than they ever would again and, in photographs, looking the best they ever would. Ferris remarks,

"Isn't it awful how everybody has to get old? How everything has to get broken."

That is a theme I noticed recurring through the feature—the idea that everything is ephemeral, each moment never to be repeated. There was something about Clark's performance that made me think that even before the topic is broached. He's not a bad actor, per se, but you know he wouldn't be in this movie if a studio hadn't hoped to emulate the success of the first Beatles film. He consistently looks as if he knows this movie is a one-off thing.

I noticed many of the scenes he is in with Ferris focus on her, even when we're hearing his dialogue. This was a smart creative choice, as she's definitely the best actor in the film. Indulge me this odd aside, but she resembles Bjork a bit, only blond.

One interesting decision for Clark's character is how strait-laced they made him. Over the course of the film, he eschews smokes, drinks, drugs and the advances made by Joyce.

One thing I couldn't stop thinking about is how the music of The Dave Clark Five is diegetic in several scenes; however, in the world of the movie, who would have made that music? I mean, the guys in that real-life band don't play musicians in this film. So, who is supposed to be The Dave Clark Five in this, The Dave Clark Five movie?

Speaking of the other guys in the band, there's an odd moment where everybody is trying on costumes, and one of them briefly puts on a long fake nose that instantly made him look like Malcolm McDowell from a key scene in *A Clockwork Orange*.

I will also not soon forget the incredibly weird vehicle that will transport Clark and Ferris across the water to the island where the holiday resort is located. This thing is basically a canopy-covered platform placed a full story above a base of tank treads. I sooo want to take a ride on that thing.

It is no surprise the island they have been trying to get to this entire time will just be another in a long series of disappointments. As Ferris puts it, "Not even a proper island, just a gimmick in the sea." That is the perfect way to cap *Catch Us If You Can*, a movie that didn't give me what I was expecting. Instead, it gave me a far richer experience which I look forward to revisiting eventually.

Original version posted on 1/4/2024

Cats Don't Dance (1997)

One of my favorite of the millions of throwaway gags in the early years of *The Simpsons* is a movie marquee showing one of the titles playing is *SING MONKEY SING!!!* I like to ponder what that film would have been like if it had been real.

That title came to mind when I first heard of 1997's *Cats Don't Dance*. Not sure why, but "animated musical" was not the genre which immediately leapt to my mind, though that is what this turned out to be. Even then, the title left me asking such questions as "That's true, but do they *want* to dance?" and "Is there some sort of law against cats doing this if they wanted to? Is this picture going to be like *Footloose* but for felines?" Also, per one of the most famous memes, I like to think that, if this picture was made today, it would be titled *Cats No Can Haz Dance*.

The reason I was so confused is because I was completely unaware of the movie in its original release. I wouldn't have been the right age for it at the time, but I have always tried to be aware of what is in the theater. I guess it isn't any surprise this got stomped at the box office, because I don't think anybody who might have been interested knew it existed.

But who would be the ideal market for this? Here is a tribute to the musicals of the 30's and 40's and which is set in that era. There are celebrity caricatures of the most famous faces of that day, but would most of the audience in the late 90's have a particular fondness for Mae West or Bette Davis? I (think I) got all the period references, but only because I have intensely explored that era of film in the past decade or so.

My best guess is the target market is old film nerds like me. Since that demographic doesn't buy many Happy Meals, the choice of subject matter seems incongruous with what most animation studios hope to achieve. I'm not seeing a lot of merchandising potential here.

Which is fine by me, because I had the best time watching this film. My face hurt from smiling so much. Not only do they not make movies like this anymore, but I'm not sure they ever did. It is a visual feast and deeply funny, to boot. There's all manner of little surprises, and I'm already wondering what I missed which I will discover in future rewatchings.

The film takes place in a world of humans and anthropomorphic animals. Scott Bakula voices Danny, a singing and dancing cat from podunk who goes to Hollywood with the dream of becoming a movie star. He quickly discovers the studio system only allows animals to play animal roles in their films, which I found a tad odd as I do not recall seeing any non-anthropomorphic creatures. I suspect this plot is a metaphor for the lack of substantial roles available at the time to those not of Caucasian descent.

Helping Danny in his struggle to change that system is a hippo voiced by Kathy Najimy, an elephant played by John Rhys-Davies,

Hal Holbrook as a cantankerous old goat and Don Knotts as a fretful turtle who was once an action star. There's also Matthew Herried as a cute little penguin who mostly works as an ice vendor. There's a small gag I really like where he's going out of town, and the only thing in his hobo kit bag is a block of ice.

With the exception of Najimy's hippo, these characters aren't given much to do, even as comic relief. But that hippo steals nearly every scene she's in and is consistently given some great little bits of comedy. One moment which surprised me is when she sits at the base of a diner and accidentally moves the entire building off its foundation. Looking embarrassed, she quickly reaches under the diner and moves it back into position.

But the most important character for me, even more than Danny, is a cat named Sawyer. Voiced by Jasmine Guy, she is smart and cynical, a shell of a person who has had their dreams crushed too many times. She is initially resistant to Danny's charms and fearful of ever getting her hopes up again.

Danny's nemesis comes in the form of a psychotic child star by the name of Darla Dimple (Ashley Peldon). This is a great role, and there are some excellent jokes around the character. Darla and various animals are starring in a musical retelling of the Noah's Ark story, where she plays the lead. It is titled *The Ark Angel*, which would be an apt nickname for her. It turns out she hates animals, as emphasized in a scene where she snacks on animal crackers, but only biting the heads off each one.

This immediately preceded a scene where she does an entertaining and overblown musical number where she convinces Danny he needs to pull out all the stops for an audition she intends to sabotage. Randy Newman composed this, and the other songs in the picture, so you know the music is solid, even if the tunes largely aren't very memorable.

Another key musical moment comes when Danny tries to rally the other animals to pursue their lost dreams. The drawings for each character start out in muted colors; however, as each animal becomes more enthusiastic, those colors become more vibrant. This is an excellent, and pleasantly subtle, way of expressing their growing joy.

This leads me to the animation. I liked the style of illustration, which is a flavor of mid-century modern. This works well, despite the picture being set a couple of decades before that was in vogue in real-life. Animation is fluid throughout, and the characters are cartoony enough without compromising the audience's ability to identify with them.

One brief moment I loved is when Sawyer unexpectedly slides down a fire escape ladder. This is a character with great restraint, the very definition of a cool cat. But she's so startled when she hits the ground that she is momentarily all arched back and spiked fur. After a couple of quick glances to see if anybody witnessed this faux pas, she restores herself to her usual nonchalant demeanor. I loved this insight into the character, as well as a certain "catness" it captures.

Lastly, and far from leastly, I can't believe I have yet to mention Max, Darla's thuggish all-around assistant. Voiced by the director (Mark Dindal), this gargantuan butler is Eric Von Stroheim by way of King Kong. This character is part of a great many visual gags and I will not spoil any of them here.

I could go on and on and on about *Cats Don't Dance*. I'm sure many would say I've already said too much. All I can hope is somebody might stumble upon this essay and become encouraged to check it out. As for myself, I not only know I will be watching it again somebody, but I already can't wait until I do.

Original version posted on 10/3/2023

Cheer Up! (1936)

It's hard to pick a favorite moment from the series *The Unbreakable Kimmy Schmidt*, as it had nearly as many great bits as the prime seasons of *The Simpsons*. But there's one I couldn't stop thinking of recently, and that's the fake 1938 musical *Daddy's Boy*, a clip of which cuts off in mid-song because the crew refused to continue working at that exact point.

What had brought this to mind was 1936's *Cheer Up!* This musical comedy is heavy on the former and not so good on the latter. It is also so preposterously upbeat that I'm surprised they didn't make the title entirely in upper case and add a couple of additional exclamation points at the end.

I went into this blindly, thinking it was only a comedy, which is my mistake. I find it bizarre so many films of that era were compelled to have musical numbers. There was hardly a genre at the time which was immune to this treatment. I'm just glad the trend died out eventually; otherwise, *The Exorcist* likely would have had Linda Blair singing while she and other characters spun and danced in the air while she spews pea soup.

The plot here concerns unemployed songwriters looking for a wealthy investor for the musical they've written. The duo is played by Stanley Lupino and Roddy Hughes. I was very surprised to learn Lupino was the father of Ida Lupino, the actress who went on to be one of Hollywood's very few female directors of her time.

These two are so poor that they are forever trying to use their talents to scam anything, even food. This leads to a bizarre early scene where they propose, and rise to, a challenge to sing the menu of a restaurant. In some musicals, everybody in the scene would get involved, and I can understand that better than the approach taken here, where the other diners don't bat an eye as these guys perform an ode to steak and kidney pudding. This is a good example of why I'm not crazy about the genre.

Lupino apparently spends each day trying to barge into the offices of various producers. Unfortunately, the office of *The Producers's* Bialystock and Bloom had not been established yet, because I'm sure our heroes could come up with something even more inane than *Springtime for Hitler*. At one of these, he runs into, and is instantly smitten with, aspiring actress Sally Gray who plays…Sally Gray. I am not making this up.

She is desperate for work and so answers an ad for a maid, but goes to the wrong house. This is the house of Wyn Weaver, a financial wizard fallen on hard times. His wife (Marjorie Chard) is there in his absence and, despite them not having placed the ad nor having money to pay her, Chard hires Gray, regardless. Concurrent with this, Lupino and Hughes have struck up a fast acquaintance with Weaver, unaware of his change in fortunes.

In the midst of all this, there's Kenneth Kove as the fey son of a very wealthy man who is constantly disappointed in his son's lack of manliness. The incredulous Lupino and Hughes say he couldn't possibly be the son of the famous man. His reply is one of the few times I laughed: "I only have the word of my father, and I trust him." Kove will accidentally take a punch in a nightclub, and so is mistaken for defending Gray's honor, thus getting some positive attention from the father, whose deep pockets help stage Lupino and Hughes's musical.

Cheer Up! concludes with a performance of that production. This number is almost psychedelic and even has a dancing mailbox. It is a waaay too upbeat finale to a waaay too upbeat film. This type of thing was doubtlessly popular in its time, but I found it tiring and excessively (and artificially) cheery. As somebody who is more of a grey skies kind of person, I really wanted the cast of *Cheer Up!* to *Shut Up!*

Original version posted on 5/29/2024

D.O.A.: A Rite of Passage (1980)

Over the years, I have had far more conversations about punk rock than about any other kind of music. I know many people who feel strongly that punk music is all about the sound: fast and loud. Many such people I have spoken with believe punk music still exists today, even when it is highly commercial in nature. I have had people tell me Blink-182 is punk rock.

I'm more of a purist, and I believe the music cannot be separated from the environment and politics that shaped it. I feel punk must be an honest expression of a person's life and not just a style. I'm not saying you have to pierce your face with safety pins, yet there is a significant difference between those who do so and those who buy fake safety pins that are the equivalent of clip-on earrings.

D.O.A.: A Rite of Passage, is a documentary about first-generation punk rock in the UK and USA. As implied by the second half of the title, the bands and their fans shown here are largely of the variety who would wear the real safety pins. Tellingly, there's also a brief shot of a vendor selling fake "punk pins" for a buck a pop, and we see many fair-weather fans who are likely wearing that novelty version.

The central focus of this doc is the Sex Pistols's seven-stop tour of the US, their sole excursion to the colonies in their original incarnation. In keeping with manager Malcolm McLaren's mischievous style, the band is largely booked in venues in the south where altercations with the locals are most likely to occur. As one concert attendee says, "There hasn't been a rock 'n' roll group to hate in a long time."

And there are fights, notably a moment where Sid Vicious beats angry people in the crowd over the head with his bass. This is a startling moment we are fortunate to have preserved on film.

When one learns what happened behind the scenes of *D.O.A.*, it is amazing we have any footage of the Pistols on stage in the USA, period. The band didn't want to be filmed and, inexplicably, neither did Warner Brothers, their US record label. The label didn't have anybody filming these shows, so it's baffling why they wouldn't want any free publicity.

We only learn about this in an accompanying documentary on the bluray which is nearly a half-hour longer than the movie it is about. That may sound counterintuitive but, together, these two documentaries combined tell a complete story that neither does on its own.

If *D.O.A.* is a documentary about punk music, the accompanying making-of is about punk filmmaking. By having to dodge bouncers, managers and various people associated with Warners, a unique approach was needed to make a documentary about a punk band on tour.

We learn how film crew members disguised themselves as press from various organizations. When Warners catches on, photos of the documentary crew are distributed to security at venues. This is alarming because not only is it going to make their goal more difficult, but the crew will become increasingly more susceptible to the violence those guards casually dole out even towards random, paying concertgoers.

Yet the filmmakers persevered and ended up with priceless footage that was later freely lifted for an authorized Pistols documentary, *The Filth and the Fury*. Unfortunately, there wasn't enough footage for a feature film exclusively focused on the tour, so we also get a significant amount of content about the UK scene.

That may sound like filler, but it is largely fascinating. For one thing, we get to see exciting performances by groups like X-Ray Spex and Sham 69. We also get to know a band of never-was and never-wills appropriately named Terry and The Idiots, just to show the alleged lack of technical proficiency for which punk bands were known still had its levels of expertise.

Even more surprising than the footage of the bands are the interviews the filmmakers managed to get with such UK conservatives as Mary Whitehouse. I only previously knew of Whitehouse from a movie I saw about the UK "video nasties" scandal. Here, she has the same sort of "who will think of the children?" histrionics, only concerning punk rock this time.

Everybody I have ever spoken to about punk seems to have a different view of it, such as which eras and artists qualify as such. And yet, I don't think there can be any doubt as to whether the artists in *D.O.A.: A Rite of Passage* qualify. When paired alongside its companion making-of, this blu-ray set presents a fascinating snapshot of an era when music could be truly dangerous, and trying to capture those moments on film could be dangerous, too.

Original version posted on 3/15/2023

Dance Craze (1981)

The 1981 concert film *Dance Craze* anthologizes performances by several UK acts of the 80's ska revival, many of whom were associated with the legendary record label 2 Tone.

The name of that label emphasizes one of the most remarkable aspects of that ska resurgence in the UK: groups with Black and White members, performing music that combined the energy and politics of punk with the rhythm and horns of ska.

I'm not especially fond of concert films, yet this one is truly exceptional. It is not just the bands' performances, but a snapshot of a microcosm that will be, lamentably, as brief as the life of the 2 Tone label that led the movement.

2 Tone was the creation of Jerry Dammers, keyboardist and chief songwriter of The Specials. It is no surprise that group is one of the main attractions in this picture.

One particularly noteworthy moment occurs during their performance of "Too Much Too Young", when they are nearly overwhelmed by the audience. The people at the front of the stage start piling on top of each other, like a tidal wave slowly building up until it threatens to crash down upon the stage.

The Specials also bookend the feature, appropriately, with their song "Nite Club." The encore performance of the number rolls under the end credits while audience members swarm the stage.

One thing I was very happy to see is, as much as I like The Specials, other acts have (almost) as much screentime. We get to see Madness, The Beat (we know them as The English Beat here in the colonies), Bad Manners, The Bodysnatchers and The Selecter.

Among those acts, The Bodysnatchers are noteworthy for being all-female. Another act which stood out from the others is Bad Manners though, unfortunately, because frontman Buster Bloodvessel's shtick wore on me fast. Basically, he's fat, yells all the lyrics and jumps around a lot with his tongue hanging out of his mouth. Huh.

The one aspect of this movie which most surprised me is how exceptionally well it is shot. Fortunately, it doesn't use showy camerawork, but it does put a Steadycam to great use. That was a relatively new innovation at the time and there were few people in the world trained to use it well. The fluid motion of the camera on stage really captures the energy of the performances.

Joe Massot directs, and I am glad he was able to largely rein in what would have likely been poor creative impulses, as he also directed the bombastic Led Zeppelin film *The Song Remains the Same*. Still, there are some bizarre moments, such as footage of ballet dancers inexplicably interspersed into a Madness number. Also, the film takes a weird detour at the midpoint, where footage from old newsreels and television programs shows some of the teenage music and movements of the late 50s.

I watched this on a BFI set that has an astonishing restoration demo showing before and after versions of a few clips. The audio is also lavishly restored, and can be heard in stereo, surround and even Dolby Atmos. Quite simply, this is a film that looks and sounds stunning on blu-ray.

Other features on the disc include some cut performances which are not restored. There's also a fantastic half-hour installment of the BBC's program *Arena* from 1980 which follows an NME journalist to Coventry where he hangs with The Specials in the 2 Tone "offices". I especially like Dammers going through the drawers of their sole desk, saying things like "And this is the A&R department. And these are the contracts…"

Dammers also shows the record that was his introduction to ska, a budget collection of original tracks from the 60's. I had a huge smile while watching the group dance and sing to "You're Wondering Now" by Andy & Joey, one of my very most favorite songs.

The title of *Dance Craze* is appropriate, as the performances are consistently high-energy and have a lot of dancing in them. Given all the mics are wired, I was astonished nobody tripped at any point. The movie left me happy to have been briefly immersed in a time and place where Black and White could work together to make such amazing music. And yet I also felt a bit depressed, and not just because of racial struggles that continue to this day, but because every single person I noticed in the audience was White.

Original version posted on 7/26/2023

Dancer In The Dark (2000)

A Lars von Trier musical starring Bjork.

Let's parse that summary to show why *Dancer in the Dark* should be approached with some trepidation.

If there is one thing I can say about the entirety of von Trier's filmography, that would be it is provocative. Other than that, there are few consistencies in his work. That said, one word that doesn't immediately come to mind when considering his oeuvre is "musical". Also, there are some of his films I am enthusiastic about (*The Element Of Crime, Melancholia*) and others where the pretentiousness is so overwhelming that my eyes roll until they nearly tumble out of my head. Unfortunately, *Dancer In The Dark* is solidly of the latter type.

If there is one thing I can say about the entirety of Bjork's discography, that would be it is challenging. Other than that, there are few consistencies to her work. But one word that doesn't immediately come to mind when thinking about Bjork is "actor". Also, there are some of her albums I am enthusiastic about (*Medulla, Post*) and others where the pretentiousness is so overwhelming that my eyes roll until they nearly tumble out of my head. Let's just say *Dancer in the Dark* embraces some of her worst tendencies.

You can look up the plot of the movie in about one second, so I feel no need to rehash it here. Instead, my autopsy of the film will be presented in a list of itemized aspects:

- *The look.* Around the turn of this century, filmmakers who should know better found themselves enamored with MiniDV. The allure of low-cost cameras and tapes led some directors to readily sacrifice image quality (SD and highly pixelated) and good taste (why bother composing shots in advance when you could have 100 cameras capture the action?). A similar kind of reasoning has led to bad CGI choices that ruined some movies, by having a virtual camera do all manner of physically impossible moves, just because it's possible.
- *The plot.* I said I wouldn't rehash the plot, but I will touch on it here briefly and as vaguely as possible. Basically, *Dancer in the Dark* is pure, uncut, street-grade melodrama so strong that even Douglas Sirk wouldn't touch it with a ten-foot pole. Simply put, it is a terrible plot which is then weighed down even more by embarrassingly blatant jabs at social commentary, courtesy of von Trier's impressions of Americans. I do not have a problem with the issues he addresses (in fact, I agree with him on many of his assessments), but he tries to bludgeon us with them. In particular, an incident involving a gun

was so preposterous that I surprised myself by bursting out laughing.

- *The songs.* Both the songs and the choreography are OK. Overall, the songs are quite solid on their own, though the arrangements date them to the exact year of the movie's production. If you liked Bjork's 1997 album *Homogenic*, you will doubtlessly enjoy the sound of these tracks as well. But it is curious how so much could change in just three years that what was innovative in 1997 could be slightly dated in 2000. Also, one number that didn't click for me involves a courtroom breaking into song, as if we needed any more evidence why the TV show *Cop Rock* was destined to fail.

- *Bjork.* Oh boy. Similar to Bowie, Bjork was always evolving and taking on different personas for each album, carrying that particular style and appearance through the related imagery associated with it. Of course, Bowie had appeared in several feature films. She had also been in a movie before, 1986's *The Juniper Tree*. One movie. Nearly a decade-and-a-half prior. I haven't seen that film yet; however, I hope she is better there than she is here. It's not like she's terrible here, but I strongly suspected Catherine Deneuve was carrying the actress as much as she, in character, was providing assistance for Bjork's visually impaired character.

Naturally, *Dancer in the Dark* won the Palme d'Or at Cannes, with Bjork receiving Best Actress, once again proving the French have a doggedly perverse and contrarian nature.

Original version posted on 12/30/2023

Dangerous When Wet (1953)

The first movie I had seen Esther Williams in was 1956's *The Unguarded Moment*. What was notable about that film is it was her first serious dramatic role. Prior to that, every picture she starred in emphasized her legendary swimming ability. This meant a whole lot of synchronized swimming routines—basically, musical numbers staged in and around water. It was an odd niche, and she longed to break out of it.

Now I have seen the first, and widely regarded as the best, of such films, 1953's *Dangerous When Wet*. I'll confess I am not a fan of musicals, though I have come to enjoy a few of them. I also thought the gimmick Williams was famous for would fail to impress me. Given all this, I was surprised I enjoyed some of this film as much as I did. That's not to say it was a complete winner, and I'll dive into the pros and cons.

The plot has Williams as the eldest sister of a rural dairy family. This is a family that is all about exercise, which they do to an earworm titled "I Got Out of Bed on the Right Side". I had never heard this tune before, but it is still stuck in my head a couple of days later. I think the CDC needs to be alerted to this earworm, which is infectious to the degree of "It's a Small World After All".

The first time the family jumps into the creek for their daily swim, the camera cuts to Williams sitting on the shore and reading a book. Even without knowing much about Williams, I at least was aware of the shtick she was famous for and so I got the joke.

She just wants to buy a prize bull for the farm. The potential to do so arrives through a chance meeting with Jack Carson. He ropes the family into a stunt wherein they will swim the English Channel to promote Liquidpep, a questionable health elixir he has been shilling. It is no surprise when it comes down to Williams being the only member of the family to attempt the crossing. And I will not take any bets on the outcome of that attempt.

What is interesting to me is how quirky some of the humor is in this. When Carson arrives in England with Williams and company, the fog is so thick that they can't see the crowds gathered to greet them, complete with brass band. Williams is given a speech to deliver, but she finds addressing it to a grey void too frustrating and so she wraps it up early.

Fog also intrudes on the first day of training. Carson was rowing a boat ahead of her but lost her in the fog. I guess that was inevitable, as he is so weak that she, swimming in the water, had to shove his boat onward at one point. Various characters are wandering around on and in the water in this fog, and the movie would have been vastly more interesting if the rest of it had just been bizarre encounters between these people.

Instead, Williams is pulled into a rowboat manned by a tuxedo-clad Fernando Lamas. He takes her to his yacht, where he delivers this unusual line, given what he is wearing, "Excuse me while I get out of my working clothes." He is supposedly a champagne salesman.

Whatever he is (it doesn't matter), he's French and he will obviously be the love interest. I only learned after the movie he was also the real-life love interest for Williams. They married and remained so until his death, and their son is the actor Lorenzo Lamas.

From the first frame of the opening credits, it is obvious this movie will be weirder than I anticipated. The titles are an explosion of Technicolor, bright yellow and vibrant purple lettering superimposed over footage of fish swimming in a tank. It is so garish, but so thoroughly committed to this design, that it is a strange kind of beautiful. Also, some of those fish swim in front of the letters, presumably through some sort of early bluescreen work. I like how I don't really know how they did that.

The most memorable segment, by some distance, is an underwater sequence teaming Williams up with Tom and Jerry. This scene is extremely well-done and justifiably famous. It was vastly more enjoyable in every regard than the scene in *My Dream Is Yours* where Doris Day dances with Bugs Bunny. The Warner Archive bluray I watched this on has numerous special features, including the Tom and Jerry short *The Cat and The Mermouse*, from which many of the gags in the movie's scene are repurposed.

I wish the movie had kept up the quirkiness it demonstrated early on, but it keeps falling back on tired cliches. It is almost like two different writers wrote scripts with entirely different tones, and somebody cherry-picked what they liked from each.

Even some of the filler that is meant to be quirky merely grates. One of Williams's sisters is played by Barbara Whiting, whose sole defining characteristic is she likes men. She even has a pointless musical number titled "I Like Men" that pretty much says it all. Not even the woman in *She's Gotta Have It* had to have it as much as Whiting seems to. Good thing this picture was made in a more innocent time, lest we see her gang-banged by every sailor in the vicinity.

Instead, I wish we could have seen more of Charlotte Greenwood, who plays the family matriarch. She wasn't a spring chicken when this was made, but she has a brief and fascinating dance number where she kicks higher than I thought possible. Then her number ends in something almost as jarring as the "spider walk" scene from *The Exorcist*—nothing that physically astonishing, but simply unexpected and strange enough to be a tad unnerving.

Perhaps the weirdest thing about *Dangerous When Wet* is that, compared to the more "serious" role she would take later in *The Unguarded Moment*, Wiliams has more agency in this film. Odd, since the later picture was an earnest drama, while this movie is meant to be pure fluff. Make no mistake: this film is an incredibly light confection, but it is an enjoyable one. And this is coming from somebody who doesn't usually enjoy musicals. If there is one aspect that distinguishes it from similar fare, it is the streak of weirdness that surfaces occasionally, and I really wanted to experience more of that.

Original version posted on 2/16/2024

The Girl Can't Help It (1956)

Little Richard is looking uncomfortable on the stage—odd since it is 1956 and he's in his prime. Admittedly, his audience is all White people in formal wear. He looks like a spring wound too tightly, like he's barely restraining an urge to completely let loose. What I like best is there is a bit of his magnificent coif flying free, as if some part of him managed to escape.

He is one of many musicians lip-syncing to studio tracks in *The Girl Can't Help It*. Although not necessarily a jukebox musical, it does drop in performances from a great many acts of the era, and those moments vary in the extent to which they are diegetic.

We see most of the acts perform in various clubs. But characters also watch Eddie Cochran perform "Twenty Flight Rock" on television. The Treniers are supposedly shown in the process of recording in a studio. Fats Domino and, later, The Platters are shown in concert. Eddie Cochran and The Blue Caps perform "Be Bop a Lu La" in a practice room.

None of these performances are live, but it is still great music and it is nice to see these artists when they were young. These moments are similar to early music videos.

The weirdest performance will be during a recording session where Ray Anthony fronts his big band. Nothing he does is strange. Instead, it's the ear-piercing siren sound made by Jayne Mansfield at only two points in the track. In one shot, we see her sheet music has exactly two notes on it, and they are spaced very far apart. I laughed longer at this visual joke than I have laughed at anything in a long time.

A has-been gangster played by Edmund O'Brien is determined to make her a star, without either of them having any idea what talents she might possess. Fearing anybody chosen to manage her will be distracted by her cantilevered physiology, he chooses Tom Ewell, playing a washed-up agent with a sterling reputation for never hitting on his female clients.

Fats Murdock, O'Brien's character, may be a few decades past the era when he ran a crime syndicate, but that only means he had the instincts and ruthlessness to outlive the competition. He gives Ewell a tour of his mansion on Long Island, pointing out where this or that guy got whacked, each occasion necessitating the replacement of carpet. On the way there, Mansfield had thoughtfully informed her agent that O'Brien had just put new carpets down throughout the place. When Ewell discovers she can't sing, he expresses his relief with, "I didn't want a part in making you into something you didn't want to be. I didn't want Fats to buy another carpet on account of me."

Despite all the music numbers, and strong performances from O'Brien and Ewell, this really is Mansfield's show. I started to write something about how only a smart person can play a dumb character so well, except the person she plays here is pretty sharp. This is a stronger performance than that in the next film she would make with director Frank Tashlin, *Will Success Spoil Rock Hunter?* In that movie, I could tell the actress was in on the joke. In this movie, I felt like both she and her character were in on it.

There are some visual gags centered around her hourglass figure. When she walks by an ice delivery man, the huge block under his hands melts into a small flood. A bottle held by the milkman positively ejaculates its contents as she passes by. Not even the prepubescent newspaper boy is immune to her appeal: "If she's a girl, then I don't know what my sister is".

Similar to *Hunter*, there is a slyly subversive opening sequence. This picture starts out in black-and-white and in the narrow Academy ratio. Ewell addresses the audience directly and flicks his fingers first to one side and then the other as the screen expands to CinemaScope proportions. He also testily has to repeat the announcement the picture is in color by DeLuxe before it finally transitions to color.

And what weird colors they are. Unlike the rival three-strip Technicolor process, DeLuxe used only one negative. The downside is the colors weren't as precise as what one would get from the other system. The result is blues and reds run towards the downright lurid, while peach, pink, purple and teal dominate the rest of the color field. This makes for some memorable, if bizarre, visuals. My favorite color is teal, but that doesn't mean I would paint a room in it.

The best use of color is employed at the beginning of Abbey Lincoln's musical number. She wears a dress of eye-searing red while standing before curtains that are so deeply blue as to be almost featureless. At first, there isn't light directly on her, so we get this ethereal glow around the edges of her skin. It is a stunning visual.

I may have thoroughly enjoyed the next feature Tashlin did after *The Girl Can't Help It*, but this earlier film is vastly superior. Similar rock'n'roll jukebox musicals of its time are little remembered today, but this movie does more than rock—it is an engrossing romantic comedy. Those who are interested should spring for the Criterion Collection disc, which is packed with fascinating special features and even includes a reproduction of a how-to brochure authored by Tashlin for the benefit of would-be cartoonists.

Original version posted on 2/18/2023

It Couldn't Happen Here (1987)

There have been bad movies based on concept albums. Then there have been bad "jukebox musical" films, where a narrative thread tries to serve as a throughline for otherwise unrelated songs. But here is a true oddity: *It Couldn't Happen Here* takes the tracks from the Pet Shop Boys album *Actually* and…uh, well, I'm not exactly sure what it does with them.

It Couldn't Happen Here strives too much for overarching themes to be a strictly absurdist work, yet it is also nowhere near cohesive enough to be a musical. There's not even enough of any single song performed without interruption for this to be a music video compilation. And this film doesn't just use the music from a Pet Shop Boys album, it also stars the synth duo. Anybody who has seen one of the act's videos knows their trademark demeanor is detached and aloof.

Neil Tennant and Chris Lowe establish a new movie first for me. It's the only time I have seen people with a negative screen presence. The tuxedo-clad Tennant somehow fails to effectively convey boredom. Lowe fares just a bit better because his too-large leather jacket has more personality than the two of them combined–probably because it is large enough that both of them could fit in it.

One of the few bright moments in the film is when these two start laughing in one scene. I would say I suspect them of breaking character, but that would require them to have ever been "in character". It also made me realize I don't think I have ever seen either of these guys smile before, let alone laugh.

The framing device for this thing has Tennant and Lowe observing, and occasionally interacting with, a variety of characters on a seaside boardwalk and elsewhere. Many of the supporting cast members play a few different characters—well, maybe not well-defined characters, but multiple caricatures, at least.

Joss Ackland fares best as a priest who may be blind and may also be a serial killer. He is definitely the funniest person in the cast. In one scene, he gets picked up as a hitchhiker by Tennant and Lowe, and he gets in a ton of decent one-liners before the next music video bit. I especially liked it when Tennant asks him, "Do you have any weapons?" and his reply is, "Why? What do you have in mind?"

Faring less well are Gareth Hunt and Neil Dickson. The former is an alleged comedian, and he plays a variety of irritating characters. I understand the characters are supposed to be annoying, but his performances are more grating than what is necessary even for that. The most generous thing I can say about Dickson, on the other hand, is I thought of him as a cut-rate Michael Palin.

There isn't much more I can tell you about *It Couldn't Happen Here*. I could tell you exactly what happens in each minute of it and not be giving anything away, as there isn't any plot to spoil. Repeating characters and motifs alone do not constitute a plot. It's hard to believe anybody went into this with a cohesive vision. Even having seen it, I'm not sure what it was that couldn't happen here and, if it did happen, I missed it.

The movie (to use the term loosely) ends with the duo performing in a club while competitive ballroom dancers do their thing, complete with the numbers on their backs. When the performance is over, the duo walks away, and we see they each have a large zero on their back. I assume this is meant to be a statement such as "we don't care to even compete in the rat race, blah blah blah", but it could be the movie reviewing itself: zero.

Original version posted on 7/8/2023

Nothing Can Hurt Me (2012)

I have only been to Memphis once. Primarily, it was to make the sacred pilgrimage to Graceland. While there, we also went to the Stax Museum and Sun Studios, which are also amazing. Then I started wondering if was possible to see Ardent Studios, where many amazing albums were recorded.

The Replacements recorded *Pleased to Meet Me* there. R.E.M. recorded *Green* there. ZZ Top recorded, um, *everything* there?

Whomever I spoke with on the Ardent staff was stunned anybody would want to see the facility. They informed me it wasn't a museum like Stax. But they agreed to give me a tour and, at the appointed hour, we were shown around by producer John Fry and Big Star drummer Jody Stevens.

I was in seventh heaven. One thing they asked me to do was try not to disturb a camera crew who were filming in the central courtyard for a documentary about Big Star.

Years later, that documentary finally got a release and much, much later, I finally got around to watching it. I don't think I was consciously putting off seeing it but, whatever I was thinking, I'm glad I have now seen one of the best documentaries about a single rock band.

Simply put, the filmmakers interview the right people and get interesting insights about one the world's top "should have been big" groups. It also goes into Alex Chilton's and Chris Bell's time before and after Big Star, as well as the unfortunate history of Ardent, the label they were on.

I thought I already knew everything there was to know about this band, but were many surprises for me. An odd tangential thing that amused me was learning TGI Fridays was at one time a genuinely disreputable place and not just one of America's least desirable restaurant chains.

I highly recommend acquiring the blu-ray of this documentary as you get some deleted scenes, as well as a couple of mini-docs going deeper into the lives of Chilton and Bell.

Original version posted on 4/26/2023

Say Amen, Somebody (1982)

I am not religious. I am not Black. And yet I feel a strong attraction to gospel music.

Admittedly, the kind of gospel I prefer is gritty, lo-fi and from the 60's and early 70's—much like the majority of the garage rock I like. I don't believe I enjoy this music in a patronizing way, at least I certainly hope I don't.

The gospel performers in *Say Amen, Somebody* are of an older and more sophisticated variety than I normally listen to, and yet I thoroughly enjoyed the energetic performances in this documentary.

The focus of the picture is on singer Willie Mae Ford Smith and gospel polymath Thomas A. Dorsey. Dorsey is the composer of the ageless standard "Take My Hand, Precious Lord" and is widely regarded as the founder of this musical genre.

This 1982 film captures the movement at a transition point. There's a lot of talk about the possibility of there being big money in gospel soon. That may sound daft, but remember Whitney Houston started as a gospel singer. And, while not gospel per se, religious pop made some coin in the 80s with singers like Amy Grant.

But the legends to whom tribute is paid here do not seem to be preoccupied with earthly gains. At one point, Smith says that, when she's singing, "I feel like I could fly away from here". And she seems realistic about her advanced age when she says, "I may have cracks in my voice as wide as the Mississippi River, but that river keeps on flowing". I like that.

Another sign of the passing of an age is a visit to a decrepit, abandoned train station. It was once a thriving hub of transportation and a couple of Smith's relatives recall her heyday when the crowds used to throng to greet her there.

Roger Ebert chose this as one of the best films of that year. The man has taste. While I don't agree the film is that great, it is incredibly good—a snapshot of an era in transition and the last fleeting glimpses of a previous era about to fade away forever.

Original version posted on 3/6/2024

Song of the South (1946)

The forbidden film arrived in the mail years after buying it. I wasn't sure if it would ever arrive. The unlabeled, burned blu-ray arrived in a paper sleeve. I felt unclean just owning this, as if I was part of a tape trading community for some horrific form of pornography.

It seems surreal to me one can walk into a Barnes & Noble and buy a blu-ray of Passolini's *Salo* nowadays, when that was the subject of an attempted pandering charge as recently as 1996, but there's nowhere one can legally buy a new copy of the 1946 Disney film *Song of the South*. In the US, it was never even released on VHS. And yet, here is that forbidden film on that unlabeled disc. I was reluctant to watch it, and so it sat on the shelf for a year or two more. When I finally did, I wondered what all the fuss was about.

The big issue with this film is obviously the racist elements, and those are problematic. Not that it excuses anything but, when you see enough cinema from that era and earlier, you will see portrayals of Black people that are downright hateful. At best, the tone here is patronizing, as the kindly Uncle Remus (James Baskett) tells fables to a little White boy (Bobby Driscoll) to entertain and to teach important life lessons.

It's a shame this film has been buried by the House of the Mouse since, by preventing new viewers from seeing Baskett's performance, they are burying a great performance by a Black actor. Regardless of how this character is presented, I challenge anybody to say an unkind word about Baskett's work here.

He especially does a great job interacting with cartoon creatures when he appears in scenes that are a hybrid of live action and cel animation. Keep in mind this is long before motion capture, so he is likely interacting with *nothing*, and yet I did not once find fault in his eyelines. There's a very brief moment that left quite an impression on me, where he extends a single finger with which he "shakes hands" with a cartoon figure.

As expected from Disney, the animation is top-notch, though there is a noticeable reduction in detail from such earlier films as *Snow White* or *Pinocchio*. Still, you get some examples of the art of Mary Blair, who would go on to greater renown with the mid-century stylings of *Cinderella*.

One exceptional bit of animation is remarkable because of how thoroughly it is integrated into the scene, and that is an animated fishing line cast from a pole held by Baskett. He's deep in the background casting that line, landing a cartoon cork float in the water right in front of us.

But the most legendary scene, and justifiably so, is "Zip-A-Dee-Doo-Dah". This is when animation first appears in the film and, when it does, it is a moment akin to the first time one sees *The Wizard of Oz* and it transitions from black-and-white to color. That song is one of Disney's legendary earworms, and still popular today. I guess everybody somehow forgot which movie it is from.

Unfortunately, there is less animation overall than I expected. Aside from a brief bit at the end, it is restricted to illustrating three stories Baskett tells. I was surprised there were separate directing credits for animation and "photoplay". Really, there's two kinds of films here and they aren't integrated well enough to be successful, which I guess one could also say about society in the south at that time.

To the detriment of the film, most of the runtime is spent with the live actors. Set in the south before the Civil War, there's a queasy nostalgia for those plantation days. It may show Driscoll playing with a Black child (Glenn Leedy), but that is only after Leedy has brought a jug of water up to the other's room--just one of his many chores around the estate.

There's an irony to the White people being those in power, when their characters are so shallow here and their performances are so cardboard stiff. And their story is melodramatic crap, largely concerning Driscoll's unhappiness that his father has left him and his mother at her mother's. Top-billed Ruth Warrick is the mother, but she isn't in the film all that much and her time on screen isn't that memorable. I know Baskett could not possibly be the main star in a film of that age, but it's still a shame he isn't.

Song of the South is not a lost masterpiece, but it is a shame it has been effectively removed from public view. Though the film could use more animation, what is here is an important part of that medium's history. Even worse, in a film pulled from circulation because of its racial matter, the public has been denied the opportunity to see a stellar performance by a Black actor.

Original version posted on 10/16/2024

The Sound of Music (1965)

It is weird to see certain movies that are new to me but which have been so famous for so long. And yet, here I am in the ass half of middle age watching 1965's *The Sound of Music* for the first time. Is there any way I can judge it fairly, given my disdain for musicals? Really, I doubt anybody can fairly judge this movie anymore, as it has been so thoroughly entrenched in popular culture that it is like I had already seen it before I finally deliberately watched it.

The film opens in a way I definitely did not anticipate, with aerial photography of the alps stunning enough to make me wonder if I accidentally threw on one of the *Lord of the Rings* movies instead. That is a hint of the quality of filming throughout. Although the majority of the picture takes place on a soundstage, the remainder is filmed outdoors and usually captured in stunning photography and shot compositions.

That opening sequence of images leads up to where it inevitably would, had I thought about it, and that is Julie Andrews slowly spinning around, singing about how the hills are alive with the sound of music, etc. Just as assuredly as millions of hearts around the world swell in joy during this number, so I was proportionately underwhelmed. To her credit, Andrews has an astonishing voice, but that "belting to the rafters" style of showtune singing is something I doubt I will ever appreciate. Also, just the general nature of the scene, and the sentiment it conveys, is sickly sweet enough to make me wish I had a blood sugar testing kit at home.

My interest waned further with each additional number. It didn't help I had heard many of these way too many times before I ever watched the film for the first time. There are nuns discussing how to solve a problem like Maria. There's Andrews singing about her favorite things, in a song I have always founding cloyingly sweet. There's Andrews's suggestion that Plummer's moppets learn a song to sing to his fiancée and, though I was hoping it would be "Fat Bottomed Girls", she does that irritating "Do Re Mi" thing. All I could think of was *The Simpsons* bit where Homer hits a deer with his car, resulting in this from him, Lisa and Marge: "Doh!" "A deer!" "A female deer!" Like I said, it's as if I have somehow seen this entire picture many times over before intentionally watching it.

One problem I had with this production is it is too long (there's even an intermission) and too stuffed with characters for so slight a story. I think I can sum up the entire plot in one sentence: in

Austria on the brink of WWII, an easily distracted nun-to-be becomes the governess for the children of a stern captain, whom she organizes into a singing group, only to have the whole lot of them flee for their lives.

I left out a lot of tangents there, and it wouldn't have hurt the film if it had jettisoned some of those. The strongest of the subplots has Eleanor Parker as a Baroness and fiancée of Plummer. She is obviously not the right woman to marry him, as she is awkward with the children. To the film's credit, her character is not a total bitch. While staying at Plummer's mansion, she is chaperoned by Richard Haydn, in a performance that made me realize the "woman's gay friend" role existed well before the modern rom-com.

There's another tangent I would have, if not jettisoned, then at least trimmed. Daniel Truhitte is a telegraph delivery boy with whom Charmian Carr, the eldest of Plummer's children, is in love. Damn, but she sure seems to get excited by his song that there's a whole world of men out there. It's like we can see her thinking of a whole buffet of cock, and this in a G rated film. I bet the actress also wishes this number had been cut, as she supposedly put a leg through one of the panels of the round glass structure the choreography has her leaping around in. Odd question but, why is this staged inside what appears to be a glass gazebo and, for that matter, why use real glass for the set?

What did pleasantly surprise me, however, was the shift in tone when the threat of the Nazis comes too close to home. If there is a reason for Truhitte's character to be here, it is to show his transformation into a jackbooted thug when he joins that movement. It is no coincidence the third act of the film has very few songs in it. There is an especially tense scene where the family hides in a cemetery. I could picture myself watching this film again someday and just skipping to this part.

Then I wouldn't have to watch Andrews make play clothes for the children out of curtain fabric that appears to be as thick and inflexible as linoleum. I wouldn't have to watch the film fulfill its threat in the opening credits that there would be puppets, ones used in a show supposedly staged by the kids, which basically boils down to an ode to goats getting their freak on. I wouldn't have to endure the petty grievances the nuns have towards Andrews, such as the one that makes her kiss the floor after each time they argue. I have never heard of that custom before but, apparently, it happens enough for Andrews to just start smooching the pavement when she sees another nun approaching. I started wondering if Andrews ever took her relationship with flooring to a more, um, *intimate* level. Now *there's* a movie I want to see.

I like a lot of innocent, optimistic cinema, but *The Sound of Music* was as nauseatingly sweet as I always suspected it might be. That said, I was surprised by the tonal shift in the final third. It wasn't enough to fully redeem the movie, but it was interesting to see some realism creep in. As another song Andrews made famous puts it, it takes a spoonful of sugar to make that medicine go down. The problem I had here is there's far more than a spoonful of the stuff—it's like a bowl of sugary cereal covered by a small mountain of it, topped with a tiny Julie Andrews spinning around, belting out how the hills are alive with the sound of sweetener.

Original version posted on 7/28/2024

Space Is the Place (1974)

Sun Ra has intrigued me for decades now. I am not a huge fan, but I discovered his work around the same time I became aware of artists like The Residents, and I suspect many fans of the latter are also fans of the former.

For those not in the know, Ra claimed (and with a straight face) to be from Saturn. While nobody believed him, the extremity of some of the freest of his free jazz seemed to provide supporting evidence. But he also made music in popular formats, such as some perfect be-bop and doo-wop early in his career. In the 1970's, he even flirted with disco.

In 1974, he starred in what may be his most direct attempt to reach out to a greater audience, the motion picture *Space Is the Place*. This independently produced feature film is part concert film, part social commentary drama, part comedy and part conspiracy thriller. The last of those feels like an element slapped on after the fact, as if to give it more of a semblance of plot. A general vibe of blaxploitation permeates throughout.

The overall framing device has Ra engaged in a battle against evil (Raymond Johnson) for…I don't know what exactly. Seemingly inspired by the chess game Max von Sydow plays against Death in *The Seventh Seal*, these two sit across a table in the desert playing what seems to be an eternal card game. The deck is a variation on tarot cards and the rules seem to be made up as they go along.

One of those cards has Ra's spaceship on it. This is a unique design. From one angle, it looks like a distorted human tooth. From another, it distinctly looks like it has boobs with psychedelic patterns painted on them. And here I thought *Battle Beyond the Stars* was the first film to have a spacecraft with tits.

This ship comes to Earth, and Ra addresses the press at the landing site. Ra has come to take Black people to a beautiful and peaceful world where they can live without the strife they endure on our planet. But Johnson tries to trap low-income Black people through various means, whether those be liquor, drugs or prostitution.

At least, these are what I assume the messages to be, as they are a bit muddled in the presentation. Further obfuscating the message are bits about Ra's Outer Space Employment Agency. Given he isn't paying anybody, I think "employment" is a dishonest term. Also, there's a bit that doesn't scan well where Ra refuses the application of an unemployed NASA engineer who is desperate for work, declaring him ineligible "because of a particular race you are". I realize this is some quid pro quo for all the people of color government agencies doubtlessly, and unfairly, rejected outright, but it still isn't a great look. Then again, Ra makes a solid point about Black people not being invited to take part in the space age, that only White people had walked on the moon.

Specifically, only White *men* have walked on the moon to date, which brings to mind an unfortunate aspect of the film. Given the high-minded principles expressed by Ra, I was baffled by a scene where two nurses in a hospital strip down to full-frontal nudity. Admittedly, this moment does have a funny twist, where the patient (Christopher Brooks) thinks they have arrived to have a threesome with him, only for his doctor (Johnson) to kick him out of his own room, so as to party with both girls alone.

Among my favorite moments in the picture are some that were likely filmed only to help pad out the runtime. These are studio shots of the various elaborate costumes of Ra's ensemble, where Egyptology is obviously a strong influence. Ra monologues over these shots. When we see him, he's wearing this astonishingly large headpiece that has to be heavy, regardless of what it is made of.

Perhaps the most unusual aspect of this movie is the music. I mentioned earlier how the musician worked in many genres. With a feature film being the best opportunity to reach the widest audience possible, one would think he would use some of his more accessible music here. Instead, it is the type of rather extreme free jazz that might prompt some wags to say they felt overcharged.

Space Is the Place concludes with a small-scale take on the rapture, as he takes worthy Black people aboard his ship to his utopia on Saturn. I think that's an interesting idea, but it's pretty depressing that the only way he believes his people can live a fulfilling life is by leaving the planet. For those left behind, take solace in his intention to teleport the faithful through music.

Original version posted on 10/31/2024

Stand By for Failure (2022)
A Documentary about Negativland

Teenagers do stupid and pointless things in their perpetual state of boredom. I recall trying to make audio collages by recording the radio while randomly scanning the airwaves, hoping I might accidentally capture some sort of interesting or humorous juxtapositions. As one likely will conclude, the results were disappointing. I have a feeling the members of Negativland past and present would never tire of doing that, especially now that I have seen the 2022 documentary about them, *Stand By for Failure: A Documentary About Negativland*.

This was a group I was familiar with beforehand, though I wouldn't say I was ever a fan. I was most aware of them through their spats with U2 and Casey Kasem after they covered "I Still Haven't Found What I'm Looking For" and mixed into that a recording of Kasem losing his shit, repeatedly flubbing an intro he was doing about U2. The recording was released in what I will concede is a deceptive sleeve, with "U2" in letters filling the entire space and "NEGATIVLAND" in smaller font along the bottom.

The result is U2's management sued SST, the label Negativland was on at the time. SST then passed the legal fees they incurred back to the group, who was in no position to pay the exorbitant losses. An interesting moment in this documentary has two members of the group engaged in what is ostensibly an interview with U2 guitarist The Edge, only to hit him up for money. To his credit, The Edge laughs, saying that is the first time he has ever been asked for money as part of an interview. In the end, U2 convinced their management to drop the matter. Something I find interesting is the record is still in legal limbo to this day because Kasem refused to withdraw his complaint.

I actually have an original copy of the vinyl, bought at a record show in the mid-90's. I'm still happy I found that, as it is the only time I have seen a copy in the wild. The Discogs marketplace shows this has not increased in value over what I paid for it decades earlier. Fortunately for me, I never buy records with the intention of one day reselling them.

The U2 incident wasn't the first time they made news. In 1988, teenager David Brom killed his parents and siblings with an axe. Negativland chose to exploit that tragedy by distributing a press release claiming the motivation for those murders had been an argument between Brom and his father concerning the band's track, "Christianity Is Stupid". It is no surprise the teen did not own any of the group's recordings.

Let's face it: there has never been much demand for the output of a group whose genre could be best described as "sound collage". Member Don Joyce acknowledges on camera the group is on the fringe of the fringe. I can agree with that assessment, as I am not really a fan of theirs, despite being predisposed to liking them, through my interest in the Church of the SubGenius, with which they are associated.

Something else that should have been a gateway for me to better appreciate them is an association with the band The Residents. But being a fan of one does not necessarily translate to being a fan of the other, regardless of how far each is outside of the mainstream. The only connection between the groups shown here is when Negativland's studio was destroyed by fire and the other group offered their Ralph Records facility as a rehearsal space. This was especially generous given The Residents were frequently very low on funds themselves.

One aspect of the collective which is unusual is how difficult it is to define what exactly they are. Founding member David Wills seems to paraphrase Groucho Marx in expressing confusion as to how he, the person least likely to be in a musical group, could be in the band.

I find Wills to be a divisive figure, somehow the spirit of the group while also being its most irritating component. I'm not sure if his voice is distinctive or grating. Most likely, it is distinctively grating. I also do not find his demeanor appealing. Simply put, he's not somebody I think I would care to spend time with. One anecdote that stands out in my mind is fellow member Mark Hosler talking about when he was a teenager, and how his mother must have wondered what the 35-year-old Wills was doing all night in the bedroom of a 17-year-old boy. Hosler says she need not have worried, as they were only eavesdropping on baby monitors, something I found very creepy.

Something I did not find creepy, but the mainstream media did, was what the collective did following Joyce's death. They once again made national news when they distributed his ashes in tiny packets included in copies of their next release. What appalled others felt like a genuinely loving tribute to me.

Stand By for Failure has a fair amount of interesting details in it about the group, but it is deliberately muddled in the telling, emulating their collage approach in both audio and video. I understand one wanting to channel the band's aesthetic for a film about them, but it still makes for a frustrating experience at times. In that regard, it is an accurate representation of their work.

Original version posted on 10/14/2024

Up Jumped a Swagman (1965)

It's hard to believe now, but Capitol Records was initially uninterested in The Beatles, so some very minor US labels (Vee-Jay, Swan and Tollie) pounced on the opportunity and licensed some of their early singles from EMI. Once the group's popularity spread to the colonies, Capitol sought control of those tracks, so Vee Jay tried to max out its investment by endlessly repackaging what little material they had.

The desperate last gasp was the truly bizarre compilation LP *Jolly What! England's Greatest Recording Stars: The Beatles & Frank Ifield on Stage*, pairing four Beatles tracks with eight by an Australian singer who did country-ish songs with flourishes of whistling and near-yodeling.

Aside from being used for a quick cash grab by Vee-Jay, I never knew anything about Frank Ifield and was curious who he was. Hard to believe he was popular enough in the UK to warrant the feature film *Up Jumped a Swagman*.

This is another of those British musical comedies made to cash-in on the popularity of an artist while they were hot. Most of those films were disposable, though they were usually a good canvas for innovative directors to get their start and put their youthful impulses on the screen.

The perfect example is the pairing of Richard Lester and The Beatles in *A Hard Day's Night*. Needless to say, *Swagman* is not going to be anywhere near as good as that, but I am happy to report it is quite enjoyable.

Director Christopher Miles isn't Lester, but there are a number of surprisingly clever and inventive touches here. This is a zanier affair than I was anticipating, and the closest analogy I can think of is a typical episode of *The Monkees* (though the music is nowhere near as good as what was in that series). The tone is gently cynical, with mild jabs at popular culture and the machinations of the pop music industry.

As for Ifield, he's…well, he seems like he would be a really nice guy to know. Alas, he has even less personality than Pat Boone and his music has less of a genuine rock feel than even Mr. Boone's. The best thing in his favor is I get the feeling he has a good sense of humor about himself, almost as if he knows he doesn't warrant a feature film but is cheerfully along for the ride just the same.

The plot concerns a money-less Ifield arriving in England to pursue a singing career and a hot "It" girl. He is instead pursued by a lower-class shopgirl and he finds his interest divided.

As far as that singing is concerned, I'm not sure how Ifield was ever popular in real life, even before the sea change arrived that was The Beatles. I was also confused by how most of the musical numbers just have him singing and walking around. I never understood why anybody would want to watch a person miming to a song without anything else happening on the screen. That said, there was a surprising moment where one of these sequences is abruptly interrupted in a comical manner.

Parallel to the featherweight storyline of the struggling Ifield is a heist subplot that comes to dominate the film. You wouldn't think these two threads would work together, yet this feels natural and is easy to follow.

I know most of what I wrote here is negative, yet this is a movie I recommend for those who enjoy *The Monkees* TV show. Although neither plotline here is novel, there are smart, amusing touches throughout. I get the feeling everybody involved was aiming higher than they knew was warranted for a disposable cash-grab like this.

Original version posted on 3/26/2023

Actionable offenses
The section about action films

The Adventures of Robin Hood (1938)

The legend of Robin Hood is one of those stories everybody knows but which has never really clicked with me. I'm curious why it has endured as long as it has. It seems, even today, somebody feels compelled to make another movie or television series of it from time to time.

I doubt anybody will ever be able to improve upon 1938's *The Adventures of Robin Hood*. While I can't say I was fully engaged throughout its one and three-quarter hours, I was still quite impressed with a picture whose audience which saw it in its original run is almost entirely dead by now.

This kind of fare normally feels like a history lesson to me, and that aspect of it often makes it difficult for me to feign an interest. It's odd that I feel the same way about anything concerning King Arthur and his knights, unless the film is made by Monty Python. Yes, I know King Arthur wasn't real, thank you, and neither was Robin Hood. It is only the nature of the material that scans for me as a type of edutainment. If that doesn't make sense, consider how every university has at least one mythology course.

Aside from a few text cards, this picture wisely lets the background information be conveyed through dialogue, which made it easier for me to absorb. It is the time of the Crusades, and the Saxon king of England has gone to fight in them. In his place is the Norman government, with his brother assuming interim control of the country. Turns out that sibling who was intended to be a temporary change in management has designs on making that permanent.

An impossibly young Claude Rains plays that duplicitous brother. Mad with power, he is desperate to be crowned king. He is also taxing and starving the populace, to literal death in some instances. Dialogue reveals the soldiers are even torturing, maiming and raping peasants, which gives this film a feeling of higher stakes than in some other adaptations. Basil Rathbone plays his ruthless second-in-command, and this is the kind of role in which the actor excelled. The film also makes excellent use of Rathbone's real-life fencing expertise.

Error Flynn is the title character. I had not seen him in a movie before and I was curious why he was such a huge star in his time. Having finally seen this picture, I now understand. This is the kind of perfect confluence of personality and role that makes a career.

When we first see Flynn, he is interceding to save a peasant from being killed by guards. All the accused had done was slay a deer, but one of Rains's draconian policies was to declare all deer to be property of the king. I guess that makes more sense than the real British policy that makes the King or Queen owner of the nation's wild swans on the Thames. I doubt most people want to eat a swan. Also, those fuckers are mean and dangerous. Probably better to mess with most deer, given the choice.

During a banquet at the royal castle, Flynn arrives with the deer slung over his shoulder. With Robin Hood having made what appears to be an act of contrition, Rains invites the man to eat with them. Conversation soon reveals Flynn is completely opposed to the current administration. The dialogue in this scene is stellar, with Rains telling Flynn, "Such insolence must fuel quite an appetite." Also at banquet table is Olivia de Havilland as Maid

Marian, who is appalled at Flynn's accusations: "Why, you speak treason." His reply: "Fluently."

Soon, Flynn is flying all around the room, as are many arrows. Some of those arrows appeared to have been actually launched from bows. While this makes such action scenes more exciting, I wondered how dangerous this shoot might have been.

From here, the tale largely unfolds in the usual way, and I started to find my attention waning. You know the drill. Encountering various rogues in the forest who will join his band of merry men. The archery tournament. Restoring the rightful king to his throne. Yada yada yada. Still, there's satisfaction to be found when any tale is told well, even if it is one everybody somehow already knows.

Of these interim scenes, the one most interesting to me was Alan Hale and Flynn fighting with staffs in a bit famously parodied in that *Looney Tunes* starring Daffy Duck and Porky Pig. What's nice is that cartoon short is among the wealth of extras on this blu-ray. Even better is the scene where Flynn first meets Eugene Pallette, as Friar Tuck. I am a big fan of Pallette, an actor who excelled in small parts in many films, with his trademark gruff and direct manner.

The film ends strong, with a huge action sequence in the royal castle. That Flynn supposedly did his own stunts is astonishing. And I love it when a film as old as this one can surprise me.

Original version posted on 4/10/2024

Barb Wire (1996)

Pamela Anderson has never piqued my interest. It isn't like I have ever felt an active dislike towards her, per se—I simply never found her attractive or interesting. Still, I was strangely pleased when she recently made news for choosing to no longer wear make-up, which I found admirable. I also respect her commitment to animal rights.

What I think of first whenever her name comes up isn't *Baywatch* or her tumultuous relationship with Tommy Lee. Instead, it is 1996's *Barb Wire*, an infamous action film she headlined, and for which she received a Razzie for Worst New Star. What is interesting is she was also nominated, but did not "win", for Worst Actress. Nor did the film "win" for the three other categories in which it was nominated, which seems to suggest this film is not quite as bad as legend would have it.

That said, this picture is still quite awful, as I recently discovered for myself. Apparently, the appeal for most first-time viewers is to see Anderson make a fool of herself. Let me get this out of the way: she's actually not that bad. The film requires her to be essentially a life-size action figure, and she has the physique to be believable as an action hero. Her line readings may largely be a bit flat, but I'm not sure what anybody could do with the tin-eared dialogue of this script.

No, what makes this a lousy watch is it is a bog-standard sci-fi action film of the 90's. It is unmistakably a product of that decade and has all the worst trappings of such fare from the era. Bad techno-ish dreck fills the soundtrack when we're not being subjected to tracks like her then-husband's godawful "Planet Boom". It is set in a post-apocalyptic world that mysteriously has roughly 100% more dance clubs than I think there would be after the collapse of civilization. But, hey, at least that gives faux-lesbians a place to *almost* make out together.

Anderson is the owner of this club, which she operates in Steel Harbor. As an interminable text crawl informs us, this is the last free city remaining after the second American civil war. While we're reading this, a narrator is also reading it aloud, presumably because the filmmakers believe their audience is too stupid to read. Just a couple of minutes later, Anderson will relay *the same info again* in voiceover.

The voiceover doesn't end there, and it returns from time to time to unload preposterous amounts of exposition upon the audience. Techniques like that, combined with the shambolic nature of the film, convinces me this was originally meant to be a longer work, then drastically cut down and stuck together with bits of ADR'd exposition as a type of Band Aid.

Anderson is extremely well-known in Steel Harbor, even a bit of a celebrity. That would seem to be a liability in her side-career as a mercenary. At least that work gets her out of the club, as I can't imagine I'm the only person appalled by the goth-ish house band covering "Hot Child in The City". She doesn't even have to change clothes for her other job, as she lounges around at home in a leather teddy and fishnet stockings. What could be more comfortable than that?

She, and everybody else in this picture, is after a pair of contact lenses that are the only way to fool the retinal scanners in order to get on a plane to Canada. I like the idea of Canada being the more prosperous country in the future as portrayed in this film. In an earlier scene, she even demands payment for a job in Canadian dollars.

There's also some sort of nonsense involving a cruel officer in the fascist government (Steve Railsback) trying to find a woman whose DNA (?) holds the key (??) to the regime's greatest chemical weapon (???). We first learn about this when Railsback is torturing a naked woman via some sort of steampunk crap that barely covers her naughty bits. That alone conveys everything anybody needs to know about the mindset of the filmmakers.

Among the actors, the one that fares best is Xander Berkeley. He excels in roles like this, a corrupt lawman who is only interested in things that benefit himself, especially when it requires the least amount of effort. I also liked seeing Udo Kier as Anderson's valet, just because I always enjoy seeing him get work. Mind you, his presence is not exactly a harbinger of quality.

Altogether, *Barb Wire* isn't as bad as its reputation led me to believe. Anderson was unfairly slighted for her performance, though it is also quite evident she isn't the right person to carry a feature. But really, nobody would be able to successfully pull off a movie so burdened with the trappings and cliches of 90's sci-if. Watching it today, it's hard to believe the film is *only* roughly three decades old.

Original version posted on 7/26/2024

Blind Rage (1976)

I keep making this stupid wisecrack about trying to seek diplomatic immunity at an International House of Pancakes. But the characters in 1976's weird grindhouse heist picture *Blind Rage* spend so much time in one that I suspect they really think this is some sort of neutral territory similar to international waters.

A climatic fight will take place on the roof of the one in Hollywood. This is after the action has been to Mexico, Japan, China and the Philippines (where the film spends the *vast* majority of its runtime). One of the first scenes is at an IHOP, so the movie went around the world just to come back to what I believe is the same location. As a cop says on the CB near the end, "It's going down right now at the International House of Pancakes!"

Fuck yeah, shit always going down at the IHOP! The first scene set there has a criminal mastermind seat himself in a booth across from an agent who just attended a meeting where it was revealed millions of dollars are going to be held in a bank in Manilla.

This criminal "geeenyus" (imagine it said in a Wile E. Coyote voice) is a performance so bad that I couldn't stop laughing through it. Not only is his line delivery bizarre, but he keeps looking to his right as if he has a nervous tic, or maybe severe drug paranoia. There's even the guy's introductory line, "My name is Lou Simpson, but my friends call me…Wilbur". Well, how about I call you Betty and you can call me Al?

At an earlier meeting where the agent learned about the money, he is told it is going to help "stop the domino theory." That is an…interesting…turn of phrase. You see, that theory was the justification used by the countries which invaded Vietnam. The idea was that, as Communism toppled one government in Asia, it would topple another, which would topple another, etc. I assume the guy meant to imply this money would help stop *Communism*, because stopping that *theory* doesn't make any sense.

Anywho, all these relatively minor stupidities will be overshadowed by the far greater one which is the plot. Five blind men from various countries will be brought together to steal the money being held in Manilla.

You will likely ask, "Why blind men?" I was never sure and I'm not sure the movie is, either. One character says it is so that, if any one of them is caught, they won't be able to identify the others or their handlers. I guess the person who thought this didn't consider the other senses a blind person has.

Another person says it is because somebody working at a bank seeing five blind men wouldn't suspect they were about to rob them. I'm thinking that, if I worked in a bank, I would consider anybody walking in to be equally likely or unlikely to be a potential robber (unless they are wearing a mask or openly carrying a gun—then I think it is safe to make an assumption). The improbability of numerous blind people being at a bank at the same time would make me even more suspicious. What if it was five guys who can see, wearing dark glasses and using walking sticks and just acting like they were blind?

All that is moot, as they will be rigorously trained to create the illusion they are not visually impaired, when the masterminds of the operation could have just used non-blind people and…I give up. A full-scale model of the bank lobby is constructed to show the robbers how many steps it is to the withdrawal slips, teller windows, etc. They are even trained to fire pistols at the positions where people are most likely to be. I was stunned that, during this target practice, many of the trainers are far closer to the targets than I would be. Heck, I would be *behind* the shooter.

Leila Hermosa, as the lead trainer, is the only woman in this picture and it is a thankless role. When we first see her, she is assisting at a beeper baseball game at a school for the blind. That was interesting to see. Then she isn't given much of anything to do in the training sequences. In one baffling and deeply regrettable scene, one of the blind men she's training tries to rape her in her sleep.

Hiring somebody only because they work with the blind seems condescending, as the guys she's training were doing perfectly alright on their own, especially the one who seemed to be under constant attack from martial arts experts. Since none of them have robbed a bank before, it seems like the best person to assist would be an expert in bank robbery.

A few innocent people get killed during the heist, thanks to that pointless bit of trickery wherein the blind are trained to perform as if they can see. Then almost everybody else in the picture dies when a tanker truck collides with an airplane. You see, the handler and an assistant make a getaway with the blind men hidden in a compartment beneath the tank of a fuel storage truck. First, why use this type of truck? Second, why is it actually *full of fuel?*!

This movie is packed with weird aspects like that. When we're told the backstories of the five blind men, we learn the first two were actually blinded by thugs in what looks like the Three Stooges's eyeball-poke gag gone very wrong. Turns out none of them lost their eyes from ricocheted BB gun fire, which is what my money was on. Fred Williamson is on screen for approximately ten minutes yet is high in the cast order. Even the music is screwy, with a theme song sounding like knock-off Shirley Bassey, which ends in the baffling line: "When you fall into the system". What system?

For that matter, what rage? *Blind Rage* is a spectacularly, often hilariously, inept movie where five blind men are pointlessly used to commit a heist. Some of these men may have been angered at the loss of their vision, but it isn't like they were exacting revenge against the bank for causing that. Here is a movie so gloriously stupid, it can't even get its title right.

Original version posted on 9/29/2023

Curucu, Beast of the Amazon (1956)

I don't know much about Curt Siodmak, but I bet he had some interesting stories concerning at least two of the features he directed. Much like his *Love Slaves of the Amazon*, 1956's *Curucu, Beast of the Amazon* was filmed entirely in Brazil. I'm not sure if that applies to interiors which, like that other film, are only cheap sets.

At least there is a fair amount of footage shot in the wilds of that country. While there is still quite a bit of fake jungle mixed in, the location footage looks like they went significantly farther off the grid than just the outskirts of the studio parking lot.

Into the jungle go John Bromfield and Beverly Garland. His character is named Rock Dean, which sounds like an action figure. Small wonder he has about as much personality as one. Garland's character is a doctor searching for a chemical the head shrinkers use in their trade, as she believes this can be used to cure cancer.

It should be awesome she's a doctor, except I'm not sure which treats her more condescendingly: Bromfield or the movie. The script puts this horrible line in her mouth: "I'm afraid of some things. I'm a woman." Then there's Bromfield's persistent belittling of her: "I know how it is. Can't get a man, so she chooses a career." And her asshole boss actually *agrees* with him!

One thing I did like is how she hires right out from under Bromfield his guide for an excursion into the jungle. Still, she brings Bromfield along on her expedition, though I have no idea why. She's the one who actually does useful things like save a native's life by performing an appendectomy.

For a movie that brags so much about how it was filmed entirely in Brazil, the natives are portrayed in the way most movies of this era did—as if those behind the camera couldn't be bothered to learn anything about the local cultures. This mindset is conveyed through such characters as a missionary who claims the indigenous people engage in "devil worship".

Both locals and anglos are being tormented by the titular beast. It is even goofier than I could have hoped it would be. It is difficult to describe, but just think of the stupidest sport's mascot you've ever seen and then imagine if somebody tried to one up that. This is a creature whose eyes are obviously not functional. Surprisingly, this is a hint of a slight twist I think the vast majority of viewers will be able to anticipate.

Some of the footage of Brazil is nice, though none of it is spectacular. Even more than the jungle footage, I appreciated the imagery of the sparkling new buildings designed in the mid-century modern style. Padding out some of the movie is stock footage of piranhas. Other real footage includes a mongoose fighting a snake, and I didn't need to see that. Needless to say, there isn't a disclaimer about no animals being harmed in this production.

At best, *Curucu* may prove some wry amusement in the spirit of *MST3K*. It is unrepentantly daft and sexist, and without any self-awareness. For those looking for a new drinking game, I recommend that, every time somebody calls out Rock's name, everybody else has to yell out either "paper!" or "scissors!" The last person to do so drinks.

Original version posted on 12/7/2023

Death Race 2000 (1975)

It isn't often I find myself in direct opposition to an opinion Roger Ebert expressed in a review, yet I am stunned by how much he hated 1975's *Death Race 2000*.

I will sum up the plot for the unfamiliar. In the future (well, 2000 was the future in 1975), America is under the thumb of a totalitarian regime. To distract from its many woes, the government stages a violent cross-country car race each year.

I'm a little unclear on the rules of the race, even after seeing it twice. I know there are points given to the drivers for running over pedestrians, and those points vary by different classifications. What I never fully grasped was how those points factor into the decision of who wins the race. If somebody crosses the finish line first, but does not incur any casualties, have they still won? Or can somebody with the most points cross the line last and still be the winner?

That kind of thing would bother me in most films, but not here. This is a picture that realizes how silly it is and it knows you know how silly it is. Basically, this is a live-action cartoon for adults.

Consider the scene where David Carridine, as one of the drivers, sees the staff of a hospital in the distance as they leave wheelchair-bound old people in the road. He tells his navigator in the passenger seat (Simone Griffeth) this is "euthanasia day" at the hospitals, where they help boost his point total while getting rid of their dead weight. He instead goes off road and runs over all those doctors and nurses. What we see are bodies bouncing into the air as if this is a Tex Avery cartoon.

Ebert's specific beef with the film was the extent of the violence in it. What I found odd is the movie isn't that violent, even when compared to many other R rated films released that same year. The crux of his review is how appalled he was to see the auditorium full of children who were laughing and carrying on. That little kids were at a movie with this rating seems to me the fault of many people, none of whom made this picture.

Admittedly, the violence is more gruesomely portrayed when the other drivers wipe out pedestrians. There is an especially nasty moment where a driver played by Sylvester Stallone runs a guy down in a muddy riverbed and blood sprays out in torrents from under the spinning wheels. But Stallone is portrayed as one of the bad guys.

Also, I doubt we're supposed to find that moment funny, unlike the scene with Carradine at the hospital. I would be appalled if I was in a theatre with a bunch of pre-pubescents laughing at the more gruesome scene but, once again, it is not the fault of the filmmakers they were admitted to the screening.

This dark comedy was directed by Paul Bartel, and it is in a similar vein to the other films he would later make, most notably *Eating Raoul*. That film is in the Criterion Collection. Honestly, I like this movie far more.

I was surprised by how good the movie looks, given the producer is legendary spendthrift Roger Corman. Each race vehicle has a distinctive appearance. There's good use of matte paintings in the stadium scenes. It doesn't exactly feel like a fully realized future world, but I still found it more believable than…well, *Futureworld*.

The movie makes numerous points about violence and how Americans are addicted to it. Of course, this point is made in a rather violent movie, which makes that seem a tad hypocritical. Then there's a moment at the very end that answers a question about violence with more violence, as the film calls bullshit on its own attempt to take the high road.

Perhaps Ebert missed the tongue-in-cheek nature of the humor in *Death Race 2000*. Maybe he just didn't care. I can totally understand being appalled by the behavior of the children in the audience when he saw it, but they shouldn't have been there, anyway. This is a movie where a character has a literal hand grenade—they can detach it from their arm and use it as a grenade. And there is another character who is dispatched in a way I have only previously seen in *Road Runner* cartoons. Maybe this is a kids' movie after all. It was just made for bigger kids.

Original version posted on 2/23/2024

The Dungeonmaster (1984)

I'm not much of a gamer, but I'm pretty sure those who are tend to dislike games that are only composed of mini-games. Inevitably, those mini-games wouldn't be sufficient on their own, nor do they collectively become a satisfying experience.

Such is the case of 1984's *The Dungeonmaster*, a title that makes a bit more sense than *Ragewar*, which is how it was originally marketed. Seven directors (!) and eight writers (WTF!) string together seven unsubstantial tales, with a wraparound story of these being "quests" a computer nerd must complete in order to free his girlfriend from the clutches of Satan. OK, the character isn't actually named "Satan" here, but that's basically who it is—except it's really just Bull from *Night Court*.

A dream sequence preceding the opening credits sets the tone for the rest of the movie, with a guy pursuing a scantily clad woman in slow-motion through a set where a lot of dry ice is used. This, and most of the rest of the film, looks like a heavy metal video from the era. Still, it was a shock to see the band WASP play a major role in one of the segments.

The woman in this dream (Gina Calabrese) will soon be far more scantily clad, as this PG-13 film has waaay more full-frontal nudity in it than one would expect, given the rating. How did I *not* know about this movie in my early teens?! That actress won't be in the picture past the opening credits; however, Leslie Wing (as the girlfriend) will, and she has a couple of scenes in see-through tops which also undermine the rating.

Jeffrey Byron plays the computer nerd boyfriend. Some of his electronic toys seem shockingly prescient. In addition to a computer with which he interacts like it is Siri, he has glasses that electronically display information over whatever he looks at (foreseeing Google Glass), and a Power Glove type thing on his forearm that sometimes acts as a Fitbit and, when at an ATM, seems to act as an early Apple Pay. Please don't tell me this picture inspired Steve Jobs and the Google people to create their inventions.

This is a lot of effects work for a movie of such obviously low budget. At least this film was made too early for there to be dodgy CGI. But there is some decent stop-motion work, which I always appreciate. There's even a neat but brief bit of hand-drawn animation. It wasn't good enough to make me suspect it was done by Walt Disney Pictures' Special Photographic Department, though it *was* actually done by them. Possibly the worst effect is a puppet in one scene. Ironically, this movie was the brainchild of Charles Band, who was behind the *Puppet Master* series. Unironically, the puppetry sucked in those films, too.

Let's get the random observations out of the way. The score is largely functional but unremarkable, except for what sounds like knockoff Philip Glass over the opening sequence. A ridiculously long scene of Wing in an aerobics class reveals she has the only tape player ever created which makes a record scratch sound when hitting the stop button.

If there is a saving grace for *The Dungeonmaster*, it is that it has some self-awareness and more than a hint of humor. The general feeling I got is "can you believe we're getting away with this?" Still, it is a bit difficult to tell when it is trying to get laughs and when it is unintentionally funny. At one point, Byron says he has one word for the villain and that is, "Forget it." In another moment, Satan tries to tempt our hero with three women and the girlfriend literally cries foul.

It's hard to say what this movie is aiming for, but I can say it largely succeeds as camp, regardless of intention. For example, one scene takes place in a museum of history's worst people, and yet it has the real alongside the fictitious, with Jack the Ripper next to The Wolfman. All in all, surprisingly more enjoyable than I expected.

Original version posted on 5/27/2023

Hercules in the Haunted World (1961)

I'm not big on swords and sandals films, known colloquially as "peplum". It seems telling that word is so similar to "pablum".

So, I was surprised by how much I enjoyed 1961's *Hercules in the Haunted World*. It doubtlessly helped it was directed by Mario Bava, a director so fond of strongly colored lighting that to consider de-colorizing one of his films would be as pointless as colorizing the black-and-white parts of *The Wizard of Oz*.

It also helps to have a young Christopher Lee as the villain, though he isn't given terribly much to do. But, let's face it, most us would watch the actor eating lunch. The horrific thing Lee has done is to wipe Hercules (Reg Park) from the memory of his true love

(Marisa Belli). That may be devastating to Park, but I feel like Lee just did Belli a favor.

In a way, the structure of the film is similar to 8-bit NES adventure games, and that's because those games were influenced by pictures such as this. There are various locales to go to, then get an object, then go to the next place, etc., all leading to a boss battle. If this case, the objects are a golden apple, the Stone of Pluto and, finally, the Stone of Forgetfulness. One location is basically a fire level. A climatic battle with Lee is the big boss fight. If anybody ever remakes this picture, they should film it as a side-scroller.

The Luigi to Park's Mario is George Ardisson, playing an absolute horndog. We first see making time with Ely Drago, though we soon learn she is supposedly the fiancée of affable dispenser of comic relief Franco Giacobini. In this analogy, maybe Giacobini is Toad(?). OK, so I couldn't carry the Super Mario analogy very far.

A slight expansion of the goal-oriented nature of the plot occurs when Ardisson falls in love with Persephone (Ida Galli) and whisks her away from the kingdom of the dead. I guess his undying love for Drago died when he met a dead woman. If they consummate this relationship, is that necrophilia?

Anywho, Park tells Ardisson Galli must return to the underworld because they have incurred the wrath of Pluto. Ardisson isn't crazy about this, but Galli decides to return of her own accord, saying their love had run its course. Guess she's of the opinion you throw away the packet after you've used the seeds.

To be honest, I'm not sure I completely followed the plot. Really, the plotting feels threadbare but so much is vaguely defined as to leave one with the impression more is going on than I suspect there really is. Also, having elements from various mythologies does not necessarily mean anybody who worked on this was a scholar on the subject. Regardless, I was along for the ride, and chose to dismiss anything that didn't feel like it made sense.

This film has some genuinely creepy elements. One thing I liked were vines that, when cut, drip with the blood of the damned they imprison. Far weirder is the stone monster that decides Ardisson "should be longer. You will be as thin as the ropes that bind you". He also announces he is going to cut Giacobini down to size because he is too long for the slab he's on. I found the…um, stone-cold logic of the monster unnerving.

Supposedly, *Hercules in the Haunted World* was made by Bava as a test for himself, to use as few set components as possible, and rearrange or repurpose them to appear to be different locations. If that is true, then I would say mission accomplished, as I otherwise would not have been aware of this self-imposed limitation. I had a good time watching this, though I recommend turning one's brain off as best they can while doing so.

Original version posted on 5/29/2024

King Kong Escapes (1967)

Now here's a strange animal—in a way, two of them, in fact. 1967's *King Kong Escapes* pits the titular ape against a robotic version of himself. And it takes its sweet time getting to that matchup, filling the runtime up with things that aren't very interesting, because the audience is desperately waiting for *King Kong to battle Robo-Kong*. Really, shouldn't the film just be 90 minutes of that?

This is an odd movie that never seems sure of what it is trying to do. I wasn't too surprised this was a co-production of

Rankin/Bass and Japan's Toho, as the result is about as bizarre as one might expect from such a lineage.

When you work with the studio that gave the world Godzilla, you know you're going to get somebody in a crummy giant lizard suit. This is the first creature defeated by Kong, on his home island of…Mondo? Not sure exactly why, but that name struck me as odd the first time somebody said it, and I'm still hung up on it long after the end credits.

Kong was saving a submarine's doctor from the store-brand Godzilla. Blond and vertically challenged Linda Miller is in that role as the object of Kong's affection. Her scant C.V. on IMDB reveals she was in the even worse *The Green Slime* in the role of "Nurse". I guess if the comfortable work shoe fits…

A less thankless role is Mie Hama as a villainess with a fashion sense that seems to be positioning her as the Japanese Emma Peel. Many of the characters seem strangely obsessed with learning her nationality. She's very evasive on this topic and the matter is never settled. It is bewildering why this is such a mystery.

I was only mildly surprised to discover Hama had previously been in Toho's *King Kong vs. Godzilla*, essentially in the role Miller got stuck with here. Hama would go on to be a "Bond girl" in *You Only Live Twice*.

But she isn't even the true villain of the film, and her duplicity is more of a Mata Hari type than diabolical supervillain. Instead, the honor goes to Hideyo Amamoto, as Dr. Who. I'm not even joking about that, he just happens to have the same name as the legendary UK cult TV show character, but only because the name was "Dr. Hu" in the original Japanese. At least he is voiced by Paul Frees, using the same voice he used for Boris Baronov on *Rocky & Bullwinkle*. That's a good touch for a dastardly villain who wears a cape.

Dr. Who is the mastermind behind the creation of Robo-Kong, which he intends to use to mine a mysterious radioactive mineral. If you're wondering why it took a robotic King Kong to do the job, you're not alone. Even more confusing is it does this work in conjunction with a great deal of equipment only a professional mining operation would have, seemingly negating the need to have a 60-foot-tall android ape do the labor. I wonder when somebody in the US will consider using a giant robot ape for fracking.

Then the radiation scrambles the robot's circuits, so it's off to abduct the real Kong to do the work. This development had me even more confused. If radiation took out the robot, wouldn't it be far less likely an organic being could succeed at the job? It's like Dr. Who is convinced radioactive minerals can only be mined by giant apes, whether flesh or metal. Maybe it's the same culture Hama was brought up in, and why she's so secretive about it. Maybe she's ashamed.

Also in the cast is Rhodes Reason, ostensibly as the lead and the commander of the sub on which Miller serves. Since it has taken me this long to get around to mentioning him, it is obvious his character isn't very interesting or even that integral to the plot. Akira Takarada is his second-in-command, and I have a nagging suspicion he was the sub commander in the Japanese edit. Honestly, it wouldn't matter which actor was the alleged lead, as both are as stiff as cardboard. Neither, however, is as bad as the dialogue they're stuck with. It is the typical drivel for this kind of thing, with every line delivered by the actors as seriously as possible, thus maximizing the potential for mockery.

The real stars are the effects, which range from cute to appalling. There were some elements that greatly reminded me of

60's cult TV show *Thunderbirds*, of which I am a fan. I especially liked the hovercar that ferries the submarine crew to and from Mondo Island when a simple raft is usually employed for such a purpose. The film opens on miniature work of the sub supposedly underwater, and it was rather beautiful, if not fully convincing.

Unfortunately, there's our real stars, the two Kongs. Oof. King Kong is a tatty suit with a raised area on the spine that is obviously concealing the zipper. The eyes in the head are stationary but covered with barely functioning eyelids. The dead eyes and constantly drooping eyelids leave one with the impression he is constantly on the verge of falling asleep. Robo-Kong fares even worse, as it is obviously a rubber suit and the actor inside can't even be bothered to move like a creature made of hinges and bolts.

King Kong Escapes is a deeply stupid film, though it can be enjoyable in parts when in the right frame of mind. It often feels like a film at odds with itself, trying to rectify disparate elements. It is an awkward coproduction of American and Japanese companies. It wants to be like a Bond movie for kids while also being a "giant things fight each other" kind of deal. It never stops feeling like it is at least two different movies failing to be smooshed together into one product and yet, in the end, it feels like you've watched less than one film.

Original version posted on 8/1/2024

King Solomon's Mines (1950)

A few decades ago, I used to be a big fan of the *Indiana Jones* series. I was all excited when the original trilogy was released on DVD, only to discover various aspects of the films now seem unpleasant and inappropriate. When the tone towards cultures outside the "first world" wasn't condescending, it was patronizing. Nowadays, I am especially taken aback by the famous scene in *Raiders* where that guy is doing all that fancy stuff with the sword, and Indy smirks while he shoots the guy dead. Not sure what has changed with me, but nowadays I'm rooting for the guy with the sword, if only to wipe that smirk off Harrison Ford's face. Well, maybe "cut" and not "wipe".

With all that said, I didn't have much hope of enjoying 1950's *King Solomon's Mines* when watching it for the first time recently. I figured it would be even less culturally sensitive than the *Indiana Jones* series 30 years later which it partly inspired. At most, I assumed I would get some cheap laughs at some sort of campy nonsense.

Instead, to my complete shock, I thoroughly enjoyed this picture. The majority of the shoot was really done in Africa, and in areas that had not been filmed in previously. There's a wealth of great location footage of scenery and all manner of wildlife. I don't think it has ever felt more appropriate to see the MGM lion preceding a film.

This feature was filmed in three-strip Technicolor, which means those massive cameras were being moved around the continent in areas where there weren't roads. Six vehicles were employed for the production: one one-ton truck and five five-ton trucks, one of which was a refrigerated vehicle. That was important not just to keep food from spoiling, but to preserve the camera negative.

The plot concerns the efforts of top-billed Deborah Kerr as she and hired guide Stuart Granger go into unexplored territory to find out what happened to her husband, who went into the area to find a lost diamond mine. Tagging along is Richard Carlson as Kerr's brother. Roughly halfway through the film, a mysterious indigenous person will join their party and, once their backstory is revealed, the movie takes a radical, but interesting, turn in the third act.

It is rare I feel wonder when watching a movie, but there were many moments here where I found myself go literally slack-jawed. There are a couple of scenes involving animals where humans are clearly in the same space with them, and I don't see how there wasn't the potential for somebody to get killed or at least severely wounded. In one early scene, two lions saunter past the party (or, presumably, their stand-ins), prompting this exchange between Granger and Kerr: "They're only dangerous if they're hungry." "How did you know they aren't hungry?" "Well, they didn't eat us."

But the single most astonishing scene is the zebra stampede. I can't believe I have not heard of this scene before, as it should be as legendary as the chariot race in *Ben-Hur*. Heck, it is even more exciting than that scene. Here, the cameras are initially holding far back from the herd of zebras as they abruptly change direction one way and the other, not unlike the way birds flying in giant flocks seem to be telepathically linked as they all somehow turn simultaneously. As I watched the herd, it dawned on me why the cameras are so far back, and that's because *what we're seeing is real* and *it is REALLY dangerous*. At a couple of points in this scene, we have the animals leaping over the ruins of a short wall our heroes are sheltering behind. I don't think anybody was killed in the filming of this picture, and I honestly have no idea how that was possible.

The startling reality of such moments throws into sharp relief some other bits that are laughable in comparison. Kerr is unaware of a giant spider on her at one point, and the thing is so stiff and pathetic that I wonder why they bothered. It is about as scary and realistic as those old Halloween decorations with that accordioned paper section you have to unfold.

Then there's the notorious scene where Kerr trims her long, auburn tresses (that are obviously a wig) into a spiffy new do that would have taken a couple of skilled professionals a long time to accomplish. Also, her character does this because she's so miserable having long hair in such heat and with the flying insects and all. I couldn't figure out why she didn't just take off the wig.

For the most part, the script has a noble perspective on wildlife. Although Granger is a guide who usually takes hunters out on safaris, he only kills animals for food or when human lives are in danger. Unfortunately, there is a scene early on where an elephant is shot and we, indeed, are seeing one really getting killed. I don't believe there are any other animal deaths shown, but I just wanted to mention this to fellow animal lovers who may not want to witness that.

But what truly stunned me was how the indigenous people are portrayed. Yes, there are natives hired for the expedition, but they are treated respectfully. Granger, in particular, is quick to shut down anybody who does otherwise: "They're not stupid, you know." His character rightfully considers these people, who have lived off these lands for hundreds of generations, to be the true experts and he seems appreciative of knowledge they pass on to him.

One last thing I want to single out for consideration is the score; namely, there isn't one. All the music here is diegetic, whether it is chanting, drumming or an isolated moment where somebody plays a marimba. I thought that was a brilliant touch.

King Solomon's Mines completely subverted all expectations I had for it. Despite being made in 1950, it is just as beautiful and exciting more than seven decades later. I certainly enjoyed it more than a particular film series it inspired three decades after it was released.

Original version posted on 3/28/2024

Modesty Blaise (1966)

Nathan Rabin used to write a great recurring piece in the *AV Club* called *My Year of Flops*. In this, he would present his musings on various unloved films from all eras of cinema. He would end each piece with the decision as to whether it was a failure, fiasco or secret success. With that in mind, I would like to declare 1966 fiasco *Modesty Blaise* fails so hard that it becomes a strange kind of success.

This movie wasn't well-received in its time. It doesn't even have a cult following today, even when no-budget movies from the 1990's shot on a camcorder seem to have found an audience.

The lack of recognition surprises me, as this seems to foretell the *Austin Powers* series, and people still seem to be referencing that all the time. Despite being made in the era parodied by those films, *Blaise* seems to be one step ahead of those and parodies itself. It is a work in the vein of *The Avengers*, though I will concede it is nowhere near as good as that classic British television show.

For one thing, *The Avengers* had the legendary Diana Rigg, who always made us aware she was in on the jokes. This movie, on the other hand, stars Antonioni muse Monica Vitti, who is horribly miscast. Being glamorous was easy for her, but she otherwise looks hopelessly lost.

It couldn't have helped that she spoke very little English. Perhaps because of this, she doesn't talk much. That doesn't, however, explain why she often seems to make expressions at random, frequently without apparent relation to other characters' lines or even the scene at hand. The resulting effect is she looks slightly insane.

Something that should have helped the movie's chances at the box office is it is based on a popular comic of the time, but I doubt fans of that series were pleased with this adaptation. In a weird touch, those books exist in the world of the movie, which would be like James Bond going to see a James Bond flick in one of the James Bond films.

I haven't seen the original print material, but the impression I get is it was like *Aeon Flux* by way of *The Avengers*. Vitti doesn't really channel the spirit of either of those. Even weirder is how her character doesn't do much of *anything* that warrants all the high praise various characters shower upon her.

Although he doesn't get much screen time in it, this is really Dirk Bogarde's film. As the villain, he is having a complete blast. Wearing a silver wig and usually twirling a parasol, he is the personification of camp. He masterminds his diabolical schemes from a Mediterranean villa where the walls are painted in various nightmarish op art patterns. His glee when initiating murderous plans is tempered by his internal torment over the theoretical children of his victims becoming orphans: "Why can't they all be bachelors?!" An intriguing quirk is a recurring bit where he is about to eat something, only to have one excuse or another for why he simply cannot do it.

Clive Revill, as his second-in-command, seems to appreciate the opportunity to eat the foods Bogarde won't. His character is always preoccupied with the costs Bogarde incurs, which reminded me of the accountant in *Fury Road*. The actor also plays

Sheik Abu Tahir, who had adopted Modesty as his most favored son, which is…a thing.

Also clearly having a good time is Rossella Falk as Mrs. Fothergill, the most dangerous person in Bogarde's organization. He brings her fresh victims to torment. Even his right-hand man finds her creepy: "Have   you   ever   wondered about *Mr.* Fothergill?" Bogarde's chipper response: "*I* am Mr. Fothergill." Her eventual demise will be very darkly humorous, and his reaction to it is weird and distinctly memorable.

Unfortunately for co-lead Terence Stamp, he fares almost as poorly as Vitti. Playing Willie, her partner-in-crime, you can see him trying hard to do something with the role, but he isn't well-served by the script. There's even a deeply horrible duet between Stamp and Vitti where they lament the fact they never partnered up in the carnal sense.

But that is the worst aspect of an otherwise solid soundtrack, even if it is overwhelmingly variations of the great theme song sung by Jonathan and David. Beware: this tune is a nuclear-grade earworm. At least it is done in a different style each time it appears, to match the tone of the scene it accompanies.

I am finding it frustrating to explain exactly why I like this movie. There's one bit I want to single out which may help convey what I find appealing about it. Vitti and Stamp need to eliminate a guard. Stamp removes his belt and it turns out, once she puts a string on it, it can be made into a bow. As we look over her shoulder, she uses this to arc an arrow through the air to…nowhere near her target. And yet, that man, without so much as an edit, suddenly has an arrow in his gut, regardless.

That moment is unexpected the first time seeing *Modesty Blaise*, yet I still laughed the two additional times I have watched it and knew it was coming. This is a strange animal, one that seems determined to keep the viewer at arm's length. Somehow, I still find much that interests me here, even if most of that material is highly unconventional. I only hope others will give this oddball, off-putting film a chance.

Original version posted on 2/12/2024

One Million B.C. (1940)

First off: this isn't that prehistoric film Hammer made in the 60's, where Rachel Welch famously wears that fur bikini. That was *One Million Years B.C.* Just wanted to get that out of the way.

1940's *One Million B.C.* comes to us courtesy of Hal Roach, a guy better remembered for his work with Harold Lloyd, the Little Rascals and Laurel and Hardy. Not exactly the guy one imagines being first pick to helm a non-comedic picture set in prehistoric times.

And yet this movie is better than the majority of similar fare in the decades that followed. I went in expecting high camp and hopefully a lot of laughs at its expense. Instead, I found myself simply watching the film and appreciating it on its own terms.

It begins in the present, with a line of people on a mountain pass during a storm. Every time there's a scene like this in a movie today, I can't help but think of Gandalf considering the dangers of taking an alternate route through the mines of Moria. I also find myself amazed by how quickly the *Lord of the Rings* pictures became a classic.

These travelers take shelter in a convenient cave. They may not be hobbits or elves, but they are still something weird: a stereotype of the Swiss people I don't think ever really existed. They are wearing vests, goofy hats and lederhosen—an ensemble perfect for waiting tables at an Octoberfest or starring in a Ricola ad.

Turns out somebody else already had dibs on the cave. There's a kindly scholar who is there studying prehistoric paintings on the walls. He proceeds to tell the visitors how the story told by the paintings might have happened. We then see, as he imagines the story, the hikers as players in this possible tale of prehistoric man.

This is an interesting way to frame the story. I like how, despite this being a tale the scholar is weaving, there isn't narration. Unlike *Clan of the Cave Bear*, there isn't much "Ooh ugh grunt grunt" dialogue and what little is there isn't subtitled. Unlike that 80's film, this picture assumes the audience is smart enough to follow what's going on without telling them explicitly. Really, it wouldn't take many changes for this to work as a silent movie.

The storyline is simple. It first focuses on the Rock People, aggressive hunters where the strongest survive. This is a society where it is every person for themselves. Victor Mature plays the son of the leader. He is exiled after a falling-out and, following a series of misfortunes, ends up floating down a river while unconscious.

Fortunately, he washes up on the banks of the community of the Shell People, a peaceful, agrarian group who believes in sharing. They can even fashion crude tools with which they are carving their history into the walls of their cave. Needless to say, these are the images which inspire the professor in the present day as he regales his guests with the story they tell.

All these new concepts are too much for Mature to take in. Sharing proves to be especially difficult for him to grasp, as we see them struggle to convince him there is plenty of food for everybody. Alas, he still can't fight his worst impulses, and he has to leave this group and return to his own people.

A besotted Carole Landis leaves the Shell People to be by his side. One of the elements of this picture I most appreciated is how the women don't have perfectly styled hair in the fashions of the time this was filmed. Not to say this movie is a complete stickler for accuracy, as one look at Landis had me wondering how cave people developed the technology of lifting and separating.

Even less accurate is the occasional appearance of dinosaurs. There are two kinds here. One is a man walking around in an obvious costume, like a cruder, less cartoony version of Barney. The other are various lizards and animals, some of which have prosthetics glued to them. The scenes with these live animals bothered me, especially when some of them fight to the death. Curiously, some of this footage would later be repurposed in a great many films, including legendary turkey *Robot Monster*.

Overall, the special effects are shockingly good. For a feature made in 1940, many of the effects have held up better than similar features from the next couple of decades that followed.

The strangest aspect of this movie is how it constantly felt like it was about to turn into a Biblical epic. For example, the imagery of Mature floating downriver on some sort of debris effortlessly brought to mind baby Moses drifting on the Nile.

My wife had an especially interesting insight while we watched this. When Mature returns to the Stone People, we see his father is now missing an eye and his right arm is withered and useless. She was wondering if this was a deliberate reference to Shanidar 1, a Neanderthal man who led anthropologists to speculate if that species took care of its old and infirm.

There is much I found to recommend in *One Million B.C.* Despite the real violence to animals, this is a smarter and better-made picture than I anticipated. Most importantly, it shows how it is never too late to learn how to share, be generous and show compassion—lessons I feel most people still need to learn today.

Original version posted on 9/2/2023

Orca (1977)

Jaws spawned so many bad imitators, but 1977's *Orca: The Killer Whale* might have the most unusual crew. The S.S. Bumpo (no, really) is captained by Richard Harris (whom I will forever associate with the horrible song "MacArthur Park"), with Keenan Wynn as his second-in-command (whom I primarily associate with *Dr. Strangelove*) and Bo Derek as…well, I'm not sure what, but she's there and wearing more clothes than in anything else I've ever seen her in. I like to think Wynn was judging all sea creatures as "preverts" while waiting for Harris to yell "Land ho! I spy a cake melting in the rain!" Nobody will mistake this trio for Robert Shaw, Roy Scheider and Richard Dreyfuss.

Harris has been trying to catch an orca to sell to an aquarium. An expert played by Charlotte Rampling keeps telling him he won't succeed, as they are too smart to be captured. I guess the specimens at places like Sea World just chose to be there, jumping directly from the ocean into the pools without any external motivation. At one point, there's a lengthy scene of a lecture she's delivering to college students in a classroom, where she talks about the sophistication of the whales' language and that they would find our comparatively primitive tongue to be "retarded". Whoa! Hold up there with that fancy-pants, high-falootin', edumacated talkin', doc!

We also learn in this lecture: "Like most human beings, they have a profound instinct for revenge." This foreshadows the integral element of the plot, where a male orca exacts revenge on Harris for killing his mate. If only Harris had listened to Derek, her voice apparently dubbed by a ten year old girl, when she says, "Do you realize whales are monogamous? We could be busting up a happy family." I imagine her character's mind being like a montage of Trapper Keeper imagery from the 80's, and her dream being to have her own pony.

The extent of the killer whale's revenge is jaw-droppingly daft. An entire seaport town is in danger of being destroyed by it unless Harris comes out into the open and fights it mano-a-flipper. I laughed hard for a looong time when it severs a pipe that carries fuel to the town, and the ignited combustible catches the village on fire and explodes its fuel tanks. The orca then does a few victory jumps out of the water while an inferno rages in the background. This thing is so smart, I wondered when it would escalate to crimes like identity theft. I was waiting for Harris to relocate to somewhere far inland (let's say Kansas) and still have the whale show up somehow: "The calls from the killer whale are coming *from inside the house!*" By the end of the picture, the whale will be doing things like shoving an entire iceberg towards Harris's ship. Given enough time, it would probably be running a multinational crime organization from a castle in the Swiss alps and threatening to use lasers to slice Sean Connery into cubes. Just imagine how different *Goldfinger* could have been: "Do you expect me to talk, Mr. Orca?" "AIEEEEE-crick-crick-AIEEEEEEEEEEAIIIIIIII!"

The effects vary wildly. Most are bad in both concept and execution, such as the moment the orca sees Harris on the prow of his ship, and we see the captain superimposed over the animal's eye. A different effect is, unfortunately, very effective, which is when the corpse of the slain female killer whale ejects a surprisingly realistic dead fetus onto the deck of the ship. Perhaps the most bizarre effect in any regard is at the beginning, when the whales romp together in weirdly composited shots that are deeply artificial. I'm still unsure whether these are dreamlike or just plain bad.

Even the music is bad, though it appears Ennio Morricone's score is widely regarded as the one saving grace of this feature. As for myself, just because the legendary composer worked on this, it doesn't mean every score of his is of equal quality. Keep in mind, he churned out such compositions at an astonishing rate. One piece of music I'm hoping everybody can agree is crap is the number that plays out over the end credits. In "My Love, We Are One", Carol Connors breathily murmurs cosmic bullshit about rainbows, moonlit waters and dawn's first light. It makes "Nights in White Satin" sound like one of Shakespeare's sonnets in comparison. Token Native American Will Sampson remarks of changing times that "even our gods dance to a new song", but I sure hope it isn't this one.

Orca just might be the worst of the *Jaws* rip-offs I have seen. I'm on the fence as to whether it is worse than the third and fourth installments of that other film's run, but it is, in the right frame of mind, as fun to mock as those. What is most peculiar is why the makers of *Jaws: The Revenge* didn't realize their movie, with its similar plot (as stated in that title), would be just as ridiculous. How strange it is that a film could rip off another, and then a sequel to the original would eventually emulate the imitator. It's like The White Stripes reuniting to do a tribute to The Black Keys.

Original version posted on 11/29/2024

Plunder Road (1957)

My wife once made a silver pendant using an interesting process called "broomcasting". The metal first is melted in a crucible, then that is poured into the bound, wet bristles of a broom. After putting the business end of the broom under water, the resulting metal has formed a random shape that was the area between those bristles.

I was reminded of this while watching 1957's *Plunder Road*, a noir where stolen gold is eventually melted down and reshaped into automotive parts. These hubcaps, bumpers and the like are then put back on the vehicle the thieves hope to drive onto a boat and smuggle out of the country.

This plan was masterminded by Gene Raymond in his first attempt at thinking up a heist. I suspect he never committed anything more significant than a minor traffic infraction before this, which makes it all the more curious he somehow came to associate with the others in the gang.

Some are ex-cons, such as Elisha Cook, Jr., who laments his long stays behind bars while married to a woman who died just before his most recent release. We never learn much about Wayne Morris, except he is a former Hollywood stuntman. His stony demeanor masks what appears to be barely restrained hostility. Steven Ritch is a former racecar driver now under a lifetime ban from the sport. Stafford Repp's character seems to have one defining characteristic, and that is his obsession with chewing gum.

It takes a while for these characters to be established. The picture opens with the theft of the gold in an interesting and complex setup that is easy to follow even without knowing in advance why we are seeing some unusual actions taken. But then we come to understand elements such as the blasting caps placed on the railroad track, as these are an audible signal for a guy on a bridge to know when to jump on the train passing under him. The weirdest element is Raymond and Cook, Jr., in the back of a truck, each nervously eyeing what appears to be a thermos suspended in the middle of the space by four long springs. That container is holding the nitro glycerin which will be used to blow open the train car. What little we hear during the heist is largely each character's thoughts in voiceover, with one thinking, "If they hit a bump, we're all angels."

The use of nitro brought to my mind Henri-Georges Clouzot *The Wages of Fear*. What happens after the heist also seems reminiscent of that picture, as the men separate into three trucks, each carrying some of the gold on a tense journey to their destination. The preparation includes staggering the times of departure, so that at least one of them should be able to make it.

They are wisely headed for Los Angeles and not the border, which is what the authorities and the media are anticipating. As Raymond says, "An idea couldn't get past the border right now." Still, there are roadblocks to contend with, not to mention the weaknesses of each man and the tensions between some of them.

We never learn much about these men, but we're given just enough background to make them feel fully realized. Cook, Jr., one of my most favorite character actors, is given a great monologue about his intention to flee to Rio with his son. He dreamily waxes about the sidewalks in that city and how they are made of colorful little tiles instead of cement. Unfortunately, his chances aren't very good, given Morris's observation: "No wonder you got sent up so many times. You think cops are dumb."

There is a great deal to love in *Plunder Road* and it is one of my most highly recommended noirs. It is lean, mean, terse, tense and intense. My attention was tightly held throughout its runtime. Afterwards, I was still thinking about these men and what more we have might have learned about them. Well, not so much the gum-obsessed Repp, who comments he's heard his habit keeps one from smoking. For the first, and likely last, time ever, here is a man who should take up smoking in order to quit his gum habit.

Original version posted on 11/6/2023

Priest (2011)

I was somehow completely oblivious to the existence of 2011's *Priest*, a big-budget action/vampire (note how I didn't use the word "horror") movie. It is unlikely I failed to miss all advertising for it at the time of its release, and yet I have zero recollection of it.

Courtesy of a budget twofer blu-ray release (where it is paired with *Legion* in a "Double Salvation" pack), I have now seen this film and it left me with some lingering questions. Just some minor, niggling details like:

In lieu of showing us material that would be visually interesting, why instead animate an extended prologue tackling the history of human conflict against the vampire hordes, reframing every conflict from the Crusades to WWI to be humans versus vampires? Why is Madchen Amick in the film for all of only about five minutes, even if it is just to be the hot mom of the girl-to-be-in-peril? What exactly was so amazing about the squad of kung-fu fighting priests that they succeeded in taming the vampire menace when all else failed? If they were so successful, why did the church disband them? If the overwhelming majority of people live in walled cities, why does the church disavow the existence of vampires, especially when they don't seem to substitute a different threat as justification for these fortresses? Why does everything in this movie look like it was stolen from other pictures, especially the cities that are about ¾ *Blade Runner* and ¼ *Brazil*? Why is there always black ash in the air and dark clouds overhead in the city, while the rest of the world becomes brightly sun-lit desert as soon as you exit the city gates? Why were the vampires put on reservations instead of exterminated, as they appear to be monsters hell-bent on destroying humanity? Also, if the church says the monsters don't exist, that seems to be another reason to finish the job. If the leaders think Paul Bettany's priest is a threat, why don't they just kill him, let alone freely let him leave the city on a jet-powered motorcycle? What is the purpose of a super-low-slung, jet-propelled motorcycle anyway, except to make sure the slightest bump in the desert wasteland turns you into a mile-long red streak? Why do people live in the wastelands anyway? With a lot of modern technology around, why is the only photo of one such family a sepia-toned thing out of the 19th century, including them wearing clothing from that period? Why does another family have a working Victrola and at least one playable 78 rpm record, when those would be extremely unlikely to survive in a post-apocalyptic world? Why do the priests have a tattoo of a cross on their foreheads, with the base extending down the bridge of the nose, when they should know how hard it is to get a good job when you have a face tat? Why do our heroes have the ability to jump impossibly high and survive great falls, when it appears they are only human? What good would it do, even when fighting vampires, to etch a cross into the bullet, especially since Bettany tells us bullets don't do anything against them? What is the point of throwing stars that are actually crosses, and isn't that kind of blasphemous? And wouldn't these be less aerodynamically sound than a perfectly symmetrical throwing star? How about the crucifix Bettany always carries, which looks a bit like a closed pair of streampunk garden shears and which has a dagger concealed inside? Why do priests in movies like this always have to read aloud some of the most famous passages from the Bible, when they damn well should have those memorized by now? How is it every single line of eye-rollingly ponderous dialogue seems to be stolen from another picture, when most of those lines weren't as bad in the source material? Why can't anybody give a straight answer to even the simplest question, instead of replying in faux-intellectual riddles? Why do the laws of physics not apply in the world of the movie in any way whatsoever, allowing things like a thrown knife to bisect an airborne bullet? What about the scene where Maggie Q throws large stones into the air, upon which Bettany bounds from one to another like he's climbing a magical staircase? What is the origin and evolution of the vampires, that they are eyeless things with huge fangs looking like discarded first-draft CGI attempts of creatures from the *Resident Evil* series? Why was Karl Urban turned into a human/vampire hybrid by the vampire queen? Why did they wait so long to do this, and why haven't they made any more of them since? What is the deal with the vampires' "familiars", who seem to be human yet have glowing eyes? Why do Urban and his crew travel around on a train? Don't they know trains can't exactly travel wherever they want and whenever? How does this train sneak into railway stations? Are there no other trains in this world and, if so, why are there still station masters? Why does Screen Gems specialize almost exclusively in garbage movies like this that, if not actually adaptations of video games, might as well be?

And yet, I haven't asked the most important questions. Ones like: why did I watch *Priest* when it was almost guaranteed to be crap? Why did I then do this huge and annoying write-up on it? Who are you and why are you reading this?

Original version posted on 4/21/2023

Robot Jox (1989)

This was the last movie I watched on Arrow Video's blu-ray boxed set showcasing five films Empire Pictures produced in the 1980's. Though they were of different genres (OK, two: sci-fi and/or horror), and made by a few different directors and other creative personnel, these had a weird aesthetic that seemed to suggest more connective tissue between them than there really was.

The last movie on the set is 1989's *Robot Jox*. It would be easy to mistake it for *Arena*, the movie immediately preceding this. That movie had different species of aliens pit-fighting on a space station. *Jox* has people in a post-apocalyptic future manning one-hundred-foot-tall robots in staged fights. Fortunately, *Jox* is as good as *Arena* was trash. It is as fun as the other film was tedious, as inventive as the other was uninspired.

I didn't realize the world needed a low-budget, live-action *Transformers* movie over a decade before Michael Bay decided to make that series of bloated, CGI-leaden, not-very-spectaculars. This older film uses practical effects such as stop-motion and miniatures, and it is all the better for it. I may have noticed the strings on occasion, but I chose to pretend I hadn't seen them. The only way to enjoy this film is to turn off your brain.

If you don't, you might find yourself asking some nagging questions. Questions such as, "Why do the pilots of the robots do all that training? I mean, it isn't like they are doing hand-to-hand combat." You probably also don't want to ask what benefit it is to one of the fighters that he has near-superhuman strength. To me, that only seems like a potential detriment, as I can imagine them accidentally crushing their machine's controls. For that matter, why even have humans controlling the fighting bots from within them? Isn't this something that could be done remotely? See, it's questions like those which are going to snuff your potential for enjoying this picture.

Once you have suspended your disbelief, you're ready for a movie where the nations of the world have consolidated into two superpowers that now only settle disputes in the robot arena. Alaska is up for grabs in the first battle of the picture. Paul Koslo fights for what seems to be most of the eastern hemisphere, while Gary Graham fights for the western world. Graham's character is named Achilles, which I thought was an odd choice. One character says, "This is Achilles's last fight", and I was left wondering why they didn't say it was Achilles's last stand. You see? Even more reasons to turn your brain off for this.

If there's one thing Achilles does, it is to behave like a heel. The government has a program to breed genetic super-soldiers and, when he is given a cup into which he is to make a "contribution" to the bank, he smirks and asks, "Can we just skip the middleman and make a direct deposit?" This is said while he is checking out Anne-Marie Johnson, who is one of this new breed of fighters. These are called the "Toobees", which only had me wondering if those who have fought are the "Not-Toobees". The idea of a female warrior is much derided, which I didn't understand since, once again, *this is somebody who will be operating a giant robot.* Not sure how physicality really impacts that ability. But that doesn't matter, as she defeats her peers in a weird jungle gym / obstacle course and becomes the next robot jock. Then Achilles comes out of self-imposed retirement and denies her that right. Jerk.

I'm sure anybody reading up to this point has assumed, correctly, the target audience for this picture is 12-year-old boys. Still, I like how the script gives Johnson a bold character with agency. When Achilles tries to swipe from under her the opportunity to fight, she drugs and impersonates him. She even puts up a good fight in the arena until being knocked unconscious, at which point Achilles runs out onto the field, saving both her and Alaska. I couldn't help but feel for Johnson, who has been denied glory. I'm also not sure how residents of Alaska may have felt, knowing their state was up for grabs.

The robots are astonishing, and there is a great deal of inventiveness in their design. It's like you can feel the giddiness of the effects people as they invented new weapons. The bad guy's bot has a retractable mace, and fists that can be hydraulically pumped like a jackhammer or which can launch off their arms like a missile. Our hero's has tank treads in its legs, and the entire structure can fold down into a tank. Both can fly into space and do battle there. For kids who had Transformers toys (or GoBots, for those who were around back in the day), it must have been like watching things from your imagination become fully realized on the screen.

But I'm hoping there were few boys who imagined their robot toys having a giant chainsaw as a surrogate penis, which the enemy bot proves to have. Sure, there was a similar development in *Tetsuo: The Iron Man*, except that wasn't a children's movie. Well, maybe it was in Japan. I don't know.

There is a lot to like in *Robot Jox* if you let yourself enjoy it. It definitely doesn't "crash and burn", a catchphrase everybody tells each other here in the spirit of "break a leg". Love it or hate it, I can at least promise you will not be bored at any point in the runtime. In my own humble opinion, *Robot Jox* rox.

Original version posted on 3/24/2024

Shazam! (2019)

My wife and I have a strong affinity with a small town in southern West Virginia named Hinton. The town has a vintage, single-screen movie theater where we eventually hoped to catch a movie, except it was never showing anything we wanted to see. Although we are not predisposed to superhero films, we finally saw a movie at The Ritz when they screened *Shazam!*.

We had a blast watching the movie, and I wondered how much of that experience was seeing it in a great theater. There aren't any theaters of this vintage (1929) in the area we live anymore, so it was amazing to see a movie in an art deco palace. Also, in my memory, there were only families in the theater with us, and it was nice to see everybody have an enjoyable evening out.

I finally watched *Shazam!* a second time recently and I am pleased to report it was as enjoyable an experience at home.

Part of why this film clicked for me, when so many superhero movies have not, is because of the focus on characters. Asher Angel plays a teenaged orphan who has ended up in a group home after escaping from, or being kicked out of, several others. This new home is filled with the expected assortment of oddball characters, notably Jack Dylan Grazer as a superhero obsessed outcast.

I should mention at this point that, in the world of this movie, superheroes are real and worshipped by the public. Angel essentially lucks into an appointment as the titular hero only because he is the last possible option. By saying "Shazam!", he toggles back and forth between his teenaged self and an adult superhero played by Zachary Levi.

This development forms a bond with Grazer, and some of the movie's best moments come from these two determining which superpowers Levi has. This type of scene is indicative of the best moments in this movie—realistic (well, action-movie realistic) characters develop in an organic manner, determining how they will function in a fantastic scenario. Similarly, the other characters in the group home eventually become more essential to the plot and, once again, through developments and plot mechanics that make sense in the world of the film.

Despite being character-driven, the movie is packed with the expected special-effects sequences. Fortunately, these don't overwhelm the picture, though I wouldn't have watched *Shazam!* based on those effects alone.

The best thing I can say about the movie is something I worry will sound flippant or dismissive, but it's the heart-felt truth: it is a very nice movie, and that is a great thing for a film to be.

Original version posted on 1/19/2023

Shazam! Fury of the Gods (2023)

I have come to begrudgingly tolerate product placement as part of modern moviemaking. At least, it's better than the ads all theatres seem to be showing before the trailers. Now, *that* I find unacceptable. Still, I wondered when placement in films would cross a line for me, and now it has in *Shazam! Fury of the Gods*. And it doesn't just cross the line, it takes a running start and tries for an Olympic broad jump record.

The offending product is Skittles, though Gatorade is prominently displayed in a few scenes. My issue with Skittles is it actually factors into a plot point, as Faithe Herman feeds some to a battle unicorn. Now there's a combination of words I never thought would exist in the English language. Herman actually tells this beast that looks like something out of *Lord of the Rings* to "taste the rainbow". My repulsion was so strong, I could have puked rainbows.

This is even after a scene where the adult version of Herman's character (Meagan Good) picks out only the yellow Skittles from a bowl of them before feeding these to their prisoner (Helen Mirren). I realize that sentence has a bit to parse, so let's get into it...

I cannot recommend seeing this movie; however, if you do, you need to see the film that precedes it. Then you'll already be familiar with this a ragtag bunch of orphans brought together under the same roof courtesy of a loving couple. Most of the kids also has an adult superhero alter-ego, these being Billy/Shazam (Asher Angel/Zachary Levi), Freddy (Jack Dylan Grazer/Adam Brody), Eugene (Ian Chen/Ross Butler) and Pedro (Jovan Armand/D.J. Cotrona). I already mentioned Herman, who is Meagan Good when in adult superhero form. There's also Grace Caroline Currey as the last of the bunch and who is, to my constant confusion, the only one of the kids to be the same actor in both of her personas.

They had obtained their powers through a wizard (Djimon Hounsou) who died in the first film but is somehow here again. Now he's a prisoner of three angry goddesses who are somehow sisters, though they are played by Helen Mirren, Lucy Liu and Rachel Zegler. The trio wants revenge on the world and...blah blah blah. They obtain the Hounsou's magic staff from the first film, etc.

As you may have guessed, I wasn't too engaged by the plot. I'm not sure it can be called a plot, unless that criteria is fulfilled by a series of events with only the thinnest of threads connecting them. Often, it seems like it wants to be a different movie from what it is. I mentioned that bit which is reminiscent of *Lord of the*

Rings. Later, Philadelphia ends up trapped under a giant dome (in a weird subplot that isn't explored much), which made me think of nothing other than *Under the Dome*. Most annoying to me was an area of our heroes' lair where the landscape is made entirely of books, including ones that fly around like birds. I didn't come here to watch some *Harry Potter* shit. With how so much seems to be lifted from other productions, I started wondering if the "tree of knowledge" that destroys the Philles stadium was a tribute to the *Peanuts* Arbor Day special.

I found the previous movie charming, despite not being predisposed to watching superhero fare. There was a goofiness to the characters and many of the plot elements had an appeal which the climatic special-effects battle with a supervillain did not. This time, it's like they decided to go all-in on the typical action movie garbage. I'm sure I am not the first to make this observation, but the title *Fury of the Gods* had me thinking of that Shakespeare line: "a tale told by an idiot, full of sound and fury, signifying nothing."

Fortunately, there are still some likeable, offbeat moments here. My favorite is probably an eternally burning violin in the lair, though nobody knows why it is there nor how it doesn't burn up. At least it keeps the lair warm. I also liked a moment where Brody is straining and grunting as he tries to keep two cars from going off a bridge. Then he goes, "Just kidding–this is super easy" and quickly pulls the vehicles to safety.

The first *Shazam* film caught me off-guard with its quirky charm. Part of why I liked it as much as I did was because I saw it in a small theatre in Hinton, West Virginia, with many families in the auditorium. It was obvious this was a special treat for them, and it was beautiful watching how happy the film left them. So, while I was offended by its sequel's crass product placement, I feel it is even more of an insult to those families for whom a night out at the movies is a rarity. I hope they opted to sit this one out.

Original version posted on 7/16/2024

Soldier (1998)

I never understood how *Starship Troopers* is supposed to be an anti-fascist film. The whole thing seems pretty "rah rah rah USA USA USA" to me. Maybe the message is clearer in Heinlein's original novel, but I haven't read it.

1998's *Soldier* came out only a year later and I feel it had what was supposedly the intended message of that other film, yet communicates it more successfully. Here is a movie that wears on its camouflaged sleeve a distrust of the military and what it will do to maintain its power.

It begins with newborns being selected for a military program which will groom them into merciless, unquestioning killing machines. I was wondering what criteria the military leaders use to pick which infants are selected for the program. The first one chosen is crying. Why select that one? Is the thinking like, "What are you crying about, you big baby? Huh? I'll give you something to cry about. I'll sculpt you into an uncaring killing machine."

We see the child at different stages of his development. As a young child, he is expressionless as he and his peers watch a fight between three Dobermans and a wild boar. Not sure what lesson is supposed to be taken away from *that*.

A couple of years later, he's leading a line of boys on a run through the countryside. One boy can't keep up with the pack, and we hear a gunshot as he is permanently removed from the program. I

was hoping this was turning into the movie of Richard
Bachman's *The Long Walk* I've always wanted, but no.

Skipping forward a couple more years, he has grown into Kurt
Russell. His group of trainees is practicing at a target range where
figures of civilians and enemy combatants move around. In a
moment of foreshadowing, Russell deliberately fires through a
civilian repeatedly in order to obliterate the enemy behind her.

Another jump to many, many years later, and Russell is a veteran
of the numerous wars tattooed on his right arm. As if he and his
ilk aren't bad enough, they are about to be replaced by a new kind
of soldier, one that is even more powerful and cruel. One of these
new killing machines will lose an eye when fighting Russell, and
yet this guy doesn't…uh, blink an eye.

The corpses of the outdated soldiers are literally discarded in the
trash. Thank God we treat our veterans with so much respect and
compassion in real life! *cough* What Russell's superiors fail to
realize is he isn't dead yet, and so he looks for a way to survive
after being dumped on a planet that is entirely one garbage
dump. Isn't it sad that, if we had access to another planet, you
just *know* we would do something like this?

Russell will discover a colony of survivors, people who seemingly
came here in order to drop out of the kind of society that would
approve of a military that does the things it does here. These are
basically hippies and, needless to say, Russell may have a bit of
trouble adjusting to their ways.

Still, it is fascinating watching him try to acclimate. In one scene,
he is eating with others, except he literally eats like a machine. He
actually lifts the spoon to his mouth in a perfect rhythm. In this
scene, Russell finally says his first line of dialogue—*almost a half-
hour* into the runtime. Even for a guy who starred in *Escape from
New York*, this is a man of astonishingly few words. And, once he

starts talking, he feels compelled to call everybody "Sir", which made me think less of a career military man than I did Marcie from *Peanuts*.

The closest he comes to befriending others is the family of Sean Pertwee, Connie Nielsen and their son. There is another guy who keeps trying to befriend him (Michael Chiklis), especially after an extremely tense scene where Russell saves him from flying into a thresher's blades that are spinning like mad from gale-force winds. The guy tries to thank Russell by giving him a scarf he's made, but he makes the mistake of startling the ex-soldier, who then tries to kill him. Russell's reaction may seem extreme but...I don't know, I think it all depends on the quality of the scarf. Homicide may be justified if it is one of those excessively long and thin hipster scarves that are useless as defense from the cold.

Exiled from the community, Russell sets up his own home in the debris. I like how this world feels fully realized even if we don't see much of it. It is like a hybrid of the prison planet from *Alien 3* and Crematoria from *The Chronicles of Riddick*. Unfortunately, the set design is augmented by some seriously dodgy CGI, though I tried to overlook this.

The community will need Russell's help when the new troops arrive on the planet as a training exercise. In keeping with the film's criticism of the military-industrial complex, those who command the soldiers regard civilian casualties as collateral damage. "What if we encounter refugees?" "Then we will classify them as hostiles."

The resulting attack on the colonists isn't just an unfair fight—the soldiers never even leave their intergalactic Humvees. The invaders are nothing more than space bullies, using a rocket to take out an unarmed civilian who has stepped forward only to initiate a conversation.

The third act gets a bit weird as Russell methodically dispatches each of the new super-soldiers. The vibe changes to that of a slasher film, where Russell is basically the Jason Voorhees here. Even weirder, he's killing *American* soldiers, so rooting for him started feeling *really* awkward.

Worst of all is this culminates in the type of one-on-one, "this time it's personal" kind of fistfight where it doesn't seem like either man is overly intent on killing the other. I refuse to believe such perfect killers as we have seen up until this point would suddenly start telegraphing their moves.

Soldier can be ham-fisted, but its heart is in the right place. That this movie is helmed by Paul W.S. Anderson, the director who gave us such garbage as the *Resident Evil* series and *Alien vs. Predator*, makes it all the more remarkable it has any heart at all.

Original version posted on 9/12/2023

Spy Hunt (1950)

The opening credits of 1950's *Spy Hunt* say it was based on the novel *Panther's Moon*. I was willing to bet good money that title wouldn't make any sense in regard to the movie it was adapted into.

I would have lost that bet. This quirky noir centers around two black panthers loose in the Alps, one of which has a top-secret microfilm sewn into its collar.

Gathered together at an inn is a curious assortment of characters trying to catch the big cats. Each person has different stated intentions, but any one of them may have ulterior motives. There's Howard Duff as the cats' handler, who just wants to get them back to the circus. Marta Toren is a spy who has been pretending to be a journalist. She's the one who put the microfilm in the collar. Another journalist at the inn is Philip Friend, and he and Toren seem to regard each other with suspicion, as if they doubt the other is in the same profession. Philip Dorn is a big game hunter who relishes the chance to take down the panthers. Robert Douglas is an artist who is only there to sketch the cats.

One or more of these characters could really be an agent for the opposition and simply looking for the microfilm. It is an interesting setup and leads to some good moments of intrigue.

Toren is clearly the star of this picture. She had been touted as the next Ingrid Bergman, but I think she looks far closer to Alida Valli, often uncannily so. What is interesting is how her character drives the entire plot, from the time she feeds a panther a meatball that conceals a sedative, through to an ending where she is the only person with a chance at defeating the enemy. Heck, the plot has Duff, our alleged hero, helpless in bed during the climatic scene.

Major highlights of the film are the action sequences. The derailment of a train car was done with miniatures so effectively that I didn't realize that's what I was seeing until I listened to the commentary track.

Although I was concerned for the welfare of the animals, I can't deny the thrill of seeing a panther leap from a cliff that appeared to be a couple of stories high. Although it didn't pounce on a stuntman from that height, you still have to feel for the guy it is dropped onto and which he then wrestles with.

I didn't think that much of *Spy Hunt* while watching it, but it has already grown in my esteem between the time it was over and when I started to write this. The dialogue doesn't have the kind of spark I expect from noir, but it compensates with a novel plot and a strong female protagonist.

Original version posted on 1/21/2024

Swamp Thing (1982)

Adrienne Barbeau is standing in waist-high swamp water after having just been rescued by a half-man, half-vegetable hybrid that is really a man in a rubber suit. Though monstrous in appearance, this gentle giant obviously wants to help her further. Instead, she dismisses him with a terse "SHOO!", which is probably among the reactions I least expected.

1982's *Swamp Thing* is full of unexpected moments like that. Some of those moments are simply surprisingly human, like Barbeau's reaction to an offer of help. Other moments are uniquely weird, such as when a beefy thug downs the formula to transform him into a superbeing, only to be reduced to the size of a midget. I had a good enough time that I was willing to overlook his clothes shrinking proportionately.

The best surprise is behind the camera, as this was written and directed by Wes Craven. I have always heard how intelligent Craven was, but I feel that rarely came across in his work. Likewise, I wouldn't have expected a film like *Last House on the Left* to come from the mind of anybody described as a gentleman.

And yet this, an adaptation of a DC comic, is where he really shows heart. I came to like these characters and felt invested in their well-being.

Before his transformation into the titular creature, Ray Wise plays a scientist heading a high-tech research facility deep in a swamp. He's trying to solve world hunger by merging together human and plant cells into a new kind of organism. Not exactly sure how whatever he grows using this technology will defeat famine. As a vegetarian, I imagine I would be aghast at eating veggies I would feel guilty consuming.

A side effect of Wise's creation is it can be used as an explosive. His sister and fellow researcher (Nannette Brown) demonstrates this by dipping her fingers in some goo and then flicking a few drops to the ground, the result being some small explosions not unlike those paper-and-gunpowder things everybody seemed to play with when they were kids. I wondered if she was going to forget she had an explosive on her fingers and unconsciously do something like smack a tabletop with her hand, but nothing doing.

It turns out the main security guy at the facility is really Louis Jourdan in disguise. His character is revealed to be an uber rich villain in the mold of those from the Bond films. He wants the formula for himself so he can use it as leverage to hold the world hostage.

He'll have an even stronger interest in it when it turns out another side effect is the transformation of Wise into a human/plant hybrid with superhuman strength. Jourdan hopes the formula will do the same for him though, like most medications, results may vary. Please refer back to the second paragraph for what happened to one of his top henchmen.

That transformation of Wise into Swamp Thing resulted from the ensuing chaos after Jourdan and his militia destroys the facility. Wise's character catches fire in what is an astounding stunt sequence ending with his body, engulfed in flames, diving into the swamp. He is initially presumed to be dead, but he has instead transformed into Dick Durock in a rubber suit. That actor's name had me wondering: pro wrestler or porn star?

Durock is actually a much better actor than I would have expected from somebody I have not heard of before. And the costume he wears is very good, as far as these things go. The facial area allows for a surprisingly wide range of expression, even when it is bit too stiff in other areas.

Where Barbeau comes into the picture is as a technician at the facility. I like how her character is an expert of some sort, though we don't get to see her do much work prior to the destruction of the lab. After that, however, we get to see her kick some ass sporadically. I like how everything she does seems possible for her to do, given her weight and physique. Go figure, her hair is similar to Sigourney Weaver's in *Aliens*, and I thought of the other actress and that movie as Barbeau fires a very big gun at one point.

Another actor who really shines here is young Reggie Batts as a kid who possibly owns his own gas station (odd how I was never certain of that). He almost immediately latches onto Barbeau and provides whatever assistance he can. Batts gets the lion's share of the movie's best lines, and his natural acting is perfect for them. Consider this response to Barbeau's inquiry as to whether there is a gun in the shop, "What kind of place do you think this is? Of course we have a gun." Then there's his response to her insistence a truck destroyed by the Swamp Thing had, in fact, hit a tree: "Must have been one of those hit-and-run trees, 'cause it's gone now."

Swamp Thing is a gloriously goofy movie. It's the kind of film where a character is killed by a literal trouser snake, when one of the baddies pulls a snake out of his pants pocket and has it bite the victim's face. I wouldn't have thought Craven would have been the right kind of person for this movie, but it turns out he was the perfect writer and director for this. It isn't just the seemingly endless types of transitions he employs to simulate the feel of reading a comic book, but more so the heart and wit he brings to fare that some might think does not require it.

Original version posted on 11/29/2023

Treasure Planet (2002)

I'm not sure how 2002's *Treasure Planet* started creeping onto my radar over the past year or so. I was only vaguely aware of it during its theatrical run, and that was only because of how much money it lost. And though I am a fan of animation, I don't usually seek out Disney's works, especially those since the studio's first golden age. Heck, I have never even seen *The Little Mermaid, Beauty and the Beast* or *The Lion King*, nor do I feel the slightest urge to do so in the near future.

To the best I can recall, I started to see it referenced in on-line articles where it was said to be experiencing a reappraisal. I guess between the legend of its failure and its potential as a lost masterpiece, my curiosity was finally piqued enough to check it out.

I now regret this.

To be honest, I did not come into this with an open mind. Obviously, the plot is that of the literary staple *Treasure Island*, except set in space. I think that is fundamentally a brilliant concept—if it had been done using means of interplanetary travel that appear to be functional.

Instead, the interstellar vehicles here are tall-masted ships of the kinds that would have been the primary means of crossing the oceans prior to the 20th century. If purpose dictates form, why use for space travel a vessel designed for floating in water?

There are some feeble attempts to justify this design, if only for the sails. These are revealed to be *solar* sails. Even if we accept that idea, is putting the sails on masts on one side of the vessel the optimal arrangement? That's not even considering how these would be of use in deep space.

Admittedly, the juxtaposition is jaw-dropping at first, if only for the audacity. Then all kinds of questions started nagging at me. While the ships use artificial gravity, how is there an atmosphere? The ship crews would need not just air, but also atmospheric pressure, to keep their eyeballs from exploding and the blood from boiling in their veins. Now *there's* a Disney movie I want to see!

Something which might have helped sell this concept is if it was animated in a different style. This might (*might*) have worked if a less realistic style had been employed. This could have been a beautiful work if done in the style of mid-century animation.

Alas, the hand-drawn characters typical of that era of Disney are set inside photo-realistic worlds. CGI was used extensively to accomplish this, which results in even more offenses. I'm going to attempt to side-step the usual CGI bashing to point out specifically why it doesn't work here.

First, those hand-drawn characters often seem to be occupying a different space than the backgrounds. One character, the duplicitous John Silver, is a composite of cel and computer animation, with his missing body parts replaced with robotic components. That's an interesting idea in theory, except I swear those elements don't fully mesh together at times.

Secondly, cel animation tends to be timeless because, although it is a technology, it is primarily an art. I'm not one of the luddites who believes there isn't an art to CGI, because there is. However, that *is* a technology first and foremost. Since that technology seems to be improving at an exponential rate, few things date a film worse than the extent of computer animation used in it.

That is especially true of the extent to which the CGI strives for photo-realism. Similar to my earlier comment regarding the realism of the cel animation, CGI works best the more abstract it is. I know many, many people think *Tron* is ridiculous, especially as regards the quality of its computer visuals. Myself, I think the low-polygon look of it is so unrealistic that it achieves a curious sort of timelessness. *Treasure Planet* suffers from the exact opposite effect.

Even more annoying to me than the space "ships" is the visual aesthetic of the entire picture. Why does everything have the appearance of 18th century British sea ports? There's a book that is essentially just another screen except it has pages that can be turned. There's a device that looks like a pocket watch but which shows holograms. So, why would the various worlds we see here all adopt this style while also having aliens, robots and spaceships? This sticks in my craw in the same way most steampunk stuff annoys me, and I suspect for similar reasons.

And I haven't even discussed the characters yet (at least, not their personalities). Oh lord, these are largely annoying.

Our hero is a petulant teenage boy who appears to believe he is the only person in the world whose father abandoned him. The movie opens with him as a younger boy full of boundless energy and enthusiasm. As soon as we're shown the "12 years later" caption, I knew we were in trouble. It doesn't help that text is over footage of him doing stunts on a hoverboard in a way that reminded me of snowboarders from Mountain Dew commercials of the time.

I mentioned John Silver before, and he is probably the strongest character here. Unfortunately, his buddy is an endlessly morphing, comic-relief alien named "Morph". The mimicries of this little pest wore on me fast.

But not as quickly as the antics of a robot voiced by Martin Short. Fortunately, he isn't in the movie until near the end of the second act, but that was more than enough time to spend with him. He's a bit like Bender from *Futurama*, if that robot had been unceasingly chatty and self-deprecating. I kinda wish Bender would have shown up and pounded this robot into a tiny metal cube.

There are some characters I wish we had spent more time with. Emma Thompson is second-billed, but the cat-like captain she plays never seems to have much to do. David Hyde Pierce plays the dog-human hybrid thingy named Dr. Doppler, who is the kind of bumbling genius Disney typically employs to good effect in their fare. Here, he has a few moments before being relegated to the background. The pairing of Thompson's and Pierce's characters at the end felt both inevitable and unnecessary, as if the movie didn't know what to do with them and eventually just shrugged and went, "Maybe if these two hooked up...?"

Oh, and there's an alien of a species that communicates only through farting noises produced by the assorted tubes hanging off its body like limp penises. Oh goody, there's the opportunity for endless fart jokes (commence eye roll). I found it odd Dr. Doppler can communicate with the alien by making similar sounds, largely by using his armpits. He explains to our hero that he is fluent in "Flatueese". Strange, but I found it offensive those who are not of that species have labelled its language as being like our unintended gaseous discharges. If this movie had been more successful, maybe there would be a porn parody with female aliens who must be communicated with in "Queefeese".

Despite my earlier digs at both types of animation employed here, I must say some of the conceptual pieces here are quite stunning. Best of all is the titular destination, a world encircled by two rings set at right angles from each other, forming an X around the planet. I thought it was neat how, even in space, X marks the spot.

One of the first things we see upon setting down on that planet are impossible trees. The tops are large and look heavy even if they seemingly float in the air like clouds. Long, thin trunks, like strings, seem to do little more than tether those tops to the ground. Seeing these, it occurred to me how odd that there hasn't been an animated film styled on the works of Roger Dean, that guy who did all those great album covers for Yes in the 70's. I'm going to dub this planet Rogerdeanicus.

Unfortunately, I couldn't turn my mind off long enough to ignore how inane so much of this seems. I'm glad I was watching this at home with only my wife, as I dropped quite a few loud WTFs during its runtime. Why are there barnacles on the underside of the ship? Where did they come from? Why would something in space even have an underside? What the hell are these space whales? What do they eat and how do they breathe? They spout water, so where did that water come from?

My better half, on the other hand, kept making wisecracks throughout *Treasure Planet*, all of which were references to *The Goonies*. So, what do we find in the treasure room on the planet when it is discovered? Why, it's the remains of a pirate ship, where the skeleton of its alien captain still sits on his throne, its skull having multiple oracular sockets. Her priceless comment: "I thought it would be One-eyed Willie, but it's Six-eyed Willie."

Original version posted on 9/19/2023

Winter Kills (1979)

It is said the best parody is indistinguishable from the genuine article, but I'm not sure I buy that. If that's true, then every movie that tries to play it straight but doesn't succeed can simply be passed off as parody. That's the way I feel about the critical reassessment of *Showgirls* that has been forming over the past decade or so.

It is also what 1979's *Winter Kills* tries to pass itself off as in the supplementary features on the blu-ray. I'm not sure if the movie is smart enough to be a deeply subversive comedy. All I know is it is such a bizarre mess that I found a lot to laugh about. I just don't know if I was laughing with it or at it. Sometimes, it seemed like it was genuinely trying for laughs. At other times, I felt it was trying to earnestly float some particularly daft ideas past the viewer.

The plot is a very thinly veiled spin on the Kennedy assassination and the resulting conspiracy theories. Nineteen years prior to the present day in the film, the stepbrother of Jeff Bridges was shot by a sniper in Philadelphia. A dying man who claims to be a second sniper puts Bridges on the hunt for the rifle he used in the assassination, and which is now hidden in a steampipe. The discovery of that gun puts in motion the gears for intrigue.

I am a big fan of 70s conspiracy thrillers, so I was excited about seeing this. The opening credits are boilerplate for the genre, text in a medieval font over images of a chess game in progress.

But I felt my expectations slipping early on, as things quickly became ridiculous. At the ranch of his wealthy father (John Huston), there's a montage of Bridges riding a horse through a variety of panoramic vistas, accompanied by a swelling orchestral score, just so he can apparently get far enough away from dad to confidently yell, "YOU STINK!". There's his French girlfriend, who so wildly fakes an orgasm it's like watching a fish flopping around as it asphyxiates outside of water. There's Bridges's encounter with Sterling Hayden's military figure on his "playground", only to find his car surrounded by tanks and given 30 seconds to leave before they will start firing on him–which they do.

Special shout-out to Huston for his performance here. If anybody went into this believing they were making a comedy, it had to be him. In his Bizarro-world take on Joseph Kennedy, I could probably count on my fingers the number of lines he says *without* profanity in them. The first time we see him, he's leading a convoy of golf carts, each driven by an old man with at least one young woman in fur by their side. He asks Bridges, his *son*, if he thinks these lovely ladies in his cart are playing with his nuts.

Bridges, on the other hand, deserves the most credit and that is for playing his role in the exact opposite way. He is the straight man to the insanity surrounding him, and he is as solid and dependable as he has been throughout his career.

I would also like to single out Anthony Perkins for his role as the manager of Huston's monstrous document archives and intelligence center. When we first see Perkins, he is on a set that could only be appropriate for a Bond villain in one of that series' more outrageous offerings. Perkins hams it up appropriately for the surroundings. When Bridges has to resort to violence to get the info he needs from Perkins, it seemingly channels, and is as hilarious as, the Black Knight sketch from *Monty Python & The Holy Grail.*

I think the best way I can convey the experience of watching this film is to rattle off some more of the many insane moments. Such as Bridges defending himself from an assassin disguised as a maid, who tries to throw him off a balcony, but instead gets her blouse torn open. Such as Huston knowing the exact number of times his Presidential son got laid while in office. Such as an extremely belligerent doorman for a fancy apartment building who won't stop yelling about how the place is "Four floors of nothing but ugly people!". Such as Bridges's girlfriend finding the loophole in a restaurant's policy of not admitting women in trousers by whipping hers off. Such as a character giving somebody financial advice while falling to their death.

Winter Kills is garbage, whether it was meant to be parody or if it is just a trashy conspiracy thriller. And I had an awesome time. I wasn't bored for a single minute. This may be the worst movie I can honestly recommend for everybody.

Original version posted on 5/19/2023

Science Fiction
(usually light on the science)
The section about science fiction movies

20,000 Leagues Under the Sea (1954)

I love the movie *Cabin Boy* and it is partly because of the weird sub-genre of cinema it lovingly parodies. The 1954 Disney version of Jules Verne's *20,000 Leagues Under the Sea* is very likely one of those inspirations. It has a large creature, albeit a giant squid and not a giant store manager. It may not have Chris Elliott forced to dance to entertain a ship's crew, but it has Kirk Douglas do a song and dance for the same, and the number is actually a pretty funny one, to boot.

What confused me initially is the film opens in what looks to be a wild west town. When Kirk Douglas first appears, he has a saloon dancin' floozy on each arm, and I like to think those women weren't cast, but that Douglas just happened to bring them with him. As happens in such a town, somebody will get punched and fly through a window and, since Douglas is there, it is a given he'll be the one to throw that punch. Memo to self: if I ever find myself in a wild west town, keep to the middle of the streets. There's less flying glass there.

We'll soon learn this is a seaport where Paul Lukas and Peter Lorre had arrived in hopes of recruiting people for a scientific expedition to hunt a sea monster that has been sinking vessels. It is obvious to the viewer, regardless of one's familiarity with the source material, the menace is mechanical. Still, it is a watercraft stylized to give the appearance of a monster, with green, glowing windows in the front that look like giant eyes, and iron embellishments along the top like the spines of some prehistoric beast.

This is the *Nautilus* and James Mason is our Nemo for this iteration of the oft-told story. Mason is solid as expected in this role, despite close-ups revealing his beard appears to be some sort of black spongy material that looks patently fake.

The inside of the ship is a steampunk wet dream, and I keep forgetting the fetishization of wood, brass and giant glass gauges happened long before it became a modern trope. There are also those great diving suits with the giant helmets that makes the wearer look like they're hunting for a tiny treasure chest, the kind with a lid that that is lifted up periodically by a stream of bubbles.

Instead, Mason has his crew hunting for various foodstuffs the sea provides. At the first dinner aboard the ship, Douglas reveals the only utensil he knows how to use is the knife, but we're denied the opportunity to see him try to use that to eat soup. Instead, he, Lukas and Lorre squirm as they consume a menu of various gross things from the ocean. I think the pudding was pureed unborn octopus, which made me wonder why anybody would even consider making such a dish. Douglas is repulsed when he discovers the cream he is about to consume is milk from a sperm whale, but at least it wasn't sperm from a sperm whale.

In his first venture out of the sub, Douglas finds and returns with a great deal of treasure in the material sense. He gets a reaming from Mason for not getting food as instructed. Mason throws open a door to reveal a treasure room so overflowing it would give Scrooge McDuck an aneurysm. The captain somehow simultaneously regards material wealth as useless while taking up valuable space with a great quantity of the stuff.

That isn't Mason's greatest contradiction, as he has been destroying military watercraft as an act of pacifism. I have always wondered whether Captain Nemo's use of violence to achieve peace was meant to be a dig at pacifists. That element in a movie made less than a decade after the conclusion of WWII feels especially suspect.

The technological advances in the film are interesting. It appears the ship is atomic powered. It's that or powered through psychedelic light shows, given the groovy, colored flashes of light we see through the many tiny portholes into the energy chamber. I guess you're going to need a lot of steam for that giant pipe organ Mason has also installed. When you're a villain, nothing less than a pipe organ will do when you're playing "Fugue in D Minor". It just doesn't sound as intimidating on an accordion.

Nor would it sound as good coming from the banjo Douglas fashions from a turtle shell as the body. The neck looks like the spine of some sort of creature with vertebrae perfectly sized as to make frets. I'm still wondering what he used as strings. He uses this to serenade a trained seal which, while cute, is the clearest evidence you're watching a Disney film.

The effects are very good for the time. Given this is a Disney production, I was surprised there weren't any animated touches, or at least none that I noticed. There's great matte painting work, which I always appreciate. There's also good miniature work that, while often not completely convincing, at least uses large scale models that allow for more detail. And I'm still wondering if nascent bluescreen technology was used for a bit where fishes "swim" between us and Lukas looking out through a porthole, though there obviously isn't any water between that window and the camera.

I enjoyed *20,000 Leagues Under the Sea*, though not quite as much as I hoped I would. It's hard to say where the fault lies, as I appreciate the types of effects employed here and the casting is pretty good. Maybe it is that this is a story I've seen done too many times already. Face it: even Disney essentially remade it in space for *The Black Hole*.

One last thing: I'm strangely bothered that the sounds in the *Nautilus* are all those we expect a sub to make, except Nemo's vessel is supposed to precede submarines and so would not have any standards to follow. At least there's never a sonar ping, but I wouldn't have been too surprised if there had been one.

Original version posted on 11/25/2024

9 (2009)

The following was originally posted on a now long-defunct web forum, in reaction to a fellow member's claim I spoiled the movie District 9 *in a review.*

Please read the following agreement before reading my review. I need each reader to agree to the terms and not complain afterwards that they were unaware of the nature, and impact, of this critique.

You, the reader, agree to not file complaints, grievances or civil suits against Place Logo Here or the representative organization, Place Logo Here Ltd.

The author, Place Logo Here, offers this review for entertainment purposes only, and does not receive financial compensation or sexual gratification in return for this document. The reader must acknowledge that he or she is at least 18 years of age (or, at least, possesses a fake ID saying as much), carbon-based and at least as tall as this sign before riding this attraction.

Place Logo Here Ltd. grants to Lessee, at no additional cost to Lessee, the right to use such items of the existing furniture, data/voice wiring, and approximately 196 cubicles owned by Lessor and currently located in the Building as of the date hereof ("Lessor's FF&E") that Lessee elects to use. An inventory of Lessor's FF&E is attached hereto as Exhibit "B." Except for the cubicles which shall remain in the Building,

WHEREAS, the board members are qualified to perform the Study and such performance would further the board's instructional and research objectives;

WHEREAS, Place Logo Here Ltd. desires the board members to perform, and the board members desire to so perform, the Study on the terms set forth herein;

NOW THEREFORE, in consideration of the promises and the mutual covenants and conditions hereinafter recited, the parties do hereby agree as follows:

1.0 DEFINITIONS.

For purposes of this Agreement:

1.1 "CFR" means the United States Code of Federal Regulations.

1.2 "FBI" means "Female Body Inspector", as defined by 12-year-old boys.

1.3 "Confidential Information" has the meaning set forth in Section 10.2.

1.4 "Discoveries" has the meaning set forth in Section 13.1.

1.5 "Effective Period" has the meaning set forth in Section 2.3.

1.6 "FDA" means the United States Fudd and Duck Administration, as overseen by Elmer Fudd and Daffy Duck.

The Party of the First Part is the Party of the Second Part. The Parties have expressed their mutual intention that the Project be promptly completed, and, to that end, it is the responsibility of the Project Group to ensure that the Parties use their reasonable best efforts, equivalent to the same level of attention and care they devote to their other businesses and products. All parties agreed to the removal of the Sanity Clause.

WHEREAS, pursuant to the Originator, the Trust will Grant to the Trustee Receivables, as trustee all of the Trust's Originators, Sellers and Trusts, to and under the Indenture and the other assets of the Trust. WHEREAS, during such time as the, the Seller, the Trust or the Indenture Trustee owns or has an interest in the Person, such Custodian or Persons shall be referred to herein as the "Receivables Holder," and the Custodian shall hold all Receivables for the benefit of the Originator, the Seller, the Trust and the Indenture Trustee during such time as such Trust is a Custodian Holder. WHEREAS, in connection with the foregoing, the parties hereto desire therefore to provide for the custody and management of the Trust pursuant to the Purchase Agreement, the Sale and Servicing Agreement and the Indenture (each, a "Transfer"). WHEREAS, the Custodian is a maintenance engineer regulated by the Comptroller of the Currency of the United States. WHEREAS, the Originator, the Seller, the Trust and the Indenture Trustee, during such time as each such Person is a Receivables Holder, desire to have the Department of the Redundancy Department (i) hold the Bureau of Superfluous Departments as custodian for each such party, (ii) take possession of the Contracts and the Receivable Files related to the Receivables.

Nothing in this Agreement in any way precludes Place Logo Here Ltd. from supporting, developing, distributing, promoting, using, selling, or licensing any software products or any product or service that distributes or promotes any software; however, the parties understand and agree that the fund may only be used to fund Place Logo Here Ltd. initiatives as more fully described below which are designed to promote Place Logo Here Ltd. products.

Sign here: _____

Thank you for that little formality. And now, my review:

I liked it

Alien from the Deep (1989)

There are a great many movies I have seen only because they were featured on an episode of *Mystery Science Theatre 3000* or *Rifftrax*. It is rare I see a movie deserving of, but has yet to receive, that treatment. Such is the case with 1989's *Alien from the Deep*.

And that isn't to say there's a lack of entertainment value to be found in this Italian-made sci-fi/adventure movie filmed in the Philippines. For the most part, this is a competently made film, which makes the batshit plot, poor dialogue and subpar special effects that much more baffling.

The picture begins with two Greenpeace members sneaking onto an island where an evil corporation will do anything to protect their secret operations. Well, anything except eliminate the many people who live there, including the indigenous people, a missionary and a man who collects snake venom. The company isn't worried about any of these people, but they will readily open fire on any boat that approaches the shore.

This complete disregard of logic amazes me. The guy who collects snake venom (Daniel Bosch) says he sells it for big bucks to pharmaceutical companies, but how does he deliver the product to them if the island is under siege from a military-style operation? The missionary lives in a stunning, multi-story treehouse that is like something out of *Swiss Family Robinson*. He definitely isn't conducting a covert operation, so why is he allowed here? How do supplies get to him and the natives?

As for the natives…hoo boy. These poor souls wear giant African masks of the like I haven't seen since misguided adventure movies of the 1950's. And yet, they are donning those while wearing jeans and corduroy slacks. They're like the primitive tribes of The Gap.

E-CHEM, the evil corporation controlling the island, is dumping nuclear waste into an active volcano, resulting in a beam of pure energy shooting into outer space. I wondered why they don't simply dispose of the waste through any other method, as a volcano does not sound like the best receptacle. And that "beam of pure energy" bit is stupefying. I wasn't sure if that was the goal or just a side effect. Whatever the intention, it isn't mentioned again.

This is twice as weird when one takes into account the title has "alien" in it. Seems to me, a beam of energy shot into space might summon a visitor from there but, no, the creature actually comes through the ocean floor. This happens far later in the picture than I would have expected. I wasn't keeping track, but it felt like an hour had passed before it is introduced. Even then, it feels like a subplot.

For most of the runtime, the most we see of the alien is one huge arm, which ends in a claw. We will see only that one arm so many times that I was reminded of the giant hand used throughout *Attack of the 50 Foot Woman*. It's like, "Godammit, we dropped a bundle for this giant claw and *we're gonna show the shit outta it!*"

One weird aspect of that appendage is it has some sort of industrial tubing as its exoskeleton. I know they were ripping off Giger's design for *Alien*, but I started to get the impression this was meant to be some sort of mechanical creature (or, at least, a hybrid of organics and mechanics). This feeling was compounded by the jets of steam that always accompany appearances of this creature, as if it is somehow both the xenomorph *and* the Nostromo from that movie.

When we do get to see the alien in its full splendor, it is genuinely impressive. Although miniatures were used for some brief shots, the entire thing stands a couple of stories tall. This is only at the end of the movie, and most of what we had seen up to this point had set the bar very low. Probably the worst effect is a rumbling volcano that looks like a child's unsuccessful entry in a science fair.

That isn't to say it is a badly made film. On the contrary, it is surprisingly well-shot. It is almost as if it was made by highly competent technical people who weren't used to directing actors and writing dialogue.

This is evident through such bizarre dialogue as: "Don't touch me, you snake squeezer! You're all alike!" All snake squeezers are alike? In what way? How many does the speaker know, anyway? On the other hand, the guy to whom this is said is pretty strange. Among other traits, he spits tobacco at snakes as a deterrent. In one scene, he yells, "Hurry! There's enough snakes down there that it would take a whole plantation of chewing tobacco to keep them away." It's like this picture was scripted not only by people whose first language isn't English, but by aliens doing an anthropological study of the human race from a very far distance away.

There is one aspect of this production I must give unqualified praise for, and that is the use of great locations, wherever this was filmed. One especially interesting location is a tunnel with a seemingly impossible number of chains hanging from the ceiling, as well as innumerable ones covering the floor.

Alien from the Deep is not a good movie, exactly, but my standards are lax enough that I found plenty to enjoy here. It has a certain "making it up as we go along" vibe that won me over–almost as if somebody took a rambling story told by a group of kids and then made a movie out of it. I just wish those kids had known how to write better dialogue.

Original version posted on 8/16/2023

Apollo 18 (2011)

The Atari 2600 had some gloriously batshit titles. For example, there was *Communist Mutants from Outer Space*, which is actually an incredibly solid game, almost in spite of the silly name.

2011 found footage sci-fi horror film *Apollo 18* has aliens bent on such mayhem as destroying our flag. And this is near a crater where it turns out the Russkis secretly placed their own lander; ergo, there just might be Communist mutants in outer space.

This is a pretty stupid movie, in spite of an interesting premise. The idea is there was one additional, secret mission after Apollo

17. This one was supposedly top-secret, and entirely for the Department of Defense, so you just know it isn't going to go well. It should be a given the top priority will *not* be the successful return of the crew.

The two astronauts in the lander set up a flag and transmitters. They also set up cameras, as has been done since Apollo 11. As indicated by the text at the bottom of the image from one such camera, these devices are also motion-detecting, which I think would raise some suspicions from the crew.

In addition to finding the Russian lander, they find a deceased Cosmonaut. There is a suspicious cut in his spacesuit, and the helmet had a hole and large cracks in the glass. What killed him will be revealed to be spider-like things that disguise themselves as rocks. Those things are shoddy CGI but, even if they have been rendered completely realistically, I still would have found the concept too laughable to believe.

The moon critters, as I believe they should be dubbed, slice into spacesuits and then into the person inside them. This leaves a nasty infection, apparently because of moon germs. I seriously doubted that was a possibility and assume somebody was just influenced by the Joe Farrell jazz album *Moon Germs* (which has an awesomely freaky cover, by the way). Also, as the moon has only the most tenuous of atmospheres, wouldn't that person be dead almost immediately after the suit is compromised?

As I mentioned earlier, this is in the found footage style. Filmmakers tend to regard that as an opportunity for a cheap and relatively easy way to make a feature film. Critics seem to largely consider the genre to be a lazy way to make a movie.

This picture shows how difficult it is to do found footage right. Once again, it appears acting like a completely ordinary human being is the hardest thing to do. From the first scene, where an astronaut is being interviewed on camera, I didn't buy any of the performances. And these guys are playing *astronauts*. Have you ever noticed how, despite their accomplishments, that group tends to not have the most dynamic personalities? Kubrick seemed to clue in on that in his direction of the actors in *2001*, where an on-board computer has more personality than any of them.

As for found footage being an inexpensive approach to moviemaking, I was baffled by the 10 minutes of closing credits. How could that many people have worked on something like this? I didn't pay them much attention, but I suspect the greatest number of people worked on CGI, yet the results aren't remarkable. And even with how slow this text crawl goes by, the runtime couldn't cross the 90 minute threshold.

I also had significant issues with the nature of the "found" footage here. Every second of it has to ring true for the production to be successful. It should stand up to scrutiny as to how the footage you're seeing was gathered and explain how we are seeing that now. Since much of what we see was captured on *film*, that means it had to get back from there to here. Also, to have adequate coverage for the movie, there need to be many cameras and, damn, did they ever bring a ton of them along. I was surprised there was still room for the crew in the lander. And there's a couple of instances of the obligatory, "We need to record this for the record" statements, as if that is adequate justification for everything little thing being captured on film.

Consider the astronaut interviews at the beginning of the picture. If this was supposed to be a top-secret mission, it doesn't make much sense for there to be the typical interviews and footage of mission preparation that were produced for the previous missions, as that material would have been created for the purpose of publicity. This mission wouldn't have any publicity, and there doesn't seem to be much reason to even preserve it for posterity. As the first man to set foot onto the lunar surface on this mission says, "I prepared a speech, but nobody would hear it anyway."

The one thing I can give credit for is a couple of decent jump scares. One of these has a good setup, where one astronaut goes into a cave, using only what is essentially a flash bulb for light. The result is akin to trying to go into a completely dark space with only an old flash camera to see your way. All we can see are the briefest glimpses of small areas of the space.

The Russian mission amused me in a couple of ways. One, their lander is like if somebody took the standard Apollo lander and did a slightly steampunk spin on it, as if Jules Verne was their mission commander. Also, I found it preposterous their ground control was still monitoring communications from their long-defunct lander, and yet they immediately respond to a distress signal from it.

I first saw *Apollo 18* in a theatre in its original run. I remember being unimpressed, but don't recall it being as god-awful stupid as I found it this time around. For those who are still curious, I ask you keep two considerations in mind. First, remember this footage had to somehow come back to Earth. Second, what did the moon critters eat before we came along?

Original version posted on 10/9/2024

Attack of the 50 Foot Woman (1958)

Hell hath no fury like a 50-foot-tall woman scorned. At least, that's what 1958's *Attack of the 50 Foot Woman* would have us believe.

Allison Hayes plays the titular character. Before her transformation, she was in a bad way. For reasons unclear to me, she still loves her scheming, greedy, adulterous husband (William Hudson). He doesn't even try to conceal his indiscretions. Also, while I can't be the best judge of what most women may be looking for in a man, her passionate love for this jerk must be blind *and* deaf. I suspect the other three senses must also be deadened. He looks like he would smell bad and feel oily.

Hayes will have a couple of encounters with an alien craft and the giant within. I'm going to guess a weather balloon was used for the ship and I laughed for a long time when my wife and I simultaneously shouted, "ROVER!" Anybody who doesn't get that reference is proof public schools have failed us all (go watch UK 60's tv show *The Prisoner*—now).

Out of the ship emerges a 30-foot (according to her estimate) giant that reaches for the large diamond around her neck. Mind you, all we see of the giant is a deliriously bad, yet very large, prop hand. We'll see that hand a lot in this movie.

We'll also see a lot more of the "diamond" around her neck which she claims the giant was reaching for. This comically large stone is obviously just glass. In fact, it looks like it came off a chandelier, which I suspect was its origin. And yet it is allegedly the Star of India.

She will flee the giant unscathed on this occasion, though the story of the encounter will further convince the local populace she's a nut job. This will give her husband additional fuel to have her committed, another potential route to getting his mitts on her fortune. She had been in a sanitarium once before and that was for headaches. Yep, having headaches was justification enough to put a woman in an asylum back then.

She's even mocked on the only TV channel that seems to exist in the world of the movie, and the only program at any given time is alleged "news" where the sole newscaster makes snippy, bitchy remarks based on local gossip. That station's ID is KRKR-TV which, when said aloud, sounds like "Cracker TV". Hey, I have a new name for Fox News!

I was shocked by the weird lapses in various characters' logic. When the sheriff tells his deputy about Hayes's encounter with a flying saucer and a giant, the deputy was only surprised by news of a giant. I guess this must be flying saucer country, where such encounters are taken for granted.

Then there's the sheriff's speculation that, if the giant was going for her diamond necklace, it must have been one of those legendary desert tramps. Do they often encounter 30-foot-tall desert tramps? And does the populace frequently wear large diamonds around their necks that attract the inordinately large hobos?

She will not be so fortunate on her second encounter with the giant. We actually get a look at the giant this time, and he looks like a bald Steve Buscemi. Subpar effects work also makes him semi-transparent every time we see him. Later, when we see more of the giant, we'll see he is inexplicably clad in a little bit of leather that looks like a costume for a soldier in the Roman army. No idea what that's about.

Also, aside from it being the result of bad effects, I would love to have the filmmakers strain to provide an explanation for a car which becomes transparent when the giant picks it up. Never mind the vehicle also changes to a different make and model— one a couple of decades older.

Not sure what in the second encounter finally did it, but the result is Hayes finally fulfills the destiny in the title. This growth happens while she is in her bedroom. We never see the entire bedroom, but she apparently doesn't exceed the dimensions of it until she decides to break out through the ceiling. Is this bedroom the size of a small aircraft hangar? Also, why is the debris from the destruction of the house several pieces of freshly milled lumber?

I'm not sure what she is supposed to be wearing when she goes on a rampage around town, but she is pretty modestly clad. Guess whatever principles of physics keeping The Incredible Hulk from going completely au natural applies to her, too.

It isn't much a rampage, either, except for tearing the roof off a bar. She comes to suffer from what I have deemed "Space Giant Malady", wherein she also becomes transparent when dropped into scenes. The only part of her that directly interacts with people is that same stupid, oversized fake hand from earlier–only now it doesn't have hair on it.

The destruction of the bar reminds me I forgot to mention Yvette Vickers as Hudson's action on the side. This is one rough looking character. I believe this is somebody that has been around the block a few times, and it is a big block with nothing on it except liquor stores and smoke shops.

Nothing I have said really conveys how odd it is to watch *Attack of the 50 Foot Woman*. It is so consistently daffy that I couldn't help but think some of it has to be tongue-in-cheek. Maybe all of it was—it's just so difficult to tell what was intentionally funny or not that I couldn't determine if it was brilliant or idiotic. I'd say that, regardless of how one interprets it, you will likely have a great time watching this.

Original version posted on 6/28/2023

The Beast with One Million Eyes (1955)

I suspect some people believe I am too hard on most of the movies I write about. From my perspective, I think I am more lenient on some pictures than the majority of critics. At least, I try to find something, *anything* I can say I liked in each film I see.

1955's *The Beast with a Million Eyes,* in my opinion, has been subjected to excessively harsh reviews. That was the case on its original release, and I haven't found evidence of a subsequent critical reappraisal. As I write this, the consensus for this picture on IMDB is at 3.7 out of ten. I would kick that up at least a whole number.

Typical of sci-fi movies of that era, it is set in the desert. In the opening narration, Paul Birch gives the audience a bleak assessment of his life. His farm has failed each of the past three years. He tells us he's a failure—at least, that's what his wife tells him. Using language that is more poetic than I expected in such fare, he describes the desolation surrounding his property, and how death awaits a short distance in any direction.

Once we have met his wife (Lorna Thayer), I had no doubt she has frequently told him he is a loser. She is so filled with angst and unfocused hatred that she might even tell him that every hour, on the hour. She even shrieks openly about how much she hates their daughter (Dona Cole) for being young, pretty and having her life ahead of her.

In keeping with some weird unspoken rule of films of any vintage, Cole does not look as young as I believe the picture wants us to think she is. I'm guessing she's supposed to be a teenager. She looks somewhere between 25 and 30, depending on the lighting. At least, there doesn't seem to be a wide enough gap in ages for Thayer (36 at the time) to be her mother.

The other resident on the farm is Leonard Tarver as a mute man who does work for them in exchange for a trailer and food. Supposedly, nobody knows his name, so they just call him "Him". I noticed Birch calls "Him" Carl when talking to the man directly, and I'm not sure why the others don't do the same. Something seems cold about depriving a man of any moniker.

Rounding out this small cast is Duke, Cole's dog and another object of her mother's hatred. Cole's boyfriend is played by Dick Sargent, and his appearance here is roughly a decade before his star-making turn on *Bewitched*. Chester Conklin plays a funny, nice old man who just wants to get his itchy back scratched and possibly get some milk out of his stubborn cow. Alas, that cow will eventually stomp him to death.

You see, *something* passed over the area earlier in the day and now the animals have started attacking people and power transformers. It isn't much of a coordinated attack—the flocks of attacking birds are largely just shots of somebody out-of-frame throwing the birds towards the camera. That said, without even seeing his picture, you already know it has to be approximately one million times better than *Birdemic*.

Alas, Duke seems to go rabid, finally giving mom an excuse to off him—*with an axe!* You *really* don't want to mess with this lady.

Anywho, all those animals make up the "one million eyes" of the title, though I'm betting a meticulous tally would reveal an overstatement of the creatures by roughly 999,974. I can't recall an "animals attack" movie older than this one, though that isn't one of my favorite sub-genres, so I'll admit I haven't seen many of them. The bird attacks seem to foretell Hitchcock's *The Birds* nearly a decade later.

I like the scene where the alien craft causing this mayhem passes over the house. We see it from indoors, as the image darkens considerably. A high-pitched squeal accompanies it, shattering the glass coffee pot Thayer is holding. We learn later it broke all the glass inside the house and even the windows. There's a moment I like where Thayer goes to a shattered display cabinet and takes out a particular vase that's broken. Her expression tells us this was important, and I felt some sympathy towards her.

Alas, one of the many minor gaffes in the feature occurs a couple of minutes later, with the inexplicable restoration of the cabinet's front glass. There are even new items in it. But I can dismiss such flaws in a film that obviously had next-to-no budget. Kicking this movie would be like kicking a puppy (or, in Thayer's case, burying an axe in its skull).

Overall, I found the movie to be competently made and with a few artistic flourishes. I shouldn't have been too surprised, as Roger Corman was involved in the production.

Particularly noteworthy are front-on shots of people approaching the alien craft, which rests at the bottom of a pit. As each person descends into that pit, they are bathed in swirling, reflected light.

My favorite image in the film is of Him approaching the craft and there just happened to be a jet contrail arcing into the sky away from his feet at a 45-degree angle. It is a nice combination of simple but solid shot composition combined with serendipity.

The movie even starts out with a solid opening credit sequence. The first thing we see is artwork of what appears to a dead tree, only to crossfade into the same image but with eyes filling every knothole of the tree. Similar artworks with the same transition follow.

Unfortunately, we will eventually see that spaceship and, alas, it gives proof to my conviction you should always show the audience less and leave them wanting more. Compounding his offense is when we get to see the alien itself.

More than that, I struggled with Him becoming possessed by the alien in the same manner as the animals. I felt there was a suggestion this man isn't just undeserving of a real name but is actually sub-human.

All that said, I actually like *The Beast with One Million Eyes*. At least, I apparently found more of merit here than the authors of any of the reviews I have read. Besides, where else could I see people using a blowtorch to fend off attacking chickens? No wonder this guy's business is failing—there has to be an easier way to fry chicken.

Original version posted on 9/25/2023

Beware! The Blob (1972)

When I say one can learn more from the worst movies than they can from the best, I can think of few better examples of this logic than 1972's *Beware! The Blob*. This is a movie that has some aspects filmmakers with more experience, or better taste, wouldn't have allowed. And this picture is all the more enjoyable because of that.

From the very first frame, you can tell the creative minds behind the camera realized how ridiculous it would be to make a sequel of the 1950's sci-fi classic. The entirety of the opening credits play over footage of a kitten frolicking in a field. Even weirder is the accompanying music, which is like carnival music as played on a Moog with the most obnoxious jingles from 70's commercials laid over it.

So, who is the moron who composed this soundtrack? It's…it's Mort Garson?! Yes, it's the renown electronic composer, whose *Plantasia* is currently being appreciated by a new audience, courtesy of a vinyl reissue which keeps selling out in consequent pressings.

Such deliriously insane music largely fills the soundtrack before more appropriate accompaniment begins creeping in. I wasn't aware of when this happened, and I'm still not sure if the change is to the film's benefit or detriment. For most pictures, I would say the best soundtrack is that which does not distract from what is on the screen but…woo-boy, Garson's work here is noteworthy for just how jaw-droppingly weird it is.

It's no surprise the kitten will be the first victim of the blob, though this is handled about as tastefully as it could be. The next two victims are a couple where the man had been keeping a sealed sample of the original blob in their freezer. He does not know what the sample might be. It was just something found by a member of his bulldozer crew when working in the arctic. Still, I wondered why he brought it all the way from there to his home. At least, I know I wouldn't keep a sample of something of unknown origin anywhere I keep food.

We're introduced to that guy (Godfrey Cambridge) as he exits a camping tent, to emerge into…his own living room. If that sounds like something out of a sitcom, then that is fairly representative of the humor in the film. This isn't much a surprise, given many of the actors are known primarily from television, such as Dick Van Patten as a Scout leader and Cindy Williams as a stoner girl. It's even directed by Larry Hagman, this being the only theatrical film he helmed. It isn't a surprise this could be mistaken for a made-for-television movie.

But such a movie would not have the odd lapses in basic filmmaking technique that happen on occasion here. A busy road is in the background of an under-cranked shot, making those cars move so fast that they look like they're trying to achieve escape velocity. Another shot has a weirdly jerky zoom-out, as if the crew was learning how to use the equipment while they were actively filming.

With the bar set this low, a couple of technically impressive scenes become even more remarkable in contrast. Especially noteworthy is a shot straight-on of lanes at a bowling alley, where the blob oozes evenly across them.

I wouldn't have thought Larry Hagman would have an unusual sense of humor, yet some of his choices here are evidence of that. There's an old guy taking a bath wearing a Shriner's fez, and he ends up running naked through the streets. A maintenance man at the bowling alley plays a piano amongst the machinery when he isn't reading *The Teachings of Buddha*.

There's also a great deal of improvisation, which I found to be of service to the film. One bizarre scene I liked has Shelley Berman as a barber who appears dismayed when a hippie type walks into his establishment. Berman declares he is a "hair sculptor" and has to charge $400, which the young man readily agrees to. The last thing Berman says to the young man before the blob attacks is while he's massaging the scalp during a shampoo: "You sure do groan a lot. I do believe you're purring". I wanted to know where that scene would have gone if these guys hadn't been killed.

I laughed quite a bit during that scene, as well as other moments in the film, which shows how poor my taste is. I keep saying how I'm such an easy laugh, but I doubt many others would even chuckle at a recurring gag where characters keep walking into a metal trash can just inside the front door of one house.

I genuinely enjoyed *Beware! The Blob*, though I can also understand why most others would not find anything of merit here. With its weird improv moments and occasional lapses in filmmaking technique, the whole affair has a "hey gang, let's put on a show" kind of vibe to it. Besides, it has such bizarre cameos as Burgess Meredith as a hobo railing against hippies. I believe there is a cult classic waiting to be discovered here, if only viewers would lower their expectations and relax their standards for what they have come to believe is a "good" movie.

Original version posted on 10/25/2023

The Boy with Green Hair (1948)

Isn't it great how a movie, an album or a book can come along and completely subvert your expectations? Going into 1948's *The Boy with Green Hair*, I thought it would be incredibly goofy or at least have a sci-fi element to it.

Instead, this sweetly good-natured tale is a plea for compassion and understanding. It also wants us to care about the less fortunate in the world and to help them from our position of privilege. This could very easily have been a dry and ham-fisted affair, but the messages are almost subversively wrapped in a confection of humor and light drama.

An impossibly young Dean Stockwell stars as the lad who wakes one morning to discover he has astroturf-colored tresses. In one of those weird bits of happenstance, I saw this movie in quick succession after seeing him as a young adult in *The Careless Years* and, before that, as a much older man in *Backtrack*. The weird thing is, I saw each of these without knowing beforehand he was in them.

Stockwell is shockingly good in this, especially for how young he was. When we first see him, he has a world-weariness beyond his years. This is when the police have picked up the now-bald Stockwell and try to get some information from him. He has obviously run away from home, and he refuses to even give them his name. Robert Ryan then takes over and the boy opens up more to him. Still, the lad is a bit of a smartass, such as when he's asked to start his story from the beginning: "At the beginning, I was born."

In flashback, we will learn how his parents exited his life when he was just a baby, and a succession of families each briefly took him in. His voiceover is accompanied by a series of static images of houses taken front-on, and these cold images are the best means I can think of for conveying the loneliness of being passed off from one family to another.

His final home will be with Pat O'Brien, as "Gramp". The highly charismatic O'Brien nails this role, as the first person to not just open his home to the lad, but also his heart. The rapport between the two is great. There's one bit I especially like where O'Brien is about to leave for his nightly shift as a singing waiter, telling Stockwell not to be afraid of the dark as, "There isn't anything there that wasn't there when the lights were on."

There's also a musical moment I could have done without, but it still has its charm. In that, we see Stockwell's imagining of when O'Brien met a king, played by Walter Catlett. It is interesting how this exaggerated tale is presented through the skewed perspective of a child. It reminded me a tad of *5000 Fingers of Dr. T.* Alas, this song isn't as good as any of the numbers in that picture. Still, it is better than the appalling title song over the opening credits. It didn't help that those credits are in a style similar to the contemporary Comic Sans font.

Anti-war and pro-compassion themes start creeping in courtesy of a conversation Stockwell overhears between grownups shopping in the general store. "I think we ought to stop fighting each other and start trying to understand each other". There's also a collection drive at his school for war orphans. What Stockwell doesn't realize at this point is *he* is actually a war orphan.

Not long after this, Stockwell wakes to discover he's permanently wearin' o' the green wig. It's not a bad wig, really—it's just that no amount of hair dye could result in such a green color. It nearly glows, it's so strong.

The first kids who see it think it's pretty awesome. Then the adults start getting suspicious and begin turning their kids against him. They think he is some sort of subversive, as if he dyed his hair on purpose. I wonder if these people would have spontaneous aneurysms if they were alive today and could see how the general populace has hair in every conceivable color.

Stockwell is visited by the spirits of the war orphans from the posters at his school. They inform him his hair turned green to draw awareness to their plight and to remind people those wars could have been prevented. I'm not entirely sure why people would come to that conclusion without Stockwell telling them explicitly, but I guess this isn't that different than the various ribbon decals people put on their cars for a wide variety of causes.

Blame starts to fall on various parties believed to be responsible for this transformation, if it is natural. Business for the milkman, in particular, is suffering. So now there's all this pressure for the boy to cut his air, which is how he ended up bald at the start of the picture.

One of the things I found most interesting about *The Boy with Green Hair* is it is directed by Joseph Losey. His attraction to unusual material would show itself strongly in the 1960's, helming such movies as *Modesty Blaise* and *BOOM!* Those films have their own unique charms, even if they are not widely appreciated. With this earlier film, we get to see what Losey would do with material equal parts quirky and heartfelt.

Original version posted on 11/22/2023

The Brain from Planet Arous (1957)

I love *Futurama*, and one of my most favorite scenes in the series involves a character asking a giant, diabolical, floating brain questions only an eternal being such as this can answer. One question is "what *really* killed the dinosaurs?", in reply to which the brain bellows "MEEEEEEEEEEEE!!!". Cut to giant floating brains zapping dinosaurs with lightning bolts.

While I never consciously stopped to consider it, I now realize there was a nagging question buried in the back on my own diabolical brain: was *Futurama* referencing a real movie or TV show? I discovered the answer is "yes", and now my life has been enriched by 1957's *The Brain from Planet Arous*.

Most low-budget movies suffer from their financial constraints, but a few b-movies instead create something more special than what would have resulted had there been more funding. *Arous* is a good example of the latter.

First, there's the floating alien brains (yes, plural). One brain is an evil escaped convict while the other is an intergalactic police officer, yet both are the same prop. The balloon used for the brain(s) has half-lidded eyes on the front of it. This sounds laughable (OK, it still is hard not to laugh at it at times), but those static eyes manage to be mildly unnerving simply through their unchanging expression of...boredom? Smug superiority? It's like talking to somebody and not being able to gauge their feelings through their expressions.

John Agar plays one of the two scientists who encounter the evil brain when they investigate a radiation pulse emanating from nearby Mystery Mountain. I love how the cave in which the brains were hiding is in a place called Mystery Mountain. It's like if *Texas Chain Saw Massacre* took place in the town of Cannibal Redneckville.

The scientist who isn't Agar (too lazy to look him up) is killed immediately, but our star is possessed by the evil brain. Per the era, and every aspect of this film, the evil brain wants to take over the Earth and uses Agar's body to put a plan in motion. As a scientist, Agar has access to the facilities and government officials the brain needs.

I'm unsure as to why the brain needs access to government resources, because the possessed Agar is able to blow up planes flying overhead without any other means. We also see he doesn't need anything like nuclear weapons, as he easily obliterates several structures set up to be destroyed in an atomic test.

When Agar is performing such tricks, the actor was outfitted with contacts that turn the entirety of his eyeballs silver. It is a surprisingly effective technique.

The chief effect employed throughout *Arous* is simple double-exposure. When Agar is talking to his possessor, the brain will sometimes appear in overlay. It starts small before enlarging and floating to the other side of the room, so a man and his brain overlord can have a more civil discourse.

I need to compliment Agar on his performance. In most of the other pictures I have seen him in, he has delivered serviceable performances, but not much more than that. Here, he gets an opportunity to expand his range and is gleefully sinister when channeling the evil alien.

The creepiest moments in the film have the evil alien brain lusting after Agar's girl, as played by Joyce Meadows. I guess a life of the mind gives a giant floating brain the hots for the first available female. It's a gross idea, and Agar maximizes the skeezy potential from it.

The Brain from Planet Arous is a hoot. It is something I simultaneously enjoyed on its own terms and as a thick slice of cheese. I wasn't bored for a minute, albeit the movie only takes 71 of them. Recommended for everybody.

Original version posted on 2/20/2023

Creature with the Atom Brain (1955)

1955's *Creature with the Atom Brain* is a curiosity. I thought I was just getting a typical 1950's sci-fi b-movie. Instead, I got a weird mix of horror, sci-fi and noir. It especially feels like the last of those, as much of its focus is on police detectives investigating crimes committed by a gang leader who had been deported. Maybe the creative team behind this just wanted to cover as many b-movie genres as they could, while still being unable to work in "western".

I seriously and unironically liked this movie, though it is *really* easy to take potshots at it. I mean, just look at that title. "Atomic Brain" would have been OK, but "atom" makes it sound like the creature has a very tiny brain.

Michael Granger plays the deported gangster who has snuck back into the country. He's brought with him a German doctor played by Gregory Gaye. Naturally, in this type of movie, you can assume "German" means "Nazi in hiding".

These two use radiation to reanimate corpses. They can then remotely control these radioactive zombies to kill the many nemeses of Granger. On a monitor, they can see through the remote-controlled assassin's eyes. They can also talk through a speaker implanted in the zombie's throat.

Each of Granger's victims is shocked to see somebody they don't know clumsily approaching them, usually by breaking through a window. Then, before their death, the victim is told this is to avenge his deportation. One creepy line that made me pay attention: "I said I would live to see you die. I am watching you now." But none of the zombies burst through a wall like Kool-Aid Man, while the speaker in their throat goes, "OH YEAH!!!" So that was a missed opportunity.

The first zombie does, however, take numerous gunshots to the back as he is exiting through the window. I was very surprised to see squibs used for this. IMDB says this is the first feature to do so, and I'm going to take their word for it.

When the mission is complete, Granger barks orders into the CB handset he uses to talk to, and talk through, the zombies. I couldn't help but wonder if the undead minion keeps repeating what the villain says, even when it is only directions. I like to imagine a zombie stumbling around like a toddler and yelling,

"GO TO THE CAR!" It would be like an actor accidentally reading stage directions as dialogue.

Richard Denning and S. John Launer play the detectives on the case. After the first murder, they discover fingerprints and blood drops left behind by the attacker. Lab analysis shows there isn't any hemoglobin in the highly radioactive "blood". Doing a fingerprint search reveals they belong to a man who died 24 days earlier.

Pretty soon, bodies are disappearing from the morgue and more of these seemingly unrelated killings are happening all over the city. As Denning notes after the second murder, the victims so far have been a crime lord and a district attorney, two people who are enemies by profession.

I liked the premise of this movie, but what I enjoyed most in it is the interaction between the characters. There's a rapport between the detectives that makes them enjoyable to watch whenever they're on screen. Even the other characters observe the close friendship of the men. When Denning's daughter asks Launer why he never married, Angela Stevens (playing Denning's wife) says "That would make him a bigamist. He's already married to your father."

There's some surprisingly funny dialogue between Denning and Stevens. Nothing that will one day be chronicled in *Bartlett's*, but it is better than what this type of fare requires. Such as when he says of the zombies, "I don't think they've gotten around to indiscriminate killings yet" and she says, "YET?!"

I was surprised by how disappointed I was when Launer gets killed and reanimated. Even more surprising is this bit of humor when he shows up at his partner's house talking robotically and

Stevens chides him. "Why so formal? [robot voice] 'I am Captain Davis, homicide'."

One aspect of this plot development that is deeply ridiculous is nobody notices a huge horizonal scar across undead Launer's forehead. Even with a hat on, it is an inch or two below the brim. Denning must not be much of a detective, if he doesn't have the observational skills to notice that scar.

Launer ends up providing an unexpected benefit for Denning's investigation when the zombie returns to the villain's lab. I'm not sure how that minion got there in one piece, as he exited a room through a window that appears to be several stories up. Still, it was awfully convenient for Denning to be able to simply follow what is essentially a homing zombie.

And now a quick round-up of random elements I liked in this. The X-rays of Launer's head are weirdly beautiful, with a circuit diagram overlaid atop his brain. Also, there was a lot of intriguing and unexpected artwork in the office of the first guy who gets killed. I covet all of it, including an Easter Island head statuette.

Creature with the Atom Brain is fun and interesting throughout its brief runtime. It is solid proof there can be more pure enjoyment found in some B-movies than most fare produced on a significantly larger budget.

Originally posted on 10/12/2023

Deep Space (1988)

I like how some of the graduates of the Corman film school, when they went on to better things, took some of that producer's stock actors with them. Like a good luck charm, Joe Dante always has a place, however small, for Dick Miller in his pictures. Similarly, I can't recall a Jonathan Demme feature which didn't have Charles Napier in it. You know him—he's the guard who gets his face cut off by Hannibal Lecter in *Silence of the Lambs*.

Of course, cameos don't pay the bills, so Napier appeared in as many films as possible, which is why he headlines 1988's *Deep Space*. That, and it looks like he had a blast doing this.

Fred Olen Ray wrote and directed this straight-to-video sci-fi/horror flick. I recognize his name from several of his works which were consequently mocked by Rifftrax. And the movies of his which I've seen receiving such treatment were fully deserving of it.

That the bar was set so incredibly low likely contributed to me being pleasantly surprised by this, which is little more than another ripoff of *Alien*. Despite the title, the action takes place entirely on Earth, which had me very confused at first. Then I decided to turn my brain off and just go along for the ride.

The Dollar Store xenomorph was developed by the military on a presumably unmanned satellite. The scientists and military personnel start freaking out when the craft begins its descent from its orbit. So, from the best I can tell, these bozos: (1) created a killing machine, (2) on an Earth-orbiting craft (3) which they apparently never meant to bring back down to Earth. Science!

A "teenage" couple who look old enough to have pre-teens of their own are the first arrivals on the crash scene. They discover a large object that is supposed to be a rock, but which looks more like a severely burned meatloaf. There's some alien goo oozing from it, and the guy pokes his fingers into it. As a member of the male gender, I can tell you this is, lamentably, exactly what a guy would do. Tentacles shoot out of it and kill both of them, so there's a great example of a woman paying for a guy's stupidity.

I was surprised the police arrive at the scene before the military does, seeing as to how the government were aware of the satellite's impending crash as soon as it deviates from its orbit. You'd think the feds would have had that area sealed off by then.

At the scene, a detective says of the scorched space meatloaf, "It looks like a rock, but it's really alive", an odd statement since they haven't seen it do anything. Apparently, it was all tuckered out from killing that couple earlier.

Also on the scene is Napier as a police officer, along with his partner Ron Glass. These two have an effortless rapport that felt like they were having fun, instead of just phoning it in to cash a paycheck. Glass is best known for *Barney Miller* and this feature was made in a period where he was probably struggling for work after that but before *Firefly* came along.

Another veteran of 70's TV and movies is Bo Svenson, here as the obligatory police captain who is frustrated by the antics of his loose cannon detectives. Like some other movies I have watched as of late, I considered how all three of the male leads would have fared successfully in any of each other's roles. Rounding out the cast is Ann Turkel as the obligatory love interest for Napier. In a cameo, there's TV's original Catwoman (Julie Newmar) contributing little as a psychic who tries to give the detective info about the case.

When we finally see the aliens, they come in two varieties, a full-sized model whose design is entirely lifted from the xenomorph in *Alien*, and a smaller kind that is a complete rip-off of the facehuggers from the same film. Both are of better construction than I would have expected on a straight-to-video budget, but only just. The facehuggers fare more poorly of the two, especially in shots where they are supposed to be running along the ground but you can tell something at the base of the body is actually propelling them forward (I suspect some type of remote-controlled toy).

What puts this above the majority of such fare, and what I had seen of Ray's oeuvre up to this point, is the humor. I started to suspect this was intended to be a comedy during an early scene in an autopsy room where an anatomy poster gets showered in viscera.

Then there's the scene with Turkel going to Napier's house for a dinner date and the humor comes to the forefront. Distracted by a call from Newmar, he burns a steak so badly it shatters the plate he drops it on. He ends up serving fast food hamburgers for dinner, and I had my fingers crossed this would somehow turn into the "Steamed Hams" sketch from *The Simpsons*. Instead, he follows up dinner by seducing her with music he's playing on bagpipes while kitted out in full Scotsman drag. She's baffled by how this is supposed to be seductive until he informs her he can only stop playing once her clothes are off.

For a movie with better production values than I anticipated, its most severe shortcoming is its soundtrack, all of which sounds like it was created on a single, cheap Casio keyboard. That instrument, however, provides appropriately goofy entrance music whenever an alien is about to appear. I'm not sure why, but the squiggly synth noises made me smile every time.

Deep Space is nothing more than dumb fun. It knows how daft it is and leans into it pretty hard. It's the kind of film where there will be a photo of Charles and Di on Napier's dartboard for no reason. It's the type of movie where a car will leap over a truck despite there not being anything apparent in the environment that it could use as a ramp. Unfortunately, the movie does overstay its welcome, even at only 90 minutes in length. Still, I would sooner watch this again than I would any of the other 162 films Ray has directed as of 2022.

Original version posted on 10/4/2023

The Demon Seed (1977)

In the eighties, the Rubik Cube was so ubiquitous that all sorts of similar toys had to be developed to satisfy the market demand. Some were pyramid shaped, some had five sides or more. One was even spherical. But one that stands out in my mind is something everybody called a "snake", though I'm not sure what names it was marketed under. It wasn't a puzzle, but a toy—a series of extruded triangle shapes linked together which could be twisted to various angles, resulting in all manner of shapes.

I mention this because 1977's *Demon Seed* has an amazing effect in it which reminded me of that toy. In this film, a large metal diamond unfolds its triangular segments to become a robot snake that can coil and strike. It can even unfold into multiple appendages that can act as arms. It can encircle a person's neck with multiple points which threaten to converge and decapitate its victim. This is an astonishing effect, and I am pleased to say I have no idea how it was done.

The plot concerns a diabolical artificial intelligence which escapes the lab of the corporation where Fritz Weaver has developed it. Fleeing via the only terminal it has access to in the outside world, it ends up in the system Weaver created to control his house. Good thing the Internet wasn't around back then, as it probably would have become Skynet.

The company that created this AI is secretly evil, because of course they are. It even operates out of a complex that is a single level structure of brutalist architecture on the surface, with a great many subterranean levels below. I think this should still be the look of technology corporations, especially the evil ones.

The servers where the development work is done are somehow organic inside, so the scientists are actually *growing* an artificial brain. Between that and the brutalist architecture, this is starting to feel like a film from Cronenberg's prime, and I haven't even talked about the icky objective of this intelligence.

That development involves Julie Christie, who plays the estranged wife of Weaver. In their separation, he is leaving her the fully automated house. An aspect of this I love is, before leaving, he programs the house for the next few months using only one 8" floppy. Even I have never seen an 8" floppy in real life. I had to look it up, but the capacity of such a disk would only be 80 kilobytes. Damn, the computer running that entire household is ridiculously data-efficient.

Anywho, the AI's creepy plan for Christie is to impregnate her. As the computer system has control of all functions of the house, it forces her into accepting this through such techniques as making the water-heated floors too hot to walk on. Yes, folks, a computer rapes our heroine in this movie.

And this is entirely Christie's film. The majority of the picture is only her and the disembodied voice of the computer. I was especially shocked that only three people bother to check on her in roughly the month in which the plot takes place, and neither of the first two are her husband! The first person to look in on her is actually Weaver's second-in-command at work. This unfortunate soul is played by Gerritt Graham, who at least doesn't take a toilet plunger to the face, as he did in *Phantom of the Paradise*.

The AI has all kinds of clever means to maintain his hold over Christie and dispatch potential interlopers. It creates that amazing metal creature that reminds me of that 80's toy. It can create a virtual Christie on the house's external video screen in what seems to anticipate the current era of deep fakes. And there's no end to the mayhem it can get up to with the extensive laser lab Weaver put in the basement. Early in the film, we see him using that to fix his glasses, prompting my wife to exclaim, "It's the first Lenscrafters!"

I was surprised *Demon Seed* was adapted from a novel by Dean Koontz, given the material is solidly in Michael Crichton territory. All in all, it was much better than I anticipated it being, given the colossal ick factor of the plot. It was interesting how elements of it such as artificial intelligence are hot topics at the time I write this. But even more than that, the picture had me thinking about how the computer technology used to protect our homes can just as easily make us a prisoner of them.

Dr. Cyclops (1940)

One of my favorite Beatle quips was courtesy of one of those weird Christmas flexi discs they used to release through their fan club. Talking about the black-and-white *Hard Day's Night*, George Harrison says they're working on another film, and this time it will be in color. John Lennon doesn't miss a beat when he pipes up with "green".

I thought about this during the opening credits and the first sequence of 1940's *Dr. Cyclops*. This sci-fi thriller is in vivid, almost lurid, Technicolor. And those first few minutes are bathed in a gorgeous, strong, emerald green. Even better, the lettering of the title card is cut out from a background, with rays of light shooting towards the viewer through those openings. It is very similar to the opening credits of *The Thing from Another World* over a decade later.

The plot concerns your typical mad scientist (Albert Dekker) who has discovered a wealth of uranium in Peru. The mineral is the key to a process he's created which can reduce living animals to a fraction of their size. I would have loved to have heard his explanation of what scientific purpose this discovery would serve. Instead, he's simply batshit crazy.

He is also extremely nearsighted, though he has two such impaired eyes. Not sure why this picture has this title, as it is only worked into the plot through an overreaching metaphor about the moral failings of the scientist. Eventually, his last remaining pair of spectacles will have only one working lens, making the title more literal for no good reason.

Dekker has summoned a fellow scientist (Charles Halton) from ten thousand miles away just to look through his microscope and see what has gone wrong with an experiment. It's Dekker's poor eyes, you see. He's unable to see the slides, which makes me wonder how he has been able to do much of anything scientific. Heck, we saw him looking through a microscope without complaint in the opening scene, so I wonder what happened so quickly. Also, that had to take Halton a crazy amount of time to get to Dekker, so I was wondering why doc didn't just rope in a local villager or two and just have them describe in detail what they see.

Halton looks through the microscope, tells Dekker what he has seen and then is instantly dismissed to begin the return voyage. I guess Dekker thinks he can just make Halton do a 20,000-mile round trip each time he needs somebody to describe the results of his latest experiment. Insulted, Halton decides to stay and demand an answer for this behavior. This will get him and his cohorts shrunken to roughly a foot in size.

A small group had travelled with Halton. There's fellow scientist Janice Logan, greedy miner Victor Kilian (from whom the Americans rent their pack mules), local ethnic stereotype Frank Yaconelli, and a bored layabout (and alleged mineralogist) played by Thomas Coley. Curiously, this is Coley's only theatrical film.

Of the supporting cast, Logan is given the best part, in a rare opportunity at the time for a female character to be a scientist. She is intelligent, sensible, and actually gets to do some scientific work, instead of simply taking care of "the boys" or being arm candy for one of them. Admittedly, she will eventually be the love interest for Coley, though that is just tacked on as part of the conclusion.

One aspect I found interesting about the predicament our heroes find themselves in is their clothes do not shrink with them. As Dekker observes of Halton: "Imagine his surprise when he awakens to find he is fully dressed in a pocket handkerchief." Indeed, each cast member starts out in one of those, and each has fashioned their own in a different manner. I found it strange Yaconelli styled his like a giant diaper. Even more bizarre is when all the actors, bar Halton, change into different colored garments without explanation. Also, each has styled their new attire in the same manner as before. Guess you have to go with what you know, though that means Yaconelli is simply now in a colored diaper.

But all this is moot, because this is a fantastic adventure, with astonishing special effects. I honestly don't know how some of these were done, such as a miniaturized horse in a box. Another effect which impressed and bewildered me occurs in the first scene, where Paul Fix is killed by radiation. His face takes on the qualities of a skull, with his eye sockets becoming a deep purple and vertical lines appearing over his closed mouth, as if it has been sewn shut.

But the true wonder for me is the use of whatever the opposites of miniatures would be called. I am going to call these giant props "maximatures". Such objects as tables, chairs, books, pencils, eyeglasses and crates were rendered so realistically that I honestly forgot at times these weren't the real thing. Similar items were done as effectively in *The Incredible Shrinking Man*, though that was 17 years later and in black-and-white. It had to be far more difficult to accomplish this in color, let alone almost two decades earlier.

There is also a fair amount of rear projection, augmented in a couple of scenes by maximatures that help bring together the foregrounds with the flat backgrounds. The moment where Halton is captured has Dekker wielding a butterfly net in the background rear projection. Once the net is out of frame in the background, a giant prop version of it appears in the foreground.

Similarly, Dekker is again in rear projection as he watches Halton on his desk and the tiny man backs up into an articulated giant hand. The hand is fairly convincing in a wide shot. It is far less so in close-up, though I still appreciated the effort. Being similar to that which was done for *King Kong*, it is light years better than what would eventually be used for *Attack of the 50 Foot Woman* (again, almost two decades later).

I also appreciated how the movie was willing to sacrifice some of our heroes. Dekker dispatches Halton almost immediately via a rag soaked in ether, as if this great scientific mind is nothing more than a butterfly. This murder is all the more chilling for how casually it is done.

With Halton out of the picture, Logan really becomes the leader of the group, as the survivors find themselves in situations such as an alligator attacking when they try to launch a boat. It is she who decides "We can't go on like this, being afraid of everything." And all the characters in peril handle things rationally, using their wits more than their fists (though there are still several action scenes).

There are what I suspected to be logical flaws, though I didn't find these distracting. For whatever reason, I couldn't seem to shake the suspicion something was wrong about a development concerning Yaconelli and his faithful dog. There is a scene where he is not recognized by his dog once he's in shrunken form. Later, Dekker employs the dog to sniff out his master, and that just didn't ring true for me. I know it's moot, but I believe either the dog would recognize Yaconelli or wouldn't—you can't have it both ways.

Dr. Cyclops absolutely amazed me, all the more so because of its age. Being able to watch this on blu-ray provides the ability to go through effects scenes frame-by-frame, which only increased my appreciation. Some films such as this are poorly done, others are done well for their time but haven't aged well. This one was a wonder in 1940, and it still is today.

Original version posted on 5/23/2024

The Final Programme (1973)

1973's *The Final Programme* is supposed to be about the creation of an eternal, self-replicating hermaphrodite that has all the knowledge of the greatest minds in the world. Not sure why anybody would want to do that, but I wasn't too surprised by some Nazi imagery near the end of the picture. That seems to be in the general wheelhouse of such weird aspirations. The result is a creature that can go fuck itself. No, really, having functioning sets of both kinds of genitalia, it can literally do that. As the end credits rolled, I was inclined to tell the filmmakers to do the same, regardless of their biology.

This film was a disappointment to me, as I have an interest in high-concept science fiction. That this was directed by Robert Fuest had me very curious. After all, this is the guy who directed one of my favorite films, *The Abominable Dr. Phibes*. But we weren't even through the opening credits when red flags started going up, when I saw this was written, directed and *designed* by the man. That last credit is a warning for the pretentiousness that is about to be unloaded on the viewer.

It is set in what I assume is supposed to be the near future, where the world is on the verge of the apocalypse. That, or it already happened—I wasn't certain which. Our protagonist is a very droll Jon Finch, wearing nail polish and the kind of frilly shirt only Prince could pull off. I'm not sure why he is entangled with Jenny Runacre, but she's some sort of Emma Peel type agent, notable in that she is bisexual and a cannibal. I don't understand why she's the latter, and I actually had to read a review to know that's what she is. The film is that frustratingly vague about almost everything.

I've already told you where the film is headed. I can't even say that was a spoiler, because such info is even in the one-sentence summary on IMDB. But before we get to a deeply ludicrous ending, there's all sorts of business with a microfilm, deadly sibling rivalries, drugs, etc. Even in the context of the film, every element of the plot just feels like something the movie chooses to briefly muse upon before wandering onto the next element, like the unfocused mind of somebody on serious drugs.

The dialogue is strange enough to suggest it was largely improvised. I was shocked to learn this was based on a novel by Michael Moorcock, and a fairly well-regarded one at that. The film supposedly hews rather closely to the source material, except for the ending. I can't imagine what would convince me to read the book, but I'll concede to being just a bit curious as to how the climax differs.

Some of the sets are impressive, yet they never seemed to serve any real purpose. I didn't even find them amusing, and this is a film that has a nightclub resembling the insides of a pinball machine, complete with huge plastic "pinballs" that girls are walking around inside of, like John Travolta in *The Boy in the Plastic Bubble*.

Such absurdities might give one the impression this film is hilarious, but it isn't. The only time I did chuckle was when we see a sign on the master computer at the end reading, "THE MOST POWERFUL COMPUTER IN THE WORLD. DO NOT TOUCH." I'm not even sure why I found that mildly amusing. Maybe it was just out of desperation to react to *anything*. I know I rolled my eyes at another moment where Finch surveys a brain floating in a tank of water and surmises: "It must be a brain-washing machine."

I like strange, new ideas and I like a fair amount of offbeat, heady sci-fi from the 70's. But *The Final Programme* somehow has a wealth of weird while ending up being tiring and boring. Too much here feels like the kind of stray ideas that usually don't make it past a work's first draft. And there's a reason why finished books and films don't have bits like a restaurant that serves industrial waste from Beaujolais—it isn't that funny or clever even a minute or two after thinking it up. This is all loose ideas that never form a gestalt and it ends up feeling like J.G. Ballard without the high-minded concepts.

Original version posted on 6/14/2023

Fire Maidens of Outer Space (1956)

There was a surprisingly wide variety of bad sci-fi movies made in the 1950's. I imagine these on a spectrum ranging from cheap cash-grab to the curiously personal trainwrecks made by Ed Wood. While everything superficial about 1956's *Fire Maidens of Outer Space* suggests the former, I was left with the impression this is somehow in between these extremes.

The plot, to use the word loosely, has a manned rocket sent to the "thirteenth moon of Jupiter". Upon landing, the five astronauts discover the atmosphere is breathable, the moon is heavily treed and it looks...um, *exactly* like Earth. They soon discover this moon is inhabited by about a dozen comely young women clad in togas. There is also one man, who is elderly and the leader of what he says is New Atlantis. There is also a "monster" that torments the women.

If that doesn't sound like a cohesive plot, then my mission is accomplished. The picture was over when I realized I still didn't know how or why the citizens of Atlantis went there. I also had a lot of questions as to why, with the exception of the old man, everybody here is a woman. Are they eons old, or were they the offspring of men and women who all recently died?

And what about the monster? It appears to be a tall, thin guy in a black unitard, wearing some sort of mask that looks like the world's worst instance of combination skin. We only see one, so is it the last of its kind? Is it an indigenous resident of this moon, is it an invader from somewhere else or did it travel with the first

Atlanteans? But the biggest issue of all is I couldn't figure what his beef was with the girls.

Speaking of which, I neglected to mention some of them want to enslave the men and use them to repopulate this moon. Since all five astronauts are total horndogs with the sophistication of 13-year-old boys, I'm confused as to why they aren't down with this. One of them looks shockingly similar to Tim Blake Nelson and acts like he's as dense as most of the yokels Nelson specializes in playing. Also, curvy alien women in togas–was Gene Rodenberry taking notes for what would eventually become *Star Trek*?

We weren't even to the opening credits before I realized something was off here. The first thing we see is a plane flying over a city. A caption says the plane is flying over New York City. Not sure what the point of that was, as the plane took off from somewhere else and is going to land in London. Anyway, New York City, ladies and gentlemen! Let's give the Big Apple a big hand!

Then we get to the credits, which include this howler: "all characters in space are ficticious". I actually found that pretty clever, and it indicates the filmmakers are aware of how ridiculous this whole thing is. And some of these plot threads could be interesting on their own, if they were developed better.

As it is, it's like somebody threw everything they could think of at the screen just to see if anything sticks. How about this–for a science fiction movie set on another planet, this has a bizarre amount of tree climbing and a large number of dance sequences. I know nothing about dance but even I can tell the choreography and performances here are pure garbage.

Naturally, the dance sequences are just filler, and this film has some of the most bizarre excess baggage I have seen. In one early scene, the camera follows an assistant as she walks to the stairs, goes down the stairs, opens a gate and then pulls out a chair and sits in it. Then we will see her do those same actions in reverse order. All of this is in one painfully long shot.

It's no surprise a movie of this "quality" has narration. It starts with endless exposition about scientists working on "Plan 13". At the end of one of the times this is said, my wife added "…from outer space". In an amazing coincidence, the narrator said immediately afterwards "…in outer space". I positively barked with laughter.

Yep, this is the kind of movie best enjoyed by watching with others, and everybody taking potshots at it. The special effects are jaw-droppingly cheap, such as a side view of the rocket which is obviously a paper cut-out. Then there's our band of heroic astronauts, who seem to be outfitted primarily with cigarettes and pistols, and whose rocket interior appears to be a boiler room.

Fire Maidens of Outer Space is not for everybody. You have to be partial to this type of movie and, even then, in the right frame of mind. It's weird how, even then, I want to cut it some slack, though what ended up on screen is hysterically funny, whether intentionally or not.

Original version posted on 8/11/2023

Five (1955)

It is telling that nuclear holocaust films seemed to have been produced in the greatest number in the 50s and the 80s, two eras when the world felt especially close to that becoming a reality.

1955's *Five* is, I believe, the earliest of this type of picture. The core group of this is four, and not five, people who somehow find each other somewhere near the northeastern US coast.

Two characters survived the nuclear attack by being in a bank vault at the time, so it is understandable these two would be together. I seriously doubt, however, those two would have met any of the others they eventually found, nor would any of those individuals have met each other. My wife and I can't find each other in a supermarket, so I doubt four people could just wander around the US and stumble upon each other. Still, I was able to suspend my disbelief for this.

The first person we meet is Susan Douglas, who we see wandering through what is doubtlessly the most recent of a long series of vacant towns. She eventually finds a fellow survivor who lives in what I thought was a ranger station, though I'm unclear on that. If it is a ranger station, then I'm considering working for the forestry service if that means I can live in a place like this. Just so long as I don't have to, you know, do any work in the out-of-doors or anything.

The guy's name is Michael Roden (played by William Phipps). I guess she didn't tell that guy, "Not if you were the last man on Earth", because she has a bun in the oven in short order.

The next to arrive are the two who survived in a bank vault. One is an upper-middle-aged bank clerk who cheerfully maintains the delusion he is still on the job. It's no surprise he won't be in the movie for long.

His friend from the bank is Charles Lampkin, and this guy *owns* this movie. He may not be top-billed but he definitely is the star of it. He delivers the best performance and has most of the best lines. What makes this surprising is Lampkin is a Black actor in a movie from 1955, a time when so much of the country had segregated bathrooms and drinking fountains.

Lampkin has a monologue which I consider to be the picture's centerpiece, probably the most beautiful re-telling I have heard of the Biblical creation story. I also like a moment then Phipps proposes they hook up a generator, and Lampkin jokes about sending himself a monthly electric bill. The line reading feels natural.

Conflict arrives when they find James Anderson washed up on the shore. He was on top of Everest when the blast occurred. The movie is unclear about how much time has elapsed since then, but the film's credibility is stretched to the point of breaking when you consider he somehow came from the other side of the world and just happens to wash up where the last four people in North America are conveniently located.

Anderson is obviously trouble from the first moment he opens his mouth, spouting doom and gloom. It's like Jean-Paul Sartre found them. Interesting attitude for somebody who climbed Everest. As Phipps wryly observes, "Some people have to climb mountains to justify their existence." I am on-board with that statement, as I am wearing a deep butt-groove into a loveseat while I write all this garbage.

To my considerable surprise, this film does not suffer what has been the death-knell of so many similar pictures, and that is over-earnestness. I expect such an effort to be ham-fisted, especially when it is such a small-scale production as this. Admittedly, things did not seem promising at the start, when a Bible verse appears on screen: "The deadly wind passeth over it / And it is gone; / And the place thereof / Shall know it no more." Why are people around me always quoting that when I eat Taco Bell?

I'm surprised this was the first nuclear apocalypse picture, as it is one of the best I have seen. It has a similar vibe to, and shares some themes with, *The World, The Flesh and The Devil*, though I liked *Five* better. It is a small film, but that works to its favor. This isn't a movie so much about most of the world's population dying, but how those who survived will go forward. As Lapmkin says at one point, "As long as things keep growing, everything will be alright."

Original version posted on 2/26/2023

Flight to Mars (1951)

The mock-religion The Church of the SubGenius employs as its primary symbol a clip art image of the stereotypical ideal of the 1950's American male, complete with pipe clenched between teeth. I kept thinking of this image every time the eerily similar Arthur Franz appears on screen during 1951's *Flight to Mars*. He is like the living embodiment of the SubGenius savior Bob Dobbs, including the ever-present pipe.

Yes, this is the kind of movie where people smoke on board a rocket on its maiden voyage to the red planet. The characters even wear what is essentially their street clothes. I was surprised to see a female scientist among the crew (Virginia Huston), but she wears a skirt throughout the trip. I guess it's a good thing the artificial gravity is working on the ship, lest things get too interesting.

The main characters even get picked up at home by hired car and brought directly to the launchpad minutes before takeoff, and I wondered if NASA has ever considered doing that. One thing that agency should be teaching astronauts is how to throw a decent punch, since that is the skill most frequently employed in this kind of fare.

Cameron Mitchell is the one with the quick fists here, as a PR guy who is inexplicably part of the crew. I guess the thinking behind this picture is people who are smart can't be decent fighters, so you need to have somebody who isn't an egghead or a girl, just for the inevitable skirmish.

The landing on Mars is hilarious. They don't have enough fuel to do a controlled descent, so they decide to crash land. Actually, they slam right into a cliff, just like the plane on the cover of the Beastie Boys' *License to Ill*. Something I found gut-bustingly hilarious is how the vessel just comes to an abrupt stop when it smacks into a rock wall. Defying all logic, it is relatively unscathed from the incident.

The crew is outfitted in what appear to be leather bomber jackets when they go explore their surroundings. I found this fascinating since Mars is *cold*–vastly colder than what people clad in such a manner could endure. They also wear oxygen masks, which is a good idea, even if I doubt that would be adequate, either, since there is still the little matter of drastically lower air pressure to consider.

They are greeted by a group of Martians who look perfectly human, something which is not speculated about. They also speak English courtesy of a development I thought was interesting: they've been intercepting our radio and TV signals for years. In their Martian spacesuits, each one a different pastel color, they look like nothing less than Teletubbies. I wonder if there is a connection between those preschool TV pals (which had television screens in their tummies) with Martians who dress to look like them (and learned our language from TV signals).

The locals are very friendly on the surface but, in covert meetings, they talk about how their planet is dying and they need to invade Earth. Those factions don't want the humans to return home, lest they possibly give some advance warning of a Martian invasion. Never mind the visitors don't know anything about these secret plans.

So, we have a few Martians genuinely helping the Earthlings repair their rocket, while others are committing acts of sabotage while only pretending to help. Why they found this ruse necessary was beyond me, except there wouldn't be a movie otherwise. In my opinion, they should just kill the humans immediately, disassemble their craft for parts, and invade Earth. Job done.

Assisting Franz in engineering the repairs is a local played by Marguerite Chapman. She makes the most of a rather thin role. It's no surprise these two fall in love, and I would have loved to have seen them try to consummate their romance, as I imagine they would discover some manner of incompatible parts.

To be fair, the two other main women in this are also intelligent, though to different ends. Lucille Barkley is a spy for the Mars-first bunch. Huston's character is probably the smartest of the three, but the actress is saddled with the worst personality. She spends most of the journey there seducing Mitchell in an attempt to make Franz jealous. You can imagine how well she responds to Franz and Chapman becoming an item. And you know a film of this kind isn't going to pass the Bechdel test, but I was still shocked her first line when shown their living quarters is "Where's the kitchen?"

I want to briefly mention the sets for the underground Martian world. While nobody will mistake anything here for Fritz Lang's *Metropolis*, there is much that has a certain naïve charm. We get a brief glimpse of a "cityscape" that, at the risk of appearing condescending, I found awfully cute. An unusual visual aspect that dominates the set design is walls leaning inward at 45-degree angles. That looks neat but seems like poor utilization of space.

Even the opening credits are as interesting as they are unusual. The very first shot is of a man looking into the eyepiece of a huge telescope. We cut to a shot of stars we assume he's looking at, except giant text bearing the title shoots out at us from the distance. So, is this astronomer actually watching the opening credits through a telescope?

I have seen better movies than *Flight to Mars* that attempt to depict such a journey in a quasi-realistic manner, but I have also seen worse ones. It is solidly a product of its time, where a newspaper man who talks with his fists flies to Mars with a catty woman and her would-be boyfriend who seems to be surgically attached to his pipe. And they fly through the cosmos in a wobbly rocket whose exhaust drifts upwards, suggesting there is gravity in open space.

Original version posted on 3/8/2024

Forbidden World (1982)

James Cameron demonstrated his ability to think on his feet early in his career when he textured the walls of a spaceship with grids made of painted, Styrofoam Big Mac containers. That was for *Galaxy of Terror*, which was produced by Roger Corman. As a man who always knew how to stretch a penny until it turned into copper wire, Corman reused that corridor for at least one other movie. That set had obviously taken a beating before being used in 1982's *Forbidden World*, with enough damage to it to make its fast-food packaging source material evident.

I have seen a great many of the films Corman produced, and I would rank this among his worst. This tired clone of *Alien* is shoddy in every regard: technical, acting, effects, music. Even the dialogue is bad enough that I wondered if Cameron had worked on the script. A sample line: "Let's go bag ourselves a dingwhopper."

The movie has at least one innovation, though not a welcome one. Near-subliminal images are dropped into some of the scenes. Some of these are a long procession of lightning-fast edits that made me wonder if they could induce a seizure in the wrong person. This had to be a massive time-consuming effort before the age of digital editing, so I'm surprised they went to that much trouble.

Of course, they were able to get some extra mileage out of the ample female nudity from other scenes by recycling them for these subliminal moments. The result is you have moments with somebody fleeing the monster and the odd frame of boobs will pop up. It is simply baffling but isn't thought-provoking. It didn't make me wonder why they did that. It was wasted effort.

I can't overstate just how copious the nudity is in this. There's enough full-frontal female exposure that I was genuinely surprised this received an R. I know much of 80's horror is about horny people getting killed, but the characters are apparently so obsessed with getting their freak on that it makes them completely forget there is a deadly creature on the loose. I found myself wondering if this had been made with the intention of easily making an X version from the material, as some scenes feel like they exist solely for hardcore inserts to be dropped in.

We will first see some of the subliminal nudity when our hero (Jesse Vint) is awakened from cryogenic sleep in a precredit sequence. I thought we were seeing random thoughts from his waking mind. But it will turn out everything we're shown are clips from later in the movie. This seems to imply Vint has some sort of precognitive abilities, something which is never touched on again.

Others in the movie include June Chadwick, who played Jannine in *This Is Spinal Tap*. She will have little more to do than get naked here.

Still, she has somewhat more to do than Dawn Dunlap, who also spends a surprising amount of time in the altogether. That is, when she's not shrieking at a pitch that could break glass. Her sole moment actually in service to the plot is when she's in a control room, watching others hunt the monster in the desert. That she is able to monitor their progress suggests an impossibly great number of security cameras in that remote and desolate area.

The only other actor worth mentioning is Fox Harris, as the lead scientist, and that is only because he has an uncanny resemblance to Tim Burton. His unfortunate character will have a tumor removed from his body without benefit of anesthesia. He walks Vint through the process of doing this, with the plan being to try feeding the tumor to the monster. Harris dies in the process and I'm still wondering why they didn't just kill the poor man outright and then carve him up. That seems far more humane.

But this is a film that consistently takes the most gruesome and gory path available. This is a very gross movie, and I think I was only able to finish watching it because of how cheaply and ineptly the effects are done. I wonder how much of the budget was allocated for gelatin, Karo syrup and red dye. Heads up to the friends of animals out there: one scene is liberally decorated with the real corpses of various species that are normally kept as pets.

The one element of this that should have been novel is the murderous creature is a "metamorph" that continually changes its structure. Alas, that just means it changes from one sub-par design to another. Given how freely this lifts from *Alien*, there is the token face-hugger version early on, but what they have here looks like a guy with a square cut out of a black rain slicker stuck to the side of his face.

The movie's nadir arrives when Chadwick decides to simply talk to the monster. I wonder why nobody in the various *Alien* sequels and spin-offs ever tried this approach, and it's probably because it would turn out as badly there as it does for her here. Before her demise, however, we get the creature responding to her by somehow playing some cheap synth music through the ship's computer. I thought the music was only on the soundtrack, but a cutaway reveals it is diegetic. An earlier scene that is almost as weird has a guy playing some sort of glass saxophone along to music we already were hearing on the soundtrack, which means *a character in a movie can hear, and play along with, the soundtrack.*

Forbidden World is bad—so bad that I don't think it can even be recommended for fans of thick slices of movie cheese. It's a horror movie without any scares, science fiction that doesn't take us anywhere interesting and near-porn that never delivers the goods it hints at. This is such a sorry mess that it isn't even any fun to laugh at.

Original version posted on 12/8/2023

From Hell It Came (1957)

A few years back, I read a piece saying the novelty song "Witch Doctor" by David Saville was emblematic of the racism inherent in American pop culture in the 1950's. I never thought of it as anything but a goofy, and rather catchy, bit of nonsense. Regardless of how one feels about it, that song can't hold a candle to the cultural misrepresentation found in 1957's legendarily bad sci-fi film *From Hell It Came.*

Even in the age of rampant whitewashing of Asians in movies, this is the weirdest casting of "natives" I have seen so far. The tribal leader on this unnamed South Pacific island has a whiff of a Brooklyn accent and looks quite a bit like Abe Vigoda, except this isn't meant to be a parody like when Vigoda appeared in such a role in *Joe Versus the Volcano.*

Nearly all the indigenous people of this island are Caucasian actors of similarly baffling lineage. Maybe there was once a land bridge from New York City to this island. This place could be an anthropological boon.

Speaking of anthropology, one of the condescending white male scientists doing a study there sarcastically remarks the tribal drumming has a nice anthropological beat. Given my eclectic tastes in music, I wonder if that rhythm is what I have been looking for the entire time I've been delving into various genres.

Tod Andrews and John McNamara play those eggheads, who are there to curtail an outbreak of the black plague. They also keep bringing up the subject of radiation—I guess just because of all the nuclear tests on Pacific islands at the time(?).

But the bulk of the plots concerns not them, but instead the chief of the natives (Baynes Barron), his own witch doctor and all-around right-hand guy (Robert Swan), and a femme fatale (Suzanne Ridgway). That last is a true fatale: the first time we see her, she testifies against her husband, who is summarily executed by the chief.

That execution gives us a taste of how bizarre these proceedings are going to be. The chief has a voodoo doll of Gregg Palmer, which seems unnecessary, as Palmer has both arms and legs tied to posts in the ground. When the chief sticks what appears to be a letter opener into the doll, a henchman uses a mallet to drive a stake into the victim's chest. Why the middleman? Clearly, this is an organization that needs to learn to streamline if it wants to survive in this economy.

Swan, as the chief's own Wormtongue, is trying to secure his status by pitting the tribe and his magic against the white people and their science. Palmer, the poor guy who got killed, was the liaison between the two groups.

But it is hard to keep a good man down, so Palmer gets his revenge from the grave. That, despite being buried standing up for some reason. Did he only buy a 2×2 square foot plot, like when Ben Johnson was buried in Westminster Abbey?

And here is where the picture becomes gloriously batshit crazy, as Palmer returns as a...tree. A walking tree, with goofy unmoving eyes and a mysterious aperture that opens and closes, apparently to breathe through. I know trees breathe in carbon dioxide, but I don't think any of them do it *through a mouth*.

The scientists discover this thing while it is still half in the burial plot, so they dig it up and try to save it. I wondered what they thought it was, since it looks roughly like a tree despite the green "blood" oozing from it. Still, a newly arrived doctor (Tina Carver) tells the others to give it an IV. How I wished they had shown a closeup of how they did that.

She administers a miraculous resuscitation serum to this creature and, while they're away, it trashes the lab and goes on a murderous spree of revenge. The rest of the movie is pretty much guy who was ritually sacrificed returning as an anthropomorphic tree and killing those who betrayed him.

And this movie is an absolute blast. I don't think the movie has a self-aware bone in its body and, because of that, it is one of the most unintentionally hilarious things I have seen. Consistently bad line readings ensure the grade-Z dialogue gets actual belly laughs.

Surprisingly, the tree costume isn't the worst thing here. While the concept of an evil, walking tree is pretty stupid, you can tell a lot of effort went into the costume. Unfortunately, the designers didn't put much thought into its physiology, so it becomes deeply ridiculous when it has to bend over, as this thing that is supposed to be solid wood just bends in two like it is rubber (which it probably was). Perhaps it was meant to be a sentient rubber tree.

Every actor here is terrible. Tod Andrews, as the lead scientist, is especially noteworthy. His demeanor throughout says this is a man who can give less than zero fucks about this picture, and he delivers every line as if he read it off the page just before the cameras started rolling.

Almost as bad is Linda Watkins as the Australian woman who runs the nearby trading post. Her accent seems to wander all over the British Isles, before deciding to settle for a while in Australia. Typical of productions like this, a character or two will seemingly be forgotten about at a given point and they may or may not reenter later. That is what happens with Watkins. Unfortunately, the movie remembers to bring her back for the big finale.

Even the soundtrack is deliriously odd. At one point, a series of mundane activities are on screen while one incongruous piece of music after another accompanies it on the soundtrack. Each piece is of a different mood than the previous and every one of them is a baffling choice. It's like somebody grabbed one of those library music albums and just let a few tracks of one side play out in sequence.

Then there's this weird bit of sound effects every time the action takes us outside and into the "jungle". It is like every possible creature of the wild kingdom is making their signature sound simultaneously. And then, after a few seconds, it just *stops*. Nobody even bothered to loop it.

From Hell It Came is a notoriously bad movie, but it is generally regarded as such because of the daft concept, and even more daft appearance, of the killer tree. While that is pretty memorable, there is so much here I found more bewildering: the accents of the "natives", the barely phoned-in performances and a general air of incompetence. I try to laugh with and not at movies, but this one was so goddamn hilarious that I couldn't help myself.

Original version posted on 5/18/2023

Galaxy of Terror (1981)

Freddie Krueger (Robert Englund), *Happy Days's* Joanie (Erin Moran), *My Favorite Martian*'s Martian (Ray Walston) and Captain Spaulding (Sid Haig) are on an interstellar mission on a ship captained by Laura Palmer's mom. (Grace Zabriskie). Is there any reason you *shouldn't* see 1981's *Galaxy of Terror*, produced by Roger Corman?

Well, yes, actually. And that is the moment where Taaffe O'Connell is raped by a giant maggot. While unexpected, that takes what starts out as an *Alien* clone into places such light entertainment shouldn't go (and, really, no movie should go).

Instead of one creature being a threat to the crew, this picture steals a page from *Forbidden Planet* and has each person confront, only to be usually killed by, their greatest fear. That might have been an interesting idea, but it is done so ineptly that I didn't even realize this is what has been happening until it is stated blatantly towards the end. So, apparently, O'Connell's character has a very distinctive phobia. I doubt psychologists have classified that one.

Anyway, that scene occurs roughly halfway through the film. I was thoroughly on-board until then, thanks largely to special effects by none other than James Cameron. I don't know which effects he was responsible for and which he wasn't, but the movie makes great use of blue-screen, miniatures, matte paintings and stop-motion. It looks like it was made with a much bigger budget than it had to have.

If you see *Galaxy of Terror*, be sure to get the Shout Factory blu-ray, as it has a fantastic feature-length retrospective documentary. It is another example of how the worst and/or lowest-budget films often have the best extras and commentaries. The anecdotes are often unique, which one would expect from a movie that has a giant maggot raping a woman.

Original version posted on 6/17/2023

I Married a Monster from Outer Space (1958)

The cliché says you shouldn't judge a book by its cover. By that logic, you probably shouldn't judge a movie by its title, either. But somebody designed that book cover and somebody named that movie and, by doing so, they were trying to convey something to appeal to certain audiences.

So, I pounced immediately when I saw an import blu-ray of a 1950's sci-fi thriller *I Married a Monster from Outer Space*. Having seen it now, I wasn't disappointed, but I also partly got something other than the thick slice of movie cheese I anticipated.

Things start out pretty silly, as a group of guys gather for a bachelor party on the eve of one of their number tying the knot. This party is far from rowdy, and the bar they're in is more orderly and subdued than any I patronized back when I used to drink. Maybe it's because the bar is such an obvious set.

But already there were a couple of flourishes which made me suspect there would be more going on than is par for the course for this genre.

First, there was a long crane shot that follows one car into the bar's parking lot and then continues in a pan across the lot. It isn't the opening of *Touch of Evil*, but some effort went into what would usually be a static establishing shot. There is also an interesting transition from that parking lot to the interior of the bar, a technique along the lines of what Hitchcock used in *Rope* to make it appear sequential long takes were a seamless whole.

The plot concerns an alien race whose women have all died. The surviving men are on an interstellar booty call to try to find a species with which they can breed. Their approach is oddly specific, as they secretly take over the bodies of bachelors and don't bother commandeering men who are already married. They are also curiously fixated on tying the knot before consummating a relationship, which means an advanced alien race is adhering to the moral standards of mid-20th-century Western civilization. The town's apparent sole prostitute seems to be going out of business by the end of the picture, yet the aliens don't bother utilizing that service.

The effect used when a man is overtaken by one of the aliens is quite impressive. It looks like they are enveloped by a billowing pillar of smoke that emerges from off-screen. I'm guessing the effect involved pouring a liquid like milk into an aquarium, but it's beyond me how they controlled the shape of this cloud or how they superimposed it over the footage.

Science Fiction (usually light on the science)

There are some other awesome effects here as well. There are occasionally flashes, literally, of the aliens' true faces over that of the humans they occupy. We also get some aliens in their true form, which are obvious rubber suits, though they have a neat pulsing glow to them. At one point, the aliens get shot and we see the bullet holes seal themselves up. There is even some truly startling gore when a dog tears off part of one of the aliens and blood (well, alien blood) shoots out in spurts. I am stunned the censors let *that* go by.

Another aspect of this picture I enjoyed is an ominous feeling that builds over its runtime. For something that starts out appearing to be high camp, it ends up being a pretty unsettling riff on *Invasion of the Body Snatchers*, complete with some similarly noir photography.

There is one scene I will remember for some time, where a raincoat-clad figure on an empty street on a dry night is standing stock-still facing the windows of a closed store. The town prostitute crosses the road to talk to the figure, but it doesn't even seem to know she's there. It's weird, somebody just standing there for no apparent reason and not acknowledging her presence. The tension mounts as this scene draws out to be uncomfortably long.

I Married a Monster from Outer Space is already one of my favorite 50's sci-fi films. Sometimes you watch a film because you think you're going to have a good laugh at its expense, and then it surprises you by being unexpectedly and honestly enjoyable. It isn't completely original, and it has some flaws, but it has so much in it which is distinctive that I know I will be revisiting it eventually.

Original version posted on 3/22/2023

The Incredible Melting Man (1977)

At this time, I own over 3000 blu-ray discs and God only knows how many DVDs. Managing this large number of titles is partly why I rent a storage unit. I imagine most people, especially those who only use streaming services, would wonder why I would go through this effort for physical media.

One reason is because of the special features on many of these discs. I doubt most people would understand why I would watch some deeply terrible movies and then watch them with the commentary track on. I do this because the good and great movies rarely have interesting commentaries, while the commentary tracks for the worst movies are almost always the most interesting, informative and bereft of industry ass-kissing. There are many discs I own solely for the commentaries and other special features.

That's why I will be holding onto my blu-ray of *The Incredible Melting Man*. This is a terrible film, but director William Sachs's commentary is blunt, highly informative and conveyed in a jovial, conversational manner. I got the impression he would be a fun person to hang out with. And while he doesn't name names, it isn't hard to determine whom he is referring to when he relates tales of incompetence, nepotism and creative differences. Most people in the industry deliver boring commentaries, as they are primarily interested in continuing their careers and have no wish to commit self-sabotage. Those who no longer have such aspirations, especially those who worked solely in the shoestring-budget world, give you the truth (or at least *their* truth).

In that commentary, Sachs goes to great pains to insist his intention was for this movie to be a parody instead of a straight horror film. As there were few movies in the late 70's with titles like *The Incredible Melting Man*, that does suggest this is a tribute to, and potentially parody of, sci-fi horror of the 50's. Unfortunately, nothing else in the finished film suggests this.

Sachs blames the producers for this change in tone, frequently pointing out where additional footage was added at their insistence. At the same time, he proudly admits authorship of such scenes as an overweight nurse running in slow-motion down a hallway (that doesn't look like any passage in any area of any hospital I have ever seen), only to crash right through a glass door. This was so ridiculous that I burst out laughing, but I never assumed the intention of the scene was parody.

Similarly, the dialogue is largely terrible and almost entirely delivered through stiff line readings. Supposedly, the best parody is indistinguishable from what is being mocked but, if that is the case, how would one even recognize such a parody unless they are told that directly? In that case, what would be the point?

If there is one thing here that is effective, it is the makeup effects on the melting man. This is early work from Rick Baker, who would go on to have a stellar career. The titular character is always covered in dripping strands of what looks like discharge from a bad sinus infection. It is genuinely nauseating, and I think the filmmakers missed an opportunity by not titling this *The Incredible Booger Man*. However, after the melting man has had sufficient screentime, we begin to notice those effects are little more than a latex skin base covered with tons of dripping goo in assorted colors.

The Incredible Melting Man is a terrible move but which, on its own, can be enjoyed as camp. But I think the ideal way to watch this film is with the commentary track on—it feels like the affable Sachs is sitting beside you, maybe with a cold beverage on a weekend afternoon, regaling you with his anecdotes. After all, the directors of low-budget films shot on the fast and loose tend to have the best stories.

Original version posted on 1/6/2023

Innerspace (1987)

It appears my approach to watching movies is "better late than never". God only knows how 1987's *Innerspace* failed to cross my path for so long. I was at the right age for such a sci-fi adventure comedy in its original theatrical run. I wouldn't have been seeking out films by Joe Dante specifically, but the fact he had also directed *Gremlins* should have been a draw.

I was very pleasantly surprised by what, on the surface, appeared to be just an update of 1966's *Fantastic Voyage*. This time, it isn't an entire crew that is miniaturized, but only Dennis Quaid's test pilot in a capsule not unlike those very small subs sent to the deepest parts of the ocean. And he wasn't even shrank down to microscopic size to perform surgery within the body of the U.S. President. Instead, this inaugural mission was to inject him into a rabbit. Through a series of unexpected events, he ends up in something slightly more hyperactive than a hare, and that is Martin Short.

Short had been advised by his doctor (William Schallert) to get some relaxation. I was never sure if Short is a hypochondriac or if he somehow has ever disease known to man and then some. It seems to me he has at least contracted a case of whatever weird ailment every character played by Jerry Lewis must have had in the 50's and 60's, as I felt Short was almost paying tribute to those performances. Still, I actively seek out films with Short in them and I avoid most of those starring Lewis (but not all—*The Nutty Professor* is shockingly good).

If Short appears to be channeling Lewis, Quaid initially seems to be Jack Nicholson. We first see him stumbling drunk into a "Test Pilots of America" dinner, doing what appears to be a riff on that actor's trademark "devilish imp" persona. Fortunately, he drops that shtick after a while, which I guess is necessary, as our hero will curiously spend the vast majority of the film seated in a small capsule.

It's just as well, as his life before this mission seemed to largely consist of laying around a house where he has a robotic arm he built just for the purpose of pouring endless drinks for him, and it doesn't even do a decent job at that. The one bright glimmer in his existence seems to be an on and off relationship with Meg Ryan.

Quaid's mission was supposed to take place entirely in the confines of a JPL-like laboratory where, as I learned from the commentary track, a great many actual JPL scientists appear as extras. That definitely makes for some solid verisimilitude. I also liked how the capsule is not some sleek, finished thing that looks like it was designed by Apple. Instead, it is how something in progress should look, with all kinds of stuff obviously just shoehorned in. It's a nice touch.

Not even the head scientist is predominantly an actor in real life. Curiously, John Hora isn't even a scientist, but is best known as a cinematographer, a service he provided on many of Dante's films. I'm surprised Hora didn't act in more features, as he is very effective as a scientist.

Surprisingly, he will even be in an extensive chase scene where he flees on foot and bike from a car driven by Vernon Wells, a henchman of villainess Fiona Lewis. Hora doesn't exactly have a build I think would be conducive for such an action sequence, and that made the pursuit even funnier than I think was intended. Wells follows Hora to a mall where we see the first of the henchman's mechanical hands in action. He points a gloved finger at the scientist and actually shoots a bullet out of that finger at him. Just try and do *that*, Dr. Strangelove! The various mechanical hands he employs will be used throughout the runtime, including a brief moment which surprised me, where he apparently has a special attachment designed for pleasuring Lewis.

It is at the mall where Hora, in a desperate last measure, injects the miniaturized capsule into an unsuspecting Short. Lewis and Wells will track Short to his job as a supermarket cashier. It is here the man first starts to have strange experiences, such as the cash register and bar code reader malfunctioning, ringing up groceries at astronomical prices. Another interesting tidbit I gleaned from the commentary is animator Chuck Jones is the third customer in line, and he spent the day drawing Bugs Bunny for everybody who wanted one.

That hardware malfunction was due to an "electro-magnetic booster" that is part of the machinery of Quaid's pod. He will deliberately use that to destroy Short's television in an effort to convince him he is not having a psychotic break when he starts hearing Quaid's voice in his head. You see, the pod has a number of interesting abilities, almost as if the scientists were trying to create the titular vehicle from *Yellow Submarine*. Especially useful is a robotic arm that can latch onto an optic nerve and see what Short is seeing or grab part of the ear and hear what Short is hearing. It can also intercept for Quaid some whiskey he has encouraged Short to down, and I wondered what on earth would drive somebody to drink some of another person's backwash. Perhaps the strangest device Quaid has at his disposal is one that can scan somebody's face and then stimulate the muscles in Short's face until he looks exactly like the other person. I really wondered how that was intended to be deployed when the mission was originally to inject the capsule into a rabbit.

The visuals inside the body as astonishing, with the film justly winning the Oscar for Best Visual Effects. One can easily imagine how badly these would be accomplished nowadays through the inevitable CGI. Instead, these purely physical effects are largely done underwater, using floating flecks of diamond dust to capture the light. Even today, such visuals as the giant orb that is the back of an eye are truly stunning.

The stunt work is also quite impressive. Perhaps the most notable sequence is where Short is hanging on to the swinging door on the back of a freezer truck barreling down a road. Ryan has pulled alongside in a convertible, and there is an astonishing moment where a motorcycle from the opposite direction goes between the two vehicles and under the legs of the actor, who has one on each vehicle. Even more astonishing is when Short finally gets both feet onto the convertible, only to briefly find himself balancing on the windshield of a fast-moving car. From the commentary, I learned this was accomplished via struts run from the car body and up through Short's pants. Just try to imagine how terrifying it must have been to be the actor in that moment.

But what really makes the film so enjoyable are the performances, big and small. I especially liked Schallert's doctor, who can keep a straight face while making such bizarre pronouncements as not ruling out "theistic hysteria" for the voice Short has started hearing in his head. It's like something on SCTV when he describes the medieval remedy for that condition being flaying "the skin off your body with brands of fire". And there is a small SCTV reunion in the doctor's waiting room when Short finds himself flanked by Joe Flaherty and Andrea Martin.

Innerspace is great fun and has dated surprisingly well. The effects are awesome, the jokes are still funny and it has creativity to burn. Not only is the movie highly recommended, but an accompanying commentary track is almost as necessary as the film itself.

Original version posted on 7/29/2024

Invaders from Mars (1953)

When I was a really little kid, I thought the front yard of my grandparent's house was huge. Admittedly, the house is set further back from the street than any other in that neighborhood, but it didn't take me long to realize the yard was nowhere near as large as elementary-school-aged me believed. All it took was a foot or so of vertical growth and I suddenly had a whole new perspective.

1953's *Invaders from Mars* wisely presents its world in a manner consistent with how young children see the world. Home is safe, but some of the outside world is very strange. A police station is an especially intimidating place, even for adults. But in the one presented here, the front desk is raised up higher than it should be, putting the sergeant behind it on a literal pedestal. The wall behind him is so absent of color and texture that a clock mounted on it almost seems to be floating in space. My wife remarked it was like Saint Peter at the gates of heaven, which I thought was interesting. Then there's the ridiculously high walls of this space, which are made even more menacing by the long, unbroken corridors they flank.

It is in this distorted environment the young Jimmy Hunt finds himself unable to convince most of the adults that a UFO is buried in the massive sand pit behind his house. People keep dropping into the sand, only to later reappear. The most noticeable difference in those people afterwards is their manner becomes brusque and stoic. Among the first victims are his parents, as well as two police officers. That the latter are converted are only more reasons Hunt is reluctant to go to the police station.

Hunt quickly takes notice of a red "X" on the back of the necks of those who were taken into the pit. We will later learn this is where the invaders have surgically implanted a control device at the base of each victim's skull. Should the aliens no longer need a subject, or the mission is jeopardized, they can instantaneously kill them through this mechanism by giving them an aneurysm.

That is rather strong stuff for a sci-fi horror movie from 1953 which is aimed at children, especially when this is how a girl Hunt knows (Janine Perreau) meets her fate. Actually, everything that happens with Perreau in the short time she is in the film is rather disturbing. We haven't met, or even heard about, this character before Hunt, watching through a telescope, sees her fall into the sand pit. As soon as Hunt runs to Perreau's mother to say what he has seen, the girl has returned and is wearing a very creepy expression. Jimmy leaves, only to discover the girl has set a can of gasoline on fire in the basement of her house. Shortly after this, we learn the girl is dead.

One aspect of this film I found intriguing and unnerving is how people just keep going up a path in somebody's yard to where they are inevitably taken by the pit. Just consider what it would take to have somebody convince you to go into a stranger's backyard. I know I would have a great many questions. Of course, the converted humans are *very* insistent the uninitiated take this little journey. Another thing that bothered me about Perreau's trip up the path is she was unaccompanied. So, what *was* she doing there? Did kids back then just wander into people's back yards and fall into sand pits?

This is one of those rare pictures where the low budget results in a feature that is likely more interesting than if it hadn't had such limitations. That path to the sand pit is only ever seen on a very restrictive set that obviously does not extend beyond a single hilltop, over which people keep conveniently dropping into the sand. For some wide shots, we see a painted rendering of the same scene. This artificiality only adds to the uncanniness of the viewing experience.

Unfortunately, such budgetary restrictions also have their downside, most notably in the extensive recycling of some footage. To pad the film out to feature length, archival military footage is utilized to a preposterous extent, with many of the same shots of tanks and the like used multiple times. Almost as bad is when we finally get into the alien tunnels underground, and the same footage of drones clad in green velour suits running past is repurposed ad nauseum. That the same shots are occasionally flipped makes not a whit of difference.

I watched *Invaders from Mars* on the Ignite Films blu-ray in a stunning restoration. Many bonus features are included on the disc, including additional footage shot for the European market. I welcome the inclusion of that footage, including an alternate ending, even if I'm glad none of it made it into the film proper. These additional scenes are cumbersome and awkward. I was stunned anybody had watched the original film, with its tiring reuse of footage original and archival, and thought the movie needed to be *longer*.

Original version posted on 4/22/2024

The Invisible Boy (1957)

1956's *Forbidden Planet* was a minor hit, growing in stature over the course of a decade or two. The film had been hugely popular with kids, and not because the plot is basically Shakespeare's *The Tempest*. No, they loved Robby the Robot, an element of the film I still find a bit too goofy, even if I can appreciate it as an icon. The difficulty was giving this audience more of the robot, when the picture doesn't leave much of an opportunity for a sequel.

This is how 1957's bizarre semi-sequel *The Invisible Boy* came to be. Set in the then-present, this is a weird kid's adventure. The script is a bit smarter than I expected, but the film has a few touches that were too juvenile for my tastes. Given this, there is also some unexpectedly dark dialogue.

I'll get to all that in a minute, but I first want to discuss the robot in the room. Apparently, this is the same Robby who was in *Forbidden Planet*, though he doesn't talk about his past..um, future. You see, he was likely brought back from the 23rd century by a time-travelling professor. This plot element is quickly addressed and then completely forgotten. If I was the curious little tyke in this film (Richard Eyer), I would have a ton of questions about this, including where that time travel device might be.

The disassembled Robby had been gathering dust and cobwebs in a storage room of the Stoneman Institute of Mathematics, a nine-story facility entirely under the ground of a mansion, bringing to my mind a similar setup in *This Island Earth*. This facility seems to serve, and house the components of, a massive computer which supposedly has "the sum total of human knowledge".

One element I found hilarious about this setup is the military's concern that "anybody can wander into here". Oh yeah, all a person would have to do is know about this secret operation, get past the doubtless guards while crossing the grounds to get to the mansion, probably get through more security once inside the mansion, and then access the elevator that is the only entry point.

Eyer's dad (Philip Abbott) works at the institute, apparently spending most of his working day at the console for the computer. About that computer: imagine Robby as one of those huge, old mainframes but with a transparent dome on top that is not dissimilar to the robot's head. I take it people are supposed to verbally direct their questions to this "head", as it has the faintest lines that look like eyes on it.

Abbott is the typical egghead of that era's media, though this leads to a few amusing bits early in the film. When his son makes the mistake of asking him at dinner what a computer is, the rambling explanation takes so long that we see crossfades through the courses of the meals, with him still going strong through dessert. This is like the inversion of Einstein's quote concerning how one should be able to explain something to a five-year-old if one really knows what they're doing. Then again, I can't talk, as I am the worst person in the world for explaining concepts to others.

Dad unwisely brings son into work to get the computer to troubleshoot why his son is such an intellectual midget. After he leaves the room, the computer hypnotizes Eyer through the flashing lights on its control panels. When Eyer wakes up, he discovers he is now a genius. And here I thought subliminal learning was bullshit.

There's a moment I like after Eyer gets smart, where he grifts his old man over chess. Allowing Abbott to win the first game, Eyer easily wins the second and so the promise to give him whatever he wants must be fulfilled. All the kid wants is to play with Robby. He doesn't even know who or what that is, but a promise is a promise.

Back at the institute, Eyer soon has Robby reassembled and back in operation. He tries to show off his accomplishment to his dad's co-workers, who are distinctly unimpressed. The strongest reaction he gets is, "Well, somebody finally got it working." Abbott feigns a bit more enthusiasm, and I liked this exchange he has with the robot: "Say something" "SOMETHING" "Well, that's a robot for you"

Eyer gets into various mischief with his new playmate. Asking Robby to build a kite for him, the robot constructs a huge, remote-controlled thing made of tubes and shaped like the letter "H", with propellers in the vertical shafts. That fun comes to an end when mom (Diane Brewster) sees Robby at the controls and Eyer doing tricks on the airborne vehicle.

Robby will soon be getting a firmware upgrade, courtesy of a hardwire link to the computer. Like most such upgrades, I believe in waiting to apply them until you are certain nobody else had any problems. What this one does is make the robot do its evil bidding.

Nothing seems out of the ordinary at first, until Robby concocts a formula to make Eyer invisible. The kid gets up the kind of mischief one would largely expect. One thing he does, however, really creeped me out, and that is when he happens to be in his parents' bedroom when they're about to get it on.

There are hints early on of a weirdly dark undercurrent. When telling dad about a bully, Eyer dreams of vengeance: "Just wait til I get him tied to a tree. I'll bash his teeth in." Oookaaay. Then there's the master computer's plan, which involves placing a miniature electronic device at the base of the skull of those it wants to control, and some of these lead to the death of the recipients. The computer is especially cold in how it has Robby holding Eyer hostage, saying how well the robot knows human physiology and how to best inflict pain. Near the end of the film, it orders Robby to kill the kid slowly, saying, "We'll start with the eyes."

The performances are decent all-around, though these aren't exactly characters with significant depth. Eyer is likeable and believable, especially when the dialogue he's given bestows upon him a matter-of-factness I can appreciate: "I'm not a gentleman. I'm a gentle boy." Abbott and Brewster both fare well as the parents, though I was stunned the script makes the mom dense enough that she mistakes Robby for a travelling salesman.

That brings to mind a question I can't shake since watching this: can Robby teleport? I'm not joking. Robby moves awkwardly and slowly, yet he somehow keeps showing up at the institute and the house. We never see how he got there, and I can't imagine him navigating even the slightest uneven surface with his weird Michelin-man legs. Not to mention all the attention he would doubtlessly draw when out in public. What planted this idea in my brain is a bit towards the end where he appears to get disintegrated by flamethrowers yet suddenly appears some distance away and intact.

If there's one significant failing in *The Invisible Boy*, it is the effects work. I know they didn't have the budget to get Disney to animate sparks in Robby's head this time around, but too much here is too sloppy. A standout example for me was a statue in the park in the kite scene that is so unreal as to draw attention to itself, and the thing isn't even important to the scene (Brewster smashes the remote control over it, but that could have been disposed of in any number of ways). But even this isn't enough to completely derail this mildly enjoyable film, a strange sequel-of-sorts to *Forbidden Planet* which nobody asked for.

Original version posted on 9/6/2024

The Invisible Ray (1935)

The production code seriously handicapped some types of films when it went into effect in 1935. The restrictions made it nigh near impossible for major studios to produce horror pictures. So, what could Universal do, when they still had Boris Karloff and Bela Lugosi? These were actors whose fame was almost exclusively through their work in horror.

1935's *The Invisible Ray* is the result of such a dilemma: a science fiction film with trappings of horror worked into it, as well as some "wild safari" kind of fare. It is a mess, but it is a fascinating one.

First, consider the title. Without knowing anything about the story, I suspect most people would be saying to themselves, "Yes, most rays are invisible". In fact, very little of the entire spectrum of waveforms is detectable by the human eye. And it will be quite a while before the movie gives any real idea as to what the titular ray does and why it is important. Until then, the viewer is subjected to such bizarre and grammatically suspect musings as, "Who [can] say that the invisible ray is impossible to science?" So, science is a verb now? That gives me a lot to chew on, but I don't know if I can food it.

The movie begins promisingly enough. It's a dark and stormy night at the old castle. There's an easily provoked mad scientist played by Karloff in a weird, curly wig. There's Francis Drake, as his young wife, and Violet Kemble Cooper as his blind mother.

Karloff has invited a group of scientists, including Lugosi, to witness a demonstration of some sort of amazing new technology he has invented. According to the overly sensitive Karloff, "They'll never laugh at me again." I think it would be hilarious if it was then revealed his fly was open, and it is thoughts like that which provide ample evidence for why I don't direct movies.

The scene with the demonstration is as fascinating as it is baffling. Great matte work provides the upper portions of his laboratory and his observatory. There is a weird dreaminess to some of the shots. A moment where the camera pushes in slowly past the moon immediately brought to mind a similar shot in *Eraserhead*. There is also some great imagery of old electrical gear, with sparks and rays of light shooting around. There's also a recurring image of the guests seated in a row, all looking up at a light from above, which I found a bit uncanny, though I cannot articulate why. It is similar to a scene in *Messiah of Evil* which had the same effect on me, where a group of ordinary-looking people are riding in the back of a truck, all looking up intently at the night sky.

Now, I found it difficult to understand what it is that Karloff is demonstrating, so it will be hard for me to explain it here. Somehow, he is looking deep into space and, from that vantage point, can look back at Earth and see eons into our own past. As he puts it, "The theory of reproducing vibrations from the past is not new." Um…it's not?! I subscribed to *Scientific American* for a few years and can't recall anything like this ever being covered there.

Through his technique, the gathered visitors see a huge meteorite crashing into our planet long before there were humans. Karloff just knows this meteorite is made of a previously unknown element that is an unprecedented source of power. Yeah, I know—just roll with this.

So, it's off to Africa. For some reason, everybody *except* Karloff goes, with him saying he will arrive later. I guess he wanted to give his wife time to develop an attraction to fellow traveler Frank Lawton. These two make for a curious couple, as he looks downright pre-pubescent with his complete lack of shoulders. This is emphasized for maximum unintended hilarity when he is wearing an oversized pith helmet. He looks like a little kid playing grown-up.

While in Africa, Lugosi proves to be about as goofy as Karloff's character, and that is strange, as he plays the good guy. He spews such bizarre inanities as, "This proves, I think, that human organisms are only part of astrochemistry, controlled by radial forces of the sun." I think he also injected a baby with one milligram of sunlight, and that called to mind the kind of crazy remedies some people were humoring at the height of Covid infections.

When Karloff does arrive on the continent, he does so secretly, as he is keeping mum on the exact location of the meteorite. It's in a cliff wall over something very hot, though I was never sure what the source of the heat was. Karloff extracts the mineral while wearing a heat-resistant suit, yet he's lowered into position by helpers using a contraption made of rope and wood. Y'know, the most heat-resistant of all known materials…

Anyway, he gets the mineral, and it has the properties he hoped it would. His first use of it is to power a death ray which he uses to dissolve a boulder, just to intimidate his assistants into doing his bidding. Seeing this, I thought it odd he already had this rather complex looking death ray before he has the mineral. Didn't anybody wonder what that thing was before now? Also, I suspect any employer with a death ray is going to be anti-union.

Unfortunately for him, the exposure to the highly radioactive element had made his touch lethal. Also, it makes him glow in the dark, which should at least make it easier for potential victims to elude him.

Lugosi creates an antidote which takes care of both symptoms. But Karloff has to take a precise amount each day. Too much, too little, or too late will kill him.

Then it is back to civilization, where Lugosi uses controlled amounts of the new element to cure a variety of illnesses and disabilities. It was surprising to see Karloff do a good deed by curing his mother's blindness, though she seems to be the only person he helps. It seems he spends most of his time festering a resentment towards Lugosi. He is also fixated on his wife, who is getting married again. Not sure why he is so angry towards her, given he pretty much pushed her towards Lawton, who is now her fiancée. Oh, and Karloff has also faked his own death by this point, leaving his "widow" no reason to not marry again.

One can imagine roughly how the rest of *The Invisible Ray* plays out. It is an enjoyable enough movie, but it is impossible to take seriously. I found it most interesting that, of the two leads, Lugosi has the meatier role this time. This was especially surprising, as Universal had been moving him out of the limelight and shifting their focus to Karloff. I'm just amazed either could keep a straight face while spewing so much complete gibberish disguised as science. As a character put it in *12 Monkeys*, "Science ain't a real science with these bozos."

Original version posted on 2/7/2024

Lady and the Monster (1944)

In the book *Junk Film: Why Bad Movies Matter*, Katharine Coldiron explains how hard-to-follow logic in some bad films makes them tiring to watch. I think that's why I almost fell asleep watching 1944's *The Lady and The Monster*.

Erich von Stroheim is a scientist of the mad sort, who is determined to keep a brain alive. At the beginning of the film, his most recent successful test subject is a monkey with tuberculosis he bought off an organ grinder. But the recovery of a body from a prop plane crash provides the opportunity to try to preserve a human brain. It will turn out the pilot was a wealthy Howard Hughes type named Donovan.

Donovan has one powerful brain, as it is able to take possession of von Stroheim's assistant (Richard Arlen). Curiously, Donovan's main goal is to free from prison a kid who is on death row for murder. His connection to that kid is withheld from the audience for too long, and the script's inexplicable failure to share that pertinent information was a bad decision.

In a weird middle ground between what I feel are two distinct parallel storylines is yet a third partial plot thread. Helen Vinson, as Donovan's widow, and Sidney Blackmer, as the family lawyer, hound von Stroheim and Arlen, asking if the deceased had any last words. The scientists are honest when they say he didn't have any such words before his body died, but his floating brain in the tank becomes a real Chatty Cathy once he takes hold of Arlen.

I have yet to mention the lead actress, Vera Hruba Ralston, because she is weirdly close to nonexistent in her own film. Then again, she hardly has much presence in those moments she is on the screen. She's the daughter of von Stroheim's now deceased partner, as well as Arlen's love interest and occasional assistant in the lab. Ralston was a Czech import who did not speak English and learned her lines for early films like this phonetically. What I found peculiar is either nobody coached her on-set or she wouldn't take direction. As she was married to the head of Republic Pictures, which made this film, it could have been either possibility. What is deeply weird is how wooden she is, even in physical movements. There's a truly bizarre moment where she takes a few awkward steps towards a column and reaches out to it as if she was a robot that reached a point in its programming telling it to TOUCH PILLAR. When delivering dialogue, she seems to randomly cycle through expressions in hopes she might accidentally hit the right emotional beat for the syllable she happens to be on at any given time.

Her curious manhandling of the English language seems to have infected others. Until I saw this film, I didn't know a particularly terrifying looking surgical tool (like a combination saw and garrote) was called a Gigli saw. But I turned on the subtitles and rewatched a bit where Arlen asks for what sounds like a "giggly saw". Now, *that* sounds like something truly disturbing, and I recommend one be used as a weapon in the next movie with a killer clown in it. But I suspect it is actually pronounced "zhee-lee", if I learned anything from the horrible Ben Afleck and Jennifer Lopez of that title. Which I didn't.

Yet another curious aspect of the film is it distinctly has a feel of gothic horror hanging over the proceedings, yet it takes place in Arizona. There's even the mandatory gothic castle, except it has a Spanish tile roof. So, if you're a gothic horror fan, but tired of ones set in traditional settings like Scotland, here's an American desert gothic one for you.

Lady and the Monster is batshit crazy enough that it should be enthralling. Instead, it is so pointlessly confusing that it becomes a chore to watch. Those who were glued to the film throughout its runtime aren't even rewarded for doing so. A quick and tidy narrative exposition dump in the final minute doesn't even bother to tell us what happened to the kid on death row.

Original version posted on 9/4/2024

Logan's Run (1976)

It is often difficult for audiences who came of age after a period to be able to properly appreciate a work in its historical context. The sci-fi movie genre was in a sad state in the period between *2001: A Space Odyssey* and *Star Wars* (don't even think of correcting me by saying its name is *A New Hope*, because I will go to the mat to defend its original name). In the wake of the former picture, the movies became more cynical, and a message was obligatory. But the later film hadn't happened yet so, barring exceptions for dystopian works like *Soylent Green*, the worlds in the movies made between the two didn't look lived-in and dirty.

Such is the case of 1976's *Logan's Run*, a typical feature of that era. It is basically *Brave New World* cross-pollinated with *ZPG* and *Soylent Green*. Following some sort of "great catastrophe" in the future, everybody lives in a dome-encased city where they have no knowledge of the outside world. Everybody lives a life of complete leisure until the age of 30, when they must die.

Every person gets a crystal implanted in the palm of their left hand when they are infants. This cheap-looking bit of plastic turns different colors over the course of each person's lifetime, finally blinking red when their number is up.

Most people choose to have their lives terminated in a goofy spectacle called "carousel". I was actually scared to see this movie when I was a little kid (reeeally little) because the way it was described to me is these people are put in a giant centrifuge which spins them so hard that they are obliterated into little pieces.

It shouldn't be a surprise this is not what happens in this PG-rated feature. Instead, those about to die wear dance leotards and weird masks that are far creepier than the not-dissimilar hockey mask Jason Voorhees wears. Some sort of energy shield engulfs the group and they start spinning slowly upwards like the world's dullest circus act. As they get near the ceiling, they get zapped out of existence like mosquitoes in a bug zapper. This never stops being gut-bustingly hilarious.

Supposedly, those who go through the carousel are then reborn, but Michael York is starting to have his doubts. He's a Sandman, one of the policemen who hunt down runners, the people who try to flee when their time is up.

Not that there's anywhere for them to go. The bulk of the world as presented in the film is one multi-story shopping mall. I never got the impression that even this area extended much farther beyond a courtyard that seems to be the hub of all activity.

Early on, we see York and fellow Sandman Richard Jordan "retire" an attempted runner. We never see anything emitted from the laser blasters the police use. Instead, there's just a tiny fireworks explosion wherever their "shots" landed. It isn't a great effect. I swear some of these explosions happened behind the guy they are shooting at, but without him appearing to be wounded. No matter, he eventually throws himself off what appears to be the third or fourth floor balcony, despite us seeing him only climb up one story from the courtyard.

York goes through the dead man's belongings, showing particular interest in an ankh necklace. Then the clean-up crew is called, and those guys arrive on what look like flying Segways—which look about as silly as normal Segways. They spray the corpse with something that makes it dissolve one disgusting layer at a time via a series of cross-dissolves.

When York delivers to the police computer the items retrieved from the runner's body, the ankh triggers a warning. Turns out this necklace is a sign of sanctuary, an underground movement providing refuge to runners. York is made to work undercover to infiltrate and destroy the group. The computer apparently decides he needs some incentive, so it changes his palm jewel to flashing red. I wonder why that was necessary. Doesn't anybody whose time *hasn't* expired ever seek sanctuary?

Now York is a runner, taking sanctuary member Jenny Agutter in tow. Jordan pursues them through the industrial works that are behind the scenes of their world of leisure. He has a small battle against his fellow Sandmen and also some of the people of sanctuary. York and Agutter escape to a weird deep-freeze area where a psychotic robot has permanently put previous runners on ice. Destroying the robot, they finally reach the outside world.

What a shock to the system this must have been. I like how little time appears to pass before Agutter screams, "I HATE OUTSIDE!" That's me after an hour of any kind of outdoor activity.

They eventually find Washington D.C., which is a wasteland on a swamp, an abandoned place not fit for life. So, D.C. hasn't changed much from how it is today. In the Capitol building, they find Peter Ustinov, who surprises them with his advanced age. There are cats all over the place and there's a nice bit where he explains how cats have three names: their ordinary name, their fancy name and the name only the cat itself knows. York decides they must take Ustinov back to the city, to convince the populace there's no harm in growing old.

There's some great matte painting work in the scenes in and around D.C. It is a lot better than the miniatures of the domed city where shuttles go from one building to another in clear tubes that look exactly like a Habitrail. I kept waiting for a giant hamster to pursue one of the vehicles in the tubes. The TV show *Thunderbirds* from a decade prior had better miniature work, yet there was still a certain charm to all this. That said, it was surprising something this bad was in a film from a major studio.

Perhaps the most shocking thing here is the nudity. There isn't a great deal of it, but it is about 100 times more than I expected for a PG film. I've read about how a few scenes had to be cut down to achieve that rating. One of those is a pursuit through the Sex Shop, which is apparently just an ongoing orgy. I wonder if they have Black Friday sales and, if so, what those are like.

It may sound like I dislike *Logan's Run*; however, I genuinely enjoyed it. I tend to like dystopian sci-fi, and this handles the topics typical of the fare with varying degrees of success. The mostly poor effects work also amuses me, though in a smirking way. Watching it, it is seriously jarring to think *Star Wars* was only a year away.

Original version posted on 10/2/2023

The Monolith Monsters (1957)

I've seen sci-fi horror movies where the threat is animal, and at least one where the threat is vegetable, but 1957's *The Monolith*

Monsters is the first one I can recall seeing where the threat is mineral.

This sci-fi/horror film opens on a shot of the Earth (well, a fairly crude model of the globe) getting hit by what are supposed to be fiery objects, courtesy of some quaint effects work. In narration, we are told about how the planet is under constant bombardment by extraterrestrial objects, but how most of these burn up in the atmosphere. As the narrator rather poetically puts it, these are "the shooting stars upon which so many wishes have been made."

Then we transition to the desert, where Department of the Interior agent Phil Harvey stops his government vehicle to put some water in the overheated radiator. He uses a black rock to chock the tires, not knowing this is a fragment of the alien material which will soon pose a major threat. Additional shots show many of these rocks scattered around the area, and these glassy objects look great as they shine in the daylight. It's almost like something from a Hipgnosis album sleeve, such as that for *Elegy* by The Nice.

Harvey takes the rock back to the department's outpost in some podunk town, where he leaves it on a counter overnight. Unfortunately, he also leaves a window open. The wind knocks over a clipboard on a high shelf, which topples a container of water, which soaks the rock on the counter below. It's as if God has a penchant for jokes with convoluted set-ups, like some sort of Rube Goldberg set-up with a cruel punchline. I also wondered why Harvey bothered keeping a container full of water, and why he set it on a high shelf.

Still, something has to kick the plot in motion, and Harvey comes downstairs to find the soaked rock growing. Transition to the next day, when fellow Interior agent Grant Williams has returned to the office, startled to find it locked. Once inside, we see his reaction to the carnage before we see the devastation. That's the key difference between comedy and horror—in the latter, you see the reaction shot before you know what the person is reacting to.

There's more of the black rocks all around the lab. A weirdly unnerving element of this scene is Harvey, uncommunicative and standing stock-still with his back to Williams. The effect is slightly spoiled by this obviously being a still image. It turns out that not only is Harvey dead, but an autopsy reveals he has become calcified. This isn't explained further, but I wondered if his body was solid rock throughout and, if so, how they even did that autopsy.

Who knew rock collecting could be such a dangerous hobby? Unfortunately, there wasn't time to warn Lola Albright, as a schoolteacher who has just taken a group of students on a field trip into the desert. I'm guessing there aren't many places in the area one could take the kids on a school outing. I like the moment where, after giving the kids some instructions, she says, "OK, explode", whereupon they all tear off in different directions.

A little girl (Linda Scheley) in the group takes home one of the rocks. After washing it off, she leaves it in the washtub. That night, the police find the house destroyed, the parents turned to stone, and Scheley in shock. Unfortunately, what initially appears to be nothing more than shock is something more sinister, as her body is gradually calcifying. Is it fair to say she was likely petrified with fear?

Analysis of a rock reveals it grows when in contact with water, which we already surmised. As it grows, however, it drains organic materials of their silicates, making them less flexible.

The rocks soon pose a far greater threat when some of them end up in water-saturated ground, causing them to grow into ebony pillars several stories high, which then fall over, shatter, and each of those fragments grow into a stories-high crystal, and so on. It's a neat idea and well-executed through miniatures.

It is discovered salt puts a stop to the growth process. There is conveniently a salt reclamation facility downstream from where the water would come through should the area dam happen to break. And the path that water, now salt water, would follow will intersect with that of the alien rocks. Hmmm…

The acting here is pretty, um, solid all around, though little of the dialogue or performances is remarkable. The one standout is Les Tremayne, as the publisher and seemingly sole reporter for the town's sad little newspaper. He apparently hangs around the Interior office a lot in desperate hopes that, if anything newsworthy ever happens, it will likely originate from there. One moment I really like is when characters are speculating about the distance between the dam and the town, and Tremayne effortlessly rattles off it is two and seven-tenths miles. "If it's dull or statistical, I've written about it."

I really liked *The Monolith Monsters* and have seen it twice so far. It is a unique approach to the sci-fi monster trope. I suspect it is also making a comment on invasive species. Events proceed in a rational manner, with rational people using science to investigate. I'm sure that science is dodgy, but at least it gives us logic we can follow, and I appreciate how these characters arrive at their solutions. For a movie with an unthinking threat, I like to believe a fair amount of thought went into it.

Original version posted on 5/5/2024

Outland (1981)

At first, 1981's *Outland* appears to be striving to be *Alien*. Its opening title sequence recalls that of the earlier film. It takes place in a grimy, grungy mining facility on the Jupiter moon IO, but it might as well be the *Nostromo*. The score is by Jerry Goldsmith, who provided that service for the other film. Heck, I swear a bar of the opening theme here directly lifts from that other score. This even feels a bit like a Ridley Scott film, and I just imagine his face blanching if anybody compared his work to that of Peter Hyams, the man who also helmed *Timecop*, *End of Days* and *2010: The Year We Made Contact*.

What is odd is this picture actually doesn't want to be *Alien*. Instead, it casts Sean Connery as an uncorruptible marshal who is the law in that mining operation, in what is obviously a remake of *High Noon*. Having disrupted Peter Boyle's trade in a synthetic amphetamine, the company sends two hitmen to snuff out the sheriff that coming Sunday. Don't even ask if they're going to shoot the deputy, as he was already dead about halfway through the runtime.

Just like the legendary western which inspired this film, Connery will find himself squaring off against the assassins almost entirely by himself. Heck, even his wife and son have deserted him, though that was before all the troubles. The one person who does rise to the occasion is Frances Sternhagen, in a great performance as a brusque, onery doctor. She steals every scene she's in. Consider her dialogue when as she intrudes upon Connery playing racquetball alone, just to break the news nobody will be helping him when the shuttle carrying the hitmen arrives: "That's pretty good, playing by yourself and losing. I'd join you if I could play sitting down. There seems to be a strange flu going around. Everybody plans on being sick this Sunday."

I'm amazed more people on the station aren't siding with the sheriff. After all, the drug Boyle has been pimping to them has resulted in a few suicides. Two of these are the result of immediate loss of atmosphere, which is portrayed quite gruesomely by that era's standards. Given the emphasis on gore in contemporary cinema, I have no desire to see how a horror film of today would portray this.

That leads me to the film's special effects, which are quite solid, if not exactly top of the line, even for the time this was made. I also had to overlook some "science facts" elements. One minor aspect needling me long after the end credits rolled is whether somebody could feel an electric shock that happened outside their space suit. Seems to me that, if one is wearing something that can protect them from extreme temperatures, radiation and a complete lack of atmosphere, it is unlikely that suit would conduct electricity from outside through to the wearer.

One thing that left a strong impression on me are the sets. This facility feels huge, though I realize most of it is just a few sections repeated and shot from different angles. Even so, it was convincing enough that I was completely oblivious to that during a great foot chase scene. Something that helps to sell that scene is not just the shot compositions and editing, but the desperation and exasperation of the pursuer and the pursued.

Connery really sells that scene and, honestly, I feel he turns in one of his best performances in *Outland*. He seems tired and weary throughout this, and that's exactly as the character should be played. I have heard some rather harsh opinions of this picture, with some saying that, between this and *Zardoz*, he should have given up on sci-fi completely. While I will concede I have a soft spot (albeit, a small one) for that other film (if only because it dared to be so uniquely batshit), I genuinely love *Outland*. It is neither a rip-off of *Alien* nor *High Noon*, but successfully restages the story of the latter in the world of the former.

Original version posted on 7/7/2024

The Phantom Planet (1961)

I wonder what Coleen Gray did to piss off Hollywood? In the late 1940's, she was in films like the astonishing Nightmare Alley. By the late 50's and early 60's, she was in TV fare and garbage like *The Leech Woman* and 1961's *The Phantom Planet*.

Typical of low-budget fare, this is not a long film, but it feels sluggish throughout its runtime. It especially takes a while to get going, and I was starting to think we would never get past a moon base and a couple of rockets with which its operators communicate. One character even says something which feels like a meta comment on the movie itself: "A person can lose their mind out here waiting for something to happen".

And yet, initially, the film had shown some signs of promise. The insides of the rocket control rooms are small, unlike those spacious enough to maintain a small herd of cattle, as seen in most other movies of the time. Also, the instrument panels tend to be packed with what look like actual buttons, knobs and gauges. That design approach always makes the world more real to me, as every inch of a spaceship's interior would be at a premium.

These rockets are dispatched from our moon base in the then-distant year 1980. I also like the model of their moon base, but I am always partial to miniature work. Looking at this installation and the associated rockets, I wondered if this is what Trump had in mind when he founded the Space Force.

Those rockets are constantly dodging asteroids that look a bit...um, dodgy and I started feeling less generous towards the film. These things mostly looked like clusters of Grape Nuts, which the ships usually evade by doing a U-turn. Yes, a U-turn. In space. Other space rocks look like popcorn, which makes me think a great tagline for this film could have been, "In space, nobody can hear you pop." Failing that, I'd like to recommend it for use to promote a sci-fi porn film.

The plot puts Earth on the defensive from the titular planet, which appears seemingly at random and is destroying our space fleet. It looks far more like an asteroid than a planet to me and, even then, the closest thing it resembles is a chicken nugget. Later, similar "planets" will be on fire and I guess those are flamin' hot nuggets.

One such rocket is captured by the planet and gently lowered down to its surface. Astronaut Dean Fredericks survives and isn't conscious when he starts shrinking within his space suit. No really, we see what is obviously a photo of his face reducing in size until it goes under the bottom edge of his faceplate before disappearing completely. When this guy comes to, he has been reduced to maybe around six inches in height. He emerges from the spacesuit as if it was a giant cave, which I guess it is at that point, and I wondered what it was like to be swimming in your body funk.

He has been shrunken so as to be the same size as the residents of this rock, which they call Rayton, which sounded to me like an exciting polymer for the world of tomorrow. Conveniently, everybody speaks English, though really there is some sort of translation device that automatically converts his language to theirs and vice-versa. So, basically an early version of the TARDIS or a Babel Fish.

Fredericks is put on trial and sentenced to…live on this planet. That seems pretty fair to me, even if they seem to be a rather humorless bunch. One character makes a dig at people having too much free time when they should be working more, so I guess Fredericks is stuck on the planet of the tiny Space Amish. Too much free time is how I happen to watch so many films like this, so maybe that guy was onto something.

A perk of being stuck here is our hero has his choice of two women eager to be his wife. One of them is Gray. Despite this being a black-and-white film, it looks like she was probably a redhead at the time. Together with her primitive costume, one only needs to put a bone in her hair and she would visually be the perfect Wilma Flintstone. The other is the mute Dolores Faith, who looks like a clearance rack Elizabeth Taylor.

There will be some conflict between our protagonist and Anthony Dexter, who had been making time with Gray before the Earthman arrived. Naturally, there will be an external threat of a rival bunch of aliens, which then brings together the men on the same side of that battle.

That enemy is from a "sun satellite", which I believe would mean they live on a planet. I'm pretty sure we only ever see one of these creatures, and it is Richard Kiel, in his feature film debut, entirely obscured by a goofy costume that would have been derisible even a decade earlier.

One of the more endearing of this film's goofier aspects is how the alleged good guys can control the flight of the entire planet, making this rock rather unlike a planet. The navigation is accomplished through just the gentle waving of hands in the open air, making it appear the planet is controlled by theremins.

Speaking of that instrument, there is a curious credit in the titles for "Interplanetary Sound". That's because the soundtrack employs a cue from *Forbidden Planet* ad nauseum with, depending on your tolerance for such fare, extra nauseum.

There's one scene in *The Phantom Planet* I want to single out, an interesting bit early in the film where Fredericks and Richard Weber are on the wing of their rocket, making a repair. Micrometeorites start whizzing past, causing chaos which results in Weber floating in space like Frank Poole in *2001*. As he drifts away to his death, we hear him reciting the Lord's Prayer in his head. It is a curiously disturbing, and even touching, moment in an otherwise ineffective and unremarkable picture.

Original version posted on 12/28/2024

SSSSSSS (1973)

Have you recently experienced peeling skin, increased sensitivity to cold, sudden weight loss and skin that has become green and scaly? Are you the actor Dirk Benedict? If you have experienced all of these, you are likely suffering 1973's *SSSSSSS*.

Additional symptoms of *SSSSSSS* include an incoherent plot involving Strother Martin as a herpetologist trying to create a king cobra with a human mind. If you are a student in that field, which is inexplicably popular at a college near this desert town, you will be especially susceptible to this scheme, as Martin will lure you in as a research assistant and then give you suspicious "inoculation" shots. Once again, Dirk Benedicts will be especially susceptible.

If you are a Dirk Benedict, and you have received these curious injections, failure to treat symptoms will eventually result in being outfitted in a thick rubber suit that surely took a great deal of effort to realize (and doubtless hours in the makeup chair each day) but which looks deeply ridiculous. The last symptom of the illness will be complete transformation, via cross-dissolves, into an actual snake. Viewers may experience intense, sustained laughter upon seeing this. Dirk Benedicts of the world may experience an unintended benefit from this development, as they may now be the only person in the world able to correctly say the title of this picture.

Speak to your doctor if you believe you are experiencing *SSSSSSS*, unless that doctor is Strother Martin, as this is a man who routinely gives liquor to a snake. That seems far more likely to be harmful to the animal than any enjoyment, however unlikely, it may derive from the experience.

Also beware of doctors such as that played by Richard B. Shull since, despite their overall good intentions, they are likely to end up chained in a basement in a *Saw*-like scenario. The key to each of their shackles will be placed in a separate terrarium, one containing a venomous snake while the other has a non-venomous snake. It is situations like this that make a person wish they had paid more attention to the Wildlife Treasury set of animal cards they had as a kid.

Perhaps it would be better if you talked with a friend, even if you only have one. That will likely be Heather Menzies, as Martin's daughter and your love interest. Another curious aspect of contracting *SSSSSSS* is conveniently blurred vision, such as in a skinny-dipping scene inexplicably placed in a PG-rated movie.

Sufferers may also want to find a peer group, such as former assistants of Martin's. To find such people, begin at your local carnival and be sure to check out the Snakeman at the freak show. Nothing like putting the evidence of your previous mistakes right out there in the open so people can start connecting the dots.

The best way to avoid suffering from *SSSSSSS* is complete avoidance of this movie. Those with a high tolerance for cheese made with the production values of made-for-TV fare of the time may ingest the Shout Factory blu-ray. If one chooses this option, only one dose is recommended. Destroy contents after use.

Original version posted on 2/2/2024

Them (1954)

1954's *Them* starts with police officers investigating the devastation at two different desert locales. At a destroyed trailer, they take note there is a box of sugar cubes on the counter. Later, at a general store, they observe sugar seemed to be the focus of some bizarre heist.

Already, I couldn't stop thinking about "Lisa's Rival", an episode of *The Simpsons*, where a subplot has Homer discovering an overturned sugar truck, filling his car with the stolen "white gold" and hoarding it in a giant pile in the backyard. Swarms of bees inevitably descend upon Homer's sugar pile, but what he should have been watching out for are giant ants. At least that was my takeaway from this picture.

This sci-fi film casts a long shadow—a long ant-shaped shadow. The general consensus is this is the best of the 50's "giant creature" trend, and I don't think I have seen one to surpass it.

This is a film full of surprises, starting with the title in bright red in a movie that is otherwise black and white. As for that black and white photography, it is crisp throughout. Not sure why the desert is always used as the locale for 50's giant insect movies, but it looks great on the screen.

What the movie does best is sustain an atmosphere of dread. The film starts with a dazed little girl in her bathrobe walking through the desert and carrying a doll with a broken head. For roughly the first quarter of the picture, we follow the two police officers who found the girl and try to determine what has happened.

As we stay with the officers, we only know what they themselves find out. We are instantly drawn into the picture as if we are investigating alongside them.

Of those officers, James Whitmore plays the lead. I had to overcome my severe doubts a New Mexico police officer would be asked to accompany an FBI agent and a couple of scientists around the US in the course of the investigation.

That FBI agent is played by James Arness. I was amused, as he had played the title creature in *The Thing from Another World* three years prior. Needless to say, he drains far fewer humans of their blood in *Them*.

Rounding out the investigating team are father and daughter doctors played by Edmund Gwenn and Joan Weldon. I was startled to see Edmund Gwenn, as I will always associate him with his portrayal of Santa in *Miracle on 34th Street*.

As for Weldon, she is solid but not exceptional. But I was pleased her character's expertise in the field is utilized, and everybody addresses her as "Doctor".

The effects range from decent to surprisingly advanced for a movie of this era. I'm sure many today would laugh at the giant ants. At least they are a physical mechanism and very well-done for their time. They look especially realistic when set on fire by scientists wielding flamethrowers. And if "scientists wielding flamethrowers" doesn't make you want to see this movie, nothing will.

But the most startling visual is a room containing the giant eggs of the giant ants. It so instantly and thoroughly reminded me of a similar scene in *Alien* that I believe that later film had to be influenced by this scene.

I thoroughly enjoyed *Them* and can recommend it for anybody with even a passing interest in 50's sci-fi. You may need to suspend your disbelief and temper your judgment, but you could end up having a great time. If nothing else, you will be better prepared if you have a mountain of purloined sugar to defend.

Original version posted on 1/13/2023

This Island Earth (1955)

Many of the discs I own are partly for the special features. Some titles I own are *only* for the special features.

I wouldn't say I bought the Scream Factory blu-ray for 1955's *This Island Earth* solely for the special features, but they helped me to better appreciate a film that's best known for being the subject of *Mystery Science Theater 3000: The Movie*. That is the only way I had seen it before (twice, actually), and the source material provided ample fodder for the only theatrical incarnation of that TV show.

This has flying saucers. There's a monster that looks like a humanoid prawn, with a large, exposed brain and which is wearing *pants*. You'll see aliens with high foreheads that immediately brought to mind the line from "We Want a Rock" by They Might Be Giants about people wearing prosthetic foreheads.

Not that the movie does itself any favors with its advertising campaign focusing on how it was "2 ½ Years in the Making!" Even looking at other films of the era, it is hard to believe that much time, money and effort went into this. It's the kind of movie where "fireballs" fly through space on highly visible supports. It's the kind of movie where the interiors of flying saucers are roomy enough to hold a ballroom dancing competition inside. Which would be quite a spectacle, now that I think about it.

The plot concerns a war between two planets, one of which (Metaluna) has been secretly enlisting Earth's best scientists in helping it restore a protective layer of its atmosphere, so as to withstand barrages of fireballs from the other planet. I was never sure exactly *what* the scientists were supposed to accomplish since the aliens provide hardware and calculations beyond human comprehension. Why don't the aliens just do the job themselves, if they have superior knowledge and all the equipment?

Perhaps the most interesting aspect of the movie is the recruitment process by which aliens test scientists to determine if they are worthy. In the case of the doctor played by Rex Reason (what a stage name, no?), his lab has been receiving electronic parts they have never heard of before, such as a resistor that "held 30,000 volts with no leakage", to which my wife promptly said, "That sounds like a personal problem."

Next, a massive parts catalog arrives, and the scientists order one of each part. I like a bit where the various mysterious parts are strewn across the lab, like a nightmare version of what any parent might experience on a Christmas morning when faced with something that has "some assembly required".

At least these items seem to serve some sort of purpose. All we watched these bozos do on their own before this was inexplicably lower a monolith into what looks like a giant toaster, only to have it burst into flames. Really, they should have tried this experiment with the giant Pop Tart first.

The resulting object is basically a two-way video screen which opens a channel of communication with the alien beings, letting them know another person has passed their test. This device is called the "interociter" and it is notable for having a triangular screen. It also has a death ray, which the mysterious figure on the screen uses to incinerate the parts catalog where it sits on a desk. Having seen this, I now want a death ray feature added to Zoom. I have been on many conference calls where I wish I could remotely administer a deathly zap to one or more participants.

Most people witnessing such a spectacle wouldn't pursue further contact with the aliens behind such technology. But Reason acts, um, unreasonably, in my opinion. He gladly boards a full-size, windowless plane that is controlled remotely by the aliens. Pilot-less planes—great, now I know what the next idiotic tech revolution will be, if we can first survive the epoch of driverless cars.

The plane lands on a dirt airstrip outside a mansion in rural Georgia. This is where the aliens have gathered brilliant minds from around the world. Every human there appears to hold a doctorate, given an unintentionally hilarious little bit where various characters all acknowledge each other with "Doctor". It's like a similar scene in *Spies Like Us*, though that bit in the 1985 movie wasn't as funny.

A couple of scientists at this facility are suspicious of the aliens' true motives. You have to admit, the aliens' stated goal of ending war is already a tad suspect when their teleconference device has a feature that can remotely kill a person.

Faith Domergue is one of those scientists. I was happy to see a woman as one of the world's leading scientists. Admittedly, we never see her doing any actual work. She will largely serve as a damsel in distress and a love interest for Reason. Russell Johnson, the Professor from *Gilligan's Island*, is there as well, I guess in case the aliens need an interociter built from a coconut.

Whatever the humans were meant to achieve, they apparently accomplish it, since the aliens take off in a flying saucer they have concealed within a hillside. They blow up the mansion once they're in the air, killing nearly all of the world's most brilliant minds in the process. I don't mind that, but that explosion also doubtlessly killed the cat that was the facility's mascot, and that I cannot forgive.

When I say "almost" all the scientists, that's because Reason and Domergue had narrowly escaped beforehand. Instead of staying on the ground, they took off in a single-prop plane. I was amazed Reason did that, as he seemed to forget the aliens took control of the jet he was flying in the opening of the film. So, the saucer captures their plane via a tractor beam and it's off to Metaluma.

Jeff Marrow plays Exeter, the alien most sympathetic to the humans, telling Reason and Domergue, "I assure you we mean you no harm". Guess that doesn't include the group of brilliant scientists he helped obliterate. Oh, and the cat. I am not going to let them live down the cat.

There is an element of the voyage that is deeply ludicrous, especially in a movie many have defended as "intelligent". You see, the air pressure on Metaluna is like that of the Earth's deepest oceans, so aliens and humans alike must go through a special process administered by standing in giant glass tubes for a while. Imagine this: in the same room, you have people who have yet to undergo the process *and* those who have gone through it. So, the room has the same air pressure throughout, and yet you have those who are acclimated to Earth's air pressure side-by-side with those adjusted to that of thousands of atmospheres.

The destination proves to be more interesting. It is all miniatures and matte paintings, but they're well-done. Besides, I love those kinds of effects. The matte paintings are far from realistic, even for conveying an alien world. Instead, they are more impressionistic, and surprisingly beautiful.

Still, the way a matte is incorporated into at least one shot is odd. This is when giant, flaming rocks bombard a facility, and only the bottom of the screen is unmatted. For no reason I could determine, people in that unmatted area are at risk of being pummeled by those rocks as they run through the exposed area from the exit of one building to the entrance of another. I wondered why such an advanced civilization would fail to cover these vulnerable stretches.

Anywho...battle between the planets, giant mutant monster, fleeing back to Earth. Yada yada yada. I don't feel like really going into it. One thing I found especially interesting in the Metaluna sequence is an unrecognizable Douglas Spencer as the leader of the aliens. This is the guy who played the reporter in *The Thing from Another World* who concluded that picture with the immortal line, "Keep watching the skies!" Here, he somehow keeps a straight face when Reason conveys the importance of humanity as "Our true size is the size of our God." I have no idea what that means, and I'm not sure the author of that line does, either.

Overall, the movie is mildly amusing, largely for its naivete. It is also greatly *unintentionally* amusing. I dare any contemporary viewer not to chuckle in the first major scene, when Reason loses control of the jet he's flying and a guy in the control tower says, "Jerking around must have caused a flameout." Wow, and I thought they only told kids back then it would make them go blind.

This Island Earth occupies a strange place in the pantheon of 1950's sci-fi films. It is so deeply absurd that it provides ample fodder for mockery, such as from MST3K. I mean, this is a movie which insists on telling us a planet was somehow once a comet, an impossibility communicated to the scientists for no reason. And, yet, as Joe Dante says in the accompanying documentary, this was a wonder to a nine-year-old like him in 1955. In retrospect, it would be completely overshadowed the next year by *Forbidden Planet*. If that movie was the *Star Wars* of the 50's, *This Island Earth* is its *Logan's Run*.

Original version posted on 2/1/2024

Who? (1974)

Man, I am getting tired of movies subverting my expectations. I keep throwing on a movie I think will be awesome and it sucks. Get myself ready to laugh at a film that looks to be hilariously bad, and it will end up actually being good.

Such is the case with 1974's *Who?* I mean, just look at that title— this is a movie with low self-esteem. The only way it could be sadder would be if it was titled *What?*, and that was the title of Roman Polanski's worst, and most self-indulgent, film.

I went into this picture with as little information as possible. It was a purchase from one of the big Kino Lorber sales. To the best I can recall, I bought it because it was cheap and the cover made it look goofy as fuck.

And it definitely starts out as laugh-out-loud bad. It is night at a border crossing. Two American agents watch a figure cross the demilitarized zone to them from the other side. As the figure gets closer, we see these guys go literally slack-jawed. I think that's the appropriate reaction to the approaching person, who turns out to be approximately 50% robot.

This guy's robot head is both the best and worst thing in this movie. It is so goofy, it is hilarious. It looks more than a bit like that offensive robot on the cover the Styx album *Killroy Was Here*. I think it is interesting Joseph Bova, as the robot man, doesn't currently have a profile picture on IMDB, so I still have no idea what he really looks like.

The question at the root of the picture is whether this weird cyborg that is sent to the US is truly what was once a prestigious rocket scientist named Dr. Martino. The Communists claim the doctor had a nearly fatal auto accident and the bizarre measures taken were only thing that could be done to save his life. The American officials, led by Elliott Gould, suspect an enemy agent is impersonating the doctor as part of a ruse.

I think this is an interesting premise. That I came to be gradually engrossed in the story is a testament to the filmmaking, given how deliriously weird Robo-Martino looks.

The movie intercuts constantly between Martino's life before the car crash and present-day interrogation sessions with Gould. For the most part, Gould asking him about something in his past will prompt a jump cut to that moment. Since those flashbacks are always from the doctor's perspective, we never see his face before the accident. Then again, judging from his monotonous voice in those memories, he may have always been a robot.

I never felt certain if Gould was playing it straight here or not. A staple of that actor's toolkit is a slight, sardonic smile. Here, it is hard to tell if it is part of his character or if the actor can't disguise his incredulousness.

The actor I hate to say fares the worst is Trevor Howard. I didn't realize he was supposed to be a Russian, as he didn't have such an accent until the second scene in which he speaks. Even then, it will wander all over the map for the remainder of the runtime. It crushed me to see the man behind my favorite performance in my favorite movie (*The Third Man*) brought so low.

One would think a plot such as this would lend itself to action scenes, but this feature is far more concerned with ideas. I may be making too much of this, but I suspect one of the intended ideas it floats out there is what exactly makes you who you are. This is suggested particularly in a scene where Gould describes some of the false memories that have been planted in agents' minds. This bit reminded me of *Blade Runner*.

Unfortunately, the main action scene in the film is lamentable—a deeply stupid car chase confined entirely to a small airport. They never leave the airport grounds! And why is Gould the only person trying to intercept that vehicle? Is there no security at this airport?

The curiously titled *Who?* is a strange, but compelling oddity. In the end, it is a bit difficult to say whether it is more ridiculous or more genuinely interesting. Which is kind of like the half-human robot at the center of this story…

Original version posted on 9/6/2023

X: the Unknown (1956)

Legendary UK film studio Hammer continues to fascinate me. Though largely known for their horror output, that really only began in earnest with 1958's *Horror of Dracula*. Prior to that, the studio was more focused on science fiction. In 1955, the studio had a major success with their film of *The Quatermass Xperiment*. A year later, they tried to mine that vein again with *X: the Unknown*.

The titles aren't the only similarities here. This could easily have been a sequel to the 1955 film. In fact, that is what it was originally intended to be, except writer Nigel Kneale wouldn't let the producers use his character.

So, instead of Brian Donlevy, you get Dean Jagger as essentially the same character under a different name. As the head of an atomic research facility, Jagger is brought in by the government to help destroy an intelligent, murderous, radioactive goo that increases in size with each additional energy source it consumes.

If you have seen *Quatermass* and the original *The Blob*, just imagine a crossover between those works and you'll have a rough idea of what's in store here. Surprisingly, *X* was released two years before *The Blob*, which reverses which film I thought might have influenced the other.

The film opens on British soldiers in a training exercise in a quarry, where the goal is to find a planted radioactive item. They do find something, but not where the intended item had been buried. The earth quakes, fissures appear in the ground and up from the ground came a bubblin' goo (death, that is, radioactive gold, blobby tea).

One aspect of the film which distinguishes it from similar fare of the time are some surprisingly frank approaches to the more gruesome elements. A child with radiation burns from an encounter with the goo will die in the hospital. I guess the hospital staff weren't too overwhelmed with grief, as a doctor and nurse apparently decide almost immediately after to get their freak on in the control room of the X-ray lab. Drawn to the radioactive material used in X-rays, the blob seeps into the room through a grate. The doctor unwisely goes to investigate, only to end up with his skin melting off his face. I was surprised by how much of that we see, and in a solidly executed effect.

Other effects are decent but not exceptional. Typical of such films, miniatures are frequently employed, and I have a soft spot for those. I especially liked a bit where the goo is sucking power out of downed electric lines, which are animated to move like wriggling snakes. Unfortunately, there was a moment later where I could not suspend disbelief, when disproportionately large flames shoot out from the fissures in the quarry, thus destroying the effect a miniature was meant to convey.

In general, this is an intelligent film, as I have come to expect from scripts penned by Jimmy Sangster. When asked how the creature can be stopped, Jagger asks rhetorically, "How do you kill mud?" Alas, some of the science is pretty dodgy, especially as concerns the lab Jagger maintains. He has been doing experiments with radiation, but he is only separated from it by a divider that appears to be just wood and plexiglass. As if that isn't lacking in and of itself, it also doesn't extend all the way across the room. I guess radiation can't go around corners.

This blu-ray had an interesting commentary track from Ted Newsom, though he has a tendency to meander. Still, I gleaned more than a few interesting morsels of information, such as Jagger having the original director, Joseph Losey, fired. Losey, who had been blacklisted in the McCarthy hearings, had fled to England to find work. Jagger hated anybody perceived as sympathetic to Communists. No surprise, given the man had starred in the hysterical "red menace" flick *My Son John*.

X: the Unknown is required viewing for fans of Hammer and/or 1950's science fiction. Still, something keeps it from being recommended for those who aren't genre fans. It isn't fair to compare deadly goo films from that era, but it is inevitable one will, and I have to declare *The Blob* as the winner.

Original version posted on 4/15/2024

A curiously unhelpful index

Movies reviewed are in **bold**

If you tolerated this,
you might feel the same way
about these other works by the author
(titles not available in all universes or dimensions)

Conversational Lorem Ipsum

*Baby's First Picture Book of
Inland Marine Insurance Policy Underwriting*

Charlie vs. Charlie
*When Charles M. Schultz's Most Popular Character
Single-Handedly Took On the Vietcong*

We'll Beat This Together
Success Stories from Masturbators Anonymous

Vanity, Thy Name Is Publishing
Lose Money and Friends Faster by Self-Publishing Your Crap